Early Medieval Europe 300–1050

Early Medieval Europe 300–1050

The birth of western society

David Rollason

Harlow, England • London • New York • Boston • San Francisco • Toronto • Sydney • Auckland • Singapore • Hong Kong
Tokyo • Seoul • Taipei • New Delhi • Cape Town • São Paulo • Mexico City • Madrid • Amsterdam • Munich • Paris • Milan

PEARSON EDUCATION LIMITED

Edinburgh Gate
Harlow CM20 2JE
United Kingdom
Tel: +44 (0)1279 623623
Fax: +44 (0)1279 431059
Website: www.pearson.com/uk

First edition published in Great Britain in 2012

ISBN: 978-1-4082-5121-8

British Library Cataloguing in Publication Data
A CIP catalogue record for this book can be obtained from the British Library

Library of Congress Cataloging in Publication Data
Rollason, D. W. (David W.)
    Early medieval Europe 300–1050 : the birth of western society / David Rollason.
        p. cm.
    Includes biliographical references and index.
    ISBN 978-1-4082-5121-8 (pbk.)
    1. Europe--History--476-1492.   2. Europe--History--To 476.   3. Civilization,
Medieval.   4. Middle Ages.   I. Title.
    D121.R65 2012
    940.1--dc23

                                                    2012001378

10 9 8 7 6 5 4 3 2 1
16 15 14 13 12

Set in 10.5/13pt Baskerville MT by 35
Printed in Malaysia (CTP-PPSB)

In memory of
R. H. C. Davis
(1918–91)
a great scholar and an inspirational teacher

Contents

List of maps   xi

List of figures   xii

Acknowledgements   xiv

Preface   xvi

PART I Introduction   1

1 Why study this period?   3
       Formative character   3
       Challenges to study   8
       This book's aims   10

PART II Empire and peoples   13

       Introduction   15

2 From Roman Empire to barbarian kingdoms: cataclysm or transition?   18
       The First Doom and Gloom Model   19
       The Second Doom and Gloom Model   25
       The Deliberate Roman Policy Model   26
       Research and study   34

3 The making of peoples   37
       The Biological Model   42
       The Constitutional Model   50
       Why did peoples form?   53
       Research and study   60

       Conclusion   63

       Time-line: Part II   65

PART III Power and society   67

       Introduction   69

4 Pagan, Roman, and Christian beliefs about kings: ideological power   72
       Paganism and kingship   72

Roman ideology and kingship   80
Christianity and kingship   84
Research and study   93

5 Edicts, taxes, and armies: bureaucratic power   96
Written documents   96
Oral communication, symbolism, and ritual   99
Government departments and staff   101
Capabilities of governments   108
Research and study   113

6 Kings, warriors, and women: personal power   117
War-bands   117
Feasting, drinking, and the hall   124
The social pyramid   125
Aristocratic elites   128
The role of women   130
Nearness to the king   132
Research and study   134
Conclusion   138
Time-line: Part III   140

PART IV The economic foundation   **143**

Introduction   145
7 Trade as a driving force?   150
Pirenne and his critics   150
The Roman economy   151
Pottery manufacture and trade   152
The economic influence of the Arab caliphate   156
Decline and revival of trade?   161
Research and study   170

8 Cultivating the land: the basis of European society?   175
The continuity of Roman agriculture   175
An agricultural revolution?   183
Research and study   193

9 Towns and cities: the functions of urban life   197
The fate of Roman cities   198
Functions of cities and towns   204
Growth of cities and towns   206
New towns   208
Research and study   220
Conclusion   224
Time-line: Part IV   226

PART V The Church's triumph   **229**

Introduction   231
The 'top-down' model   231
The 'bottom-up' model   232

10   Conversion to Christianity   234
The Roman Empire   234
The barbarians within the Roman Empire   242
Conversion outside the former Roman Empire   251
Research and study   255

11   The success of monasticism   258
'Bottom-up' model   259
'Top-down' model   264
Research and study   275

12   The power of bishops and popes   278
Bishops and popes in the Church hierarchy   278
The resources of popes and bishops   282
Bishops and popes in the world   289
Research and study   297

Conclusion   300

Time-line: Part V   302

PART VI Scholarship and art   **305**

Introduction   307

13   Scholarship and literature   309
Scholars   309
The language of scholarship   312
Scripts   314
Syllabus   315
Educational system   316
Research and study   320

14   Art and architecture   322
Architectural forms   322
Sculpture, decoration, and painting   326
Barbarian styles   331
Research and study   333

Conclusion   336

Time-line: Part VI   338

PART VII   341

Conclusion   343
Original sources   346
References   351
Index   384

Supporting resources

Visit **www.pearsoned.co.uk/rollason** to find valuable online resources

Companion Website for students
- Tips for learning and revision
- Glossary, Biographical Notes on key figures and Timeline
- Guidance on key reference works for seminar preparation
- References and links to primary sources in print and online
- Images and commentary on how to read non-written sources – building, sculpture and artifacts from the period

For instructors
- Tips on organising and conducting effective seminars
- Sample seminar outlines giving guidance on content, essay titles and further reading for students

For more information please contact your local Pearson Education sales representative or visit **www.pearsoned.co.uk/rollason**

List of maps

1 The extent of the Roman Empire   4

2 Europe around 1000–1050   6

3 Europe in 500   16

4 The distribution of later Roman Empire cities   30

5 The barbarian invasions   38

6 Treaty of Verdun   56

7 Charlemagne's itinerary   106

8 Expansion of the Arab Moslems   147

9 Distribution of pottery from La Graufensque   153

10 Rivers between the Baltic Sea to Black Sea and the Caspian Sea   164

11 The principal Carolingian polyptychs for the northern part of
the Carolingian empire   177

12 York, showing the components of the Roman settlement   200

13 Archaeological remains at Haithabu (Hedeby)   212

14 Winchester in the period 993 to 1066   217

15 The city of Trier in the Early Middle Ages   292

List of figures

1   Portchester Saxon Shore fort from the air   21

2   The *liburna* (oxen-powered paddle-ship) from the anonymous 'On Military Matters'   22

3   Cremation urns from the cemetery of Sancton I (Yorkshire East Riding)   45

4   The skull and hair of a man recovered from a bog at Osterby (Schleswig-Holstein, Germany)   49

5   Replica of the seal-ring of King Childeric   76

6   Sutton Hoo Whetstone-Sceptre   78

7   San Vitale, Ravenna and the palace-church of Aachen   83

8   Reconstruction of the palace of Ingelheim (Germany) as built by Charlemagne   84

9   Scene from the ninth-century Sacramentary of Metz, illustrating the text of the service for the inauguration of the king   86

10   Detail of a modern reconstruction of a mosaic forming part of Pope Leo III's decoration of his new Lateran Palace in Rome   89

11   Emperor Otto III enthroned   90

12   Harold Godwinsson's oath to Duke William of Normandy represented in the Bayeux Tapestry   100

13   A Merovingian and a Carolingian coin   109

14   A section of Offa's Dyke, near Clun (Shropshire), looking south   110

15   The Sutton Hoo Mound 1 ship as excavated just before the Second World War in 1939   121

16   Ships represented on coins   169

17   The village of Chaussy-Épagny in the valley of the River Somme, photographed from the air by Roger Agache   182

18   Model of a Roman plough in use from Arezzo (Italy)   187

19   A mould-board plough represented in the margin of the Bayeux Tapestry   188

20   Tower 19 (the 'Anglian Tower') in the fortifications of York   202

21 The forum at Rome   205

22 Aerial view of Burford (Oxfordshire)   209

23 Reconstruction of the layout of Hamwih   211

24 Aerial view of Wallingford, Oxfordshire   218

25 Arch of Constantine, Rome   236

26 Franks Casket, left side of the front   250

27 The Gosforth Cross, Gosforth churchyard (Cumbria), detail showing
    the punishment of thc god Loki   252

28 'Triumphal Arch' at Lorsch (Germany)   269

29 The east end of St Peter's in the Vatican, reshaped by Pope Gregory
    the Great   286

30 *Codex Amiatinus*, detail of the text of the Gospel according to St Mark   311

31 Interior of the Roman basilica at Trier (Germany)   323

32 The nave of Brixworth church (Northamptonshire), interior looking west   325

33 Ruthwell Cross, Dumfriesshire. Detail of the inhabited vine-scroll
    with a version of the Old English poem, *The Dream of the Rood*   327

34 St Andrew's Sarcophagus   328

35 Lindisfarne Gospels, preliminary pages to the Gospel of St Matthew   329

36 The Godescalc Evangelistiary, miniature of Christ enthroned   330

37 The Coppergate Helmet (Yorkshire Museum, York)   332

Acknowledgements

We are grateful to the following for permission to reproduce copyright material:

Figures

Figure 1 courtesy of Jim Bramble, Portsmouth Technical High School; Figure 3 from Hull & East Riding Museum: Hull Museums; Figure 4 from Archaeologisches Landesmuseum, Germany/Munoz-Yague/Science Photo Library; Figure 5 from Ashmolean Museum, University of Oxford, UK/The Bridgeman Art Library; Figure 6 © The Trustees of the British Museum, all rights reserved; Figure 7a © Domkapitel Aachen (photo: Ann Münchow); Figure 7b © 2011 Photo SCALA, Florence; Figure 8, model of the Kaiserpfalz Ingelheim am Rhein, © Hartmut Geissler, Historischer Verein Ingelheim; Figure 9 © Photos 12/Alamy; Figure 11 © Domkapitel Aachen (photo: Ann Münchow); Figures 12 and 19, detail from the Bayeux Tapestry, 11th century, by special permission of the City of Bayeux; Figure 13a from Classical Numismatic Group, Inc., www.cngcoins.com; Figure 13b from Mary Evans/Rue des Archives/Tallandier; Figure 15 courtesy of Colchester and Ipswich Museums; although efforts have been made to find the copyright holder of this image, this has not been possible; Figure 16 from *Frühmittelalterliche Handelsschiffahrt in Mittel und Nordeuropa* (Ellmers, D. 1972), p. 56, reproduced by permission of Prof. Dr Detlev Ellmers and the Council for British Archaeology; Figure 17 from Roger Agache – DRAC de Picardie; Figure 18 © The Art Gallery Collection/Alamy; Figure 18 © The Art Gallery Collection Alamy; Figure 22 © English Heritage (NMR) Wingham Collection; Figure 23 from John Hodgson; Figure 24 © English Heritage NMR; Figure 29 from The shrine of St Peter and its twelve spiral columns, *Journal of Roman Studies*, xlii (Ward-Perkins, J. 1952), Cambridge University Press; Figure 30 from Walton Sound and Film Services, Adrian Beney; Figure 35a © INTERFOTO/ Alamy; Figure 35b from Heritage Images; Figure 36 © The Art Archive/Alamy; Figure 37 from York Archaeological Trust.

Where no acknowledgement is made, photographs are by David and Linda Rollason.

Maps

Map 4 from Jones, A. H. M., *The Later Roman Empire, 284–602: A Social, Economic and Administrative* Survey, *II*, © 1964, reproduced with permission of Blackwell Publishing Ltd.; Map 5 from Porcher, J. and Volbach, W. F., *Europe In The Dark Ages* (Thames and Hudson, 1969), Photo UDF/© Gallimard; Map 11 from Pounds N. J. G., *An Economic History of Medieval Europe* (Pearson Education Ltd., 1976); Map 12 from *An Inventory of the Historical Documents of the City of York 2: The Defences*, Stationery Office Books (Royal Commission on Historical Monuments (England), 1973), courtesy of Her Majesty's Stationery Office; Map 14 from Parsons, D. (ed.), 'Felix Urbs Wintonia: Winchester in the Age of Monastic Reform', in *Tenth-Century Studies: Essays in commemoration of the Millennium Council of Winchester and Regularis Concordia* (Phillimore & Co, 1975), courtesy of Professor Martin Biddle.

In some instances we have been unable to trace the owners of copyright material, and we would appreciate any information that would enable us to do so.

Preface

This is a book intended to provide guidance and assistance to undergraduate students embarking for the first time on early medieval European history. It is not intended to be a definitive statement of research results, or even a distillation of the author's own interpretations, but rather a road-map to the ideas, questions, scholarship, and sources which make up the heady mix of study and research.

Each chapter is focused on themes and historical problems, brings students into close contact with written and non-written evidence, and offers a 'research and study' section to guide their work by posing questions, by dividing the topic of the chapter up into manageable study-blocks, and by offering commentary on what the author considers to be the most exciting and appropriate reading. Each of the book's parts provides a time-line appropriate to the themes of the chapters in question.

The book's emphasis is on developing students' confidence in making historical research their own, in fearlessly developing their own ideas in a clear and structured way, and in using a wide range of sources to support their arguments. For students for whom a single course or module will be their only encounter with this period, the book aims to help them clarify the broad underlying issues of human society which the period raises, but which may be equally applicable to work they may move on to undertake on other periods or geographical areas.

These are ambitious aims, but I have tried to be realistic as to what is possible for students in the context of a single course or module aimed at beginners. For the book's guidance on reading and research, I have selected only works in English, with apologies to those students who read other languages and may be anxious to use them. Even so, the number of works available is often daunting and overwhelming. I have further tried to select books and papers which seem to me to take students to the heart of issues, without bogging them down in technicalities and detail which are beyond what is needed at this stage of study.

I have also selected the source-materials used and recommended, both written and non-written, on the grounds of how practical it is for students who read only English to acquire in-depth understanding of them. For written sources, for example, this is not just a question of the availability of translations into English, but also the availability of readily accessible and usable commentaries on them. The result of this, however, is that the book's emphasis is heavier than I might have wished on north-western Europe, with much use, for example, of Bede's *Ecclesiastical History of the English People* and Gregory of Tours's *History of the Franks* (or, more accurately, *Ten Books of Histories*). There are, of course, exciting sources and issues relating to more southern areas, such as Spain and Italy, and students may well wish to pursue with regard to those areas the ideas and questions developed in this book.

Supporting and assisting such wider explorations, and in general providing support and confidence, are the aims of the website which is the partner of this book. This offers resources for lecturers (including guidance and templates for seminars); resources for students (including revision projects); reference aids to give students access to works of reference as well as providing assistance with technical terms, historical personages, and dates; and pointers to visual and documentary source-materials. The website is intended to underline the book's intention to be a starting-point for students (and their teachers) and not an end.

It is a great pleasure to acknowledge the role in the writing of this book played by over thirty generations of Durham University history students. Their enthusiastic response to lectures, their sharp-minded, critical approach to seminars, and their unfailing commitment to scholarship have guided and inspired me throughout my career, and it is a huge satisfaction to commit some of what they have given me to print and to the web. Colleagues at Durham and elsewhere have been unfailingly generous and helpful. To Robin Frame, I am immensely grateful for his patience and understanding over the many years during which we taught early medieval history together. He has very generously read and commented on this book, and it is tighter and clearer for his efforts. I am similarly grateful for their time and comments to Bob Moore, who shares with me affectionate memories of the book's dedicatee, Ralph Davis, to Christian Liddy, to Conrad Leyser, to John-Henry Clay, to Len Scales, and to Barbara Crawford. My school-teacher, Andrew Thomson, who first instilled in me the importance of clarity of thought and analysis, has also read and improved the book, close on fifty years after he first taught me. Finally, I must record my thanks to Mari Shullaw at Pearson Education, who first suggested the book and the website, and has been unfailingly helpful and supportive, and to Melanie Carter and her colleagues for doing so much to make the publication of this book an easy and pleasant process for the author.

David Rollason
History Department
Durham University

PART I

Introduction

1

Why study this period?

Formative character

The aim of this book is to explore how far for the development of Western Europe in political, religious, cultural, social, and economic terms, the period from 300 to 1050 was one of the most formative in its history.

Consider, first, how in 300, Western Europe was dominated politically by the Roman Empire (Map 1). Its frontiers stretched from the Atlantic Ocean on the west to the Rivers Tigris and Euphrates on the east, from Hadrian's Wall in the north, to the Atlas Mountains of North Africa in the south.

By 1050, the political map of Western Europe was very different (Map 2). In place of the unitary might of the Roman Empire, which had come to an end in Western Europe in the late fifth century, a series of often very fragmented kingdoms had come into existence and we can perhaps dimly perceive underlying this development the beginnings of modern political geography, with the kingdoms of France, England, and Germany, for example, already appearing in embryonic form.

Developments in the eastern Mediterranean had been equally far-reaching. After the break-up of the Roman Empire in the west, the eastern Roman Empire continued to exist as an important state, with its centre in the great city of Constantinople (modern Istanbul); and, from at any rate the seventh century onwards, it is generally known to modern scholarship as the Byzantine Empire. It was itself reduced in size when, following the rise of Islam in the early seventh century, Arab armies burst out of the Arabian peninsula and robbed it of the provinces of Syria, Egypt, Libya, Tripoli, and the remainder of North Africa, as well as destroying the Kingdom of Persia and taking over its lands. In 711, Moslems from North Africa invaded Spain, where the Byzantine Empire still had a foothold, destroyed the kingdom of the Visigoths there, and subjected

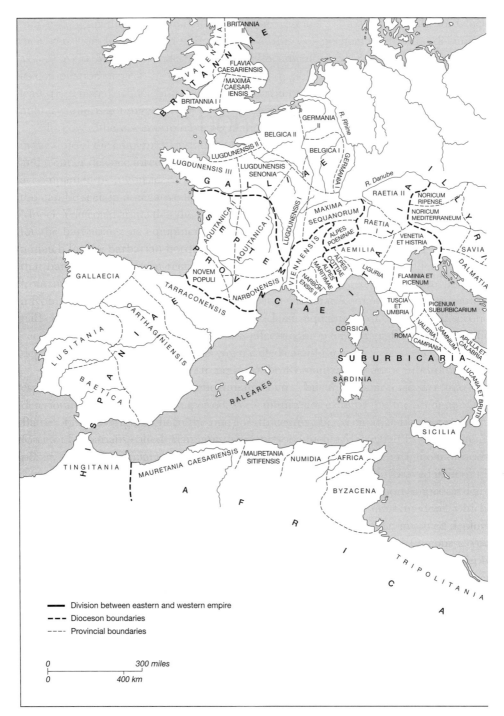

Map 1 The extent of the Roman Empire with the governmental units called provinces and dioceses marked as in Late Roman documents.

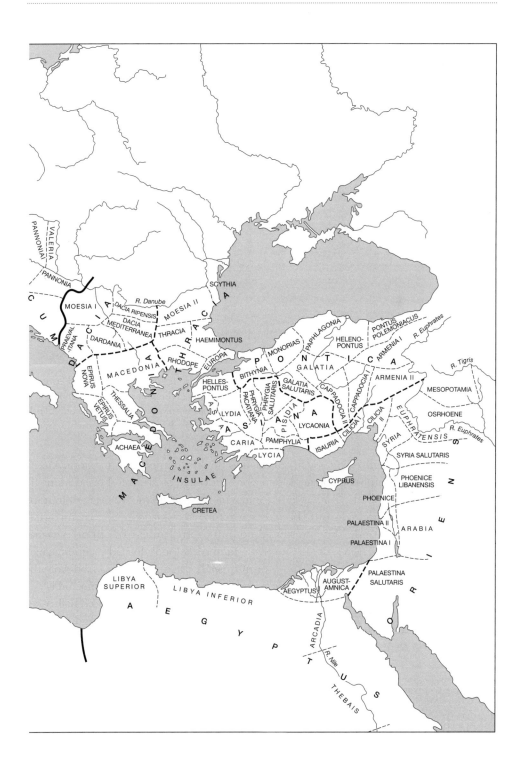

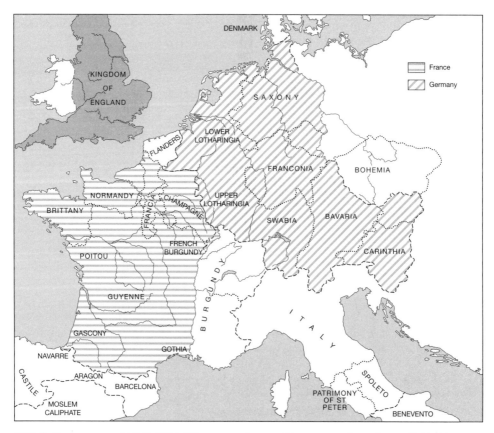

Map 2 Europe around 1000–1050. What was to become France as we know it was divided into a series of duchies such as Flanders, Normandy, and Aquitaine, and Aquitaine itself was subdivided into Poitou, Guyenne, and Gascony; but nevertheless it was at least notionally under the rule of a king whose centre of power lay in the area around Paris, the Île de France, or 'Francia' as it was known and is marked on this map. Germany was also fragmented into duchies such as Saxony, Swabia, and Franconia, but nonetheless a clear political distinction was emerging between the western and eastern parts of Western Europe. To the east lay areas such as Bohemia whose status and connection to Germany were still fluid. To the south, lay the kingdom of Italy, also very fluid and occupying broadly northern Italy, with duchies such as Spoleto to the south, and also the 'Patrimony of St Peter', which was the pope's lands, the nucleus of the future papal states. To the south-west of the Pyrenees, the Christian kingdoms and counties of Navarre, Aragon, and Barcelona (with Castile to the west of this map) were pressing against the Moslem caliphate and emirates to the south.

almost the whole of the Iberian peninsula to their rule. The Byzantine Empire was reduced to Asia Minor, the Balkans, and parts of Italy and the Mediterranean islands (Map 8 below). These events were potentially formative for Western Europe in subsequent centuries, and into the modern period, and we shall need to ponder their significance.

We may also be seeing crucially formative changes in the development of political institutions. In 300, Western Europe was dominated by the institutions of the Roman

Empire, the emperor or co-emperors at least notionally at its head, and the exercise of power in the hands of a paid civil service and a standing army. By 1050, it was dominated by kings, their households, and their military followers. Although Roman writers knew of kings as the leaders of their barbarian allies or enemies, kingship as we know it may have begun in this period, including the shaping of its rituals, regalia, and ideology. Certainly, the 1953 coronation ceremony of Queen Elizabeth II of the United Kingdom had its roots in the ninth century, when the various rituals of the ceremony first appeared, notably in the ninth-century inauguration ceremony of Charles the Bald, king of West Frankia, in broadly what is now France. Was the period of this book then one in which the political structures of Western Europe were shaped in broadly the form in which they were to remain for centuries to come?

The social and economic organisation of Western Europe may have been changed in this period in similarly radical ways. Although modern scholars have sometimes emphasised the European aristocracy's continuity with the Roman world, the change in its character and structure was nevertheless striking, and many of its branches believed that they had originated in the course of this period, notably in the ninth century. Likewise, the organisation of rural life no doubt owed something to the Roman past; but, by 1050, we may be seeing in many parts of Western Europe the manors, villages, and pattern of fields, in which rural life was to endure until the agricultural and industrial revolutions of the modern age. As for urban life, there has of course been a major transformation produced by modern industrialisation; but we may nevertheless be seeing the origins of the pattern of much modern urban development in this period, not least the concentration of cities in the valleys of the Rhine and adjacent rivers, and in north Italy, and the emergence already by 1050 of cities like London, York, Dublin, and Paris.

Most dramatic of all, however, was the change in religion. In 300, Western Europe was dominated by the paganism of the Roman and classical world, which had often absorbed and made its own the pagan cults of indigenous Celtic inhabitants. By 1050, Christianity, which had in 300 been a minority religion, until very recently the victim of campaigns of bloody persecution, had secured a monopoly as the religion of Western Europe, even in lands outside the former Roman Empire, like Ireland, which had been converted to Christianity already in the fifth century, and Scandinavia, which was converted by the early eleventh. Intolerant of other religions, Christianity had succeeded in crushing both classical paganism and Germanic, barbarian paganism, and it had become the defining characteristic of European civilisation. Europe was Christendom by 1050, and its eastern frontiers were frontiers against pagans beyond. Only in Spain was Christianity challenged, there by the religious and political power of Islam, following the conquest of Spain by Moslems from North Africa at the beginning of the eighth century.

Christianity's dominance was not just a matter of belief. It was also a matter of organisation and wealth. Some bishops were certainly already functioning as 'prince-bishops', and the popes had gone a long way to achieving a position of dominance in Western Europe. Also, monasticism, originating in the Nile Valley in the fourth century, had risen to considerable prominence in Western Europe, with a dense distribution of monasteries and an astonishing proportion of the productive land in their hands.

As for the learning, scholarship, and culture of Western Europe, this new dominance of Christianity may have proved seminal for the way in which the learning of the ancient world was transmitted across the centuries, fused with new Christian scholarship, in forms which were to shape European culture throughout the Middle Ages. This culture was largely founded on the Latin language, as Roman classical culture had been. But our period also saw the rise of the vernacular languages. The very first texts in the ancestor-languages of French and German belong to the ninth century, as does one of the earliest texts in the Old Norse language of Scandinavia. The earliest texts in Old English belong to the eighth century, and that language came to be widely used in writing from the ninth century onwards.

In this book, we need to explore the case for the importance, or otherwise, of each and every one of these changes. Modern scholars have refined our understanding of their nature and extent, and they have sometimes disputed their importance. We need to examine their findings in depth, and we need to be aware that we are everywhere surrounded by controversy and debate. We shall have to argue whatever case we choose to make – powerfully and vigorously. But there can be no doubt that, however we might want to answer the questions raised, however much we might want to finesse our answers and conclusions, we are looking at a period which is potentially a central one for understanding what Western Europe is and has been.

This period is, however, arguably crucial to our understanding of history more widely. We can study it for the joy of discovery, for the fascination of looking at a remote and often exotic period. But we should never forget that it has been of crucial and often sinister relevance to political ideas and ideologies up to the present day. The imperial robes of the Emperor Napoleon were decorated with jewelled insects inspired by those found in the tomb of the fifth-century king Childeric; Napoleon's predecessors who ruled France through the later Middle Ages and the early modern period believed that the oil used in their coronations was miraculously the same oil used to baptise their first Christian predecessor, Clovis, king of the Franks (c.481–c.511). The ideologues seeking to build a late medieval German nation drew on Roman writers of our period, and Hitler and his fascist colleagues used the history of Germanic peoples in and before our period as the basis of their ideology of the Aryan race. History, however remote, is never irrelevant and never neutral. This period has had more than its share in the shaping of Western European political ideology, and an understanding of it is crucial to appreciating how that developed.

Challenges to study

At first glance, the study of such a remote period can be daunting. There are few archives of records surviving, and there never were helpful documents such as censuses, or guides to popular feelings such as newspapers, which are the life-blood of the history of the modern period. In some parts of Western Europe, notably Scandinavia, there was little or no use of writing at all for most of the period. The volume of evidence is thus spectacularly less than that for modern centuries, when the problem for historians is often its sheer scale rather than its scarcity.

But that presents a challenge rather than a handicap, for it offers you the possibility of mastering a significant proportion of that evidence. And, given the remoteness of the period, it is rich and vivid. It includes unrivalled writers of history, such as the sixth-century Gregory of Tours, whose *History of the Franks* provides a rich picture of royal and aristocratic life in the area of modern France and western Germany, or the eighth-century Bede, whose *Ecclesiastical History of the English People* is justly celebrated as a subtle, wide-ranging, and influential work. We possess in addition, for example, accounts of the lives and deaths of saints, detailed surveys of landed estates and the peasantry who lived on them, and documents casting light on the organisation of land and power.

Moreover, the small size of this base of evidence, and the remoteness and strangeness of the period, will compel you to analyse it deeply and imaginatively in a way which is rarely possible for students of more modern periods. You need to think of our sources as radio stations broadcasting from the past. To what channel are they tuned? In whose interests were they written? What were their underlying purposes, and what light can that cast on the mentality and patterns of thought of those who wrote them?

For this period you will also be forced to move beyond written evidence. You will need to treat surviving buildings, monuments, and art-objects as every bit as important. Why were they created in the way that they were? What message were they intended to convey and to what audience? What light do they cast on the ideas and outlook of those who created them, those who commissioned them, and those who saw them? You will need to know them, to explore them, to appreciate their significance every bit as much as you will need to look closely at our written sources. And you will need to be broad-minded and imaginative. When the great King Offa of Mercia (757–96) built an enormous earthen dyke between England and Wales, for example, was he establishing a practical military frontier or was he seeking to rival the long-dead ruler of Denmark, his supposed ancestor King Offa of Angeln, who had similarly created a frontier in Denmark. When the gruesome story of maiming, rape, and decapitation which is the story of Weyland the Smith was carved on the whalebone casket known as the Franks Casket alongside a carving of the visit of the Three Kings to Christ (Fig. 26 below), what pattern of ideas was present in the mind of the carver and his patron?

As these questions suggest, you will need also to range beyond the areas of expertise sometimes regarded as those of history, to engage with the dating and technical analysis of buildings, sculpture, and painting, and with archaeological excavation to under-stand the evidence which it has produced, especially since the Second World War. You will need too to understand the approaches of literary scholars to the poetry of this period, including *Beowulf*; to have some appreciation of coins as evidence for the past; and to have some insight into the work of anthropologists, whose conclusions about peoples in the modern age have often been applied by scholars to the development of the society of Western Europe in our period.

This book's aims

The outline of history

Seven and a half centuries is a long time and a great deal happened in Western Europe during it. This book does not aim to give a 'what happened next' narrative account, which has often enough been written before, but rather it aims to give you a sufficient grasp of the course of events and developments for you to be able to appreciate the broad themes and debates which are at the heart of modern scholarship. To facilitate this, each part has a time-line relevant to its theme.

You will obviously need to expand on this for whatever research you are conducting. The clearest narrative account is a venerable textbook by R. H. C. Davis, recently revised with additional sections updating the interpretations of each chapter (Davis and Moore, 2006). More modern accounts are provided by Collins (1999) and Innes (2003); both are rather dense, and the latter more a work of analysis than a narrative account. A survey by Wickham (2009) considers much more than just Western Europe, and is also more analytical than descriptive. All three of these modern works are useful to read, but they do not do the job of giving you instant familiarity with the whole period as well as Davis does. Brief, easy to read accounts, but which are rather thin on material, are those by Rosenwein (2009) and Olson (2007). The quite different type of survey by Smith (2005) is a more specialised work; it is probably not the best starting-point, but it deals in depth with particular issues, notably gender (ch. 4). Brown (2002) is a stimulating survey, concentrating on religious history, but also discussing other topics.

Historical atlases are extremely useful not only for mastering the political changes in the broad shape of Western Europe, but also for appreciating the interrelationships between different states, the importance of land-routes, river-routes, and sea-ways, and other aspects of the geographical context. Useful general ones are Mackay and Ditchburn (1997), Almond, Black, Fernandez-Armesto, et al. (1994), and Barraclough (1990). The best for our purposes, however, are Moore (1983) and the *Großer Atlas zur Weltgeschichte* (Anon., 1997b). The second of these has the drawback of being in German but, if you can cope with that, it is a brilliant atlas with very illuminating, detailed maps.

Questions, models, and experiments

The real aim of this book, however, is to direct your attention to big questions of history in the context of this period. Why do people live as they do? Why do they think as they do? Why do they believe what they believe, and why do particular practices arise from those beliefs? Why do they accept authoritarian political structures which are, in the history of mankind, quite recent? Why is economic production organised as it is and why are some economically subservient to others? Questions like these relate to all human history, and the answers you may get when you pose them of a period as remote as 300–1050 can still be relevant to our perception of human life and human society today. But, because the period is so remote, you can take nothing for granted, and so you are more likely to ask the big questions in a probing way.

To understand how it is possible to tackle them, it is important to appreciate that history is more like science than many other 'humanities' subjects. Just as scientists begin with a hypothesis about how some aspect of the universe works and then test out that hypothesis by running experiments, so historians begin with hypotheses – we shall call them models – about how human society functioned. With the model formulated, it needs testing alongside the various types of evidence which remain from the past – the records, chronicles, coins, archaeological sites, buildings, art objects, and so on. Is that evidence consistent with the model? If it is not, the model will have to be rejected or modified and tested again. If it is, then the model can stand, although others will be constantly seeking to disprove it or reshape it, as they seek to look at the past in different ways, to draw new evidence into play in connection with the model, or indeed to bring in new evidence (like the results of archaeology) or evidence which has been ignored (like the mysterious text overlooked in some ancient library). Of course, historians are inevitably biased by the preoccupations which each new generation brings to the past; but this is not an excuse for sloppy approaches to the evidence.

Sources and methods

To run the experiments in science you need the test-tubes, the fundamental particle accelerators, and the electron microscopes, and you need to know how to use them. In history too, you need the techniques to run experiments. You need to understand what our sources can or cannot tell us, how they are constructed as they are, and what can be known about their dates, who created them, and so on. A whole series of technical skills (called on the Continent auxiliary sciences) exist to make this possible. Palaeographers, for example, are specialists in handwriting and can date what scribes in our period wrote, often quite precisely, and sometimes can even name the scribes. Codicologists understand the way that manuscript books were made from calves' leather or sheep's leather, and they can discover how the texts which have been preserved in these books came to be there and how they related to each other. Numismatists specialise in the study of coins and understand when particular issues of coins were made, how they were made and how they relate to each other, and how much precious metal was used in them. Art historians understand the dating, origin, and meaning of works of art and buildings from the past. Archaeologists specialise in the physical evidence of the past, whether it is the grains of pollen from the earth of an early settlement, or the palace of a king, or the bones of animals in the rubbish-pits of a town. And archaeoclimatologists specialise in the history of climate change and have, for example, identified a remarkably favourable period of climate (the French call it the 'thermal optimum') in the middle part of our period. Historians have to draw on all these 'auxiliary sciences'. They cannot possibly master all or even any of them, and this book is certainly not asking you to do so. But it is aiming to give some understanding of how they work and of the sort of things which they can – or cannot – tell us about the past.

The progress of research

To assist you to read and explore further, perhaps in quite different directions from those followed in this book, every chapter has a section devoted to 'Research and study' which aims to list and comment briefly on the most helpful, exciting, and accessible books and papers. The sections provide guidance at two levels, first to broad approaches, and then to more specialised investigations if you want to go further. They are not intended to be comprehensive, and you must explore further and in whatever directions you wish, following up the references in the footnotes and bibliographies of the works you are reading. You need nevertheless to realise that the number of works published is huge, and you should not even try to read all of them. Your key aims must be to have a clear view of what questions you are seeking to answer as you read, and how the evidence we have might be used in connection with them. The 'Research and study' sections are intended to help by formulating questions, although you must feel free to formulate questions of your own as your experience and confidence increase.

Being confident

All this requires a confidence which at the beginning you may find hard to acquire. So, if there is one over-arching aim of this book, it is to engender that confidence. The history of this period, as of any other period, is overshadowed at every turn by great authorities from the past and the present, whose contribution is or was very great in terms of the research they have undertaken and the ideas they have explored. But history is not made by individuals, however distinguished, and its continuing vigour depends on your willingness to form your own ideas and interpretations, to ask your own big questions, and to look at the writings of any authority in the spirit of what is wrong with them rather than in a spirit of deference and acceptance.

That is above all what this book seeks to encourage you to do. Everything you do must of course refer to the evidence available, it cannot be merely speculative, but you must not be inhibited in developing original ideas, reviving old ones, or differing from the views of established authorities. You need to engage with the evidence and to enjoy the process of letting your mind range across it. In your seminars and classes, you will often be playing a sort of game of cards, where the cards are the items of evidence you are using. As you develop an idea or give a paper, you need to play those cards skilfully; you need to be aware of what counter-cards your colleagues might play in the course of the discussion; you need to be alert to the possibility that cards might be drawn from other decks. History is a serious subject, of course, but if it is to stay alive as a subject for us, you need to feel in control of it, and to have an awareness that your activities, serious as they are, are also a sort of game.

PART II

Empire and peoples

Introduction

We glanced in the last chapter at the Roman Empire as it existed in 300 and noted the enormous changes in the political geography of Western Europe that had occurred between then and 1050. But equally impressive were the changes that occurred between 300 and 500. If we compare the map of the frontiers of the Roman Empire (Map 1) with that of the political shape of Europe in 500 (Map 3), we can see that in the eastern part of Europe, at the level of frontiers at least, little had changed.

There is the Byzantine or east Roman Empire, with its centre at Constantinople (modern Istanbul), on the Bosphorus between the Aegean Sea and the Black Sea. Its territories extend across the Balkans to the Adriatic Sea, and on the east they include Asia Minor (broadly modern Turkey), as well as modern Syria, Israel, Egypt, and Libya. But, to the west, the political geography has undergone very considerable changes. The Roman province of North Africa, centred on the ancient city of Carthage, and the Mediterranean islands of Sardinia, Corsica, and Minorca, have become the kingdom of a barbarian people called the Vandals. Similarly, the northern part of the Balkans together with Italy and Sicily have become the kingdom of the Ostrogoths, with its principal centre at Ravenna. Westward again, the area of modern Switzerland and south-eastern France around and east of the River Rhone is now the kingdom of the Burgundians, while the northern part of modern France and the western part of modern Germany, extending some way east of the Rhine, form the kingdom of the Franks. Modern Spain is chiefly dominated by the kingdom of the Visigoths, which extends along the Mediterranean coast eastwards into modern France, and includes much of south-western France, although not the area known as Aquitaine, which it lost to the Franks shortly after 500. It shared the Spanish peninsula with the kingdom of the Suebi and, along the north coast, with the Basques and the Cantabrians.

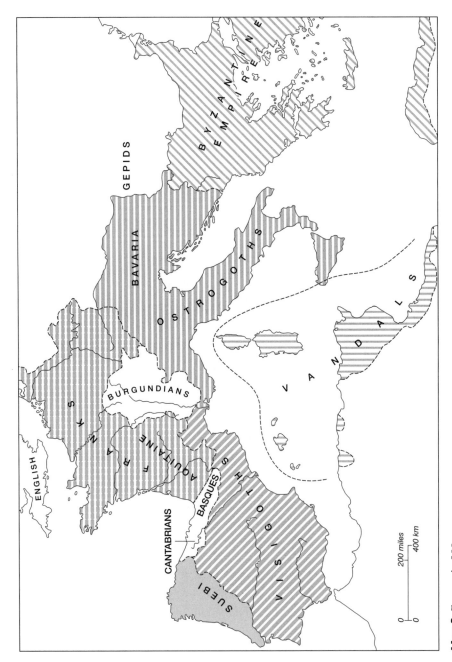

Map 3 Europe in 500.

What were the processes by which the Roman Empire in the west came to disintegrate in this way while its eastern part remained intact? Was it the culmination of a long process of decline, or the result of an immediate crisis caused perhaps by hostile invasions, or the result of a change in the policy of the Roman emperors? Secondly, how did Western Europe come to be divided between a series of kingdoms named after such barbarian peoples as the Franks, Visigoths, Ostrogoths, Burgundians? Did these kingdoms represent parts of the former Roman Empire taken over by invading and conquering peoples which had formed outside the empire? Or was there some more subtle process which resulted in inhabitants of the empire assuming new identities as members of one or other of the peoples in question, those people therefore being quite new groupings of humanity? Although these questions have often been raised specifically in the context of the end of the Roman Empire in the west, they are in essence more widely applicable to the processes by which, throughout our period, the political map of Western Europe changed and new kingdoms emerged, and we need to think broadly.

2

From Roman Empire to barbarian kingdoms: cataclysm or transition?

How and why did the Roman Empire in the west disintegrate in the period following the late fifth century? In crude terms, historians have used three interpretative models to answer these questions. The first and second, which we shall nickname the Doom and Gloom Models, embody variants of an interpretation according to which the Roman Empire in the west was destroyed by forces which were irresistible and beyond its control. The thesis of the first is that there was a general process of decline and disaster in all aspects of the Roman Empire, which had been going on since the third century, and which so sapped the empire's strength that it was unable to resist the fragmentation of its western territories amongst incoming barbarians. The thesis of the second is that the power of the Roman Empire was not sufficient to withstand one or all of the waves of barbarians which stormed against its frontiers, and the invasions which resulted brought about its demise in the west. According to this model, the barbarians were just too numerous, too powerful, too ferocious to be resisted, and so the Roman Empire was forced to admit them within its frontiers, and to cede its western provinces to them to form the new barbarian kingdoms. What happened to the Roman Empire could be explained by either of these models by itself, or by both of them working together. There is, however, a quite different model which we can nickname the Deliberate Roman Policy Model. According to this, the division of the western Roman Empire into the barbarian kingdoms was the result of deliberate policy pursued by the Roman government and supported by the Roman aristocracy of the West. It consequently involved very little real change or disruption, but was a process of transformation rather than one involving a serious break in the way Western Europe developed.

The First Doom and Gloom Model

To test out this model, we need to consider, first, how far Late Roman government showed symptoms of such decline and disaster, and, secondly, how far the empire as a whole did.

Late Roman government

The Emperor Diocletian (284–305) presided over radical changes in Roman government. In many provinces he made the responsibilities of the governor (*praeses*) entirely civil, encompassing chiefly law and taxation, while leaving military responsibility to a duke (*dux*); he subdivided many provinces to make them more manageable, while grouping them into dioceses each under a vicar; he expanded the central civil service; and he undertook a major reform of the taxation system.

Supporters of the First Doom and Gloom Model regard these changes, which seem on the face of it to be an expression of imperial power, as evidence of weakness, for – they maintain – the civil service was now too large and too burdensome on the imperial finances. Such an argument seems impossible to assess; and you may be more impressed by the achievements of the Late Roman government. In 301, for example, Emperor Diocletian issued an Edict of Prices, which defined prices for commodities throughout the empire; it was certainly widely known, appearing for example on an inscription at Aezani in Phrygia. It is possible to regard this in a negative way – as a deleterious state intervention; but you might wish rather to be impressed by the governmental power and confidence which such an edict implies. It is of course also possible to emphasise the Edict of Prices as a symptom of inflation in the economic system, although how far inflation extended and how far it was really a threat to the Roman Empire we do not have the data to decide.

In any case, against such an interpretation is the fact that Diocletian's successor, the first Christian emperor Constantine (306–37), introduced a gold coin, the *solidus*, which appears to have brought considerable stability to the Roman imperial coinage. Before its introduction, there clearly had been a problem with the declining precious metal content of coins, so that they had become little more than bronze coins washed in silver or gold; but the *solidus* retained its gold-content across many centuries in the eastern Roman Empire, it was stable and successful in the west until the Empire disintegrated, and even had a major impact on the currencies of the barbarian kingdoms which succeeded it.

There are more major landmarks in the achievements of the Roman imperial government in this period. A considerable achievement was the *Code of Theodosius*, a very substantial compilation of Roman law issued since 312, made under the emperor Theodosius II in 437. We might equally be impressed by the evidence we have, fragmentary as it is, for the military organisation of the Roman Empire from 300 onwards. The *Notitia Dignitatum* is a document quite different to the *Code of Theodosius*, but it is in many ways equally impressive. It sets out in great detail the disposition of Roman military units in the east around 401 and in the west in 425, apart from Italy, for which there must surely have been information but this was not included in the document as we have it. We can wonder whether the document is accurate; but the very fact of its compilation suggests a government of considerable ambition and capability (or, at least, pretension), while – if it does represent reality – the density of the distribution of military units is not suggestive of a state in disastrous decline.

Moreover, there seems to have been a major reorganisation of the army, probably in the time of the emperor Constantine, into mobile forces (*comitatenses*) on the one hand, and frontier defence forces (*limitanei*) on the other. This reorganisation was apparently accompanied by a considerable increase in numbers of troops. These developments too can be seen in a negative light from the viewpoint of the First Doom and Gloom Model. You could argue that the Roman army, numerous as it was, was really no match for the barbarians; its equipment was too light; its drill was inadequate for it to be a match for the barbarian hordes. But none of this is easy to take seriously. We know that barbarians had been recruited into the Roman armies on a considerable scale from an early date, so it is hard to accept that there was really such a disparity between a Roman army and a barbarian one. While it is true that Roman military equipment had changed by the fourth century from the classic equipment of the first and second century, it does not follow that it was less effective, or even lighter, for we hear of the deployment of heavily armed cavalrymen called cataphracts.

As for drill, one of the great strengths of the Roman army had been its discipline, especially in the execution of tactical manoeuvres, but there is no evidence that this deteriorated in the late Roman period. We can turn, for example, to the account of the Battle of Strasbourg fought in the mid-fourth century between a Roman army and a force of barbarians called Alamanns, the start of which is described by the contemporary historian Ammianus Marcellinus (Book 16, section 11.12). He gives no indication here of lack of drill, referring rather to the Romans' trumpets having 'brayed in unison', with the Roman infantry 'covered by squadrons of cavalry'. Still more impressive are his accounts of the emperor Julian's campaign against the Persian Kingdom, which, although unsuccessful as a result of the chance killing of the emperor, involved deploying land-troops coordinated with naval vessels on the River Euphrates. Of course, you can be sceptical of this reading of Ammianus on the grounds that he was a man deeply learned in Latin literature of the past, and that he was representing this and other battles as if they were classic Roman encounters of an earlier period; but that would be no more than a conjecture.

Equally significant for the military capabilities of the Roman Empire in this period were the programmes of building new fortifications and refurbishing old ones along the Roman frontiers and coastlines. On the northern British frontier, for example, Hadrian's Wall appears to have been extensively repaired and refurbished in the Late Roman period. Excavations at one of its forts, Housesteads, have shown not only the addition of interval towers along the walls of the fort in order to bring it more into line with state-of-the-art fortification; but also substantial reshaping of the barrack blocks.

Figure 1 Portchester Saxon Shore fort from the air. The wall surrounding the fort is 10 ft thick and over 20 ft high. The rectangular structure in the top left-hand corner is a medieval castle which was built to make use of a small part of the surviving Roman walls.
Source: Courtesy of Jim Bramble, Portsmouth Technical High School.

Excavations at the Roman city of Winchester have shown the creation in the Late Roman period of massive platforms, presumably intended to provide for the installation of the great Roman shooting-machines, the *ballistae*, which were capable of firing large missiles over considerable distances. At York, the great multangular tower which survives in the Museum Park to the south-west of York Minster has been shown by excavation to be only one of an impressive line of state-of-the-art towers built along the fortifications bordering the River Ouse.

The south-east coast of Britain was equipped with a chain of massive forts, the so-called Saxon Shore forts (Fig. 1), supported by a system of signal stations to warn of approaching danger along the coasts to the north, around Whitby and Scarborough, for example.

The exact dating of these developments is open to question, but they probably belong to the third century and later. Those convinced of the later Roman Empire's weakness can see them as ineffective displays rather than real exercises of power, or symptoms of desperation rather than signs of control. But considering the remoteness of Britain from the centres of Roman imperial power, development of fortifications on this scale may well strike you as impressive testimony to the Roman Empire's capabilities even towards the end of its existence in Western Europe.

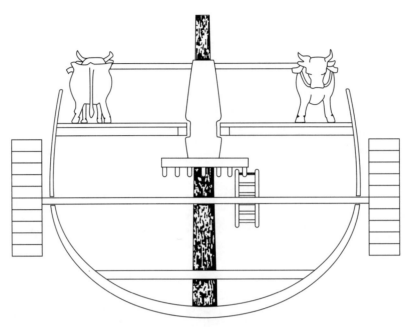

Figure 2 The *liburna* (oxen-powered paddle-ship) from the anonymous 'On Military Matters'. This modern reconstuction of this invention represents it as a cross-section of the ship amidships. The oxen are yoked to a bar which goes through the top of the capstan. As they walk in a circle on the deck of the ship, the capstan turns, and the large cog-wheel below the deck engages with another cog-wheel (seen vertically on to us) which drives the axle on which the two paddle wheels to the right and left of the vessel are attached (Thompson and Flower, 1996).

The inventiveness of Roman fortification towards the end of the Roman Empire in the west is as impressive as its scale. In the use of flanking towers, for example, we are seeing the first appearance of a feature of fortification which was to dominate castle-building in the later Middle Ages. The Roman Empire had not been prone to exploit the technological potential of new inventions, its failure really to use the water-mill being an example. But there is evidence that it could nevertheless be vigorous and imaginative in the mid-fourth century, for we have a remarkable tract by an anonymous author of that period called 'On Military Matters'. This tract was intended to provide advice for the emperors on how they could re-invigorate their armies. It offers a series of inventions, including a warship on which oxen turned capstans to drive the paddle-wheels (Fig. 2), a portable bridge for use on military campaigns, various sorts of firing engines, and a chariot which had a mechanism for automatically lashing the horses.

The emperor

We might equally be impressed by the position and power of the emperor. The third century had been dominated by a series of military usurpations and short rulerships.

But towards its end the emperor Diocletian drastically reorganised the whole system underpinning the emperor's position. He divided the empire into two parts, the western empire and eastern empire with the divide running across the Balkans (Map 1). Each half was to be ruled over by an emperor termed an *augustus*; and each *augustus* was to be assisted by a subordinate emperor to be known as a *caesar*. This college of two *augusti* and two *caesars* was never entirely stable. Diocletian's successor, the emperor Constantine (306–37), in fact ruled over the whole empire after his victory over the eastern emperor Licinius in 324, and so too did Theodosius I the Great (379–95). But Diocletian's college of emperors nevertheless had a certain reality, and the frontier survived as that of the Roman Empire in the east, following the dissolution of its western counterpart. Of course, there was political instability, as in the case of the usurpation of the imperial throne by Julian (360–3), or the usurpation of Eugenius (392–4). But perhaps we should be impressed rather by Diocletian having the power to make a reorganisation on this scale, and we might conclude that his successors were all the stronger for it. Moreover, the instability affecting their position in the course of the fourth and fifth centuries could be seen as much less than the chronic instability which had affected emperors of the third century, with for example a whole series of usurpers between 232 and 284, or than that which had prevailed in the bloody series of civil wars and usurpations between 67 and 69.

Maybe the fact that the emperors so drastically changed their own religion and that of the Roman Empire as a whole was another sign of power. At the beginning of the fourth century, Christianity was a minority religion, not well entrenched in the dominant groups of the Roman Empire, and just emerging from an extended period of persecution. Yet the emperor Constantine adopted it, choosing to favour it at the expense of paganism; and his successors (with the exception of the brief reign of the pagan emperor Julian) laid the basis for making Christianity the official religion of the Roman Empire, which was achieved when the emperor Theodosius the Great prohibited pagan worship by law in 391. Of course, there may have been trends within the development of Christianity and within the Roman Empire itself which made all this feasible; but, on the face of it at least, it does look as if the emperors' adoption of Christianity represented the exercise of a very considerable power, which did not baulk at unsettling and eventually banning the pagan religion which was so embedded in Roman culture and Roman heritage. And it had the power to promote the development of a wealthy and powerful Church hierarchy which was to have such a dominant effect on subsequent centuries.

The emperors were also impressive builders. Anyone who has stood inside the ruins of the massive basilica completed by the emperor Constantine in the ancient forum at Rome cannot fail to be struck by its scale, dwarfing earlier buildings on the forum. Equally impressive was the palace of the later Roman emperors at their centre of power in the city of Trier on the River Mosel (Germany), a small part of which now forms Trier cathedral; or the great imperial residence which the emperor Diocletian built for his retirement on the Adriatic coast at Split. It is hard to escape the conclusion that such rulers had real power, even if supporters of the First Doom and Gloom Model can still argue that it was not sufficient for the problems they faced.

The Roman Empire as a whole

The view that the empire as a whole was in the process of terminal decline in the later Roman period and that this explains its dissolution in the West rests on various types of evidence. First, that for supposed dramatic falls in population in the later Roman period, sometimes being calculated at as much as from seventy millions for the population of the empire as a whole in the time of the emperor Augustus to fifty millions by the time of the emperor Diocletian, with further falls thereafter. The problem with such figures is how they can possibly be verified when we do not have anything approaching census data, or any statistical data at all for the empire as a whole. We have figures for the city of Rome, which do indeed show very considerable declines in the city's population. But for the Roman Empire as a whole discussion has to rest on evidence such as that of inscribed tombstones to assess the death-rate, and such evidence is extremely partial and difficult to interpret. It has also rested on the frequent references in imperial documents to *agri deserti* ('deserted fields'), which evidently concerned the Late Roman government deeply. Some claim that this means that lands actually were being deserted because there were not enough people to cultivate them. But others argue that these *agri deserti* were not lands actually deserted, but lands which were not paying tax to the government, so that they are evidence for tax-gathering problems rather than population decline.

Secondly, evidence supposedly showing that the tax-burden, increased as it was by the emperor Diocletian's expansion of the civil service, was crushing and sapped the Roman Empire's strength. This evidence consists largely of the complaints of tax-payers, particularly aristocratic tax-payers whose writings are generally all that we have, and whose complaints may be evidence less for the tax-burden than for the unwillingness of those liable to pay taxes actually to pay them. We have looked already at the reform of the coinage, and we should perhaps be impressed by the Roman Empire remaining an essentially monetary economy, even though it is true that some payments were made in kind, such as the *annona militaris*, a system of in-kind payments used to support the Roman army.

The First Doom and Gloom Model has also found ammunition in the supposedly peasant revolts of the later Roman Empire, especially those of the so-called *Bacaudae* in Gaul, which Marxist historians have woven into an image of class conflict undermining and weakening the Roman Empire. But it is by no means easy to see the *Bacaudae* or any other peasant insurrections as evidence for such conflict. The *Bacaudae* may not even really have been a peasant movement – many of the references in the sources are merely to brigands, while those in the fifth century seem to be to rebels of middling status, the only individual amongst them known by name being a doctor. Disruption of war within the empire may explain their activities much better than class conflict.

More ammunition can be found in the series of usurpations which constituted the so-called 'third-century crisis', characterised as it was by civil wars and barbarian incursions. But aristocratic families such as those of the Rufii Festi and the Anicii seem to have lived their lives undisturbed, so we may be struck rather by the strengths and continuities of the aristocratic life of the later Roman Empire. In the letters of the great Roman senator Symmachus (*c*.345–402), for example, we find him using his great wealth to organise the most traditional of Roman aristocratic activities, such as circus games for his son in which a group of captive Saxons were made to strangle each other (the violence of Roman games was part of their traditional appeal). We have the same sense from great villas like that at Piazza Armerina in Sicily with its magnificent mosaics.

It is, then, possible to envisage the later Roman Empire in a much more positive light: to see it rather as the springboard of European history, and as providing the foundations for the continuing success of the east Roman Empire for nearly a millennium after the dissolution of the western empire. In that case, however, the problem of why that dissolution took place at all becomes all the more acute.

The Second Doom and Gloom Model

In its crudest form, this model maintains that the Roman Empire in the west was violently swept away by the overwhelming force of waves of barbarians breaking across its frontiers. This had supposedly begun already in the third century, but was to reach a dreadful climax in the late fourth and fifth centuries as a result of the people called the Huns moving westwards across the great steppe plains of central Europe. This initiated a sort of domino effect amongst the barbarians living east of the Roman Empire's frontiers, and, by the mid-fifth century, it culminated in the military incursions of Attila, king of the Huns, leading his army of fearsome mounted warriors from his headquarters in central Europe deep into the Roman Empire. The domino effect is supposed to have caused the people called the Goths to cross the River Danube into the eastern Roman Empire in 376, defeating a Roman army and killing the Roman emperor Valens at the Battle of Adrianople in 378, and going on to sack the city of Rome itself in 410, and on again to establish the kingdom of the Visigoths in Spain and south-west France. In 407, a great confederation of barbarians had crossed the River Rhine and proceeded to take control of much of Roman Gaul in a fierce and destructive campaign. By the end of the fifth century, the barbarian kingdoms had largely taken their initial shape, with the kingdom of the Burgundians emerging by 443, the kingdom of the Ostrogoths appearing in the area known as Pannonia (between the rivers Sava and Danube in modern Hungary and Croatia) by 454 and embracing Italy by 493, and the kingdom of the Franks appearing in the area of north-east France and Belgium by the later fifth century. As Britain had already been given up by the Roman government, perhaps in 410, all this effectively marked the dismemberment of the Roman Empire in the west, which was represented symbolically by the deposition of the emperor Romulus Augustulus in 476 at the hands of a barbarian ruler called Odoacer, whose rule in Italy preceded that of the Ostrogoths.

How strong is the evidence for this model? First, the images of 'waves' and 'tides' of barbarians piling up against the empire's frontiers assumes that these barbarians were seriously numerous. But the only actual figures we have for the number of a barbarian people is that given, by the Latin writer Victor of Vitensis in 484 and the Greek writer Procopius about fifty years later, for the people called the Vandals, who entered the Roman Empire in 407 and in 429 crossed the Straits of Gibraltar from Spain to North Africa, where they established a kingdom. They numbered, according to our writers, 80,000, although it is not clear whether women and children were included in this figure, and Victor observes that the figure was a ruse to trick the Romans who were providing the shipping. The fourth-century Christian writer, Jerome, says that 80,000 barbarians came up the Rhine in 370, and various sources give the number of barbarians who crossed the Alps under the leadership of Radagaisus in 405 in hundreds of thousands. It is, of course, very difficult to know what to make of these numbers, and to decide whether the Roman writers were just guessing or giving fanciful figures. Nonetheless, when the barbarians were within the Roman Empire, the Roman authorities had to deploy very large armies against them, suggesting that they numbered tens of thousands of warriors.

It might be possible to estimate the number of barbarians settled on Roman soil from their cemeteries, for barbarian funerary practices involved the use of grave-goods which may perhaps enable barbarian dead to be identified and counted. Such cemeteries are very unevenly spread through the former western Roman Empire from the fifth and sixth centuries, so that even on these terms it does not look as if the numbers of barbarians settling in the empire were very great, except in relatively limited areas such as south-eastern Britain, north-eastern France, and parts of Spain. But it is possible to undermine even this evidence, by arguing that the style of the grave-goods buried with the deceased in these cemeteries was as much Late Roman as it was characteristically barbarian. So these cemeteries need not be evidence at all of barbarian numbers. They could contain the graves of members of the indigenous Roman population, whose styles of dress and jewellery had come to be indistinguishable from those of whatever barbarians there may have been, who were themselves influenced by Roman style. So there is no really solid archaeological evidence that very large numbers of barbarians were pressing against the Roman frontiers and pouring into Roman territory (below, Chapter 2). Nor is there evidence of any unity between them. In the first century, the Roman writer Tacitus, in his *On Germany*, described the peoples east of the Roman frontiers and called them all 'Germans'. But he himself makes it clear that he was describing a kaleidoscopic array of peoples. Reciprocal hostility between them was probably the norm, and there is certainly no evidence that they felt any empathy with barbarians serving in the Roman armies, and thus constituted a particular threat to the empire's security.

The Deliberate Roman Policy Model

To understand this third model, we need to remind ourselves of a crucial aspect of the background to the dissolution of the Roman Empire in the west, that is the division of the empire into a western and an eastern empire implemented first by the emperor Diocletian. Despite the two empires being brought together again under the emperor Constantine and other emperors, the east–west division was a continuing reality. From the reigns of Honorius in the west (395–423) and Arcadius in the east (395–408), the empire was always split. It was, of course, the western emperor, Romulus Augustulus (475–6), whose removal by Odoacer formally ended the western empire.

The model rests first on the absence of any military response from the east Roman emperors to the barbarian incursions and the establishment of the barbarian kingdoms in the west. At no point in the fifth century did an east Roman army attempt to destroy a barbarian kingdom in Western Europe. It was clearly not that the east Roman emperors could not have done this, for they did send armies into the former western empire, at the beginning of the fifth century against the newly formed kingdom of the Vandals in North Africa and again in the middle of the century in the reign of Leo I (457–74). Moreover, Theodosius I, who ruled the whole empire from Constantinople, despatched an army in 394 to Italy to put down an attempted usurpation by a certain Eugenius. Otherwise, the east Roman emperor did not intervene at all in the west in the fifth century; and specific policy-objectives probably underlay the emperor's Vandal campaign. North Africa was an area of immense importance to the empire because of its capacity to produce grain for shipment across the Mediterranean, a process which could equally benefit the eastern empire.

Secondly, there is evidence that the barbarian kingdoms were established under Roman supervision. When the Visigoths settled in south-west Gaul, a contemporary chronicler called Hydatius says that this was done on the initiative of the Roman patrician Constantius, who handed over to those barbarians' king, Wallia, an area of land for his people to settle. As for Burgundy, we are told that the people called the Burgundians were defeated by the Romans in 443, and that the survivors of their defeat were given an area called *Sapaudia*, which may have been part of what became Burgundy, so that they should divide this 'with the natives'. All this was apparently under the direction of another patrician, Aetius. Later, in 457, their king Gundioc seems to have enlarged their territory, and the chronicler Marius of Avenches says that this involved dividing the lands with the Romans resident there. In the case of Italy, we hear from the sixth-century Byzantine writer Procopius that there was a coup d'état there led by Odoacer, a barbarian who made himself king, and deposed the last Roman emperor in the west, Romulus Augustulus. Although this was not managed by the Romans as the cases of south-west Gaul and Burgundy seem to have been, Odoacer was nevertheless a member of the emperor's bodyguard, so this looks much more like an internal Roman coup than any sort of particularly barbarian conquest. When, in 488, the Gothic leader Theoderic led his people into Italy, eventually to defeat and kill Odoacer in 493 and to make himself king, he acted initially at least with the encouragement of the east Roman emperor Zeno, and he seems throughout his reign to have maintained close contact and collaboration with the Roman senate. In each of these cases, then, the creation of barbarian settlements can be seen as fitting quite well with the Deliberate Roman Policy Model.

Other barbarian settlements are less easy to interpret in this way. The creation of the kingdom of Lombardy in the late sixth century was certainly the result of a Lombard invasion of Italy shortly after it had been conquered by the armies of the east Roman emperor Justinian; but even so the eighth-century historian Paul the Deacon refers to division of land between Romans and Lombards. Other barbarian settlements and kingdoms originated after the end of Roman rule in the west, as was the case with the kingdom of the Visigoths in Spain, and the kingdom of the Franks in Gaul, although this people had been closely in touch with the Roman authorities for as much as two centuries before.

We can of course paint a picture of invasion and pillage, and there is no doubt that the establishment of the barbarian kingdoms did involve these, and did have deleterious effects on the Roman standard of life. But everything suggests that the east Roman emperors could have expelled the barbarians, or at least could have made serious efforts to do so, but chose to settle them on Roman soil in their own barbarian kingdoms. At the very least, this suited the east Roman emperors; at the most, it reflected a deliberate policy.

To support the model, however, we need a hypothesis as to why such a policy of dismembering the west would have seemed appropriate to the eastern emperors. It is instructive to consider that one of the great achievements of the emperor Constantine was the establishment of the great city of Constantinople as the principal city of the empire in preference to the old centre of Rome. He based it on the pre-existing city of Byzantium, but he invested immense funds in building it to every bit as high a standard as Rome itself. It was in many ways an inspired choice, for Constantinople occupied a site between the Bosphorus, the Sea of Marmara, and the inlet known as the Golden Horn, which was both easily defensible, and also strategic in that it controlled the routes out of Asia Minor in the east and out of the Balkans in the west, where they came down to cross the straits of the Bosphorus. It rapidly established itself as the favoured residence of Constantine while he ruled the united empire, and of his successors as rulers of the eastern empire or, in the case of Theodosius I, as rulers again of the united empire.

This emphasis on Constantinople as the centre of the empire in succession to Rome harmonised with the fact that its centre of gravity increasingly lay in the east. Map 4 shows how much greater was the density of cities in the east than in the west – with the exception of North Africa, which may in part explain why that was the only western province which the fifth-century emperors sought to recapture from the barbarians. The east was certainly wealthier than the west, for it was on the eastern Mediterranean coast that the great trade routes from central Asia terminated, and it was the east which had access to the gold mines of the upper Nile Valley and of the Caucasus. It was in the east too that Roman imperial interests lay, especially with regard to the military confrontation with the great kingdom of Persia, which seems to have been regarded as a worthy adversary of the Romans in a way which the barbarians were not. The Persian wars sporadically occupied emperors campaigning in the area of the Rivers Tigris and Euphrates until the destruction of the kingdom of Persia by the Arabs in the seventh century.

The emperors' concern with Christianity also led to an increased focus on the eastern empire, for that was where the religion was strongest in the Late Roman period, and that too was where there arose a series of doctrinal disputes which greatly occupied the attention of the emperors from the fourth century onwards. These included the one about the nature of Christ, called Arianism after its originator, the theologian Arius (died 336) from the school of Alexandria in Roman Egypt.

In short, perhaps it was the eastern empire which really mattered, and the western empire looked, by comparison, unimportant or even deleterious to imperial interests. The western empire was not only less intensely Christian than the eastern, it was also more resolutely pagan, at least at the social level which most concerned the emperors. Many of the aristocrats who were the members of the ancient senate, the body which had governed the Roman state before the time when there were emperors at all, were staunchly pagan, and they clashed with Theodosius I, who was ruling the empire as a whole, when he wanted to remove the pagan Altar of Victory from the Senate House in Rome. As the ancient capital of the Roman world, Rome was deeply impregnated with paganism; and when the first Christian emperor Constantine wanted to build Christian churches in it there was simply no space for this in the central area to do so.

Worse still, from the point of view of the emperors, was the militarisation of the western empire with its enormous armies along the frontiers, and its predilection to produce usurpers who would lead those armies to seize the imperial throne, whether of the west, the east, or of the empire as a whole. This is exactly what Constantine himself had done. After he was made co-emperor (or *caesar*) by the troops stationed at the Roman legionary fortress at York in 306, he led an army to defeat the emperor (or *augustus*) Magnentius at the Battle of Milvian Bridge outside Rome in 312, and then, in 324, to defeat the eastern Roman emperor Licinius and to take control of the whole empire. This was what Constantine's relative Julian did in leading troops out of Gaul to make himself emperor in 360. In 383, Magnus Maximus launched an attempted usurpation from Britain; and three would-be usurpers of imperial power, Marcus, Gratian, and Constantine III, emerged – also from Britain – in 406–7. The risk of violent usurpation of imperial power which the west posed may be the real difference between the east and the west. It may most obviously explain why the eastern emperors were so willing to hand over the western provinces to barbarian rulers who were very unlikely to claim the emperorship.

The possibility that this was imperial policy is strengthened by the fact that there were no comparable barbarian settlements in the eastern empire, despite the very serious Hunnic attacks on it, despite the temporary settlement of the Ostrogoths there in 382, and despite the Gothic victory at the Battle of Adrianople in 378. Such a difference of policy may also have been perceived by the new barbarian rulers in the west, who generally used Roman coins and, as in the case of Theoderic and in the case of Clovis, used Roman official titles, *magister militum* in the case of the former, *consul* and *augustus* in the case of the latter.

To strengthen the model, you could argue that history was rewritten in the sixth century as the result of a series of military campaigns launched by the east Roman

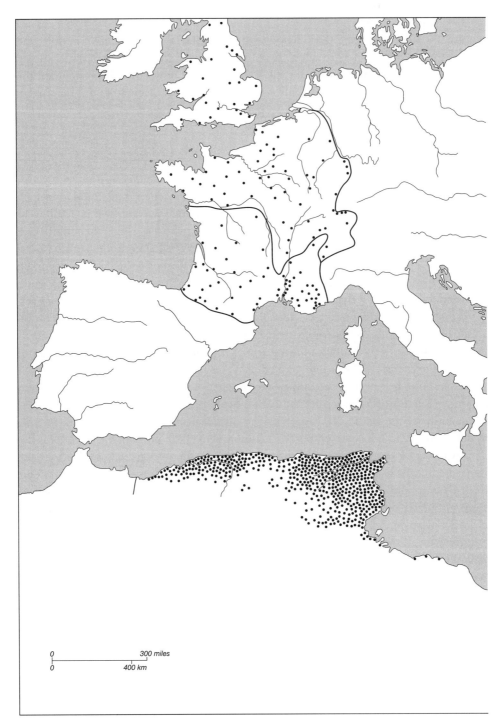

Map 4 The dots show the distribution in the later Roman Empire of cities, that is, urban centres with their surrounding territories. The blank for Italy and Spain is because the appropriate evidence does not survive. Notice the density of dots in the eastern Mediterranean as compared with their sparseness in Gaul and Britain. Of the western provinces, only North Africa is known to have had

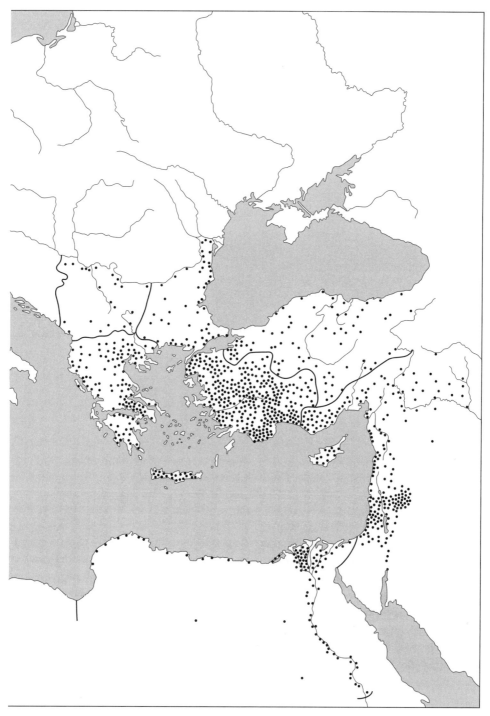

real concentrations of cities, which may account for the determination of the east Roman emperors
to re-take control of it from the barbarians.

Source: Adapted from Jones, A. H. M., *The Later Roman Empire, 284–602: A Social, Economic and
Administrative Survey*, II © 1964, reproduced with permission of Blackwell Publishing Ltd.

emperor Justinian (527–65) to recapture the lands taken by the barbarian kingdoms in the west. These were successful in restoring North Africa to imperial control and destroying the kingdom of the Vandals; they established an east Roman foothold in the southern coastlands of Spain; and they destroyed the kingdom of the Ostrogoths in Italy, although in fact imperial control over much of the peninsula was itself destroyed by the invasion of Lombards and the creation of the kingdom of Lombardy in the late sixth century. In line with the model, it is possible to regard Justinian's campaigns as a new departure in imperial policy. To justify them, you could argue, the Byzantine court historian, Procopius, wrote a *History of the Wars*, which represented them as a natural response to barbarian aggression, and thus deliberately concealed the fact that fifth-century imperial policy aimed at establishing the barbarian kingdoms in the west. It would then have been this picture created by Procopius which influenced subsequent attitudes to the barbarians down to our times.

We are still, however, faced with a problem. We may be able to make a case that the establishment of the barbarian kingdoms and the dissolution of the Roman Empire in the west was desirable for the emperors, who, from their centre of power in Constantinople, now had their attention focused on the east, and who regarded the west as a liability. But why was that dissolution not resisted by the powerful aristocratic landowners of the west, who were apparently so committed to Roman rule and to Roman culture? This may be explicable in terms of the way in which barbarians were actually settled within the Roman lands in the context of the formation of the barbarian kingdoms.

There is a little evidence about this. For Italy, we have two remarkable contemporary letters from the reign of Theoderic. In one, Ennodius, the Roman bishop of Pavia, praises the Roman prefect Liberius for the way he has handled Gothic settlement:

> You have enriched the countless hordes of Goths with generous grants of lands, and yet the Romans have hardly felt it. The victors desire nothing more, and the conquered have felt no loss.
>
> (Jones, 1964, p. 251)

A second letter is from the Roman senator Cassiodorus to the Roman senate, referring to the fact that 'the sharing of estates seems in this case to have produced harmony' (Jones, 1964, p. 251). We have no such explicit statements of satisfaction from the Romans in south-west Gaul and Burgundy, but equally we have no evidence that the barbarian settlements caused difficulties amongst them, let alone causing them to revolt against their new masters.

Cassiodorus's letter talks of 'thirds' (*tertiae*) which were given to the barbarians, and this seems to be echoed in the barbarian law-codes relating to south-west Gaul (the code of King Euric), and to Burgundy (the laws of King Gundobad). The former refers to the 'allotments' (*sortes*) of the Goths, and the 'thirds' (*tertiae*) of the Romans. So it seems reasonably clear that there was some sort of a systematic division of landed resources between the indigenous Romans and the incoming barbarians which was satisfactory to both parties. It may be that the legal basis for this was the Roman laws concerning the billeting of soldiers on civilians. The relevant law in the Code of Theodosius deals with how a billeted soldier should have one-third of the civilian's house to which he is assigned, which is of course reminiscent of the proportions for barbarian and Roman land-holding after the settlements referred to in the barbarian law-codes mentioned earlier. If billeting was indeed the legal foundation for the barbarian settlements, then it was actually a division of the land itself between Romans and barbarians which formed the basis of the settlement of the latter. Thus a barbarian being settled on the land of a Roman aristocrat would be assigned, effectively in ownership, one-third or two-thirds of his lands (depending on where this was). In either case, it is very hard to see why this took place as such a peaceful process as it apparently did.

It may be, however, that the Roman system of billeting is not at all relevant to the barbarian settlements. The law in the Code of Theodosius explicitly forbids soldiers from accepting anything more from their billets than warmth and shelter. Since they were prohibited from taking food, it is not easy to see what connection there could have been between this and the actual taking over of Roman land which is envisaged in the barbarian settlements. So it may be that what was actually shared out between Romans and barbarians was not land as we normally understand it, but rather the tax-revenues which the land owed to the imperial government. In other words, barbarian settlers on Roman territory were granted not one-third or two-thirds of the actual land, but rather those proportions of the tax-revenues from it. If we assume that the barbarians settling in the empire were not so much entire asylum-seeking peoples, but were rather groups of warriors with their dependants, such a system would have made excellent sense from their point of view. They could have continued to provide military services, as they had previously done in the service of the emperor, rather than concerning themselves with agriculture. And they could have been guaranteed an income since they would have collected the taxes directly from the tax-payers, rather than waiting on payments from the imperial government.

Equally importantly, such a system would have made excellent sense from the point of view of the aristocratic Roman landowners, whose position would in fact have been very little affected. Whereas previous to the barbarian settlements they would have paid their taxes directly to the imperial government, which would have used them in part to pay the salaries of soldiers, including barbarian mercenaries and federates, to protect the landowners, they now paid a proportion of their taxes directly to those barbarians. Barbarians had been used as Roman troops for a long time, so no one would have found this exceptionable. And it may well have seemed to the aristocrats much more satisfactory to be, as it were, cutting out the middle man, and to be supporting military forces to protect them on the spot rather than supporting those of an often distant emperor, who might use them not at all in the interests of the landowning aristocrats of the western empire.

Whatever you resolve, the debate around these three models must focus attention on how far the end of the Roman Empire in the west was more an organic change than a violent upheaval, more a transformation than a revolution and, if you go in that direction, there are many implications for how far Roman institutions and Roman forms of organisation continued to dominate Western Europe even after the Roman Empire had ceased to exist there. But it raises questions also of what the barbarian peoples really were and how they were formed, and it is to those that we must turn in the next chapter.

Research and study

Broad research questions

Was the disintegration of the Roman Empire in the west the result of long-term decline (First Doom and Gloom Model)?

Was it due to the force of barbarian pressure from outside of it (Second Doom and Gloom Model)?

Was it what the Roman emperors in Constantinople and the senatorial aristocrats in the west wanted (Deliberate Roman Policy Model)?

Books and papers to begin with

Very influential as a counter-blast to the First Doom and Gloom Model has been the massive, but surprisingly readable, work of Jones (1964); and you can get some sense of what he was reacting to in, for example, Moss (1935, pp. 1–37). Another, quite different counter-blast was delivered by Brown (1971) in an equally influential book, arguing that the later Roman Empire was a very creative and innovative period, notably in spiritual and religious development. Of more recent books, Mitchell (2007) builds excellently on Jones's work. Ferrill (1986) presents a rather crude version of the Second Doom and Gloom Model, while Heather (2006) offers a much more subtle view of the importance of the barbarians. The most extreme recent argument emphasising the effects of barbarian force and damage to the Roman Empire is Ward-Perkins (2005). The most recent statement of the case against the importance of the barbarians in the end of the Roman Empire in the west is Goffart (2006, especially chs 2, 5, and 7). The titles of two quite general books, Heather (2009) and Halsall (2005), indicate the extent to which they are preoccupied with this discussion. On Goffart's side, and very helpful, is Wolfram (1997). Also useful are Jones (1966), Cameron (1993), Moorhead (2001), and the relevant chapters in Cameron and Garnsey (1998) and Cameron, Ward-Perkins, and Whitby (2000).

Pursuing more specific aspects

Late Roman military capabilities

How effective was the late Roman army in fighting wars and defending against barbarian attack?

On the Roman army and fortifications, see Southern and Dixon (2000). On the *limitanei* specifically, there is a good discussion in Elton (1996, ch. 5). On fortifications, see Johnson (1983), and, for the Late Roman refurbishment of Hadrian's Wall, Johnson (1989). The Saxon Shore forts in Britain can be pursued in Pearson (2002). Also worth looking at is Reece (1999). Goldsworthy (1999) has some helpful material on the Roman army, for example its performance at the Battle of Strasbourg. Ferrill (1986) provides a clear Doom and Gloom statement of the case for the deficiency of Late Roman military capabilities.

Late Roman governmental capabilities

How effective was Late Roman government?

Useful and easily accessible are the sections in Bowman, Cameron, and Garnsey (2005) and Cameron and Garnsey (1998). Kelly (2004) enables you to go deeper into the nature of Late Roman government. On Late Roman coins, including the *solidus*, see Kent (1978). The role of the emperors in the conversion of the Roman Empire to Christianity is discussed below, Chapter 9. For the emperors' ambitious use of architecture in promoting themselves (Constantine's basilica, for example), see Wheeler (1964), Hannestad (1988), or Elsner (1998).

Social tension in the later Roman Empire

How far did social tension and peasant revolt weaken the later Roman Empire?

Ideas of decline resulting from social tension were developed by the Soviet historian Rostovtzeff (1957) and the American Walbank (1969). The latter discusses the *Bacaudae* as a symptom of class-warfare, but there is a more modern study, revising this interpretation, in Drinkwater and Elton (1992, ch. 18). The dominance of the aristocracy in the Roman west can be pursued in Arnheim (1972) and in a rather heavyweight book by Matthews (1990), summarised in a review by Wormald (1976). A book on this topic which, although old, is engaging and readable, bringing you closely in touch with the evidence, is Dill (1933).

The barbarians

What were the mechanisms by which the barbarians were settled in the Roman Empire?

The most outspoken statement of the thesis that the barbarians were settled peacefully as a result of Roman policy is Goffart (1981). The argument that their settlement, at least in Italy, Gaul, and Spain, cannot have been based on Roman billeting, but must have involved the diversion of tax-revenues from the Roman government to the barbarians themselves, is set out very lucidly in a longer work (Goffart, 1980). Goffart (2006) is a response to criticism of this in the previous twenty-six years. Chapter 6 'revisits' the argument about diversion of tax-revenues, and seeks to refute the critics who have, as Goffart points out, paid little attention to his rejection of billeting as the basis for barbarian settlement, and have therefore left a void in the interpretation which he believes his thesis regarding tax-revenues fills.

A lucid paper in opposition to this, maintaining in the case of Italy that land and not tax-revenues was what was diverted, is Barnish (1986). There is a useful summary of the debate in Halsall (2005, pp. 422–6). In some ways, though, the best thing is to consider the actual texts on which this debate is based. You can see them in translation interspersed in the text of Goffart (2006).

3

The making of peoples

What makes a people and why do peoples form? What did it mean to be a Visigoth or an Ostrogoth or a Burgundian or a Frank? What were the origins of the peoples in question? What sort of groupings of humanity were they? Did they represent genuine groups of people bound together by particular ties, or were their names just labels used by kings and members of the elite as a matter of convenience without any real basis in the relationships between the people assigned to them? These questions are amongst the most complex, shifting, and sometimes subjective that we have to address, and there are many avenues which you can pursue, only some of which can be touched on in this chapter. We shall begin with the problems of how and why peoples developed in the context of the end of the Roman Empire in the west and the emergence of the barbarian kingdoms, which offer us such a kaleidoscope of peoples to consider. We can illustrate this with a map such as Map 5.

Here you can see in graphic form the way in which the history of the barbarian peoples was envisaged in terms of actual migration and settlement. Take, for example, the Goths. You can see their supposed origin in Scandinavia, and their migration, supposedly around the middle of the second century AD across the Baltic Sea, and so on southwards across what is now Russia, until at some point in the third and fourth centuries they were separated into the Ostrogoths, settled to the north of the Black Sea, and the Visigoths, settled to the north-west of the same sea, on the northern banks of the River Danube. There a great Gothic confederation arose, which was driven southwards and westwards into the Roman Empire by the remorseless pressure of the supposed migration of the people known as the Huns. The arrow emerging from the east marks this migration, with the date 375, which is the year given in Roman sources for the first appearance of this people.

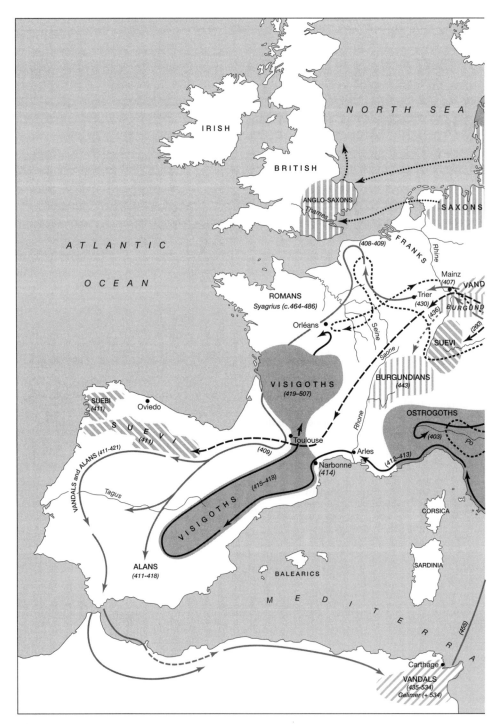

Map 5 A map of the barbarian invasions.
Source: Adapted from Porcha, J. and Volbach, W. F., *Europe in the Dark Ages* (Thames and Hudson, 1969). Photo UDF/© Gallimard.

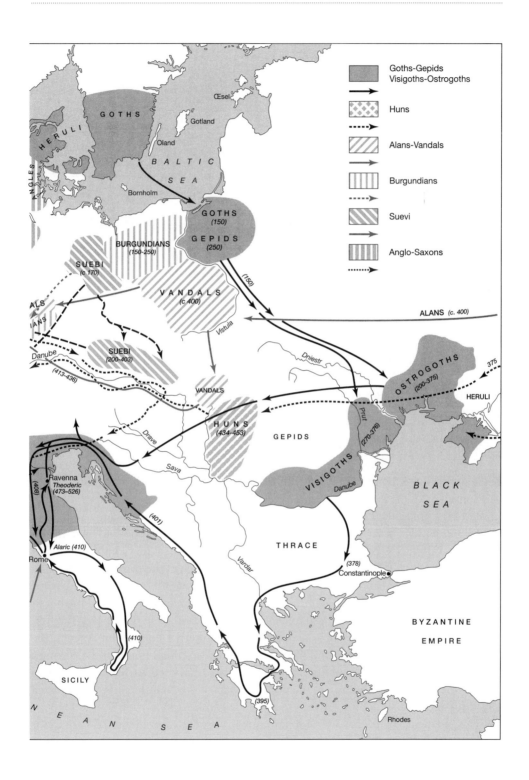

Legend:

- Goths-Gepids / Visigoths-Ostrogoths
- Huns
- Alans-Vandals
- Burgundians
- Suevi
- Anglo-Saxons

Map labels:

GOTHS
HERULI
ANGLES
Œsel
Gotland
Oland
BALTIC SEA
Bornholm
GOTHS (150)
GEPIDS (250)
BURGUNDIANS (150-250)
SUEBI (c. 170)
VANDALS (c. 400)
Vistula
SUEBI (200-403)
VANDALS
ALS
IANS
Danube
(413-436)
(150)
ALANS (c. 400)
Dniestr
OSTROGOTHS (200-375)
375
HERULI
Drave
HUNS (434-453)
GEPIDS
Prut
(270-376)
Sava
Ravenna
Theoderic (473-526)
(408)
(401)
VISIGOTHS
Danube
BLACK SEA
Alaric (410)
Rome
(410)
THRACE
Vardar
(378)
Constantinople
SICILY
(395)
BYZANTINE EMPIRE
N E A N   S E A
Rhodes

After the Visigoths had crossed the River Danube with Roman permission in 376, they settled briefly in Thrace (you can see the name on the map), but they revolted against the Romans and defeated them at the Battle of Adrianople in 378. After that victory, the arrow marking their movements goes remorselessly on, bringing them into Italy, where they sacked Rome in 410, and so on to Spain, where they were defeated by the Romans and settled in 418 in south-western Gaul. Later, however, they again expanded into Spain, forming the kingdom of the Visigoths, which lasted (in Spain at least) until it was destroyed by Moslem invaders from North Africa in the early eighth century. As for the Ostrogoths, you can see their settlement in the area called Pannonia (between the rivers Sava and Danube in modern Hungary and Croatia) in 454, and then their entry into Italy to form the kingdom of the Ostrogoths from 493.

Meanwhile, the pressure of the Huns continued to increase as they established a great hegemony over the peoples of central Europe east of the Roman Empire. In 407, that pressure is supposed to have driven a whole group of barbarian peoples westwards across the River Rhine. Of these, the Burgundians, as we have seen, were eventually defeated in northern Gaul by the Romans and were settled in the area of Switzerland and the Rhone Valley to form the kingdom of the Burgundians. The Suebi, originating from the upper valley of the River Danube, moved to establish the kingdom of the Suebi in what is now Portugal and north-west Spain. The Vandals were driven on through Gaul and Spain, across the Straits of Gibraltar in 429 to become military allies (federates) of the Roman Empire in the Roman province of North Africa, only to revolt against the Romans and to establish the kingdom of the Vandals, centred on the city of Carthage.

Finally, you can see the pool representing the Franks around the valley of the River Rhine, with those Franks known as the Salians around its mouth and those known as Ripuarians to the east of its central section down to its banks. Less affected by the power of the Huns, the Franks had long been settled in these regions, being noted there by Roman writers as early as the second century AD, and they appear to have begun to settle within the Roman Empire from an early date. Under their king Childeric in the later fifth century, however, they came to occupy much of the provinces of Roman Gaul called Germania and Belgica, and under his son Clovis (486–511) they established a kingdom of the Franks which embraced much of Gaul and was to expand further in the course of the sixth century. Also unaffected by the Huns were the Angles (English) and the Saxons, whom you can see coming from southern Denmark (or Angeln, the supposed home of the Angles) and from Saxony (the supposed home of the Saxons). The map might also show another people who are supposed to have migrated to Britain, the Jutes, whose home was the northern part of the Danish peninsula, the area called Jutland.

This sequence of events was not fantastical, for the movements of barbarians it represents are described by contemporary and near-contemporary historians who, like the draughtsmen of such maps, assumed that they were dealing with distinct barbarian peoples, which had distinct places of origin in the distant past, and had, sometimes under the pressure of another migrating people, migrated en masse into the Roman Empire where they had established kingdoms peculiar to the various peoples. Underlying this was an interpretation of the nature of peoples which Patrick J. Geary (2002, p. 42) calls the Biological Model, defined as: 'standing largely outside the process of historical change . . . based on descent, custom, and geography'. The first part of this definition relates to the idea represented by the map that the barbarian groups were coherent peoples with histories reaching deep into the past, or in other words that they had not been affected across the centuries by 'historical change'. The second part of the definition, together with the label Geary gives it, underlines the idea that a people was a coherent group in terms of its members being related to each other biologically, more closely at any rate than they were to members of other peoples. According to this model, a people is a biologically, racially pure entity, which also has a defined area of origin and residence (hence Geary's reference to 'geography'), and coherent and distinctive customs which have not changed over time.

Geary calls his alternative model the Constitutional Model, and defines it as: 'based on law, allegiance, and created by the historical process'. So the issuing of laws in the name of a people – or for the exclusive use of a people – may be part of this process of people-formation, as may be allegiance to a particular leader, a king declaring himself to be ruler of the people in question, for example. The 'historical process' refers to the ways in which peoples evolve over time, so that they are not necessarily ancient entities at all, but may be the product of a series of historical events, such as conquests.

When it comes to explaining the emergence of the barbarian kingdoms, the Constitutional Model can itself be broken down into two submodels:

> Mass-Migration Submodel: There were migrations, mass-migrations we could call them, around and into the Roman Empire, but these were of neither racially pure nor long-established peoples, but rather of groups in a constant state of change and evolution. So the formation of peoples was the result of identity-change, but within a context of actual migrations.

> Military Elite Submodel: There were no migrations. All that happened was that barbarians, either those who had served in the Roman armies, or those forming barbarian armies in the service of Rome, established the kingdoms which succeeded the Roman Empire, and they themselves were the rulers and the social elite. They duly assigned to those kingdoms new identities which derived from their own barbarian associations. The Roman populations of the areas of those kingdoms gave their allegiance to these new barbarian rulers and elites, and thus assumed new identities deriving from their barbarian associations. Thus new peoples were formed by negotiation and agreement.

You may want to develop intermediate or variant versions of these models and sub-models as you consider the problem of how and why peoples formed at the end of the Roman Empire in the west. But let us take them as they are for the moment, and begin to test them out against the evidence we have.

The Biological Model

The Biological Model, then, involves mass-migration of peoples founded on descent, custom, language, law, marks and fashions and geography.

Descent

Common descent as a characteristic of peoples, or in other words the concept of the blood-purity of peoples (or races), was quite widely accepted by scholars, implicitly and explicitly, before the mid-twentieth century, but it ceased to enjoy support, partly because it came to be associated with the horrific policies of the German Nazis for the genocide of peoples like the Jews who were considered not to be of pure 'German' blood, and for the expansion of the German state to areas like the Sudetenland, which were considered to be part of the ancient homeland of the 'German people'. Early medieval history, interpreted on the lines of the Biological Model, provided an important intellectual justification, as it had done for the whole process of the rise of modern nationalism since the nineteenth century.

Another reason for the rejection of common descent as an indicator of peoplehood has been because studies of modern peoples have shown the extent to which members of any one people are often the descendants of very varied groups who have come together as a people because they regard themselves as being members of it rather than because of any blood relationships with other members. For the ancient past, this was obviously the case with the Romans themselves, for Roman citizenship had been extended by imperial decree to everyone within the empire, regardless of their ancestry – with the result that the Roman people was a mixture of groups who had simply come to assume the identity of being Roman.

Nothing, however, is simple. Modern research on DNA, which is the matrix in all our cells which carries the genetic code for our bodies, opens intriguing new possibilities that it really might be possible to evaluate scientifically the relative interrelationship of members of peoples. A recent project on samples of present-day populations of England, Wales, and Frisia has considered the code contained specifically in the Y-chromosome, that is the male chromosome which is passed from father to son, based on blood-samples. The results show that the English samples have Y-chromosomes which are much more like those in the Frisian samples than in the Welsh. One explanation might be, of course, that there had been a migration of a more or less interrelated people from Frisia to England, the result of which was that the native British were killed or displaced to the west, where they became the Welsh. This would partially confirm the spirit at least of what is represented for Britain on Map 5, and it would mean that the formation of the English was really about the migration of a racially defined people.

Aside from the fact that the scientific methods involved are in their infancy and the research project involved only samples, there is, however, a very serious objection to accepting such an interpretation. Although the researchers assumed that the supposed migrations at the end of the Roman Empire were the context for the introduction of the dominant Frisian DNA into England, there is no way of proving this. The DNA tested came from the present-day populations, and we simply cannot know whether its distribution really originated in such a remote period, or whether it is the product of some process or processes extending over many centuries. It is possible to suggest statistically that the DNA pattern may in fact have resulted from quite small numbers of people coming into England from Frisia, and establishing themselves in dominant positions so that their DNA was more likely to have been passed on to their children than that of native people lower down the scale who were less likely to have had families. There is no certainty here, but research into DNA clearly has potential.

Custom

Custom is the idea that membership of peoples had been for long advertised, so to speak, by particular customs or practices.

In the case of cemeteries, it is possible to analyse both the way in which bodies were disposed of – by cremation or inhumation (that is burial), for example – and also the objects which were in some places and periods placed in the graves or with the cremated ashes. In the case of buildings, it is possible to suggest categorisations of style and design which might have been customary to particular peoples.

We can take three examples to consider the difficulties and the possibilities. First, the cemeteries and settlements which have been associated with the Goths as a people outside the Roman Empire. According to Map 5 above, they originated in Scandinavia and then lived for a considerable time south of the Baltic Sea in an area where archaeologists have identified a culture of disposal of the dead and of buildings which they call the Wielbark culture. It is characterised by mixed cemeteries of crema-tion and inhumation, by the practice of not burying the male dead with weapons, and burying the female dead with jewellery, especially with characteristic pairs of brooches. Now, Map 5 represents the account in the written sources of how the Goths moved south to the area north of the Black Sea, and it is there that we find a culture of burial and settlements which is known as the Čjernachov culture and has many similarities with the Wielbark culture. So it is possible that we have evidence here for exactly what the Biological Model proposes, namely that the Goths really were a people with distinctive customs moving as a mass-migration from their original homeland to a new area just beyond the Roman Empire's frontiers. But certainty is impossible. Are the Wielbark and the Čjernachov cultures really so similar as to permit such an interpretation? And how can we be sure enough about the dating of either to be certain that they are evidence of a migration rather than of parallel and contemporary development in two relatively unrelated areas?

The second example is that of the Row-Grave cemeteries of north-eastern Gaul, which consist of inhumations in rows (hence the name), with the male bodies equipped with weapons and the female bodies adorned with jewellery. These cemeteries begin in the late fourth century and cease to be found after the mid-fifth. Because we know from historical sources that north-eastern Gaul was an area where the Franks were present in the Late Roman and post-Roman period, we could argue that these cemeteries are Frankish, and that the laying-out of graves in rows together with the inclusion of weapons and jewellery is a distinctive custom of Frankish people. Thus the cemeteries would be evidence for the arrival within the Roman Empire of a distinctive and coherent people, namely the Franks. If so, they seem to have come as federates (that is, military allies) of Rome, since the weapons of the men are often of Roman manufacture, and their bodies were often dressed with characteristically Roman military belts.

There is, however, a serious objection to this interpretation, in that no such burials are found in the areas around the mouth of the River Rhine and to the east of that river, from which the Franks are supposed to have come. So there is no reason for thinking that this type of burial was a marker of membership of the Frankish people, especially as many of the weapons found in the graves seem to be of Roman manu- facture, or at least are similar to those found in graves known to be those of Romans. So it is entirely possible that the Row-Grave cemeteries do not indicate any sort of migration or movement of a people into the Roman Empire, but rather a change in burial-practices made by the native Roman population. Why that population should have made such a change is a matter of conjecture, but it is possible that in the unsettled circumstances of Late Roman Gaul members of the Roman elite adopted the custom of putting weapons and jewellery into their graves as a means of emphasising their (perhaps increasingly threatened) status in society.

The third example we can take from the archaeology of cemeteries is that of crema- tions in fifth- and sixth-century England. These consisted of ashes buried, sometimes with objects such as tweezers, in pottery urns, which were made by hand rather than on the potter's wheel and were usually decorated by stamping patterns on the clay. Cremation was not a native British rite, so the existence of these graves in England suggests at once that they represent the disposal of the dead of an incoming population. Moreover, it is possible to compare the urns in terms of their shape and their patterns with contemporary or earlier cremation urns excavated in the areas from which the English are supposed to have migrated. Notable similarities are visible, as in the urns shown in Fig. 3.

So does this prove that there really had been a migration into Britain of a defined people from a defined area of origin with a defined culture? It is a possible inter- pretation, and you may want to argue that the Biological Model really does apply to the creation of England within Britain (as the DNA research noted above also suggests). But here too serious objections are possible. It may be, for example, that the distribution patterns of cremation urns were simply a result of the organisation of their manufacture. Maybe a group of potters produced urns like this and was successful in marketing them both in England and in the supposed homelands of the English (Denmark in the case of Fig. 3). Indeed, the question applies in essence to the whole study of cemeteries. How far in the grave-goods are we looking at a pattern of distribution of objects rather than of the movement of peoples? And how far in the organisation of cemeteries are we looking at the spread of fashion, or maybe of different beliefs, rather than any indicators of peoplehood as such?

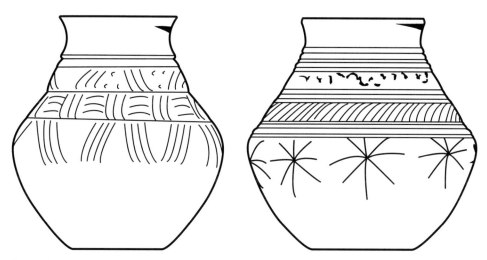

Figure 3 Cremation urns from the cemetery of Sancton I (Yorkshire East Riding). Note the incised and stamped designs on the urns, which are not wheel-thrown. The left-hand one particularly resembles urns from a cemetery at Funen (Denmark), which is thus evidence for contacts across the North Sea.
Source: Courtesy of Hull & East Riding Museum: Hull Museums.

Language

Long-standing peoples with defined areas of origin ought, you may think, to have had distinctive languages which were part of their attachment to a people, as common language has often been in modern nations. So did the Goths bring a language called Gothic with them from their homelands, the Franks a language called Frankish, and so on? There is a very serious impediment to answering this question in that these peoples were almost entirely without writing, so that we have virtually no texts in whatever languages it was that they spoke. Our earliest text in a barbarian language is the translation of the Bible into the language of the Goths, made by a missionary to that people called Ulfilas in the fourth century. After that, we have virtually nothing on the Continent until the version of the New Testament, the *Heliand*, written in an ancestor-language of modern German in the ninth century. But this was produced long after many of the peoples of the Late Roman period had ceased to exist, so that it is really not much help to us. In England, however, we do have writings in Old English from at any rate the early eighth century, notably the poem on the Creation by the poet-cowherd, Cædmon, which was copied into a manuscript of Bede's *Ecclesiastical History of the English People*. Thereafter, England had a considerable tradition of writing in Old English. A tradition of writing in the language which scholars call Old Norse also developed in Scandinavia, but the earliest texts belong perhaps to the ninth century, and the bulk of them are much later.

So we really have very little chance of tracing back any languages which may have distinguished particular barbarian peoples from each other. What the texts we do have seem to show is that, although there probably were differences in language between barbarians, these did not necessarily correspond to the peoples who appear on our map. Old English is a case in point. According to our written sources, the migrants to Britain came from Saxony in what is now eastern Germany, Angeln in central Denmark, and Jutland in northern Denmark. They may have spoken different languages, or at least different versions of 'Germanic', but when we first have texts in Old English it seems a remarkably unified language, albeit with dialect differences between north and south in particular. Its evidence brings us much closer to the Mass-Migration Submodel than to the Biological Model. It looks more like a language created in England by a fusion of groups to mark out a new English identity for themselves, than a language which was carried unchanged from an original homeland. As for the Continent, there is really not much we can say beyond noting the existence of Ulfilas's Bible in the language of the Goths; but texts in Germanic languages we have for later centuries show the emergence of a broad language known as Continental Germanic, with a northern relative in Old Norse. So again we seem to see broad language-groups rather than individual people-specific languages.

Language evidence does not therefore seem to do much to support the Biological Model, but it may be that we could use it to support the Mass-Migration Submodel. If we can see barbarian languages being adopted in Western Europe, this would create a presumption that large numbers of barbarians speaking those languages had settled in Western Europe. Complex and technical as linguistic history is, there does seem to be a reasonably clear pattern running through the distribution of Western European language-families. On the Continent, that pattern is dominated by the so-called Linguistic Frontier, which divides the Romance languages (that is, chiefly French, Italian, Spanish, Portuguese, and Catalan) from the Germanic languages (that is, chiefly German, English, Flemish, and the Scandinavian languages). In the present day, the frontier cuts across Belgium, running from the North Sea coast to near Liège, and dividing Walloon-speaking Belgium (Walloon being a Romance language) to the north, from Flemish-speaking Belgium to the south (Flemish being a Germanic language). The frontier then turns south, following the border between Germany and France, but in earlier times, indeed as late as the late nineteenth century, it lay to the west of that, which meant that the eastern French provinces of Alsace and Lorraine were linguistically Germanic, as the German character of many of their place-names shows. The frontier runs on across Switzerland, dividing French-speaking Switzerland from the German-speaking part to the east.

This frontier is potentially of great interest to us because the Romance languages spoken on the west side of it are essentially derived from Latin. To the east of the frontier, however, the Germanic languages derive from the group of languages spoken by barbarians such as the Franks and the Goths. There is no doubt that the frontier has changed in the course of the centuries, and there is equally no doubt that languages on either side of it have been consolidated. But the fundamental pattern seems to be ancient to judge from the language of the place-names found on either side of the frontier, and you may find it hard to escape the conclusion that the replacement of population following the end of the Roman Empire in the west in the areas west of that frontier cannot have been very great. Whatever changes in language there may have been across the centuries, you may think that the dominance of Romance, Latin-derived languages west of the Linguistic Frontier must signal the survival of a Latin-speaking population. Similarly, you may think that the dominance of Germanic languages east of the frontier must point to significant settlements of barbarians in those areas, such that Latin was replaced by whatever ancestors of the modern Germanic languages the barbarians spoke.

Law

A number of the rulers of barbarian kingdoms produced codes of law at quite an early date in their history. Thus Clovis, king of the Franks, produced the Salic Law (that is, the Law of the Salian Franks) in the early sixth century; Æthelberht, king of the English kingdom of Kent, produced a code of law around 600; the kings of the Burgundians produced two codes in the sixth century; and so too did the kings of the Visigoths. In the seventh century, the Law of the Ripuarian Franks appeared, and other laws assigned to particular peoples followed in the eighth century.

You could interpret the issue of such laws as showing that individual peoples had laws which were particular to them and which had been carried with them as distinctive of their identity as peoples in the course of their migrations in the spirit of the Biological Model. You could argue further that such laws were not just issued in particular barbarian kingdoms but were exclusive to the people concerned. So a Salian Frank would have to be judged under the Salic Law, a Visigoth under the Visigothic codes, and so on, whereas a native Roman would be judged under Roman law even after the end of the Roman Empire in the west.

To these interpretations, too, there are serious objections. On the one hand, the content of the laws does not suggest that they came from the ancient traditions of peoples, for many of them draw very extensively on Roman law in the form of Roman Vulgar law (that is, common law in everyday use in the Roman Empire), so that they seem to relate to the period of the creation of the barbarian kingdoms within the empire rather than to some ancient past. Indeed, many of them also show strong Christian influence, which must have been very recent. King Æthelberht of Kent (died 616), was the first of the Christian rulers of an English people, for example, and his law-code begins with the statement: 'The property of God and the Church is to be paid for with a twelve-fold compensation' (Whitelock, 1979, no. 29). Bede says that these laws were produced 'after the Roman manner' (Bede, *Eccl. History*, II.5), which does not suggest that they embodied the ancient traditions of a people.

Marks and fashions

Marks and fashions could be used to denote membership of a particular people, such as weapons which were distinctive of a people, hair-styles and costumes, and jewellery which might be similarly distinctive. The sixth-century scholar in Spain, Isidore of Seville, connected the name 'Frank' with the use by the Franks of a throwing axe called a *francisca*. For Isidore, then, this axe was a symbol of the ethnic identity of the Franks, and was indeed the origin of the name of their people. Similarly, Widukind of Corvey, a German writer of the tenth century, connected the Saxons (those at any rate who had been living from an early date in the area of Saxony in central Germany) with the short, one-edged sword called a *sax*, which was accordingly held to be characteristic of them.

You might see this evidence as supporting the Biological Model to the extent that there really were distinct peoples with long-standing traditions, but equally you could be sceptical that such associations were real. They would have been artificial creations, of the sixth century in the case of Isidore, and of the tenth century in the case of Widukind. Why, especially in the case of the Saxons, is this association only mentioned at such a late period unless it had been invented then as part of some quite late process of negotiating the creation of a people? And why, in the case of the Franks, is Isidore the only writer to mention it, when writers like Gregory of Tours, writing his *History of the Franks* within the Frankish kingdom in much the same period, make no allusion to it?

As for hair-styles and costumes, one of the chief pieces of evidence we could use to make this support the Biological Model is provided by Tacitus's *On Germany* (ch. 38), which does indeed treat hair-style as a mark of ethnic identity. Tacitus writes, for example, that it is the 'special characteristic' of the Suebi 'to comb the hair sideways and fasten it below with a knot. This distinguishes the Suebi from the rest of the Germans', although Tacitus goes on to say that it is only the freemen of this people and not the slaves who wear their hair in this way. It is naturally very difficult for proponents of the Biological Model to test out such claims, let alone to verify that such styles of hairdressing were a lasting mark of a people. Occasionally hair is indeed recovered on human remains of an early period, as in the case of the bog-bodies from the Schleswig region of Germany (Fig. 4), but it is impossible to map such sporadic remains against the areas where particular barbarian peoples were known to have been settled at the period from which such remains date.

Nor have we any evidence that such hair-styles were still potential signs of ethnicity in the barbarian kingdoms after the end of the Roman Empire in the west. In the sixth century, Gregory of Tours in his *History of the Franks* says that the kings of the Franks were long-haired (Gregory, *Hist. Franks*, II.9) but he says nothing of the Frankish people as a whole. In any case, if you want to argue for the Military Elite Submodel you could maintain that hair-styles and costumes really have nothing to do with the Biological Model, but were just part of the artificial creation of peoples. Their function was to make its members feel that they belonged to it, so that they were the equivalent of wearing a tie or a sweatshirt to announce, and to reinforce, membership of a college.

Geography

In a few cases, it is possible to suggest that barbarian peoples had moved from defined areas of origin which were peculiar to them. In the time of Tacitus, around 100 AD, there was a people called the *Gothones* south of the Baltic Sea, and this name does seem

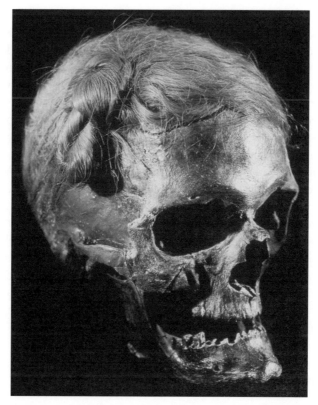

Figure 4 The skull and hair of a man recovered from a bog at Osterby (Schleswig-Holstein, Germany). The man lived at about the time of Tacitus (late first century AD). His long hair had been tied into a knot such as Tacitus describes for the Suebi by being divided into two parts, which were then twisted together and tied to form the knot.
Source: Courtesy of Archaeologisches Landesmuseum, Germany/Munoz-Yague/Science Photo Library.

to be the same as that of the Goths who appear in our sources north of the Black Sea in the fourth century. But, in fact, the name 'Goths' itself covers a more complex picture, and Roman writers describe two subgroups, the *Teruingi* and the *Greuthingi*, in that area. It looks very much as if the Goths were really a grouping, perhaps an artificial grouping, of these and other peoples, including Sarmatians from farther east and maybe, as the Goths came into the Roman Empire after 376, native Romans too. We have much the same sort of information as to the emergence of a Hunnic federation, that led by Attila the Hun, in the first half of the fifth century.

Much the same may be true of the English. Bede's *Ecclesiastical History of the English People* tells us that they consisted of three peoples, the Angles, the Saxons, and the Jutes, who settled in different parts of Britain (Bede, *Eccl. History*, I.15). Bede was aware of distinctions between these peoples, but the title of his book shows that he was envisaging the emergence of a consolidated English people, which had no antiquity but was the result of whatever form the arrival of Angles, Saxons, and Jutes in Britain had taken. As for the people of the Alamanns, who took over the area of the Roman Empire called the *Agri Decumates* (the triangle between the Rivers Rhine and Danube) in the fourth century, their very name points to the same conclusion, for it means 'all men', strongly suggesting that we are looking at the *ad hoc* assemblage of a new people, rather than the movement of an ancient one.

These confederations were not so very far outside the Roman Empire, and it may be that the forming of peoples in the context of them was strongly influenced by the Roman Empire itself while they were still outside it. The frontiers of the Roman Empire were probably not absolute barriers, but were porous, allowing influences – as well as traffic and commerce – to pass in both directions, so that a similar fusion of barbarian and Roman forms is discernible on both sides. Moreover, barbarians sought employment, goods, and sometimes plunder across them, so that there must have been constant movement. Thus the barbarian peoples might well have formed, under Roman influence passing through the frontiers, while they were resident just outside the empire, as the Franks, for example, seem to have been for centuries before the fall of the Roman Empire in the west. Roman influence might have been a very important part of the complex changes that took place in the groupings of humanity which we see under the names of peoples.

The Constitutional Model

You can of course pursue these types of evidence further and in different directions, but you may think that they are generally pointing away from the Biological Model and towards the Constitutional Model. If you decide, however, that the barbarian peoples were indeed of recent creation, you may still reach the conclusion that, in line with the Mass-Migration Submodel, they were engaged in mass-migrations, even if the nature and membership of the peoples in question were constantly changing.

Mass-Migration Submodel

The evidence that there was mass-migration is, first of all, circumstantial. In the third century, the Roman Empire found itself faced with a threat from outside its frontiers which was clearly very serious and required very large Roman forces – and concessions of territory too – to neutralise. This was the period when the empire gave up the *Agri Decumates* (the triangle between the Rivers Rhine and Danube) and the province of Dacia north of the River Danube, and when there were very extensive raids on the eastern part of the empire, including the sack of the city of Marcianople by Goths in 249. The threat seemed equally great in the fourth century, when the empire was forced to admit Goths across the River Danube, and when in 378 a Roman army was defeated and its general, the emperor Valens himself, killed by these Goths at the Battle of Adrianople. Such information can be used to suggest that the empire was not dealing with just a few people, but rather with a major movement of people which amounted to a mass-migration.

Secondly, some Roman sources give impressively large numbers of barbarians entering the empire, difficult as these numbers are to evaluate in terms of their accuracy and value to us (above, Chapter 2). Some sources too specifically refer to the barbarians within the Roman Empire being accompanied by wives and children as if their movements were real migrations rather than just campaigns by war-bands or armies. The fifth-century writer Malchus, for example, refers to the large numbers of non-combatants in the army of Theoderic of the Ostrogoths, and there is possibly reference in connection with the crossing of the Vandals to Africa to the dependants of the warriors (above, p. 26).

The case can be strengthened on circumstantial grounds. Migrations have certainly occurred in the modern period, and the population of the United States of America consists very largely of migrants. The Roman Empire was much richer than the barbarian lands to the east and north of its frontiers, and it is entirely plausible to argue that it must have exerted a pull on potential migrants just as modern Western Europe does on Third World countries, or the United States of America did on Western Europe, or does now on poorer Latin American countries to the south of it. Moreover, there are hints in the sources that migrations in the Late Roman period followed the same pattern as some modern migrations, with advance groups establishing know-ledge of the target area, which they then communicated to much larger groups which followed them. But these lines of argument rest principally on circumstantial evidence; as we have seen, the more concrete evidence which might confirm them is almost always ambiguous.

Military Elite Submodel

What then of the Military Elite Submodel, according to which there were very few barbarians involved in the creation of the barbarian kingdoms, but deliberate changes of identity by the native Romans produced the barbarian peoples which we see in our sources? This submodel is itself very difficult to evaluate, because it carries the implication that nothing was what it seemed. The more someone claimed to be a Goth or a Frank or a Jute, the more explicit they were in their use of custom or language or culture, the more likely that they were in fact natives adopting a new identity. Your view on this will be crucially affected by the decisions you take on the issues raised in Chapter 2 above. If the break-up of the Roman Empire took place along the lines of the Deliberate Roman Policy Model, with the support of the Roman aristocrats of the west, you may find the scenario envisaged in the Military Elite Submodel much more plausible. The more we can show that barbarian kingdoms were created by a trans-formation rather than a destruction of the Roman Empire, the more we can show that Roman aristocrats were crucial to their government and to sustaining their kings, the more we can show that Roman culture persisted in them, the more likely it is that the Military Elite Submodel is valid.

A type of evidence which may be very important here is that of origin-myths, which consist of accounts of the origins of peoples usually embedded in more general histories. In his *Gothic History* (ch. 4), the sixth-century writer Jordanes tells how the Goths came 'from this island of Scandza, as from a hive of races or a womb of nations . . . long ago under their king, Berig', and how when they landed on the mainland they 'straightaway gave their name to the place'.

We could interpret this in various ways. First, it may embody genuine traditions about the history of the Goths which have been transmitted across the centuries, and carried by the whole Gothic people on its migrations. You would have to accept, for example, that Jordanes's reference to naming the place where the Goths landed after them is not his own piece of fantasy based on the similarity of names, but a genuine, ancient tradition. If you can proceed in that way, the evidence would support the Biological Model. Given the heterogeneity of the Goths as we have seen them, however, this seems implausible, but we can still argue in favour of the Mass-Migration Submodel by maintaining that there were indeed genuine ancient traditions in the myth, but that these were carried not by a whole people, but only by the topmost elite, who preserved them intact, as the migrating people below them changed its character, drew in new members to its numbers, and so on. To accept this, you would need to be convinced that there really were genuinely ancient Gothic traditions in the myth.

The alternative interpretation, which would much more support the Military Elite Submodel, is that the myth was really a fabrication, made to flatter the few Goths who were the military leaders of the new Ostrogothic kingdom in Italy by native Romans seeking to create a new Gothic identity. In favour of this is the fact that, although Jordanes was a Goth, he wrote his book in Constantinople after the destruction of the Ostrogothic kingdom in Italy by the emperor Justinian; and the book itself is by his own account based on a now lost work by a Roman senator, Cassiodorus, who was a very important figure at the court of King Theoderic of the Ostrogoths.

Another example of such an account of a people's origins is in Fredegar's history of the Franks, written in the seventh century. According to this, they had migrated to the area east of the lower and middle Rhine from the ancient city of Troy, which they had left after the Greeks captured the city (Fredegar, *Chronicle*, II.4). This seems like a myth created within an elite which knew Virgil's *Aeneid* (the Latin epic poem describing Aeneas's eventful journey from Troy to the place where he was to establish the city of Rome) and used the basic theme of this to create a Frankish origin-myth. The aim was perhaps to give the Franks just as illustrious an ancestry as the Romans themselves, since both peoples could be seen as in origin refugees from the Trojan War.

But one of the richest collections of accounts of the origins of the peoples is in Book 1 of Bede's *Ecclesiastical History of the English People*, written around 731, which deals with the end of Roman Britain and its aftermath. According to Bede, four peoples were involved in this: the Angles (English), who had conquered most of the area which is now England in the middle of the fifth century; the Britons, who were the indigenous inhabitants of Britain from the period before the Roman Conquest of 43 AD, but who had become restricted to Wales, the south-west peninsula of Devon and Cornwall, and southern Scotland; the Picts, who lived in Scotland north of the Firth of Forth; and the Irish (or Scots as they were called), who were the indigenous inhabitants of Ireland, but who had established an Irish kingdom, the Kingdom of Dalriada, in the western part of Scotland and the Hebrides.

Of the Britons, Bede states that they had 'sailed to Britain, so it is said, from the land of Armorica, and appropriated to themselves the southern part of it'. There is no other evidence for this statement, and it is hard to avoid the conclusion that it is based on a story deriving from the fact that Armorica was also called Brittany, a name which would have suggested to a story-teller that it was the area of origin of the indigenous inhabitants of Britain. Bede then goes on to give an account of the origin of the Picts. According to this, as the Britons were taking possession of Britain from the south, the Pictish race came from Scythia and 'sailed out into the ocean in a few warships and were carried by the wind beyond the furthest bounds of Britain, reaching Ireland and landing on its northern shores'. Bede states that the Irish race refused them permission to settle in Ireland, but advised them to go east and settle in Britain, which they did in the north 'because the Britons had seized the southern regions'. The Picts then asked the Irish for wives, which were granted on condition that the Picts should 'elect their kings from the female royal line rather than the male' (Bede, *Eccl. History*, I.1).

Finally, Bede relates the coming of the English to Britain. In 449, after the Roman Empire had abandoned Britain as one of its provinces, 'the race of the Angles or Saxons . . . came to Britain in three warships', at the invitation of the British leader Vortigern, who granted them 'a place of settlement' in return for their military assistance. They were joined by others, however, who came in three ships from 'three very powerful Germanic peoples, the Saxons, the Angles, and the Jutes'. After 'hordes of these peoples eagerly crowded into the island', they revolted against the Britons who had invited them and were paying them as mercenaries or federates, and they either killed the Britons, forced them into slavery, or left them to lead 'a wretched existence, always in fear and dread, among the mountains and woods and precipitous rocks' (Bede, *Eccl. History*, I.15).

Bede's reference to the 'three ships' strongly suggests that the account is indeed a myth and, although it is possible in principle to take seriously his accounts of the Picts, the Irish, and the Britons, these too sound like myths, especially the story of the negotiations between Picts and Irish over women. But were these ancient myths carried by either whole peoples or by their elites? Or were they a creation of Bede's time or thereabouts for purposes of establishing and projecting particular identities of peoples? It seems very possible that Bede was participating in the creation of a series of identities of peoples in Britain.

Why did peoples form?

You have, then, choices to make between the Biological Model and the Constitutional Model, and within the latter between the Mass-Migration Submodel and the Military Elite Submodel. Your judgement may be affected by considering the second question of this chapter, that is why did peoples form? If, let us say, the moving force was a small barbarian elite taking over the reins of Roman power, why should it have opted for an identity cast in the form of 'Goths' or 'Franks'? And why did later kingdoms, such as those of England and France for example, see themselves as based on peoples?

A range of possible answers presents itself. First, if you adhere to the Military Elite Submodel, you may decide that it was because that elite was carrying ancient traditions of a people and transmitting them to its newly created kingdom. The other inhabitants of that kingdom then changed their identity to that of the elite because it was beneficial to them to align themselves with it. Secondly, it may be that in some way regarding oneself as a member of a people became an essential part of the spirit of the age. Classical writers like Tacitus and Pliny operated in a framework of ideas which automatically classified humanity into peoples, and so did the Old Testament, populated as it is by a series of peoples, the Jews themselves but others too such as the Canaanites and the Assyrians. To judge from Tacitus on the one side and *Beowulf* on the other, the notion of peoples was also deeply embedded in the outlook of the barbarians. So maybe becoming a people was a sort of intellectual inheritance.

There is, however, a third possible answer: peoples were essentially products of political organisation. In our period, it is striking the extent to which their survival or disappearance seems related to their political and military success. The Ostrogoths, for example, disappeared as a people with the destruction of their kingdom by the Byzantine invasions of Italy initiated by the Emperor Justinian in 536. The Visigoths likewise effectively disappeared as a people following the Moslem conquest of most of Spain at the beginning of the eighth century. The kingdom of the Burgundians was destroyed as a political unit by the Frankish kings in the second half of the sixth century and, although the name Burgundy had a long future down to the present day, the Burgundians as a people effectively disappeared from history. The Franks, on the other hand, had a considerable future, and, by the time of the First Crusade in the late eleventh century, the name 'Frank' could be applied to all the crusaders, wherever they came from in Western Europe, as was done in the anonymous Norman account of the First Crusade called the *Deeds of the Franks*. As for the English, we have already seen how the constituent peoples described by Bede, that is, the Angles, Saxons, and Jutes, were merged into a single people of the English (Angles) at any rate in Bede's presentation of them; and by the end of our period a kingdom simply of England was in existence.

The Franks and the English are amongst the most interesting cases. The rise of the Franks as such a dominant people in the history of this period has everything to do, you could argue, with their military and political success. The conquests of King Clovis (481–511) and his sons and their successors down to the early eighth century established Frankish power throughout most of Gaul, and into an area reaching east of the Rhine to take in Frisia, into Thuringia as far as the upper valley of the River Elbe, and southwards along the valley of the River Danube to take in what was known then, and is now, as Bavaria (Map 3 above).

This expansion was then continued under the great Frankish ruler Charlemagne (768–814), who extended Frankish political and military power eastwards by the conquest of Saxony to the River Elbe, expanded to a lesser extent south-westwards into the area of the Pyrenees, and conquered the kingdom of the Lombards, incorporating it into the Frankish realm. This massive expansion created the largest political unit since the Roman Empire in the west, and, although you need to think about how cohesive and unified it really was, it laid the foundations for the inhabitants of Continental Western Europe being called simply 'Franks', as they were in the context of the First Crusade.

There were, however, more complicated developments in the establishment of peoples stemming from this great expansion of Frankish power under Charlemagne, his father Pippin III (751–68), and his son and grandsons. In the first place, we may be able to perceive Frankish political power engaged in shaping the identities of subsidiary peoples within the Frankish realm, just as the Romans might have been doing with their barbarian military allies. For one of the activities of these kings was the issuing, or at least re-issuing, of law-codes for particular peoples. Thus we find from the eighth century a re-issue of the Law of the Salian Franks, which originated around 500, together with new, or at least revised, versions of the Laws of the Alamanns, the Bavarians, the Ripuarian Franks, the Burgundians, and the Visigoths. The peoples to whom these laws applied had ceased to have any real existence in the history of Western Europe, so it is possible that the Carolingian rulers were using ethnic names to organise the inhabitants of their enormous realm into what were in effect subsidiary administrative units, referred to by ethnic names, and all subsumed under the overarching category of Franks. If so, we have here the creation of peoples as in the Constitutional Model, but driven from above by political and military power.

Equally striking is the history of the Frankish realm through the late ninth and the tenth centuries. After Charlemagne's death in 814, what was then his empire (he had been crowned emperor by the pope in 800) passed intact to his only surviving son, Louis the Pious (814–40). This ruler made a series of attempts to arrange for the division of his realm between his heirs after his death. Towards the end of his reign, and following a second marriage, these heirs were three in number: his eldest son Lothar, his second surviving son Louis, and his youngest son, the child of his second marriage, Charles. The emperor's intention had been to leave the whole empire to Lothar, with the other two in subordinate positions. Following his death, however, civil war broke out between them, and this was resolved only in 843 at the Treaty of Verdun by the division of the Frankish empire (Map 6).

Lothar was to rule over the so-called 'Middle Kingdom', including Italy and a corridor of territory reaching northwards into the middle and lower Rhine Valley, and known subsequently after him and his like-named son as Lotharingia. The territory west of this was to be ruled over by Charles, known as Charles the Bald, and the territory east of it was to be ruled over by Louis, known as Louis the German. This arrangement did not, however, prove lasting, for Lothar soon died, and his son Lothar proved too weak to defend himself against his uncles to his west and east, so that they soon absorbed the Middle Kingdom in the Treaty of Meersen in 870. The result was that Western Europe was divided between the west Frankish kingdom of Charles the Bald and the east Frankish kingdom of Louis the German, with Italy established

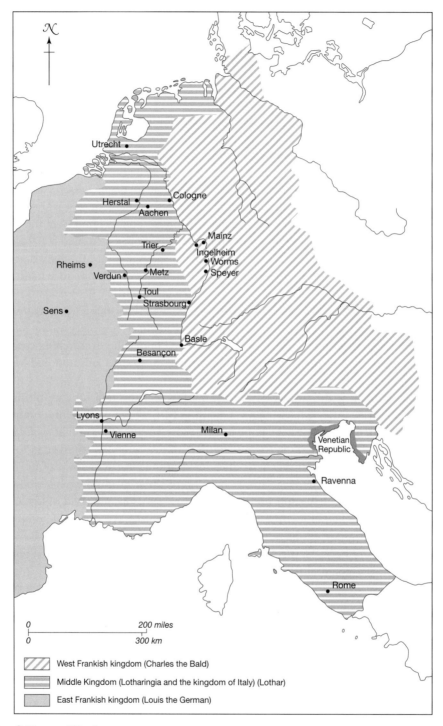

Map 6 Treaty of Verdun.

as a separate kingdom, although notionally a subkingdom of one of the two Frankish kingdoms. You may think that the implications of this for the emergence of a west Frankish people, viewed by the medieval kings of France as the ancestor of the French, and of an east Frankish people, viewed by the rulers of the medieval German empire as the ancestor of their people, are considerable.

It is possible to envisage the process of forming peoples in the British Isles as similarly driven by political and military processes. The first of these may have been to do with the hostility between the indigenous Britons, the Celtic-speaking inhabitants of Wales, Cornwall, and south-west Scotland (Strathclyde), and the Germanic speakers of Old English, who constituted the people who became known as the English. That hostility is a major theme of Bede, who praises even the pagan king of Northumbria, Æthelfrith, because he 'ravaged the Britons more extensively than any other English ruler' and he 'subjected more land to the English race or settled it, having first either exterminated or conquered the natives'; and Bede deplores the activities of Cædwalla, the British king of Gwynedd (North Wales), who 'with bestial cruelty put all to death by torture and for a long time raged through all their land, meaning to wipe out the whole English nation from the land of Britain' (Bede, *Eccl. History*, I.34, II.20). Bede was of course writing an essentially ecclesiastical history, as the title of his work indicates, so it is possible to argue that this hostility to the native Britons was generated simply by disapproval of their religious practices, for we know that Bede condemned their method of calculating the date of Easter, a live and very important issue in his time. But we may think that it is hard to reconcile this with the words Bede uses, redolent as they are of nothing less than genocide. And it is also hard to reconcile with the parallel hostility to the English displayed in texts by British writers. The sixth-century tract by Gildas, the *Ruin and Destruction of Britain*, sees the English as the scourge of the sins of the Britons, and in that role as the source of the destruction of the island. The early ninth-century *History of the Britons* supposedly by a writer called Nennius is equally condemning of the destructiveness and untrustworthiness of the English 'thugs' as the writer calls them (ch. 63). And one of the underlying themes of the poems of the British bards Taliesin and Aneirin is warfare between English and British. Aneirin's poem *The Gododdin* tells of the gathering of the subsidiary British people called the Gododdin in a great hall at the British fortress at Edinburgh, from where they rode down to die heroic deaths fighting against the English of the kingdom of Deira at the 'great sadness of Catraeth', usually identified as Catterick in Yorkshire. The poems of Taliesin embody parallel sentiments, speaking in their praise of a British king called Urien of how:

You cause havoc
when you advance;
before dawn
houses aflame . . .
The English are without protection
because of the most courageous stock
you are the best.
        (Taliesin, 'You are the best')

How real this hostility was throughout Britain is open to discussion, and Bede himself records an important alliance between the English leader Penda of Mercia and the British king, Cædwalla of Gwynnedd. But it is hard to escape the conclusion from our texts that the hostility came to be a formative element in the development of Welsh peoples to the west and English peoples to the east. It was like a fault-line running down British history, graphically emphasised by the construction in the late eighth century of Offa's Dyke, a massive fortification along the western frontier of what was to become England. We may think that, given the political power which such a construction over many miles would have necessitated, this is an excellent pointer towards the relationship between the formation of peoples and political power.

The second political and military process which you might wish to identify in the formation of the English people is that of the aftermath of the great Viking invasion of the late ninth century. That invasion, which was principally by the military force which the contemporary *Anglo-Saxon Chronicle* called the 'Great Army', began in 866. By then the kingdoms of Bede's time had become consolidated principally into a group consisting of those of Northumbria, Mercia, East Anglia, and Wessex.

The Great Army effectively destroyed all of them except the kingdom of Wessex, whose ruler, Alfred the Great, led the resistance from the depths of the marshes of Somerset, as is heroically described in the *Anglo-Saxon Chronicle*, and in his biography, the *Life of Alfred* by the churchman at his court, Asser. That resistance was ultimately successful, in the words of the *Anglo-Saxon Chronicle* for the year 886:

> King Alfred occupied London; and all the English people that were not under subjection to the Danes submitted to him.

The *Anglo-Saxon Chronicle* was either actually written at the West Saxon royal court or in the orbit of it, so it was presumably saying what Alfred wanted it to say. In that context, the reference to the English people submitting to him is very striking. England at that time was not at all unified, and the only surviving English kingdom was that of Wessex. It looks very much as if a concept of a people of the English was being developed as a political tool in connection with Alfred's wars against the Vikings who were occupying much of the rest of the former English kingdoms. The same process may have continued under Alfred's successors, especially his son Edward the Elder, who conquered (reconquered, he would no doubt have thought of it) much of midland England from the Vikings, absorbing it into what was to become the kingdom of England. In 942, Alfred's grandson, King Edmund, appears in the *Anglo-Saxon Chronicle* as the 'lord of the English' when he captured the five Viking garrison-towns (or boroughs) of Leicester, Nottingham, Stamford, Lincoln, and Derby. Thus we could well argue that the consolidation of the idea of a people of the English was intimately tied up with this military and political expansion of the West Saxon kings, who made themselves kings of the English as a result.

Your judgement of the argument that peoples are the product of the exercise of political power, however, will depend on how you envisage that power relating to society at large. If you are envisaging society dominated by small elites which had very few lines of communication with people lower down the social scale, you might want to argue that any ideas of peoplehood really only belonged to the elites. Below them the populations of their kingdoms had no sense of identity or belonging to the peoples in question. At its most extreme, you could argue that there were no peoples, in the modern sense which attaches to the word 'nation', in our period, and perhaps indeed not before the nineteenth century when the rise of modern nationalism was fuelled by spectacular improvements in communication (mass printing, for example), and organised education, which made possible the creation of widespread consciousness throughout society of belonging to a nation.

But it may be that, even in the Early Middle Ages, sufficient lines of communication existed within society for nations to be a reality. Needless to say we are not dealing with societies possessing anything like the communication potential of newspapers, let alone of the electronic media. There is no question of awareness of belonging to a nation being anything like so insistently impressed on the nation's inhabitants as it has been from the nineteenth century onwards. It does not follow, however, that we are not looking at something similar in character, if less intense, in the peoples we have been considering. Mechanisms of communication which could have bound peoples together were not wholly lacking, for the Christian Church was capable of reaching across the social spectrum. Indeed, you could argue that the Church's close relation-ship with the kings made it particularly suitable as a vehicle for diffusing the ideas of belonging to a people which may, as we have seen, have been part of the political processes initiated by those rulers. Churchmen may have been particularly willing to develop the idea of peoples because of the background provided by the Bible. The Old Testament, as well as being a history organised around peoples, took it as normal that kings were the rulers of these peoples, just as they were of the peoples we are con-sidering. So it may be that churchmen were actually in the lead in developing ideas of peoples in close association with kings. Bede's *Ecclesiastical History of the English People* is the most striking example of a churchman's work which, even in its title, makes much of the emergence of an English people which was, from a political point of view, a development of the future rather than of the writer's time. Then England was politically disunited with a whole series of English kingdoms, including those of Northumbria, Mercia, and Wessex. Yet Bede deliberately used a single name, English, for the whole population of what was to be England, and referred to them as a single people, the people of the English. It would be hard to find clearer support for the idea that, at least under some circumstances, churchmen were precocious in giving momentum to the idea of peoples.

If the making of peoples was, or became, part of an essentially political process in our period, then its efficacy – the extent to which the peoples in question were in any sense like modern peoples – must have depended not just on the Church, but also on the extent to which the institutions of the states which identified themselves with these peoples were sufficiently developed really to bind them together. It is to that and related issues which we must turn in Part III.

Research and study

Broad research questions

How far did peoples foster amongst themselves 'kernels of tradition' establishing their identities by reference to the past?

How much did the making of peoples depend on top-down military and political action?

How different from each other and distinctive in biological origin, law, culture, and customs were peoples?

How important was language in making peoples?

Books and papers to begin with

Useful starting points are Geary (2002) and Webster and Brown (1997). A balanced and lucid discussion of the barbarians is James (2009, ch. 5), and there is a very helpful essay by Heather (2008). A spirited assault on the Biological Model and the Mass-Migration Submodel is made by Goffart (2006), supported in part at least by Wolfram (1997). Halsall (2005), despite the book's title, is really in the same camp. Heather (2009) ranges much more widely in time and space, and argues by contrast that there really were barbarian migrations, even if the peoples in question were shifting and recent creations. A very insightful and stimulating book about the function of frontiers and frontier-zones in the making of peoples is Whittaker (1994).

Pursuing more specific aspects

Collections of learned papers

Drinkwater and Elton (1992) contains an admirably organised series of papers about Gaul in the fifth century; chapters 5–8 are particularly useful for considering what sort of people were the Goths who settled in Gaul, and the contrast between chapter 6 by Nixon and chapter 7 by Liebeschuetz is especially revealing.

Pohl and Reimitz (1998) contains an important article by Pohl on distinguishing marks. Goetz, Jarnut, and Pohl (2003) includes a paper by Wormald on the significance for ethnicity of barbarian laws, and papers on a range of peoples. All the contributors are supporters of the Constitutional Model.

Smyth (1998) contains a useful paper by Collins on law and ethnic identity. Mitchell and Greatrex (2000) contains papers ranging across the East as well as the West. Especially useful are those by Matthews (ch. 3), Harries (ch. 4) on law and identity, and Greatrex (ch. 17) on Roman identity.

Gillett (2002) has papers dealing with more general themes, including a paper by Goffart, a paper by Murray on the work of the earlier historian Reinhard Wenskus, and a paper by Gillett on the politicisation of ethnicity. There is a useful summary by Brather of work on the Alamanns.

Finally, Garipzanov, Geary, and Urbańcyk (2008) contains papers on the Franks but also, very usefully, on Scandinavia. A paper on frontier identities by Garipzanov is especially thought-provoking.

Individual peoples

Taking the broad research questions set out above, a series of works make it possible really to get to know individual peoples (along with the collections of papers noted above); for the Goths, Wolfram (1988), Heather (1996), Burns (1984), Barnish and Marazzi (2007); for the Ostrogoths, Amory (1997), whose work is perhaps more easily accessible as an article on names (Amory, 1994) and another on law (Amory, 1993). The Čjernachov culture is clearly illustrated and discussed by Heather and Matthews (1991, ch. 3). For the Lombards, Christie (1995); for the Franks, James (1988, 1982) and, for their later development, McKitterick (1983, 2008); for the Continental Saxons, Green and Siegmund (2003); for the Alamanns, Wood (1998); and for the English, Hines (1997), Foot (1996), Wormald (1994), and Brooks (2000) on Bede's approach to the English.

Scientific and medical research

How important to understanding the making of peoples is scientific and medical research?

The results of the University College London DNA project are most accessible on the internet at: www.ucl.ac.uk/tcga/. You can also look at Weale (2002) and, for the latest interpretation of the results, Thomas, Stumpf, and Härke (2006). There is a summary in James (2009, pp. 182–4).

Cemeteries and material culture

How far does the evidence of cemeteries and material culture support the idea that peoples were created through identity-formation rather than biological origin?

Useful introductions are Halsall (1995) and James (1988, pp. 19–28, 109–17). Halsall (1992) sets out his views on Row-Grave cemeteries, the discussion summarised by James (2009, pp. 210–14). On Anglo-Saxon cemeteries, there is an excellently clear treatment in Welch (1992, chs 5–7). Hamerow (1994a) offers a spirited defence of the view that the evidence of cemeteries (and that of settlements) proves that migrations occurred, at any rate into Britain. To go further by looking at the material itself, there are rich catalogues of exhibitions with maps, introductory essays, and photographs with commentary: for example, Aillagon (2008) and Menghin (2007).

Origin-myths

Did origin-myths reflect historical reality or were they tools in the making of peoples?

A seminal paper is Reynolds (1984). There is thought-provoking if rather technical commentary in Goffart (1988). Goffart (2006, ch. 4) provides further commentary on Jordanes's origin-myth of the Goths. Howe (2001) concerns myth-making and migration of the English.

Conclusion

In this part of the book, we have focused on the question of the nature of the end of the Roman Empire in the west on the one hand (Chapter 2), and the related question of the development of peoples on the other (Chapter 3), and we have extended discussion of the latter question into the later centuries of our period. As we move on to other topics, we need to keep these questions in sharp focus, for they have wide-ranging implications, and the answers we give to them will inevitably affect the way we see other developments of our period. And we need to see the questions also in a wide chronological perspective if we are to assess fairly what our period amounted to.

The nature of the end of the Roman Empire in the west raises the broad question of how far Western Europe in subsequent centuries was based on what that empire had bequeathed to it. We have taken the discussion so far in Chapter 2, but you may want to pursue it further and in a wider context. Did Western Europe acquire a sense of unity because its roots were essentially Roman, and the whole framework of its existence originated in the Roman world? Or was it rather the case that the developments of our period shattered the Roman framework, not least because the various kingdoms of Western Europe expanded far beyond the former Roman lands, as did the kingdom of the Franks reaching east of the Roman frontier on the River Rhine already by 500 (Map 3), or emerged quite outside the former empire as did the kingdoms of Scandinavia? Did the real impetus for the development of Western Europe come in a much wider variety of ways, including ways drawn from the Germanic barbarian world beyond the Roman frontiers, than just continuation of Roman forms of organisation? Was it from areas outside the former Roman Empire that the most formative influences were coming – perhaps from the Moslem world, or from Ireland and the northern lands? And did the expansion of the kingdoms of our period, southwards into Moslem Spain, and above all eastwards against the Saxons, the Slavs, and others, mean that forms of organisation quite different from Roman ones grew up in the frontier societies which formed as a result? Were these forms of organisation the ones which then shaped Western Europe as a whole? You need to keep these questions in mind as you research and study, but, in pushing your answers further, you may find it useful to look at the stimulating comments of Peter Brown (2002, pp. 1–34), and to widen your chronological perspective beyond our period with the help of the exciting discussion of the importance of frontier societies by Rob Bartlett (1993). It is very instructive to compare the conclusions of this book with those of Whittaker (1994) relating to the Roman period.

As for the development of peoples, we have been examining how this may have come about and what 'peoplehood' meant in our period. Here, too, we need to keep these issues in a wide perspective as we research and study. How far were the peoples which emerged in our period the same as the peoples (or nations) of later centuries and indeed of the modern period? We touched on this in Chapter 3, but the problem needs further thought, particularly in the context of the issues we are going to examine in subsequent chapters. If peoples were produced by states, were the states of our period strong enough to create them? Might it not have been until the later Middle Ages, with greater efficacy of government organisation and bureaucracy, that peoples really developed – or, indeed, might it not have been until the modern period with the rise of mass communication? Much will depend on our view of how sophisticated government in our period really was, compared with that of later centuries, and much will depend also on our view of the nature of society – was it, for example, dominated by a small aristocratic elite with little in common in cultural terms with its inferiors? Was the development of vernacular literature in our period an indication that peoples were forming with their own distinctive writing and language, or must we wait until much later, until the age of Chaucer in the fourteenth century, perhaps, for this to be significant? We can widen our perspective and develop our comparative understanding by considering the arguments of sociologists and historians of the modern period, which have been very influential. For the former, see Anthony Smith (1986, 1995, 2000); for the latter, arguing that we cannot speak about 'nations' (in much the same sense that we are using 'peoples' in this chapter) before the modern period, see John Breuilly (2005) or Ernst Gellner (1983). There is also an important discussion of medieval peoples' relation to modern peoples by Bartlett (2001).

Time-line: Part II

55–c.120	Tacitus (P. Cornelius Tacitus)	
	97/98	Publication of *On Germany*
235–84	The 'third-century crisis' of usurpations and revolts	
284–305	Reign of Emperor Diocletian	
	286	Empire divided between two *augusti*: Diocletian in the East, and Maximian in the west
	301	Edict of Prices, shortly after an edict on tax-reform
306–37	Reign of Emperor Constantine	
	306	Constantine elected emperor ('raised to the purple') at York
	312	Battle of Milvian Bridge; conversion of Constantine to Christianity
	324	Founding of Constantinople
c.345–402	Symmachus, senatorial aristocrat in the west	
360–3	Reign of the pagan Emperor Julian	
	357	Battle of Strasbourg
	363	Julian killed in the course of a Persian campaign
364–78	Reign of Emperor Valens in the east	
	c.375	Arrival of the Huns east of the Roman Empire
	376	Visigoths cross the River Danube and settle in the Roman province of Thrace
	378	Valens defeated and killed by the Goths at the Battle of Adrianople
379–95	Reign of Emperor Theodosius I the Great	
	383	Attempted usurpation from Britain of Magnus Maximus
	379–88	Ruler in the East
	388–94	*De facto* ruler of the whole empire
	391	Prohibited pagan worship
	394	Battle of the Frigidus and defeat of the usurper, Eugenius
	394–5	Sole emperor
395–423	Reign of Emperor Honorius in the west	
	405	The Goths cross the River Rhine led by Radagaisus
	406–7	Attempted usurpations from Britain of Marcus, Gratian, and Constantine III
	407	The Vandals, Burgundians, and Suebi cross the River Rhine
	410	Alaric, king of the Visigoths, sacks Rome
	411	Settlement of the Suebi in north-west Spain
	418	Settlement of the Visigoths in south-west Gaul

395–408		Reign of Emperor Arcadius in the east
408–50		Reign of Emperor Theodosius II in the east
	437	Code of Theodosius issued
425–55		Reign of Emperor Valentinian III in the west
	429	The Vandals cross the Straits of Gibraltar to North Africa
	439	The Vandals capture Carthage
	443	Settlement of the Burgundians in Switzerland and neighbouring areas
	449	Date given by Bede for the arrival of the Angles, Saxons, and Jutes in Britain
	451	The Huns invade Gaul under Attila
	454	Settlement of the Ostrogoths in Pannonia
473–5		Reign of Julius Nepos, emperor at Rome
475–6		Reign of Romulus Augustulus, emperor at Rome
	476	Deposition by Odoacer
476–93		Reign in Italy of Odoacer
493–526		Reign in Italy of Theoderic, king of the Ostrogoths
481–511		Reign of Clovis, king of the Franks
532–4		The Franks invade and destroy the kingdom of Burgundy
527–65		Reign of Justinian, emperor of Byzantium
	536	Invasion of Italy
568		Establishment of the kingdom of the Lombards in Italy
616		Death of Æthelberht, king of Kent
711		Moslem invasion of Spain and destruction of the kingdom of the Visigoths
751–68		Reign of Pippin III, king of the Franks
768–814		Reign of Charlemagne, king of the Franks and from 800 emperor
814–40		Reign of Louis the Pious, emperor
	840–3	Civil wars between the sons of Louis the Pious
	842	Oaths of Strasbourg between Louis the Pious's sons, Charles the Bald and Louis the German, and their followers
	843	Treaty of Verdun
870		Treaty of Meersen absorbs the Middle Kingdom in the kingdoms of East Frankia and West Frankia
871–99		Reign of Alfred the Great, king of Wessex
	866	Arrival in East Anglia of the Viking Great Army

PART III

Power and society

Introduction

The origin and nature of power in human societies is one of the most fundamental problems of human history, vividly outlined by the sociologist Michael Mann (2003), who looks across the aeons of time since man evolved as a species, and underlines the apparent unwillingness of human society to develop and accept political power. Even when such power began to emerge in the Neolithic period of approximately 5000 years ago, the evidence of archaeology can be read as showing that people were reluctant to accept its exercise and reverted to their stateless condition whenever they could.

Why did this change? How was it possible for complex societies with highly centralised political systems, of the type we are accustomed to, to grow up and come to be dominant in the world? Mann's analysis ranges in most detail over what were clearly the crucial periods in the evolution of complex states, that is the third and second millennia BC, which saw the development of sophisticated political structures in the Nile Valley, in the valleys of the Tigris and Euphrates, in India, and elsewhere. Although Mann's attention was less focused on it, we may think that our period offers great potential for addressing the question, since it saw so much change in political organisation. We have already looked at the end of the Roman Empire in the west and the rise of the quite new – and very fluid – entities which were the barbarian kingdoms, followed by the development and amalgamation of some of those kingdoms to create the embryonic political geography of Western Europe. Of the emergent kingdoms of France and Germany, the former was ruled by the descendants of Charlemagne, the Carolingians, until the accession of a new dynasty, that of Hugh Capet, in 987, while the latter passed in the early tenth century from the descendants of the Carolingian Louis the German to the dukes of Saxony, whose family ruled it as the Ottonian kings of Germany through the tenth century and the early eleventh. Both kingdoms remained in our period very fragmented into a series of quasi-independent duchies and other political units, so that their development offers rich possibilities for studying both the power which created them and the centrifugal forces which inhibited their development.

Equal potential is offered by other areas of Western Europe. Italy's disintegration into a series of duchies without real central power belongs to the period following the break-up of the Carolingian empire in the mid-ninth century, although the rulers of Germany still sought to maintain their kingship in Italy, sometimes ruling from Rome as the Roman emperors had done. England offers the possibility that we are looking at a precocious and particularly successful attempt at state-formation, while Ireland remained stubbornly locked into a political pattern consisting of a mosaic of small kingdoms. Spain offers us a Christian kingdom, that of the Visigoths, swept away by the invasions of Moslems in the early eighth century, and only reconstituted as a Christian kingdom as a result of military campaigns conducted from footholds in the north, beginning in the last years of our period. Scandinavia presents yet another opportunity, since it was an area which retained its paganism until the tenth and eleventh centuries, so that we can examine the growth of the kingdoms of Denmark, Norway, and Sweden to some extent outside the environment created by Christian organisation and teaching.

In considering the nature and origins of the power which underlay this kaleidoscope of political developments, we need to focus particularly on the political institution that characterised our period, that is kingship. And we need to focus on the social structure which underlay that institution and how it related to it – hence the title of this part of the book. But we need first to define the different types of power that we may be looking for, so that we can interpret the evidence we have to best effect. We need, in other words, a series of models for what constitutes power and how it works, so that we can test these out against the evidence.

Such models can be developed in a variety of ways, and you should feel free to think critically about (and modify or replace as you wish) the three which are intended to form the basis of the following chapters. They are the following:

Ideological power. This label is used here as shorthand for power which derives from the beliefs of those who accepted it. Such beliefs may be, for example, that the holders of power have been divinely endowed with it, and that failure to obey them may risk supernatural retribution. They may also owe their position to being members of a family or kindred which occupies a special position in the eyes of God or the gods; or they may be representatives of a particularly revered political order. The key thing here, however, is that power derives from beliefs and ideas.

Bureaucratic power. This too is a shorthand label, used here to refer to power which is based on what we in the modern period would call the machinery of government. Such power, which is essentially the type of power we are used to in modern states, derives from an impersonal system of offices and office-holders, and is regulated by impersonal procedures, regulations, and laws.

Personal power. This third label is equally a shorthand, this time for the sort of power which depends on personal relationships between the holders of power and those subject to them. These relationships, which may be created, for example, by oaths of loyalty, or by bonds of financial or other dependence, thus form the essential framework for the exercise of power.

These three models of power will be tested out in the next three chapters respectively. Even if you accept them, however, you need to ponder the extent to which they are or are not mutually exclusive. Power may, in other words, be exercised through different mixes of two or more of them. And, whereas we shall be taking broad sweeps across the period, you may want to ponder also the extent to which we can see change in the models of power most appropriate to the different sub-periods and areas of Western Europe.

If you want to go more deeply than is possible here, you can pursue Mann's approach further in Hall and Schroeder (2006), of which the first chapter provides a summary of his views, and the other chapters consider the nature of his influence on ideas about power. The three models of power used here are adapted from the highly influential formulation of models of power (or authority) developed by the great German sociologist Max Weber (1947, pp. 297–333, or in another translation 1968, I, 212–45). They were: charismatic authority, which rested 'on devotion to the specific and exceptional sanctity, heroism or exemplary character of an individual person, and of the normative pattern or order revealed or ordained by him'; legal authority, which rested 'on a belief in the "legality" of patterns of normative rules and the right of those elevated to authority under such rules to issue commands'; and traditional authority, under which 'obedience is owed to the *person* of the chief who occupies the traditionally sanctioned position of authority . . . [and] the obligation of obedience is a matter of personal loyalty'.

A quite different approach to categorising power – or at least states – is proposed by Chris Wickham, who distinguishes between: (1) 'strong states . . . based on taxation and a paid army as an independent resource for political power'; (2) 'weak states . . . with a landed army but also a strong sense of public power acting as a focus for political legitimation'; and (3) 'the pre-state system . . . where royal centrality was for a long time much more *ad hoc*, much more personal' (Wickham, 2005, ch. 3, especially pp. 56–62, see alternatively Wickham, 1984). Founded on the notion that power derives fundamentally from control of material resources, this system of models of power gives great importance to whether or not states could impose taxation, or at least extract material resources from subject peoples. We need to have Wickham's models in our minds as we consider the topics of both Parts III and IV of the present book, and you may want to pursue them further. But I have found the three models based on Weber's work, as set out above, more useful and wide-ranging in their approach, and it is on those that the following chapters will focus.

4

Pagan, Roman, and Christian beliefs about kings: ideological power

Ideological power, then, derives from beliefs and ideas. Our first written evidence for the nature of kingship extends back to the first century BC, when Julius Caesar wrote about kings as part of his account of his conquest of Gaul, and around 100 AD, when Tacitus also described them amongst the barbarians east of the Roman Empire and in Britain before the Roman conquest. (There had been no kings as such in the Roman state since the quasi-mythical past of the foundation of Rome.) There is also archaeological evidence beginning in the same sort of period, although we have to recognise that it is not always easy to be certain that it relates specifically to kings.

Our evidence, then, begins in the pagan period, so we need to start with the question of how far royal power was rooted in pagan beliefs. But we know, of course, that the Roman Empire was very influential amongst barbarian peoples, so we need to ask too how far the ideology of kingship was rooted in Roman imperial ideology, and how far it continued to be a reflection of it throughout our period. The other great influence on kingship was Christianity, which came to be very concerned with the ideas and behaviour of kings. We need to consider how far that religion altered the ideology of kingship to create in effect a new beginning in royal ideology.

Paganism and kingship

Was acceptance of the power of kings rooted in beliefs that the power of kings somehow derived from pagan gods? Such beliefs might have involved envisaging kings being priests of pagan gods, or being descended from such gods, or even married to one of them, and developing the practices and rituals of kingship in such a way as to make such supposedly divine connections explicit.

Very important to discussing this is the Roman writer Tacitus's *On Germany*, published in AD 97/98, and describing the various barbarian peoples east of the River Rhine. This is a notoriously difficult source to use, first, because it is not clear how much Tacitus really knew about the Germanic barbarians; secondly, because his Latin, although much admired in terms of style, is extremely sparing in words, often making appreciation of its precise meaning problematic; and thirdly, because he seems to write about the barbarians to underline deficiencies and immoralities which he perceived in Roman society, rather than to give a dispassionate account of them. Nevertheless, the book has remarkable resonances with the testimony of later sources which suggests that, for all its faults, it may not be without value to us. Tacitus's most famous passage on this subject begins:

> They [the barbarians] choose their kings (*reges*) for their noble birth, their leaders (*duces*) for their valour.
>
> (Tacitus, *On Germany*, ch. 7)

The leaders owe their 'special admiration' to 'their energy, their distinction, or their presence in the van of the fight'. But the kings owe their position to descent from a particular family-line rather than to military prowess, so the king need not have owed his authority to his military activity. That his office may have rested on pagan religious functions is suggested by Tacitus's description of 'auspices and casting of lots' amongst the Germanic barbarians wishing to foresee the future. These could involve the use of horses which, Tacitus explains, were:

> kept at the public expense in sacred woods and groves . . . they are pure white and undefiled by work for man. The priest and/or king and/or chief of the state (*sacerdos ac rex vel princeps civitatis*) yoke them to a sacred chariot and go along with them noting their neighings and snortings.
>
> (Tacitus, *On Germany*, ch. 10)

Here the Latin is especially infuriating, because the words *ac* and *vel* can both mean 'or' as well as 'and', while the word *civitatis* (literally 'of the city') raises difficulties because we know that the lands of the Germanic barbarians were at this period not at all urbanised. Romans, however, understood the word 'city' to mean rather 'city-territory', so Tacitus may be using it to mean just 'territory', here translated as 'state'. But what of *sacerdos ac rex*? It could mean that the priest and the king accompanied the horses together, but it could equally mean that the priest and the king were one and the same person, that is the person who would take this augury. So the king may have had a close association with a pagan god or gods, and presumably was believed to have derived his authority in part at least from it or them.

If such ideological power existed in Tacitus's time, did something similar persist throughout our period? The evidence is problematic because it is mostly late in date, derived for example from the Old Norse literature of Scandinavia, most of which was not written down until the twelfth or thirteenth centuries. But the fact that earlier Christian writers, who are the overwhelming majority of our informants, would inevitably have been unwilling to report such aspects of the kings of their period should perhaps make us more not less sympathetic to at least posing the question.

First, is there evidence that kings themselves were believed to be descendants of pagan gods? For England, we have in a ninth-century copy the genealogies of royal families back to Woden, presumed to be the pagan god who appears in Old Norse texts as Odin. The only exception is the genealogy of the kings of Essex, which reaches back to Seaxnot, who was probably also a god. Bede refers to such genealogies when he tells us that the first leaders of the English, Hengest and Horsa, were descended from Woden, 'from whose stock the royal families of many kingdoms claimed their descent' (Bede, *Eccl. History*, I.15). His apparent insouciance in relaying this might show that a belief in the descent of kings from Woden had been fully absorbed by even so Christian a writer as himself; but we might on the other hand conclude that this shows that it was just an ancient tradition which had long since been drained of meaning. The same doubt arises when the ninth-century compiler of the *Anglo-Saxon Chronicle* for the year 855 gives the genealogy of the royal family of Wessex. He extends this back to Woden, and he goes on to give a genealogy of Woden himself which reaches back to a son of the biblical figure Noah born on the Ark, and so back to the first man, Adam of the Book of Genesis. Was the compiler trying to accommodate a belief from the pagan period which was still of considerable importance to the authority of the kings of his own day, or was he too just relaying a fanciful and meaningless tradition?

We find suggestions of the descent of kings from gods in Continental writings too. For the Merovingian kings of the Franks, the seventh-century Frankish writer Fredegar (*Chronicle*, III.9) states that the ancestor of the Merovingian Frankish kings, Merovech, was conceived when his mother was bathing at the seaside, and:

> a beast of Neptune resembling the Quinotaur [= Minotaur] sought her out. As she conceived right away, either by the beast or by her husband, she afterwards gave birth to a son called Merovech, after whom the kings of the Franks were later called Merovingians.

Interpreting this story, however, is equally problematic. Not only is Fredegar ambiguous at the crucial point of who exactly was Merovech's father (although the underlying point must surely be that it was the 'beast of Neptune'); but, more seriously, the story sounds as if it derived as much from classical mythology as from anything in barbarian paganism. It was a regular practice for the classical god Zeus to come out of the sea in the guise of a swan or a bull to mate with a woman on the shore, or to abduct her as he did in the case of Europa, and Fredegar's use of the name of the classical god Neptune in connection with the beast (as well as the comparison with the Minotaur of classical mythology) rather reinforces this impression. It may be, of course, that what we are seeing is a learned, Christian, Frankish author imposing a classical framework in order to neutralise what was really a very Germanic barbarian story rooted in pagan belief;

but we cannot be sure – and if we adopt that interpretation we are left wondering why he told the story at all.

We have similar problems of meaning and ambiguity with the eighth-century Lombard writer, Paul the Deacon, who tells a story in his *History of the Lombards* (I, 15) about how a certain *lupa* gave birth to seven boys, one of whom grew up to be king. The Latin word *lupa* can mean 'she-wolf', so the point of the story would be that at least one Lombard king was descended from the goddess Frea, known from Norse mythology and appearing as a she-wolf in some sources. However, *lupa* can also mean 'woman' in a pejorative sense, or 'prostitute'. If that was what Paul meant, the story need not relate to any pagan belief about power.

When we turn to Scandinavia itself, which (unlike the kingdoms we have looked at so far) was pagan until the tenth and eleventh centuries, we have a fragment of evidence which is equally difficult to interpret. *Ynglingatal* is an Old Norse skaldic poem, probably of ninth-century date, listing twenty-seven early Scandinavian kings back to a certain Fjolnir. The poem does not identify this person as a god, but if we turn to the thirteenth-century Icelandic writer, Snorri Sturlusson, we find that he states that Fjolnir was the son of Yngvi-Freyr, who was probably a god in Scandinavian mythology, and that the first three rulers of the Swedes were this Fjolnir, together with Othin and Njorthr, the last two of which were certainly gods. But did Snorri know what he was talking about? Was there a lost beginning section of *Ynglingatal* which he knew but we do not, and would have given him this information? As with the other evidence we have discussed, there is deep uncertainty, but there is perhaps enough consistency in what we have to keep the question of a continuing, underlying belief in royal descent from gods at least open.

Were there indications in the appearance of the kings of our period to indicate that their power was based on pagan beliefs? The one possibility is the long hair, which Gregory of Tours gives as a distinguishing mark of early Frankish kings (Gregory, *Hist. Franks*, II.9), and which is prominent on the seal-ring portrait of the late fifth-century Frankish king Childeric (Fig. 5). In Gregory's time (late sixth century), long hair was evidently a sign of throne-worthiness, for example in the story of how the reigning kings Childebert and Lothar murdered their nephews to prevent their sister-in-law claiming the throne on their behalf. They sent a certain Arcadius with a sword and a pair of shears to offer their mother the choice of either having them killed or having their hair cut off. She replied: 'If they are not to ascend the throne, I would rather see them dead than with their hair cut short.' So Arcadius savagely murdered them (Gregory, *Hist. Franks*, III.18). Long hair clearly indicated that the wearer was a potential claimant to the throne. It is possible too to argue that the removal of the last Merovingian king, Childeric III, in 751 by the Carolingian Pippin III also indicates the importance of long hair as a sign of royalty, since Childeric is explicitly said to have his hair shaved at his deposition (*Royal Frankish Annals* for the year 750).

It is possible to argue that long hair reflected some pagan belief in the source of royal power. But, if so, it seems to have been limited to the Merovingian kings of the Franks. The shaving of the last Merovingian king may really have been because he

Figure 5 Replica of the seal-ring of King Childeric from the great treasure discovered in his tomb under what is now Tournai Cathedral in the seventeenth century. Most of this treasure was subsequently stolen and not recovered, but this cast of the seal-ring had been made before the theft. The Latin inscription, which is back-to-front so that it would appear correctly when imprinted on wax, reads 'Of King Childeric'. The image of the king shows him with two impressive plaits of long hair, armed with a spear, and wearing a patterned garment which may be Roman-style armour. *Source*: Courtesy of Ashmolean Museum, University of Oxford, UK/The Bridgeman Art Library.

was to be imprisoned in a monastery, presumably as a monk, which would have necessitated his being tonsured. It may be also that wearing long hair really did derive from very early in the pagan period of barbarian history, but was not a sign of pagan belief underpinning power, but rather simply an archaic fashion which the kings had preserved – rather as the present monarch of the United Kingdom wears old-fashioned costume to open parliament. Tacitus seems to refer to wearing long hair as normal practice amongst some barbarians (Tacitus, *On Germany*, ch. 38); and it has even been preserved in some of the first-century bodies of barbarians buried in the bogs of Schleswig in northern Germany (Fig. 4 above).

Did the rituals and ceremonies which were used to inaugurate kings in their offices suggest pagan beliefs in their power? In the twelfth century (when Ireland had long been Christian), Gerald of Wales described the inauguration of a king in the district of Kenelcunill (Tír Conaill) in northern Ireland. This involved the king-to-be having 'bestial intercourse' with a white mare before all his people while 'professing himself to be a beast also'. The mare was then:

> killed immediately, cut up in pieces, and boiled in water. A bath is prepared for the man afterwards in the same water. He sits in the bath surrounded by all his people, and all, he and they, eat of the meat of the mare which is brought to them. He quaffs and drinks of the broth in which he is bathed, not in any cup, or using his hand, but just dipping his mouth into it round about him. When this unrighteous rite has been carried out, his kingship and dominion have been conferred.
>
> (Ger. Wales, *Ireland*, III, 102)

This all sounds pretty pagan, for the king was engaging in some rite of marriage with the mare, who may have represented a goddess (notice Tacitus's emphasis on the sacredness of horses in Germanic barbarian society); and the ritual seems to involve sacrifice and sympathetic fusing of the king and his people with the flesh of the animal. The problem is that Gerald was intent on presenting the Irish as a barbarous and uncivilised people, and telling a story which its readers are likely to have regarded as barbarous and savage may simply have been part of that.

Nevertheless, if there were some such beliefs, this might explain the choice of sites for inaugurating kings to their office which were prehistoric and therefore possibly had pagan associations, for example the great prehistoric forts of Tara and Navan Fort in Ireland, the former in particular set in a landscape replete with prehistoric monuments such as the great burial chamber of New Grange; or in Scotland the mysterious site of Scone, where the focal point of the inauguration seems to have been the famous Stone of Scone, once removed to Westminster Abbey but now returned to Scone; and in England the mysterious inauguration-site of Kingston-on-Thames, the reasons for the choice of which are obscure, but may have been connected – as at Scone – with a sacred stone.

Did kings use symbolic objects, regalia in other words, which indicated belief in their power deriving from pagan gods? One possibility, and it is a striking one, comes from the early seventh-century ship-burial, which was very richly equipped and is presumed to have been that of a king, excavated originally in 1939 in Mound 1 of the great East Anglian mound-field at Sutton Hoo. This is the so-called whetstone-sceptre (Fig. 6), the core of which really is a whetstone for sharpening knives, although as can be seen from its condition it has never been used for this. At its base is a metal mount, which is concave like a cup and appears to have been intended to allow the base of the whetstone to rest on the knee of a seated person. So it was probably a sceptre which a king could have held in his hand while he sat on his throne. The base and the top of the whetstone are carved with heads, and the whole is surmounted by a metal ring which is capable of being rotated, itself topped with a metal stag.

The boldest interpretation of this object is that of Michael J. Enright (2006) who interprets the sceptre as deeply rooted in pagan Celtic religion. A sun-cult is suggested by the fact that other whetstones are decorated with swastikas, which are symbols of

Figure 6 Sutton Hoo Whetstone-Sceptre.
Source: © The Trustees of the British Museum. All rights reserved.

the sun. The Sutton Hoo whetstone has a rotating ring, perhaps representing the sun's apparent rotation round the earth, while Celtic material from the Val Camonica (northern Italy) associates stags with the sun, so the stag on the whetstone may have a similar association. Moreover, the sceptre may also have been bound up with the cult of the human head, which seems to have been prominent in the early Celtic world. Diodorus Siculus, writing in the first century BC, describes how the Celts embalmed the heads of their slain enemies and kept them in a chest, while sculptures now in the museum of Aix-en-Provence (in southern France) show piles of severed heads in what may be ritual contexts. Close inspection of the heads on the whetstone-sceptre suggests that their hair is represented as drawn round under their chins. Enright interprets this as showing that they are severed heads and the hair has been arranged in this way to prevent blood dripping from them. If he is right, we are looking at a notably pagan symbol of kingship, which implies both some connection with the sun-god, and an involvement in the cult of severed heads.

But there is inevitably a mass of problems, with Enright's interpretation and the evidence from very different periods that he uses, but also with the problem of why the whetstone-sceptre was buried in Mound 1 at Sutton Hoo at all. Was it really the dead king's sceptre, or was it simply an exotic treasure amongst a whole host of exotic treasures randomly collected from Europe, Byzantium, Coptic Egypt, and elsewhere?

Were the kings of our period believed to have magical or miraculous powers? Beliefs in these may be evident in the claims of medieval kings from the time of King Robert II the Pious of France (996–1031) and King Edward the Confessor of England (1042–66) to be able to cure scrofula (a disease of the neck-glands) by touching the sufferer. There may be an earlier example of the appearance of a similar sort of power in Gregory of Tours's story of how a woman who cut a few threads from the cloak of Guntram, king of the Franks, was able to use them in water to cure her sick son (Gregory, *Hist. Franks*, IX.21).

You may, however, want to take the view that the appearance of such powers in the eleventh century arose from the immediate political circumstances of Robert the Pious and Edward the Confessor, and that its continuation into the Middle Ages was a product of the increasingly Christian aspects of kingship (that is, representing kings as having something in common with Christian saints) rather than as reflecting what may have been ancient pagan beliefs that kings had god-like powers because they were descended from gods. Indeed, Edward the Confessor was successfully canonised in the twelfth century, and the purpose of Helgaud's biography of Robert, in which the story of his curative powers appears, may well have been to achieve the same result. By that period, the working of miracles was an essential qualification for canonisation. In the case of King Guntram, a similar interpretation is possible, since the first part of the story about him is strongly reminiscent of Christ curing the woman with the flow of blood when she touched his robe unperceived in the crowd, and the whole account clearly assigns to Guntram Christ-like wonder-working powers. It is possible to argue that what we are seeing here is the Christian Church responding to the pagan, sacral nature of early medieval kings by making Christian saints out of them in order to give an acceptable face to their supposed relationship with the divine. But that argument is hard to sustain, for Guntram's power of curing is not attributed to any other king until much later.

Finally, do we have evidence that kings were regarded as being responsible for the overall well-being of their people in such a religious or magical way that you might think that this derived from belief that their authority came from pagan gods? Belief that the king was magically responsible for natural events may be reflected in an Irish text of around 700, the *Testament of Morann*, which makes the king responsible for keeping at bay 'plagues and great lightnings' as well as promoting good harvests, good fishing, and so on (Enright, 1985, pp. 51–2). Another Irish text which was often quoted by Christian writers in the Carolingian period is *The Nine Abuses of the World*, one of which is the unjust king, whose injustice leads, amongst other things, to scattering of herds of domestic animals, and storms and lightning which damage the crops (Jonas Orl., *Royal Institution*, ch. 3). On the other hand, both these texts were composed in Christian contexts, and we could interpret what they say as simply a reflection of the fate of kings in the Old Testament who suffered plagues and other afflictions for their failure to heed the words of God's prophets.

In the fourth century, the Roman writer Ammianus Marcellinus wrote of the early kings of the barbarian people called the Burgundians that they could be deposed for failure in battle or, perhaps more significantly for our question, if the crops failed; and twelfth- and thirteenth-century Scandinavian accounts of the pagan period suggest that kings were sometimes sacrificed when things went wrong, for example when the harvest was not good.

So we are faced with a dilemma which only individual judgement can resolve. On the one hand, every piece of evidence we bring forward in support of the idea that the authority of early medieval kings stemmed from pagan ideas of sacrality and priestly functions as reflected in Tacitus's *On Germany* is problematic and can be interpreted negatively. On the other hand, we may be surprised that we have as much evidence as we do when the writers we are chiefly drawing on in our period at least were Christian and had every reason to mask any such elements in the power of kings.

Roman ideology and kingship

Did the power of kings have an ideological basis in their close association with Roman emperors? Theoderic, king of the Ostrogoths, who had been in Constantinople as a hostage and had spent his childhood and youth there, was sent by the Byzantine emperor Zeno to Italy, effectively as an imperial representative, to attack the barbarian king Odoacer, whom he lured to a banquet and killed, making himself king of Italy. Theoderic's kingship seems to have been shaped in Roman ways. His court was similar to that of the Byzantine emperor's and resided in the old Roman palace at Ravenna; and he celebrated imperial triumphs and rituals in Roman manner, being buried in a mausoleum resembling the mausoleum of the Emperor Hadrian at Rome.

We may, however, be being misled by Roman writers who are providing the overwhelming bulk of the evidence which we have, and who wanted their readers to think that barbarian kings were more Roman than they really were. If the Deliberate Roman Policy Model (above, pp. 26–33) is valid, Roman aristocrats like the historian Cassiodorus had deliberately opted to accept barbarian rule. It would have been very much in their interests to believe that the barbarian rulers were respectably Roman even if really they were not. In this connection, it is very striking that, although rulers like Odoacer and Theoderic were Christians, they persisted in their adherence to the Arian form of Christianity, even when it had ceased to be dominant amongst the Romans, as if they wanted to keep their distance from the empire. Indeed, Theoderic began to persecute Catholics, who were of course Romans, at the end of his reign.

Moreover, there was a strange after-life to his kingship. In later medieval literature and myth, he appeared as a great barbarian hero, Dietrich of Bern (a Germanised form of the name Theoderic of Verona), and still more strikingly his name was used on a runic inscription on the great stone of Rök from pagan ninth-century Scandinavia. According to that inscription, Varin the rune-master dedicated his son to Theoderic in expectation that the spirit of the long-dead would grant him vengeance for the death of another son Vemod, at the hands of twenty sea-kings. The sentiment and the process were clearly pagan and barbarian, and Theoderic's rule, Roman as Cassiodorus and the Romans may have wished to present it, may have had aspects which permitted the king to be regarded posthumously as a pagan god-king, capable of inflicting supernatural vengeance as this inscription envisaged.

As for the Franks, their king Clovis, son of the pagan Childeric, became converted to Christianity at the end of the fifth or the beginning of the sixth century. Gregory of Tours wrote of him that, following his victory over the Visigoths at the Battle of Vouillé in 507, he was received at the church of St Martin at Gregory's own city of Tours, and:

> he stood clad in a purple tunic and the military mantle, and he crowned himself with a diadem. He then rode out on his horse and with his own hand showered gold and silver coins among the people all the way from the doorway of St Martin's Church to Tours Cathedral. From that day he was called consul or augustus.
>
> (Gregory, *Hist. Franks*, II.38)

The 'purple tunic' was the classic symbol of Roman emperorship, no less than the military mantle and the diadem which especially the emperors of the later Roman Empire had worn. Equally Roman was Clovis's distribution of gold and silver coins in the context of a procession. This had been a characteristic ceremony which the Roman emperors had engaged in to emphasise their generosity and their care for their subjects. Clovis was here, as king of the Franks, behaving for all the world like a Roman emperor, and Gregory states that he was called 'augustus', which was actually the name of the first Roman emperor and which had come to be a title applied to all subsequent emperors. The use of the term 'consul' is admittedly a confusing element here, since consuls were officials of the senate rather than of the emperor, but the general gist of this passage was nevertheless that the king of the Franks behaved every bit as a Roman emperor should do. Indeed, Clovis's entry into Tours was entirely in line with the Roman emperor's victory ceremonies, the use of which can be detected amongst many other barbarian kings, and continued to be of importance to the Byzantine Empire, which was probably influencing western kings in this respect.

The most striking example of ideology of power deriving from Roman (or at any rate Byzantine) association is provided by the events following the deposition by the aristocracy of the city of Rome of Pope Leo III in 799. He fled north to Paderborn in Saxony, then the residence of the court of Charlemagne, king of the Franks, with whose help he was restored to the papal office. Later, Charlemagne came to Rome, and the pope crowned him emperor in the papal church of St Peter in the Vatican on Christmas Day 800. We have various accounts of this coronation, but the most detailed is the following:

> On the most holy day of Christmas, when the king rose from prayer in front of the shrine of the blessed apostle Peter, to take part in the mass, Pope Leo placed a crown upon his head, and he was hailed by the whole Roman people: To the august Charles, crowned by God, the great and peaceful emperor of the Romans, life and victory! After the acclamation the pope adored him in the manner of the old emperors.
>
> (*Royal Frankish Annals* for the year 800)

The striking thing about this coronation as emperor is that it consisted of three elements. First, the coronation itself; secondly, the acclamation by the Roman people; and, thirdly, the adoration by the pope, which presumably involved the pope prostrating himself on the ground before the new emperor, as Byzantine mosaics show the emperor himself 'adoring' Christ by prostrating himself before Him. These three elements were new in Frankish royal inaugurations, but they were characteristic of the inaugurations of Byzantine emperors. In the Byzantine inauguration ceremony the coronation was performed by Pope Leo III's Byzantine equivalent, the patriarch of Constantinople, in the church of Haghia Sophia, the equivalent in Constantinople of the church of St Peter in Rome. The formal acclamation of the new emperor by the Roman people was a normal component of the inauguration of Byzantine emperors, as was the adoration. So Charlemagne was unequivocally being represented as a Roman emperor in a ceremony clearly designed to emphasise the ideological aspects of his power. Coronation as emperor remained important to the rulers of what was to become Germany. Otto I, for example, was crowned emperor in Rome in 962, as were Otto II in 967 and in 996 Otto III, who took the Roman basis of his rulership so seriously that he established a residence in Rome.

The idea that the power of early medieval rulers derived in some way from their similarity to Roman emperors, including the contemporary Byzantine emperors, is clearly articulated in some surviving royal palaces. Most spectacular is Charlemagne's palace at Aachen, of which the great stone hall survives as the town-hall, and so too does the palace-church, amazingly little altered, as the church that quite recently became Aachen Cathedral. The hall had all the proportions, and (to judge from its surviving east end) the architectural style, of a Roman hall or basilica such as the one which survives at Trier (Germany).

The Aachen hall can only have been built to emphasise the Roman character of Charlemagne and his successors. The palace-church, moreover, is very specifically modelled on Roman architecture, either on Late Roman buildings in the great Roman city of Cologne (Germany), or (as most scholars have thought) on the church of San Vitale in Ravenna (Italy), which was built under the conquering Byzantine emperor Justinian in the sixth century (Fig. 7). The whole Aachen palace-complex was laid out in a geometrical and proportioned way to look for all the world like a Roman complex.

(a)

(b)

Figure 7 San Vitale, Ravenna (above), and the palace-church of Aachen, now Aachen Cathedral (below). Both images show the interiors of the churches looking east towards the high altar. Notice the polygonal shape of both buildings and the way that arches with classical columns are used both at ground-floor level and in the first-floor gallery, which is a feature of both buildings. At San Vitale, you can see the short eastern arm of the church in the centre of the image. Aachen is now quite different because its eastern arm was rebuilt in Gothic style in the fourteenth century, but it was originally the same sort of size as that of San Vitale as excavation has shown.
Figure 7a source: © Domkapitel Aachen (photo: Ann Münchow).
Figure 7b source: © 2011 Photo SCALA, Florence.

Figure 8 Reconstruction of the palace of Ingelheim (Germany) as built by Charlemagne.
The hall in the form of a Roman-style basilica, with its apse (or semi-circular ending) is at the back,
on the left. The Roman-style semi-circular, two-storey corridor and ceremonial gateway are on the
right. They have been partially restored as a result of extensive archaeological excavation. Note the
round towers, very late Roman in form, attached to the outside of the corridor.
Source: Model of the Kaiserpfalz Ingelheim am Rhein, © Hartmut Geissler, Historischer Verein
Ingelheim.

Other palaces were equally strikingly Roman, such as that of Ingelheim, where the
hall survives as another Roman-style basilica, and the buildings of a great Roman-
style semi-circular complex and ceremonial gateway are partially preserved (Fig. 8).
But even away on the northern fringes of Europe, beyond the frontier of the Roman
Empire, the seventh-century Northumbrian palace of Yeavering had, alongside its
timber halls, a remarkable timber replica of a Roman theatre where the king is
thought to have addressed his people, and possibly to have passed judgment.

In all this, there is clearly a strong case to be made for the influence of Rome
on Western European kingship, but there is an important question as to whether that
influence represented continuity with the former Roman Empire in the west, or
whether it represented contemporary influence from the surviving Roman Empire in
the east. Did the kings, in other words, look backwards to ancient Rome, or sideways
to contemporary Byzantium? The answer you return to this question has a bearing
on the nature of the end of the Roman Empire in the west (was it simply a process of
transformation or an abrupt change?) and on the extent of east–west communications
and channels of influence in post-Roman Western Europe.

Christianity and kingship

Inauguration rituals

We have already considered the imperial coronation of Charlemagne in 800 for its
Roman connotations, but we could equally emphasise that it was as much a Christian

as a Roman ceremony. It took place, after all, in the church of St Peter's in Rome, and it was carried out by the pope. Moreover, although it closely resembled its Byzantine equivalent, it was not identical. The chief difference was that in Charlemagne's coronation the acclamation by the people followed the coronation by the pope, whereas in Byzantium the acclamation preceded the coronation by the pope's equivalent, the patriarch. You could argue, then, that Charlemagne's coronation was deliberately emphasising the role of the Church in the making of the ruler.

This degree of ecclesiastical dominance in coronations certainly varied in later ceremonies. Another one which is very well recorded is the inauguration of the German king, Otto I, at Aachen in 936, described for us by Widukind of Corvey. This follows a sequence more like the Byzantine version: first, election: the men of the realm chose Otto; secondly, enthronement in the portico of the palace-hall at Aachen and oaths of fidelity; thirdly, consecration or anointing in the palace-church at Aachen. Nonetheless, the ceremony's climax occurred in the church and an archbishop was a principal actor in the ceremony, clearly signalling the belief that the king's power was coming from God.

Widukind's account shows, however, that another important development had taken place by this time, that is the introduction of what became an almost indispensable element of royal inauguration ceremonies, namely the consecration, or anointing with holy oil, of the king by a bishop, archbishop, or pope. In the late seventh century, the Visigothic kings in Spain had introduced this. The destruction of their kingdom by the Moslems in the early eighth century had put an end to it, but the idea appeared in Ireland in the early eighth century, when the Irish abbot, Adomnán, seems to refer to it. The anointing mentioned in his writing may not in reality have happened, but his account shows that the idea was present, as does a passage in the *Collection of Irish Canons* of about the same time which sets out the procedure for it. But royal anointing really had its origins in the Carolingian period. When in 751 the last Merovingian king of the Franks was deposed to be replaced by the first Carolingian king, Pippin III, the latter was anointed by Archbishop Boniface by permission of Pope Stephen, and then anointed again by the pope himself in 754. Such anointing was used sporadically after this, but from 848 (the anointing of Charles the Bald as king of Aquitaine) onwards, it became almost a necessary part of king-making.

It was by definition an ecclesiastical ritual. A bishop or an archbishop or a pope had to perform it, because only they could bless the oil which it required. It carried the clear message that the king's authority was God-given, and its establishment in the mid-ninth century went hand-in-hand with the appearance of texts for coronations which were performed by bishops and archbishops and strongly emphasised the Church's view of the king's position and duties. We have, for example, the text for the ceremony of inauguration of Charles the Bald as king of Lotharingia in 869, which refers to God himself anointing 'priests, kings, prophets', the last being an allusion to anointings in the Old Testament (Herlihy, 1970, pp. 128–31).

The belief that God himself inaugurated kings is graphically represented in the ninth-century Sacramentary of Metz, a book of services including that of the anointing and coronation of a king by a bishop or bishops (Fig. 9). In the miniature, the point is made very strongly that the bishops were only representing God, for they stand on

Figure 9 Scene from the ninth-century Sacramentary of Metz, illustrating the text of the service for the inauguration of the king. (Paris, Bibliothèque nationale de France, MS lat. 1141, fol. 2r)
Source: © Photos 12/Alamy.

either side of the king, who is actually crowned by the hand of God which reaches through a cloud, and is clearly intended to be coming down from heaven.

Another sacramentary, that of Henry II, ruler of Germany (1002–24), represents him with a bishop on either side of him supporting his arms, which hold respectively the sword of power and the Holy Lance, both being handed to him by an angel. This lance was an actual object, now preserved in the Imperial Treasury in Vienna, which was believed to have within it the lance which was used to pierce Christ's side during the crucifixion.

All this provides strong evidence for the idea that the Christian ideological power of the early medieval king was important. But our sources, both written and visual, are exclusively by Christian writers and artists, which must create a suspicion that they are heavily biased in favour of the role of the Church. We should note that at least one ruler, Henry I the Fowler, king of Germany (919–36), declined to be anointed. Moreover, the prominence which the process of election, in which the nobles chose their new king at least in a formal way, retained in royal inaugurations might suggest that the God-given nature of kingship was more apparent to churchmen than to the upper level of society as a whole.

Royal styles

That the king's power was derived from God was most explicitly signalled by the use of the title 'king by the grace of God', which was adopted by Charlemagne (768–814), and widely used by his successors in the Frankish kingdom and elsewhere in Western Europe, sometimes in variant forms. In writing a formal letter to Abbot Baugulf on the cultivation of learning, for example, Charlemagne begins: 'We, Charles, by the grace of God king of the Franks and the Lombards' (*Capitularies*, no. 12). In his equally formal letter to Bishop Ghaerbald on famine, he begins: 'Charles, most serene Augustus [i.e. emperor], crowned by God' (*Capitularies*, no. 16). In 857, King Burgred of Mercia began a charter with a more elaborate title: 'I, indeed, Burgred, by concession of the most omnipotent God, king of Mercia (*Charters*, no. 92). In a charter of 934, King Æthelstan of England took the title: 'I, Æthelstan, king of the English, elevated by the right hand of the Almighty, which is Christ, to the throne of the whole kingdom of Britain' (*Charters*, no. 104). In Germany at about the same time, Henry I referred to himself more simply but equally pointedly as 'by God's grace king' (Hill, 1972, no. 1), even though he had declined to be anointed.

Palaces

In discussing the Roman origins of the ideology of power, we examined the evidence of palaces as statements of the beliefs of the ruler and his court as to the sources of power. Aachen is particularly evidence for Roman-based ideological power; but equally it is capable of providing evidence for that power's Christian origins. The palace-site is arranged with the hall at one extremity, linked by a two-storey corridor to the palace-church. The king or emperor would presumably have left his private chambers on the first floor of the hall-building, proceeded along the first floor of the corridor, and entered the church at the level of the western gallery, where a great marble throne atop a flight of stairs is still preserved. That throne commands a direct view down on to the original high altar of the church, and up to the mosaic in the great dome (a modern replacement of the original) which represents Christ in Majesty, a celestial king mirroring the real king on his throne in the gallery. The message is clearly intended to be that the real king's power derived from God, or perhaps from Christ the King. His throne, in the church and raised up above the people, was a clear statement of that.

Other surviving palaces provide parallel evidence, as for example that of Paderborn in Saxony (Germany), Frankfurt-am-Main (Germany), and (from the eleventh century) Westminster in England, where the royal hall and chambers were directly linked to a palace-church, as at Aachen. Moreover, we have a number of monastery-churches which seem to have been equipped with a western gallery, perhaps for a throne for the king when he visited them. The best example is the church of the royal monastery of Corvey on the River Weser (Germany), where a western gallery looking down across the nave towards the high altar has on its west side an even higher raised gallery where the king's throne may have been.

Representations of kings

Just as palaces may be statements of how the sources of royal ideology of power were perceived, so too may be representations of kings, either in art or in writing. We have looked already at two artistic representations of the inaugurations of kings, but there are numerous, richly informative examples. A mosaic which Pope Leo III installed in the papal palace of the Lateran in Rome shortly before 800 showed, on one side, Christ giving to the first Christian Roman emperor, Constantine, a lance, and to St Peter, the keys of the Kingdom of Heaven; and, on the other, St Peter giving the pallium, the white shawl of office, to Pope Leo III himself and to Charlemagne a lance (Fig. 10). This was clearly intended to represent the idea that royal power came from God, although the pope was presumably emphasising that the king's responsibility was for secular and military affairs, the Church was the preserve of churchmen, and kings were ultimately subject to the Church, here represented by St Peter. This was the doctrine of the 'two powers', the secular and the ecclesiastical, which had been expressed already by Pope Gelasius I in a letter to the Roman emperor in 494.

Representations of the king's power deriving from the hand of God are also found in other pictures of manuscripts in the ninth century. For example, the *Golden Book of St Emmeram*, a copy of the gospels made for King Charles the Bald in 870, has a whole opening with on one side the king enthroned with the hand of God reaching down to him from heaven, and on the other the Lamb of God with the twenty-four elders as set out in the New Testament in the Book of Revelation; the king is looking devoutly across at the Lamb (Mütherich and Gaehde, 1977, plates 37–8, fols. 5v–6r). In fact, this may be a representation of the original mosaic on the dome of Aachen palace-church before it was changed to represent Christ in Majesty (probably in the tenth century), and it may be that the miniature shows the king seated on the throne in the western gallery looking up at it.

But perhaps the most dramatic example of such miniatures is folio 16r of the Aachen Gospels, made at the monastery of Reichenau on Lake Constance in southern Germany at the end of the tenth century, and now preserved in the treasury of Aachen Cathedral (Fig. 11). This shows Otto III enthroned with the hand of God reaching

Figure 10 Detail of a modern reconstruction of a mosaic forming part of Pope Leo III's decoration of his new Lateran Palace in Rome. The main subject, to the left of this detail, is Christ giving their mission to his apostles. To the left of that is a scene which matches this detail and shows Christ giving the Keys of Heaven to St Peter and a lance to the first Christian emperor, Constantine. The scene illustrated here is on the right of it, and it shows St Peter himself (whom you can recognise by the keys on his lap) giving the white shawl called the pallium to Pope Leo and the lance, with a banner attached to it, to Charlemagne.

down to crown him. Around him are the symbols of the evangelists who wrote the gospels: the lion of St Matthew, the eagle of St John, the bull of St Luke, and the angel of St Matthew. Below the level of his throne are two kings apparently subservient to him, and below them are churchmen and lay warriors. Most striking of all is the veil held by the bull and the lion, which can be interpreted as the Veil of the Temple which, in the Old Testament, sealed off the innermost tabernacle of the Temple. If that is what it represents, then the ruler was being represented as almost in heaven, so great was his holiness and closeness to God. So you can even argue that the ruler, set in a mandorla (the oval-shaped frame around him), was being treated as if he was Christ himself.

Figure 11 Emperor Otto III enthroned. (Aachen, Cathedral Treasury, Aachen Gospels, fol. 16r)
Source: © Domkapitel Aachen (photo: Ann Münchow).

Images of kingship in writing may be as important as pictorial images in presenting kings' power as God-derived. Bede's *Ecclesiastical History of the English People* is full of images of kings, for many of whom the clear implication is that their power, or at least their military success, was a grant of God. Oswald, king of Northumbria (634–42), was presented by Bede as 'the most Christian king' (II.5), and he won his kingdom after setting up a wooden cross to win a God-guided victory against his enemies, who included the pagan Penda, king of Mercia (III.2). By contrast, his predecessors, kings of the two constituent kingdoms of Northumbria, Osric and Eanfrith, had abandoned Christianity to revert 'to the filth of their former idolatry, thereby to be polluted and destroyed' (III.1).

Charlemagne and his Carolingian successors were similarly presented as close to God, closely associated with churchmen, involved in Christian learning, and intent on doing God's will in their kingdoms. Charlemagne's General Admonition of 789, which sought to raise the religious standards of his people, began with the words:

> Considering . . . the abundant clemency of Christ the King towards us and our people, and how necessary it is not only to render unceasing thanks to His goodness with all our heart and voice, but also to devote ourselves to His praise by the continuous practice of good works, that He Who has conferred such great honours on our realm may vouchsafe always to preserve us and it by His protection.
>
> (*Capitularies*, no. 5)

The image of a king's functions embodied in this is reflected in Jonas of Orléans's statement that: 'No king governs his kingdom by virtue of succession from his forefathers. Rather, he must truly and humbly believe that it has been given to him by God' (Jonas Orl., *Royal Institution*, ch. 7). A strikingly similar picture of royal power is presented by the biographer of King Alfred of Wessex, in an account of the king which represents him as committed to Christian learning and to the will of God (Asser).

Yet, we must be alert to the possibility that contemporary views of the nature of royal power were not necessarily consistent. Churchmen would naturally have leaned towards interpreting it as derived from God, but others may have differed. At the same time as Jonas of Orléans was writing, a former member of Charlemagne's court, Einhard, was writing a biography of Charlemagne (Einhard, *Life Charl.*), modelled on a first-century work by a Roman pagan writer, Suetonius, *The Twelve Caesars*, which it draws on so heavily that it seems clear that Einhard was presenting Charlemagne as the direct successor of those first-century emperors of Rome. He certainly presents Charlemagne as pious, telling us that he went to church morning and evening with great regularity. But his piety was restricted to his private life. Regarding his wars and political affairs, the qualities attributed to him seem very different. His wars 'were directed by Charlemagne with such skill that anyone who studies them may well wonder which he ought to admire most, the king's endurance in time of travail, or his good fortune' (Einhard, *Life Charl.*, II.8). The reference to good fortune rather than to God's intervention could not be more striking. This was surely a very different view to the one presented by Bede and Jonas, a view emphasising the king's own abilities and the role of fortune as the sources of his success, rather than the benign intervention of God on his behalf.

Another source pointing to the currency of a quite different view of kingship from that articulated in the work of the Church writers was the Old English epic poem *Beowulf*. Written in England between the mid-seventh century and the date of its manuscript, that is *c.*1000, it is principally concerned with the legendary adventures of the Scandinavian hero and later king, Beowulf, whose career was set in the sixth century. The poem begins with an even earlier and largely legendary Danish king, Scyld Scefing, whose claim to be a 'good' king is set out as follows:

> There was Scyld Scefing, scourge of many tribes,
> a wrecker of mead benches, rampaging among foes.
> This terror of the hall-troops had come far.
> A foundling to start with, he would flourish later on
> as his powers waxed and his worth was proved.
> In the end each clan on the outlying coasts
> beyond the whale-road had to yield to him
> and begin to pay tribute. That was one good king.
>   (*Beowulf*, lines 5–12)

Scyld Scefing's claim to be a good king is clearly based not on his performance of Christian duties or on his belief in any divine derivation of his power, but on his warlike powers and his ability to extort tribute-payments from those subject to him. Are we then dealing with different perceptions of the source of royal power, and did different models of authority exist in parallel to each other?

The evidence we have been considering for the nature of the ideological power of kingship in our period raises a series of questions which you will need to ponder as you go forward with your research and reading. How far has the nature of the source-material distorted kingship as we now see it? How far, in other words, have Church writers made it seem much more Christian, and more rooted in civilised Roman practices than it was? Or, alternatively, had it been so completely captured by the Church and its teaching that after the rise of Christianity it was every bit as Christian as the Church writers presented it as being? The Roman aspects of our subject present equally challenging problems. With them, it is not just a case of what distortions our sources may be introducing, but there are also questions of whether what Roman influences we are seeing are coming from the former Roman Empire in the west, or whether they are being imported – perhaps as quite new developments – from the Byzantine Empire.

As with so many other discussions in this book, you also need to be alert to the potential importance of differences between different parts of Western Europe and between different phases of our period. We have been discussing kingship as if it was a continuing institution from beginning to end. Are you convinced that that was the case, or do you rather think that the kingship of, say, the Carolingian period and later had little in common with the kingship of the fifth and sixth centuries? Do you think that it is valid to bring together evidence from the far-flung regions of Ireland and that from the heart of the Carolingian Empire? If you do not, you may want to break our field of study up into distinct parts as many scholars have done. But you may alternatively want to explore the (I think) exciting possibility that kingship was continuous and consistent across our period, and that we are seeing in it a fundamental and long-lasting manifestation of power.

Another question you need to consider, which underlies everything in this chapter, is that of the importance of ideological power. Do the beliefs and rituals we have been looking at add up to authority, or do they just represent outlooks and fancies which lacked meaning? Do you, in other words, think that ideological power was real power, because it reached to the very core of what people believed, or do you prefer to see real power consisting rather in the bureaucratic and personal power to which we must now turn?

Research and study

Broad research questions

To what extent was the ideology of kingship buttressed by that of the Roman emperors?

In what sense, if any, can kingship in our period be described as sacral?

How formative was Christianity on the ideology of kingship?

What were the most effective means by which the ideology of kingship was expressed and communicated?

Books and papers to begin with

A very important and influential series of lectures remains that of Wallace-Hadrill (1971b), who begins with barbarian kingship and the Roman attitude to it, and then follows its development under what he considered to be very effective Christian influence down to the time of the ninth-century kings Charles the Bald of West Frankia and Alfred the Great of England. An equally important set of lectures by Ullmann (1969) broadly follows the same line but regards the real period of the development of Christian influence on kingship as the Carolingian Renaissance in scholarship of the late eighth and ninth centuries. The turning-point was the removal of the Merovingian kings of the Franks by the Carolingians in 751, and the employment from then on for the inauguration of kings of the ritual of anointing with holy oil. This ushered in, Ullmann argued, a period when the king was believed to have been reborn in the glow of God's grace, but at the same time his sovereignty was stunted because he now depended for his position on the Church, which alone could offer the ritual of anointing. Ullmann's view is summarised in the context of his other work, and also criticised, in a very useful review-article by Oakley (1973). Ullmann's student, Janet L. Nelson, has published many discussions, the most useful for the present subject reprinted (Nelson, 1986, especially nos. 10–14), in conjunction with what is perhaps Nelson's most important paper (1987) on the importance of anointing and its relationship to other aspects of royal inauguration such as election, and to other symbols of royal power, such as hunting. Smith (2005, pp. 239–52) discusses the influence of churchmen on kings, and Robinson (1988, especially pp. 288–305) examines the papacy's view of its relationship with rulers, including the doctrines of the 'two powers' and the 'two swords'.

The most full-blooded case for pagan beliefs underlying royal power even after conversion to Christianity is made by Chaney (1970), but there is a classic, succinct discussion by Binchy (1970). The importance of Rome to the ideology of barbarian kings is set out by Wormald (2005), and developed in relation to 'victory' and 'arrival' rituals by McCormick (1986).

Pursuing more specific aspects

Pagan ideology of kingship

Are our sources sufficiently rich and appropriate to allow us to identify and understand what pagan ideology of kingship there may have been?

For a very useful summary of the way that scholarly debate about pagan kingship has developed, especially with regard to Scandinavian material, see two papers by McTurk (1975–6, 1994), the one updating the other. An enthusiastic statement of the pagan foundations of royal power is given by Enright (2006) in relation to the Sutton Hoo whetstone. To explore the evidence for kingship offered (at least potentially) by the supposedly royal burials at Sutton Hoo, you can consult Carver (1998) or Evans (1986), or, for more detail, Carver and Evans (2005). If you want to tackle the original report on Mound 1, browse the three volumes of Bruce-Mitford (1975–83). An argument in favour of the significance of another object from Mound 1, the axe-hammer, as a sacrificial tool serving as a symbol of pagan kingship is developed by Dobat (2006).

Inauguration rituals

How significant are inauguration rituals for understanding the ideology of kingship?

Aside from the work of Ullmann and Nelson cited above, you can explore this further with a very interesting, if controversial, book by Enright (1985) and a collection of papers edited by Bak (1990). Very useful for Charlemagne's imperial coronation is Folz (1964), with an invaluable appendix of translated texts at pp. 231–44. If you want to argue that rituals are not really suitable for understanding the fundamental ideology of power, you can look at a deliberately controversial book by Buc (2001), summarised in a paper (Buc, 2000).

Representations of rulership

Did rulers use representations of themselves as a means of justifying their power to their subjects?

Elsner (1998, ch. 3) discusses very helpfully, and with excellent illustrations, the way Roman emperors used not only representations of themselves, but also new buildings associated with them, to boost their power. For painted images of kings, see the relevant plates in Mütherich and Gaehde (1977), Dodwell (1993), and Mayr-Harting (1991b), although you will need to think about the significance of these images for yourself. There is, however, a general discussion of this evidence by Bullough (1975). On the significance for kingship of Roman monograms and symbols, there is an excellent discussion by Garipzanov (2008, ch. 4). On literary representations of kingship, there is a study of Bede's kings by McClure (1983), and of kingship in *Beowulf* by Whitman (1977).

Palaces as representations of royal ideology

Were palaces and other royal sites intended to constitute statements of royal ideology?

There is a summary of what is known of Carolingian palaces by Lobbedey (2002). For Irish palaces (or at least royal sites) and their possible relationship to the pagan past, you can look at Bhreathnach (2005) or Aitchison (1994). Driscoll (2004) discusses the coronation stone of the Scottish kings at Scone. It is well worth getting to know the seventh-century Northumbrian palace of Yeavering with the aid of Frodsham and O'Brien (2005).

5

Edicts, taxes, and armies: bureaucratic power

Bureaucratic power, as we have defined it (above, p. 70), derives from the sophistication and efficacy of the machinery of government. To help us to assess whether government was based on such power, we can turn to a definition of bureaucracy provided by Max Weber (1948, pp. 196–7): a form of governmental organisation in which there are 'fixed and official jurisdictional areas', that is clearly delineated departments with specialised governmental staff, involved in 'regular activities . . . distributed in a fixed way as official duties', and 'based upon written documents'. Were early medieval kingdoms bureaucratic in these sorts of ways? We can tackle this by exploring how important in government were written documents as compared to oral and symbolic means of communication, which would seem to be much less related to bureaucratic power; how complex were government departments and their structure of staff, and how strong were the links between central and regional government; and whether what governments were capable of achieving indicates that they must have had a level of bureaucratic organisation even if we cannot always see that directly in our sources.

Written documents

The case for the importance of written documents in early medieval kingdoms rest on quite an impressive survival of such objects from them. In the kingdom of Theoderic of the Ostrogoths in the fifth century, for example, there was clearly quite widespread use made of written documents in the form of royal edicts and pronouncements, which were drawn on by the Roman senator Cassiodorus in his *Variae*. We will perhaps not be surprised by this in view of what we know about the close links between Theoderic's government and the Roman senatorial aristocracy of Italy, of which Cassiodorus himself was a member. It is possible, however, to see evidence also from less obviously Roman-like kingdoms. From that of the Visigoths, we have a series of quite extensive written law-codes, including the *Breviary of Alaric* and the *Laws of the Visigoths*. And there are law-codes from other kingdoms, such as the laws of the Burgundians from the fifth and sixth centuries, the Law of the Salian Franks from the early sixth century, the laws of the Ripuarian Franks and the Bavarians (written down at any rate in the course of the eighth century, but probably earlier), and the series of English laws beginning with those of Æthelberht, king of Kent (died 616), and continuing through laws of kings of Wessex such as Ine, through the laws of King Alfred the Great (871–99), and down to the laws of the English kings of the tenth and eleventh centuries.

From the time of the Carolingian rulers of Frankia we have quite an impressive series of documents called capitularies, which are arranged in chapters (hence the name 'capitulary') recording the meetings of royal councils or assemblies, sometimes of both lay and ecclesiastical composition, sometimes just ecclesiastical. We also have written land-surveys called polyptychs, which recorded in detail the enormous landed estates of monasteries – they were not in themselves royal documents, but the monasteries in question were often closely associated with the rulers and it seems very likely that the production of the polyptychs was stimulated by them and that these documents were to all intents and purposes an integral part of their government.

We have also an impressive number of charters and writs, many of which were issued by kings and were clearly instruments of royal government. Charters were documents granting land or privilege, usually to churches but sometimes to laymen; they have often been preserved in later copies in manuscript-books called cartularies, but we sometimes have them as the original single sheets of parchment which were officially issued. Writs were a king's instructions to his officials and we find them, for example, from eleventh-century England. Still more striking from the period of the Merovingian kings of the Franks is a compilation called the *Formulary of Marculf*, which is a collection of blank forms for creating governmental documents.

We have from the Carolingian period another compilation which was evidently a guide to the production of written documents for royal use, in this case a survey of a royal landed estate. The compilation in question is the *Brevium Exempla* (literally 'examples of briefs') which includes surveys of five royal estates. As not all the names of the estates are given, the document appears to have been intended to be used as a model for recording in writing and in great detail all the buildings, equipment, and crop-stores of such estates.

On the one hand we can be very impressed with this evidence as showing the extensive use of literacy in early medieval kingdoms, and we can be surprised by how much there is of it, given that no royal archives as such have survived from our period. On the other, this evidence is often only giving us one side of governmental activity through written documents. Often what we have are either the commands or the models for written documents, and we have no real way of knowing whether the commands were implemented or the models were used. We have, in other words, very little of the sort of royal archival material that we have from later centuries which shows us government by written document actually working. There are some monastic archives such as those of Lorsch in the Rhineland or St Gallen in Switzerland which do, however, make it possible to see something of the use of written documents in land-transactions which sometimes involved royal government; and very occasionally we have some direct indication of the actual working of royal government by written document, as in a set of written responses which were dictated by Charlemagne himself in response to queries from one of his officers, a *missus dominicus* (*Capitularies*, no. 30). Nor can we be sure whether the documents we have were always written with a view to putting them into effect in a practical way. This is particularly the case with the law-codes, where it is not always clear whether they really were practical codes or whether kings issued them as objects of prestige, to broadcast their importance rather than really to control the functioning of their kingdoms.

There are deeper problems too. First, the question of whether royal documents would even have been comprehensible to the king's subjects, whether, in other words, literacy was sufficiently widespread as to have made their use practical or effective. The documents we have were exclusively written in Latin on the Continent; in England, they were mostly written in Latin (except the law-codes, which were in Old English) until after the late ninth century when they began to be written in Old English. Who could read, or even understand, Latin in our period? The question is bound up with a much wider one about the development of language in Western Europe, and in particular when Latin ceased to be a vernacular language. It is possible to argue that, if we accept a 'transformation of the Roman world' interpretation of the origin of the barbarian kingdoms, Latin remained the basic spoken language of the new kingdoms, including the barbarians who had (according to this interpretation) been mostly members of the Roman army in some form, and so would have spoken Latin as much as the indigenous Romans. If this were the case, the documents we have in Latin could have been comprehensible, at least when read out, to the population at large. It may be, however, that the development of scholarship and learning in the eighth and ninth centuries, which is generally known as the Carolingian Renaissance, caused written Latin to become so academic and formal that it ceased to be comprehensible to those who spoke vernacular Latin as an everyday language. This vernacular Latin then evolved into such Romance languages as French, Italian, and Spanish, leaving written Latin as a language which was comprehensible only to those who had studied it.

So there might then have been only a relatively limited part of our period when the use of documents written in Latin could have had really widespread utility, unless those documents were mediated by members of the Church who were necessarily trained in written Latin, for Latin continued as the main ecclesiastical language. It is possible to argue that it was the Church which principally promoted and facilitated the use of written documents in royal government. We know that churchmen were very prominent in royal palaces. In a work written in 882, Archbishop Hincmar of Rheims describes the important churchmen who were there, with the archchaplain (or *apocrisiarius*) being one of the principal officials, responsible for recording 'in writing the imperial commands' (Hincmar, *Organisation of the Palace*, sec. 16). In the Ottonian kingdom of Germany, surviving documents from which are admittedly much rarer than for the Carolingian kingdom, the importance of churchmen in government was also very great, with the emperor Otto I giving high office to his brother, Archbishop Bruno of Cologne, and typically using churchmen as royal officials. So it may be that it was the role of the Church in government which made the continuing use of written documents in a bureaucratic way possible, at any rate after the Carolingian Renaissance had 'improved' written Latin. But it may be also that the writings and activities of churchmen are giving us a distorted view of the importance of written documents. For the overwhelming majority of our surviving documents come from Church archives and were produced in the context of Church affairs.

Oral communication, symbolism, and ritual

Beyond the picture given by these churchmen with their command of Latin, there may have lain a very different world in which oral communication, symbolism, and ritual were much more important than the written documents. We can see a hint of this in some of the Carolingian capitularies, for example the Aachen Capitulary for the Missi of 802 (*Capitularies*, no. 14), which contain clauses such as:

Clause 6. Concerning the secular laws: that everyone is to know by which law he lives and judges.
Clause 7. Concerning perjuries.
Clause 8. Concerning homicides.

It looks as if the oral pronouncements were what were really important here, and these clauses of the capitularies do not represent the sort of governmental instruments that Weber had in mind, but rather *aides-mémoires* for the decisions taken. The real mechanism of diffusing instructions would then be oral communication rather than writing.

Very important too may have been symbolic acts, which in themselves required no writing at all. Take, for example, a charter of the 670s by which King Cenred of Wessex granted land in Dorset to a certain abbot Bectun. In the text of this, the king records his grant and then states that he has 'placed for more complete security sods of the above-mentioned lands on the gospels' (*Charters*, no. 55). This symbolic act, presumably to invoke divine power in respect of the grant being made, may (we could argue) have been more important than the actual document. We seem here to be a very long way from the sort of bureaucratic use of written documents which Weber envisaged, and to be rather in a world of religious belief and symbolism, a world in other words of ideological rather than bureaucratic power.

The use of the relics of saints, either whole bodies of saints or fragments of those bodies or objects which had been in touch with the bodies and were believed to have absorbed the power of the bodies themselves, in what we would regard as governmental processes may be another indicator that symbolism and ritual were more important than was writing. Relics were, for example, used in the swearing of oaths, clearly an important part of early medieval government. The Bayeux Tapestry was embroidered in the late eleventh century, probably in southern England, to provide a picture-strip narrative of one interpretation at least of the Norman Conquest of England in 1066 and the events leading up to it. One of its most famous scenes concerns a key moment in those preliminary events. It shows Earl Harold Godwinsson, who eventually took the throne of England in 1066, and Duke William of Normandy, who defeated and killed him in the same year to become King William I.

In the scene on the tapestry, Harold is engaged in swearing an oath of fidelity (or fealty) to William with one hand touching a reliquary, or casket of saints' relics, on an altar, and the other touching a portable shrine (or reliquary; Fig. 12). It was the breaking

Figure 12 Harold Godwinsson's oath to Duke William of Normandy represented in the Bayeux Tapestry. The fixed altar is on the right, and appears to have on it a casket, presumably containing saints' relics. On the left, you can see the handles of what was evidently a portable shrine for other relics. It is in the form of a little house with crosses on it in the characteristic way of early medieval shrines.
Source: Detail from the Bayeux Tapestry, 11th century, by special permission of the City of Bayeux.

of this oath, solemnised by the presence of relics, which (in the interpretation of the Norman Conquest proposed by the Bayeux Tapestry) justified William's invasion of England in 1066. Such a use of relics is widely documented. For example, the words 'By the Lord, through whom this relic is holy, I will be faithful and true to N' is a formula for an oath-swearing found in Old English, and the laws of King Æthelred the Unready (978–1016) require a witness in a legal case to swear an oath while handling a relic.

Relics were also used in manumissions, that is the freeing of slaves, and a manumission granted by Æthelstan, king of England (924–39), refers to relics used in the process, in this case relics which the king himself had collected. Even more striking is the use of relics in the judicial ordeal, a process developed from the early ninth century onwards as a means of determining guilt in cases where evidence was lacking. There were four types of ordeal: the ordeal by fire, in which the accused was made to carry a piece of red-hot iron, and was found guilty if the resulting burn did not heal cleanly; the ordeal by boiling water, in which the accused had to reach into boiling water to retrieve a pebble, and was found guilty if the resulting scald did not heal cleanly; the ordeal by cold water, in which the accused was bound and thrown into water, and was found guilty if they failed to sink; and the ordeal by bread and cheese, in which the accused was required to swallow pieces of these without choking. In all these processes, relics were involved or were invoked for purposes of solemnising the ordeal.

Government departments and staff

Government officers

Central government was constituted by what our sources call the royal palace, not in the sense of a building but in the sense of the personnel and organisation of the king's immediate entourage. For the ninth century, Hincmar describes the various officers of the palace with their functions and responsibilities in a way which on the face of it sounds quite close to the type of bureaucracy envisaged by Weber. The part of the text dealing with the personnel of the palace begins with the sort of hierarchy which we might represent in a modern management diagram: at the head of the palace staff were the archchaplain (*apocrisiarius*) with 'under his supervision and direction all the clergy of the palace', and 'associated with him' the archchancellor, under whom were 'wise, intelligent, and faithful men, who were to record in writing the imperial commands'. As we read on we may think that the picture changes, for Hincmar names the officials subordinate to these officers as: the chamberlain, the count of the palace, the seneschal, the wine steward, the constable, the master of lodgings, four chief hunters, and one falconer, with:

> under them or associated with them . . . other officials, such as the porter, keeper of the purse, dispenser, and keeper of the utensils. Also some of these latter had subordinates or deacons, or others associated with them, such as wardens of the forest, keepers of the kennels, hunters of beavers, and others in addition.
>
> (Hincmar, *Organisation of the Palace*, secs 16–17)

We may think that the titles of these officials do not suggest a bureaucratic machinery of government, for they mostly imply essentially domestic roles. Chamberlain means 'the person responsible for the king's bedchamber', constable 'the person responsible for the king's stables', the master of the lodgings 'the person responsible for the king's accommodation' as he moved from palace to palace, and seneschal simply 'old man'. We might be struck too by the number and specialisation of hunters on the palace-staff. Hunting seems on the face of it to have little to do with bureaucracy. These titles may of course have been traditional rather than reflections of reality, and they certainly became that in later centuries; but they convey the impression that the palace was essentially conceived of as a household, a domestic home, housing a wide circle of the king's immediate family and his faithful men who were almost on familial terms with him, rather than a bureaucratic structure.

Royal finances

It is hard to perceive a developed bureaucracy for the management of the royal finances. Hincmar does mention the 'keeper of the purse', but that is the only mention of anything to do with finances, apart from references to gifts. These latter, it appears, were given annually to the officers, and to the king by his subjects when they came to his palace. We might conclude that these were in fact salaries and taxes which were called by tradition 'gifts'; but we might equally think that, much as Hincmar may have wanted to represent the palace as based on legal authority, it was in fact much more concerned with traditional authority, here represented by a system of gift-giving. Such a system of gift-giving certainly seems to have been the means of support of the servants of the palace, for of the first 'class' of them the text notes that, 'The kindness and concern of the senior officers provided them with food or clothing or gold or silver, sometimes too with horses or other gifts' (Hincmar, *Organisation of the Palace*, sec. 27).

As regards taxation, there is a very striking passage for the sixth century in which Gregory of Tours tells the story of how Chilperic I, king of the Franks (561–84)

> decreed that a new series of taxes should be levied throughout the kingdom, and these were extremely heavy . . . The new tax laws laid it down that a landowner must pay five gallons of wine for every half-acre which he possessed. Many other taxes were levied, not only on land but also on the number of workmen employed.
>
> (Gregory, *Hist. Franks*, V.28)

The people of the city of Limoges called a meeting and resolved to kill the tax-collector, which they would have done if the bishop had not saved him, although they burned his 'demand-books' which led the king to inflict great punishment on the city. We can reasonably argue that there was something quite bureaucratically sophisticated here: a combination of a land-tax and a head-tax, administered with the aid of written documents, even though the payments were in kind and therefore not of modern type in that respect.

In the case of the Frankish kingdom from the mid-ninth century and England from the late tenth century, we may be able to see a new system of taxation, probably based on land. This took the form of a tax called on the Continent the 'Norman Tribute' and in England the 'Danegeld', and it was notionally at least paid to provide the kings with money to bribe Viking armies to cease attacking the kingdoms in question. The Frankish *Annals of Saint-Bertin* record the payment of £7,000 in 845 and £5,000 in 877. In England, the *Anglo-Saxon Chronicle* records even larger sums: £10,000 in 991, £16,000 in 994, £30,000 in 1007, perhaps £48,000 in 1012, and the truly staggering sum of £72,000 in 1018, all these payments being made during the reign of Æthelred the Unready (978–1016) which was much troubled by Viking attacks. The problem with all this is that the source of our information is narrative accounts, which may have exaggerated the amounts and in any case give us no direct information about how the money was raised, so it remains open to dispute whether or not we are seeing here a modern-type taxation system capable of raising these sorts of amounts in revenue.

The system of tolls levied by kings on the movement of commodities or the movement of ships and carts may also be close to a financial system driving a real machinery of government. We find evidence for its operation from, for example, the kingdom of Kent, where Æthelbald, king of Mercia (716–57), granted to the church of Rochester remission of toll due on one ship at London (*Charters*, no. 66). Normally the king would presumably have been levying this toll.

In the Carolingian kingdoms, there is evidence of the existence of toll-stations and customs-houses. For example, the Capitulary of Diedenhofen (Thionville) of 805 or 806 refers to a series of named customs-houses, each under a named official, dealing with 'merchants who travel to the territories of the Slavs and the Avars'. The capitulary prescribed penalties for merchants found trying to export arms and coats of mail to the Slavs (*Capitularies*, no. 17, clause 23).

Regional government

As regards regional government, we have fairly clear evidence of the existence of what were known on the Continent as counties, but appear (at any rate from the early tenth century) as shires in England. The county was governed by a count, who had under him (in the Carolingian lands at least, where the evidence is richest) subordinates known as vicars, each responsible for a vicariate, and hundredmen, each responsible for a hundred manses. A manse was, notionally at least, the area of land required to support one peasant family (probably an extended family). It seems clear that most, if not all, of Western Europe was divided into such units, which were known as 'hides' in England. As for the English shires, these too were divided up into subsidiary units called hundreds, each of which consisted of a hundred hides. Below that the evidence from the later part of our period shows that these English hundreds were divided in their turn into units of ten men (perhaps ten hides) called tithings, the members of which were mutually responsible to the king for each other's behaviour.

It is possible to interpret all this as fully consistent with the existence of bureaucratic structures. But we may have doubts as to how lasting such structures were across Western Europe, for our evidence is very much concentrated in the Carolingian world of the late eighth and ninth centuries, and in the England of the tenth and eleventh centuries. We may also have doubts about the underlying reality which this evidence represents. We know, for example, that by the tenth century on the Continent counties were generally hereditary, in the sense that the count's son would normally succeed him in that office, and we are left wondering whether the system was actually much more based on personal relationships than on bureaucratic structures.

We may have the same doubt about hides and manses, and about hundreds. Were these units really elements in a bureaucratic structure, or were they ancient forms of organisation which went back into the mists of time and the very beginning of settlement in Western Europe? If so, they may have been used by kings but have really had no direct connection with the creation of a machinery of royal government. The fact that these units are found so universally might perhaps incline us towards the latter view, although we may still be impressed by the kings' use of them in their systems of administration.

Links between central and regional government

Itineration

Royal palaces (in the sense of kings and their entourages) were almost always itinerant, moving several times a year, from one palace (in the sense of a building) to another. There were exceptions to this, notably the period when the palace of Charlemagne was fixed at Aachen from the late eighth century until his death in 814, or when the palace of the kings of the Lombards was more or less fixed at the city of Pavia in the Po basin in northern Italy; but generally speaking some movement at least was the norm for kings. We could argue that the king moving round his kingdom was a means of connecting the palace with regional government. The king's very presence, in other words, was a means of transmitting his authority. But was a bureaucratic organisation possible with the palace in such regular motion? And can we be sure that the king was moving for governmental purposes in a systematic way, or were his travels only to do with military campaigns or his desire to visit hunting forests? When later medieval kings developed what were certainly bureaucratic organisations, such as the exchequer in medieval England, they established them in a fixed way (the English exchequer at Westminster), but they themselves and their entourages remained itinerant.

Moreover, it is not easy to reconcile the idea of the itinerary as a means of communicating power with its rather limited geographical extent. Charlemagne, for example, certainly travelled quite widely (Map 7), but equally he did not travel routinely throughout his kingdoms, but rather favoured particular palaces, after 794 almost exclusively Aachen. The Ottonian rulers of Germany certainly did travel throughout their realm, but the majority of their movements were focused on Saxony, which was the core region, or heartland, of their power. The remote regions of their realm, for example Bavaria and Franconia, were visited much less frequently, although they were linked to the core region by what we can call 'transit zones', in which royal monasteries in particular provided them with bases of power and facilities for accommodation (see also below, pp. 267–71).

The same is true of the early kings of England, whose itineraries were notably concentrated in the southern part of England.

Royal assemblies

We know that early medieval kings regularly held such assemblies, known sometimes as councils or diets, and as *witanegemots* ('meetings of the wise men') in England. These were supposed to be attended by all the king's subjects, at least all the free men of his kingdom, so that in principle they were indeed a means by which the king could communicate his authority throughout his realm. But were these assemblies bureaucratic in any sense? The capitularies, which are our best evidence for their functioning, are very unsystematic in their compilation and often, as we have seen, incomplete in their recording. Is it really possible to regard these assemblies as methodical instruments for communicating authority? Moreover, it is clear that they were often manifold in their functions, and in origin at least they were assemblies of the king's army prior to a campaign, even if later they did assume more governmental functions. Finally, we can only rarely be clear what the attendance at them actually was, and whether in fact they assembled even a decent proportion of the king's subjects. We do have some evidence, notably the lists of witnesses to English royal charters, which must effectively have recorded those present at the royal assembly at which the charter was granted, but much research needs to be done on this.

Missi dominici

Missi dominici were royal officers appearing regularly in Carolingian capitularies. Their role seems to have been to go out from the palace and to check that the king's wishes were being implemented in the regions of his kingdom. The Capitulary of Nijmegen of 806, for example, orders that 'every *missus* [singular of *missi*] is to take the greatest care to examine, order and settle matters in his district in accordance with God's will and our command' (*Capitularies*, no. 19). After 802, Charlemagne reorganised the system of *missi dominici*, laying down that they should have defined areas of inspection (*missatica*), that they should make tours through these three times a year, and that they should work in pairs, one of each being a count and the other a bishop who acted as *missi*.

It is possible to doubt, however, that *missi dominici* were a crucial tool in the communication of authority. For one thing the period during which they functioned was not a long one, nor were they a universal feature of governments. They appear in the Frankish kingdom around the middle of the eighth century, and they are found no more after the 870s. It is hard to believe that any such officials were central to early medieval government in general. Moreover, the reform of the system of *missi dominici* in 802 was itself an equivocal one. First, the *missatica*, that is the areas designated for

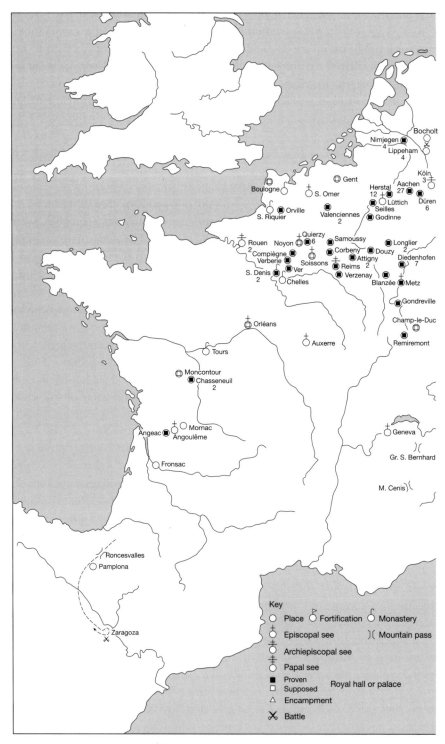

Map 7 Charlemagne's itinerary. The Arabic numeral by the name of a place indicates the number of times that Charlemagne stayed at it. Where there is no numeral, this means that he stayed there only once. The dense concentration of stays in Saxony is the product not of routine itineration but rather of the military campaigns against the Saxons, which stretched over many years. The stays in Italy are to do with military campaigns, for example against

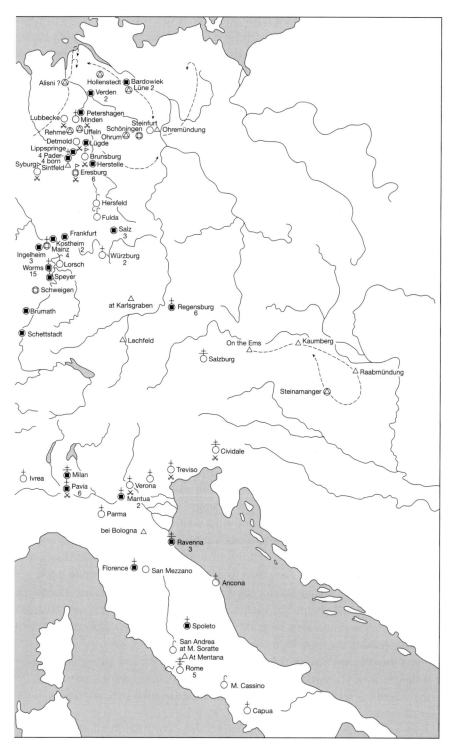

the duke of Benevento in the south, or with visits to Rome, while the brief incursions into Spain and into the lands of the Avars are also to do with military campaigns. If these are disregarded, it is immediately apparent that the ruler's itinerary was overwhelmingly concentrated on the area around Aachen, the area of the middle Rhine valley, and the Paris basin – that is, the core Frankish areas of Austrasia and, to the west of it, Neustria.

inspection by pairs of *missi*, can only be traced in the heartland of Carolingian royal power, especially round the valleys of the rivers Rhine, Mosel, and Meuse. If *missatica* were limited in this way, was the system about communicating royal authority, when it was apparently limited to the area where that authority needed least communication, the area where the king owned extensive estates and where his palace was frequently resident? Secondly, it is clear from the 802 Capitulary for the *missi* that the pairs were, at least in those cases where we know their identity, the local count and the local bishop. You could argue that more local knowledge was consequently focused on the job of inspection. But it seems equally likely that, whatever the *missi* were really intended to do, challenging local interests and autonomy, which the local count and the local bishop must have represented, in favour of the communication of royal authority, was not what was primarily intended, or at least achieved.

Capabilities of governments

Two areas of activity have left significant evidence of the capabilities of early medieval governments: the minting of coins, and military organisation, including the construction of defensive works.

Minting of coins

Our principal evidence for the minting of coins is the coins themselves, which survive in considerable numbers, from archaeological sites, from hoards of coins which were buried for whatever reason, and as stray finds, often today as a result of the use of metal detectors. They were minted in numerous mints all over Western Europe, apart from in Scandinavia, Ireland, and the eastern fringes of what became the kingdom of Germany. They are a crucial type of evidence for our period, and they have been extensively studied in very sophisticated ways by numismatists, that is, specialists in coins.

The designs and inscriptions on the coins offer clues to the power of the government under which the coins were minted. For example, do the coins give prominence to the name of a king, with perhaps a consistent representation of the king or some other symbol of royal power; or do they carry only the name of the individual moneyer without any reference to the king under whose suzerainty he nominally was? Are the coins of a high and consistent quality suggesting a consistency and efficacy of royal control over moneyers; or are they of poor quality and shoddy design, suggesting a lack of royal supervision over minting?

The significance of these questions can be seen in the evidence provided by coins from the kingdom of the Franks under the Merovingian kings, where the coins of, for example, the seventh century were of poor quality in terms of design and had only the name of the moneyer and of the mint on them (Fig. 13).

Comparing these coins with those of the first Carolingian king, Pippin III (751–68), and of his son Charlemagne (768–814) is highly instructive, for the Carolingian coins

(a)   (b)

Figure 13 Obverse faces (or heads) of a Merovingian and a Carolingian coin. On the left is an early eighth-century *denarius* (i.e. silver denier or penny) minted at Rouen in Normandy. The execution of its full-face bust is very crude. The cheeks, for example, are merely blobs, and the nose is irregular. By contrast, the obverse of the Charlemagne Class IV *denarius* on the right is very fine and really does resemble quite closely a Roman coin, especially one of the first Christian emperor, Constantine's. Notice the fine profile bust, with the laurel crown, and the words *Karolus Imp. Aug.* ('Charles, august emperor') inscribed around it.
Figure 13a source: Courtesy of Classical Numismatic Group, Inc., www.cngcoins.com
Figure 13b source: Courtesy of Mary Evans/Rue des Archives/Tallandier.

are all very consistent in design, and that design executed to high standards, and all have the name of the king, sometimes in the case of Charlemagne's coins with a consistent monogram or (in the case of his Class IV coins) a bust (Fig. 13). This seems a clear indication of the difference in the efficacy of royal government between the time of the Merovingian kings of the Franks and that of the Carolingians.

But the research of numismatists allows us to go further, for it has also been concerned with the weight and precious-metal content of early medieval coins. It is important to emphasise that, whereas modern coins work on the basis of their face-value rather than what they are actually made of, the key thing about early medieval coins was precisely the precious metal which they contained. Indeed, when payments were made, they were probably often made through the hands of moneyers, who would melt down and remint the coins to confirm their content. So we can at least in theory obtain an index of the level of royal control by examining these aspects of coins.

Two results of such research are revealing. The first is the change in the weight from 1.3 g to 1.7 g of Charlemagne's coins between his Class II coins and his Class III coins, which probably occurred around 794. Allowing for wear and tear to the coins, and the clipping of them which often happened as a fraudulent activity, this weight-change was consistent, and is surely a demonstration of the power (not to say the wealth) of Charlemagne's government. The second result is that from research into the contents of hoards of coins of the tenth-century English kings, which gives an indication of the coins in circulation at particular points in time (that is, the points at which each hoard was deposited). It has shown that these coins were reminted regularly at intervals of approximately six years, and that the coins issuing from each reminting were consistent in weight and showed significant changes in weight between mintings. This can only have reflected a situation of royal power and organisational capability.

Figure 14 A section of Offa's Dyke, near Clun (Shropshire), looking south. The path in the foreground is running down the original ditch itself. The great earth bank rises on the right, and would originally have been much higher, probably with a wooden palisade at the top. You can see the Dyke running on up the facing side of the valley in the distance. The way in which its builders accommodated their work to the lie of the land is not the least impressive aspect of this monument.

Military organisation

It is striking to consider early medieval logistical and tactical capabilities. The *Royal Frankish Annals*, for example, describe how in his 787 campaign against Tassilo, the rebellious duke of the Bavarians, Charlemagne deployed no less than three armies to surround him on three sides:

> Then the Lord King Charlemagne with the Franks . . . set out on a campaign into Bavaria with his army, and came in person to the Lechfeld above the city of Augsburg. He ordered another army to be raised consisting of East Franks, Thuringians and Saxons, which was to assemble on the Danube at Pförring. He ordered a third army to be raised in Italy. He also commanded King Pippin to advance with this army as far as Trent, to remain there himself, and to send his army ahead in full strength as far as Bolzano.

The logistical sophistication involved in such a complex exercise is impressive, and suggests the existence of an effective governmental organisation, perhaps of bureaucratic type. Amongst a series of comparable annals in the *Royal Frankish Annals*, that for 801 is particularly striking, since it describes a two-year siege by the Frankish army of the Moslem-held city of Barcelona. A siege of that length suggests organisational capabilities and was a demanding exercise at any period.

As regards the ability of early medieval governments to carry out major works, Charlemagne's government, for example, was capable of undertaking an immense project to build the Fossa Carolina, a canal creating a route between the rivers Main and Danube by linking together two of their tributaries. This is recorded in the *Revised Royal Frankish Annals* for the year 793; the project was not a success, but the excavations for it can still be seen as earthworks, and a considerable amount of work had evidently been undertaken before it was abandoned.

In late eighth-century England, on the other hand, a project of even greater ambition, namely the construction of Offa's Dyke along the Welsh borderland, was actually carried out, apparently by King Offa (757–96). It is not certain that the dyke extended the whole length of the Welsh borders, since the section which was once thought to have run down the Wye Valley to the Bristol Channel may in reality never have existed; but an impressive length was nevertheless built (Fig. 14).

On the face of it, a king's ability to execute a work on that scale would seem to suggest that he was in control of a bureaucratic machine to organise the labour and supplies required. The same kingdom seems also to have built town defences, like those at Hereford, and such building was an even more impressive activity of the kingdom of Wessex under King Alfred and his successors (see also pp. 216–20).

One defensive earthwork, however, raises a particularly interesting question. It is the great linear earthwork called the Danevirke, dated by dendrochronology (dating based on tree-rings, in this case of wood excavated from within it) to the eighth century. It runs across the southern neck of the Jutish peninsula (across what is now the German province of Holstein), and is arranged with a massive bank on the north and a ditch on the south, clearly intended to defend what was then the kingdom of Denmark against aggression from the south, presumably on the part of the kingdom of the Franks. But, unlike the Carolingian and English earthworks which we know were undertaken in kingdoms where there was some literacy and which therefore may have had a proper bureaucracy, the Danevirke was built in a kingdom which was not to have any real acquaintance with literacy until the eleventh century. However its construction was achieved, it was clearly not by a bureaucratic machine using written documents to organise the labour and supplies.

This may sow in our minds a seed of doubt as to whether the sort of governmental effectiveness that the earthworks bear witness to could only have been produced by bureaucratic organisation. It may be that the kingdom of the Danes used a comparable organisation that was dependent only on oral instructions. Or it may be that a completely different system was used, one much more based on personal relationships and personal obligations rather than on obligations administered by a literate, bureaucratic machinery. If that was so of Denmark, we may ask whether it was also true of the Carolingian and English kingdoms, where, although the operation of a literate bureaucracy was possible in theory, in practice quite different mechanisms of power and organisation may have operated.

The same problem – that of whether or not the achievements of early medieval governments presuppose the existence of bureaucratic organisation – affects the whole question of how armies were raised. We have seen that, at certain periods at least, those armies could be very effective, and clearly quite sophisticated in their organisation. Certain of the Carolingian capitularies, those from the early ninth century in particular, convey a picture of sophisticated bureaucratic-style organisation of military recruitment and deployment. A capitulary of 807, for example, represents military recruitment as being based on land-assessment, involving a system of spreading the assessment in the case of small land-holdings, so that every freeman with three, four, or five *mansi* should 'come to the army', but where two men have less land than this they are to club together to provide one man for the army (*Capitularies*, no. 23). We find the same picture in England, where the Domesday Book records for the county of Berkshire that 'if the king sent an army anywhere, only one soldier (*miles*) went from five hides' (*Domesday Book*, p. 136 (i.56v)). 'Hide' was the English equivalent of *mansus*, the area of land to support one family. So both these texts suggest the existence of a system based on a consistent assessment of land which, as we have noted already, could be seen as evidence for the existence of a bureaucracy.

In addition, the Carolingian capitularies in particular suggest quite detailed royal control of how the king's army was equipped and provisioned. A clause in the capitulary of 802 or 803 deals with how 'the king's provisions are to be transported in carts, as are those of the bishops, counts, abbots and *optimates* of the king: flour, wine, flitches of bacon and victuals in abundance; whetstones, stone-cutting tools, axes, augers, slinging machines and such men as know how to make them throw well'. The need for the army to have fodder and to cross rivers is also attended to, for 'each count is to reserve two-thirds of the grass in his county for the needs of the army and is to have sound bridges and sound boats' (*Capitularies*, no. 15).

All this suggests a bureaucratic organisation of the royal army. But there are two possible objections to this interpretation. The first is that the capitularies also have clauses which refer to *fideles*, that is, counts and others of high status, bringing their *homines* to the army, as, for example, in a clause in the capitulary of 807 (*Capitularies*, no. 23). The Latin word *homines* (singular *homo*) just means 'men' or, rather, 'human beings', but here it seems to mean something more like 'retainers' or 'vassals'. So the clauses in the capitularies which refer to *homines*, and they are quite numerous, may be reflecting a system of military organisation involving obligations to perform military service based on personal relationships, rather than on bureaucratic organisation administering universal obligations to serve in the army.

The second objection is that the capitularies detailing the organisation of the army really only come from the first years of the ninth century. Yet we know that the Frankish armies conquered great areas of Western Europe before that time. It may be that we do not have the documentation for earlier, and indeed for later periods, and the survival of the early ninth-century capitularies is a lucky chance. But it may alternatively be that the armies of our period were not normally raised by land-assessments and in a bureaucratic way, but were based on personal relationships, with their soldiers driven by a desire for rich gifts from their leaders derived from the booty they would win. Maybe, we could suggest, the system detailed in the ninth-century capitularies was really aimed at self-defence against the Vikings, who were particularly menacing the Frankish kingdom at that time, and was exceptional rather than normal. It seems likely that armies in the Scandinavian kingdoms were raised by personal relationships, given the lack of literacy in those kingdoms to support a bureaucratic organisation.

We have, then, reviewed some of the evidence for the existence – and importance – in early medieval kingdoms of systems of bureaucracy. That evidence is naturally mixed, and there seem to be some kingdoms to which it cannot apply at all; but it is in its entirety nevertheless quite impressive. But it also may not be as important as it seems at first sight. It is naturally the principal evidence we have, because we rely so much on written evidence. Yet, it may be that quite different systems of organisation were much more important but much more poorly documented. It is to that possibility that we must turn in the next chapter.

Research and study

Broad research questions

How genuinely bureaucratic and sophisticated was government?

How effective was government?

How did kings chiefly communicate their will throughout their kingdoms?

How dependent was government on the bureaucratic support of the Church?

What was the importance on of written documents in comparison with that of symbols and ritual acts?

Books and papers to begin with

For a maximal interpretation of Frankish government in the Carolingian period as based on bureaucracy, classic studies are Ganshof (1968, 1971a) and Halphen (1977, ch. 6). In the same vein is McKitterick (1983, ch. 4) and, with reference to more recent reseach, McKitterick (2008, chs 3–4). There are lucid and balanced overviews, encompassing other interpretations, by Nelson (1988, 1994, 1995). Later Anglo-Saxon government is classically interpreted as a full-blooded bureaucratic structure by Campbell (1975, 1987). It is very revealing to look at the excellent maps of mints and governmental organisation, with concise commentaries in Hill (1981, nos 135–53, 164–6, 171–8). There were bound to have been considerable differences between periods and areas of Western Europe, and the government of Ottonian Germany may have been much less bureaucratic than Carolingian or late Anglo-Saxon government (Leyser, 1981, Reuter, 1991, pp. 84–94).

Against all this in the context of the Carolingian kingdom, Innes (2000) uses the local archives of the monasteries of Lorsch and Fulda relating to the Middle Rhine area to argue that Frankish government was based much more on networks of kinship and patronage developed at local level than it was on bureaucratic structures, although the Carolingians achieved a considerable amount in formalising and organising these networks, and making them dependent on the royal palace. Innes even disputes that counties were really administrative districts under the control of counts, whose power he sees as much more based on personal connections. The book is detailed, but well worth wrestling with (albeit in a critical spirit!).

Underlying the work of Innes is that of Althoff (2004), who argues that power in the Middle Ages was based not on bureaucratic state-machinery, but rather on 'political and social bonds' formed by kinship, membership of a lord's retinue or a sworn guild, or resulting from agreements of formal 'friendship'. We need to consider this more in Chapter 6, but for the present discussion it is worth looking at Althoff's survey of historical approaches to the state (pp. 4–7). There is, however, a wider question relating to all this. Were the kingdoms and empires 'states' in any real sense, and what are the criteria for the definition of a 'state'? If they were not 'states', how are we to define and categorise them? A useful starting-point is provided by a debate between the late Rees Davies (June 2003) and Susan Reynolds (December 2003), although you should concentrate on the ideas being discussed rather than get bogged down in all the references given.

Pursuing more specific aspects

Written documents, symbols, and ritual acts

How important for power was writing?

A useful collection of papers covering a range of the barbarian kingdoms is McKitterick (1990), who has also written a full treatment of literacy in the Carolingian kingdoms (McKitterick, 1989), which builds on and expands an important paper by Ganshof (1971b). If you want to pursue individual areas of Western Europe further, there are specialist studies on Lombardy (Everett, 2003), England (Wormald, 1977), and Celtic societies (Pryce, 1998). The last of these is especially interesting since Celtic societies have often been regarded as leaning essentially on orality and memory. The question of language development is summarised in McKitterick (1989), and she develops the topic in an interesting (but rather technical) way in McKitterick (1991).

For the general issues relating to symbolism and ritual acts, the major contribution in English was made by Clanchy (1993). His book goes beyond our period, but it has many implications for us. For the use of relics, see Rollason (1989, pp. 188–95, 1986).

There is an excellent book on the judicial ordeal by Bartlett (1986). Innes (1998) provides illuminating discussion of the general issues, although his article is principally concerned with oral and literary aspects of history-writing in the context of Notker the Stammerer, *Life of Charlemagne*.

Taxes and tolls

What was the role of taxation in shaping the character and capabilities of states?

The partial continuation into the barbarian kingdoms, and then cessation, of Late Roman taxation is central to the interpretation of political development advanced by Wickham (2005, ch. 3). This long chapter is worth wrestling with for the evidence it provides, for example about taxation in the kingdom of the Visigoths. There is a great deal of information about tolls in McCormick (2001; use the index under 'tolls'). For the Kentish tolls, see Kelly (1992). There is a series of stimulating articles on the size of the Danegeld (Gillingham, 1989, Lawson, 1984, Metcalf, 1989); on the Norman Tribute, you can look at Joranson (1923).

Itineraries

Was royal itineration primarily a social, ritual, or governmental process?

Well worth studying in detail are the maps of Anglo-Saxon royal itineraries, with commentaries, in Hill's atlas (1981, nos 154–63, 167–9). A critical view of the idea that Charlemagne was itinerant is set out by McKitterick (2008, pp. 157–204), who maintains that the ruler's itineration was not as extensive as has been supposed, and that he depended much more on resident notaries to deal with royal documents in his absence. This is possible, but needs our critical attention. On the itineration of the Ottonian rulers, there is a very detailed but worthwhile book by Bernhardt (1993).

Coinage

What was the function of coins in royal government?

A consummate master of numismatics, and a great communicator, was the late Philip Grierson. By him, you can look at a brief, but masterly and well-illustrated, survey of coins (Grierson, 1991), and a collection of his specialist papers (Grierson, 1979). His paper 'Money and Coinage under Charlemagne' (1965b) is particularly helpful for the reforms of that ruler's coinage, especially the change from 1.3 g to 1.7 g, although it is quite technical and requires perseverance. If you want to go further, there is a very useful catalogue with many illustrations and an excellent introduction to the development of coinage in Grierson and Blackburn (1986), and a summary by Blackburn (1995). For English coins, the most useful and accessible catalogue is North (1994).

he tenth-century English coinage and its regular remintings were fascinatingly studied by Dolley and Metcalf (1961).

Military organisation

How bureaucratic was the organisation of armies?

For the organisation and tactics of early medieval armies, see Halsall (1998), and a useful collection of papers by a range of authorities in France and DeVries (2008). Halsall is very critical of earlier books, which can nevertheless be useful, for example Verbruggen (1996). You may want to think critically about Halsall's arguments that the earliest armies of the barbarian kingdoms were really former Roman armies which had settled down; and that the dominant form of military recruitment in later centuries was on the basis of the amount of land individuals held rather than their personal networks. For a maximal view of military organisation, there is a brilliantly clear exposition of the Carolingian evidence by Ganshof (1968, part 2). Further on Frankish warfare, you can consult Bachrach (2002), on Carolingian and Ottonian warfare Reuter (1999) and Leyser (1993), on Anglo-Saxon warfare Hooper (1989) and the full and balanced study by Abels (1988). On the importance of plunder, very stimulating is Reuter (1985).

Fortification

How important are the remains of fortifications as a key to understanding the character and extent of royal power?

There is very little in English on either the *Fossa Carolina* or the Danevirke. Roesdahl (1982) has some discussion of the latter, and also of the other Danish royal fortifications such as the great forts of Fyrkat and Trelleborg. For Offa's Dyke, the classic survey is Fox (1955), which is brilliant if you really want to get the feel of the Dyke. But, for up-to-date modifications to Fox's interpretation, useful is Hill and Worthington (2009), although you may think rather fanciful its interpretation of how the Dyke was built. For the English *burhs*, fortified towns appearing from the late ninth century onwards, there is an excellent map and discussion in Hill (1981, no. 149). But if you want to pursue them further, there is a collection of papers edited by Hill and Rumble (1996).

6

Kings, warriors, and women: personal power

We have defined personal power as power which depends on personal relationships between the holders of power and those subject to them. Was government based on power of that type? Did, for example, rulers depend on aristocratic elites obedient to them by virtue of bonds of personal obedience and loyalty? And, if so, how was power and the way it was exercised affected by the nature of those aristocratic elites and their dependence or otherwise on the rulers?

War-bands

Tacitus

We can begin with Tacitus, who writes about 'chiefs' of the barbarians who were the leaders of what he calls the *comitatus*, generally translated as 'war-bands' (Tacitus, *On Germany*, ch. 13). He describes first the induction ceremony of a young warrior who will join such a war-band:

> When the time comes, one of the chiefs or the father or a kinsman equips the young warrior with shield and spear in the public council. This is with the Germans the equivalent of our toga – the first public distinction of youth.

He then explains that such young warriors are 'attached to the other chiefs, who are more mature and approved', and that the war-band so constituted has 'its different grades, as determined by the leader, and there is intense rivalry among the companions for the first place by the chief, among the chiefs for the most numerous and enthusiastic companions'. And he summarises its importance in Germanic barbarian society:

> Dignity and power alike consist in being continually attended by a corps of chosen youths. This gives you consideration in peace-time and security in war.

He explains that the war-band can carry considerable prestige, not only in one's own people but also in neighbouring states (or territories, *civitates*):

> Nor is it only in a man's own nation that he can win name and fame by the superior number and quality of his companions, but in neighbouring states as well.

In ch. 14, Tacitus emphasises the importance of gift-giving within the society of the war-band:

> The companions are prodigal in their demands on the generosity of their chiefs. It is always 'give me that war-horse' or 'give me that bloody and victorious spear'. As for meals with their plentiful, if homely, fare, they count simply as pay. Such open-handedness must have war and plunder to feed it.

Tacitus's picture is thus of barbarian society dominated by war-bands based on personal loyalty to chiefs. His *On Germany* is a problematic source (above, p. 73), and it does not at all follow that the society of the barbarian kingdoms after the end of the Roman Empire in the west was necessarily related to that of the barbarians east of the River Rhine at the end of the first century.

Beowulf and the *Battle of Maldon*

But the fact remains that Tacitus's picture seems to be quite closely reflected in Old English literature, when that appears, especially in the epic poem *Beowulf*, written in England sometime between the conversion of that country to Christianity in the mid-seventh century and the date at which it was copied into its sole surviving manuscript, that is around 1000. It is a poem of over 3000 lines in length, which concerns events supposed to have occurred in Scandinavia, apparently in the sixth century. Beginning with an account of the early Danish kings, it goes on to tell how Hrothgar, king of the Danes, built the great hall of Heorot, which was haunted by the monster Grendel to the extent that the firmness of Hrothgar's followers was undermined and his power waned. His plight came to the attention of Beowulf, nephew of Hygelac, king of the Geats of southern Sweden, who came to Denmark with his own war-band, slept in the hall of Heorot, and fatally wounded Grendel by tearing off his arm when he was attacked by him. The king's rejoicing at this was cut short by the events of the very next night, when a raid was made on Heorot by Grendel's mother in revenge for her son's death. Beowulf, however, pursued her even to the bottom of the mere where she lived, and killed her too. Laden with gifts, he returned to the land of the Geats and was given land by his uncle King Hygelac. He became guardian of Hygelac's son after the king's death, and eventually king himself, reigning for fifty years. At the end of this period, a dragon-hoard was robbed and the dragon disturbed so that it began to ravage the land. Beowulf encountered it and killed it, although he was himself mortally wounded in the struggle.

We cannot but be struck by the emphasis in the poem on personal relationships between kings and their men, and leaders (such as the young Beowulf) and their men, of a type which seems to conform with an interpretation of the war-band as the primary driving force of political development, as implied by Tacitus. This is quite explicit in the poet's account of King Hrothgar's war-band:

> The fortunes of war favoured Hrothgar.
> Friends and kinsmen flocked to his ranks,
> young followers, a force that grew
> to a mighty army.
>
> (*Beowulf*, lines 65–8)

Notice here not just the picture of the king's war-band but the image of it growing by a sort of snowball effect of recruitment. The more successful the king, the more powerful his war-band – which is more or less what Tacitus says about it.

Beowulf also seems to reflect Tacitus's emphasis on the importance of gift-giving within the war-band. The poet tells us that King Hrothgar, the 'ring-giver', shared on the floor of the hall of Heorot 'the gifts God had bestowed on him with young and old' (lines 72–3); he gave Beowulf sumptuous gifts after his victories over Grendel and his mother (lines 1019–23; 1870–3); and Beowulf's own king, Hygelac, gave him on his return to the land of the Geats an ancestral sword and a substantial landed estate (lines 2190–6).

As for the centrality of the war-band, and of the loyalty which it entailed, the poet presents this most unequivocally in the context of Beowulf's preparations for his fight with the dragon near the end of his life. Then, we are told, he is deserted by all but one of his war-band out of fear. The dire results for the deserters are underlined by the speech of Wiglaf, the one steadfast member of the war-band, who tells them that they shall become 'wanderers without land-rights' (*Beowulf*, lines 2884–91).

The same image of the centrality of the war-band is projected by another Old English poem, the *Battle of Maldon*, written about the time that *Beowulf* was copied in the form we have it, that is around 1000. This tells of how the ealdorman, Byrhtnoth, was with his army on the coast of Essex to prevent a Viking landing. When he challenged the Vikings, they represented to him the unfairness of their not being allowed to land so that they could fight properly. Byrhtnoth accordingly let them land, fought with them, and was defeated and killed. The bulk of the poem (or at least the bulk of the part we have, for the end is lost) consists of a series of speeches by his followers declaring their undying loyalty to Byrhtnoth even after his death, as for example:

> I swear that from this spot not one foot's space
> of ground shall I give up. I shall go onwards,
> in the fight avenge my friend and lord.

Beowulf is of course fiction, a tale essentially of monsters and dragons, and you might argue that to try to learn about early medieval kingship from it is the equivalent of using a cowboy movie for information on the American West. On the other hand, we may think it unlikely that the poet would have presented aspects of the organisation of society which would have struck his audience as implausible, or at least would not have chimed with their values, so you could argue that, although the stories of monsters and a dragon are clearly fiction, the social context and the system of values in which the struggles with them are set are not. Likewise, the fundamental context in which the *Battle of Maldon* is set must have been in tune with the values of contemporaries to make the followers' attitudes and behaviour plausible, even if the chief purpose of the poet was to present Byrhtnoth as being as heroic as possible.

In the case of *Beowulf*, this view found startling corroboration in 1939 with the discovery of the ship-burial in Mound 1 at Sutton Hoo in Suffolk. At the beginning of *Beowulf*, the poet tells of the burial of the early (and probably mythical) Danish king, Scyld Scefing:

> At the hour shaped for him Scyld departed,
> the hero crossed into the keeping of his Lord.
> They carried him to the edge of the sea,
> his sworn arms-fellows, as he had himself desired them
> while he wielded his words, Warden of the Scyldings,
> beloved folk-founder; long had he ruled.
> A boat with a ringed neck rode in the haven,
> icy, out-eager, the atheling's vessel,
> and there they laid out their lord and master,
> dealer of wound gold, in the waist of the ship,
> in majesty by the mast. A mound of treasures
> from far countries was fetched aboard her,
> and it is said that no boat was ever more bravely fitted out
> with the weapons of a warrior, war accoutrement,
> swords and body-armour; on his breast were set
> treasures and trappings to travel with him
> on his far faring into the flood's sway . . .
> High over head they hoisted and fixed
> a gold standard; gave him to the flood,
> let the seas take him.
>
> (*Beowulf*, lines 26–48)

This burial is represented here as involving the actual launching of the burial-ship on to the sea, which sounds improbable since no one could have prevented the treasures being robbed at sea, and may have been an image connected with the mythical origins of Scyld, who was (as the poet tells us) supposed to have arrived as a child from the sea (lines 43–5). But in other respects the correspondence with Sutton Hoo Mound 1 was very striking. Both burials involved a ship (Fig. 15). Like Scyld's ship,

Figure 15 The Sutton Hoo Mound 1 ship as excavated just before the Second World War in 1939. The wood had entirely decayed away, but the impressions of the planks are clearly visible in the soil, and the iron rivets were still in their places. The outline of the chamber, where the burial itself and the treasures were, can be seen amidships.
Source: Courtesy of Colchester and Ipswich Museums; although efforts have been made to find the copyright holder of this image, this has not been possible.

the Sutton Hoo ship was equipped with a 'mound of treasures from far countries', including the great silver Anastasius dish from Byzantium, the two silver bowls from the eastern Mediterranean, and the great gold reliquary-buckle, possibly from England, possibly from somewhere else in early medieval Europe. Similarly the grave had the 'weapons of a warrior', in the shape of a great sword and shield and spears. It even had a standard (although not a gold one as in the poem) if the iron object so-called by its excavator really is such. The 1939 Sutton Hoo excavation then gave credence to the idea that at some level *Beowulf* was reflecting contemporary society, or at least its values.

The Gododdin

If we accept that literary sources have such an importance for us, we can extend our investigations further. From the Celtic world, we possess an epic poem in Brittonic, the ancestor of modern Welsh, called *The Gododdin*. This is preserved only in a thirteenth-century manuscript, and it is thought to have been composed in at least two stages over a period of centuries, although the oldest layer may date to as early as the late sixth century. Its title refers to the British Celtic people called the Gododdin (in Latin, the *Votadini*), whose kingdom seems to have lain in the area of the Firth of Forth and Edinburgh, until it was conquered by the English kings of Northumbria in the first half of the seventh century. It tells of how their king, apparently at the end of the sixth century when the kingdom of Northumbria was just emerging, held a great feast of warriors in his hall, and how they then set out on an ill-fated military campaign to attack the Deirans, that is (probably) the southern Northumbrians, but were in the event massacred. The bulk of the poem consists of a series of laments for the fallen warriors and the tone of this, as of the references to the feasting that preceded the campaign, are strongly reminiscent of the ethos of the war-band which Tacitus evokes.

Song of Roland

From the Frankish world, we possess a literary work which can also be viewed as evidence for the importance of the war-band in kingship. This is the *Song of Roland*, another epic poem, this time in Old French and from a little after the end of our period, around the year 1100. It tells the story of another military expedition, that in 778 of the Frankish ruler Charlemagne to Zaragoza in what was then Moslem-held Spain. This expedition, which is described in other sources, notably the near-contemporary *Royal Frankish Annals* for the year 778, was at first successful, but the Frankish army was attacked as it was returning across the Pyrenees. That misfortune is the principal subject of the *Song of Roland*. Charlemagne, the *Song* tells us, put his nephew, Roland, in command of the rearguard, which was attacked by Moslems (the *Revised Royal Frankish Annals* make it clear that the attackers were in reality Christian Basques). Roland and his companion Oliver heroically defended themselves at the Pass of Roncesvalles in the Pyrenees, but in vain. The dying Roland eventually sounded his horn, the Olifant, to summon Charlemagne's aid, but before that ruler could arrive with reinforcements, Roland had smashed his sword Durendal against a rock which he split in the process, and as he died he had knelt and handed over his glove to God who reached from the heavens to take it.

Aside from the heroism of Roland and Oliver, the real themes of the poem are all to do with the behaviour of Charlemagne's *palladins*, that is his immediate followers, or, as Tacitus would have put it, his *comitatus*. One theme is that of treachery, especially of the man who betrayed Roland to the Moslems by making possible the attack on him. But the other is the duty of Charlemagne himself to protect the members of his war-band, or in the technical legal parlance of the end of our period, to 'warranty' for them – a duty which, the poet implies, was of immense importance but not fully attended to. The *Song of Roland* is not of course of any real value for the organisation of the war-band in the time of Charlemagne himself, but arguably it casts a very intense light on a war-band ethos which was continuing as the dominant element of elite society in Europe through to the end of our period and beyond. The picture it paints of the dying Roland handing his glove to God emphasises the importance of formalised personal relationships between a lord and his military retainers, for Roland's gesture effectively acknowledges that God also enjoys his personal loyalty and obedience, just as Charlemagne does.

Ammianus, Hincmar, and the *Anglo-Saxon Chronicle*

In exploring the importance of the war-band in the centuries after Tacitus's time, we need not be entirely dependent on literary texts such as these. The account given by the fourth-century Roman writer Ammianus Marcellinus of the battle fought between Romans and barbarians at Strasbourg in 357 strikingly reflects the evidence we have looked at thus far. When Chnodomar, king of the Alamanns, was surrounded by Roman forces and surrendered, Ammianus tells us that:

> His attendants to the number of 200, together with three very close friends, also surrendered, considering it a disgrace to survive their king or not to die for him if the occasion required.
>
> (Ammianus, 16.12.60)

This sounds like a war-band, bound to its leader by extreme ties of personal loyalty. Moreover, Bede describes how warriors flocked from all over to serve the Northumbrian king Oswine (died 655) (Bede, *Eccl. History*, III.14). The similarity to what *Beowulf* says of Hrothgar's war-band is very striking.

Equally striking is Hincmar's *On the Organisation of the Palace* (secs 27–8), which describes the servants at the Carolingian palace as much as anything else like a war-band. The 'first class' of them was supported by the 'kindness and concern of the senior officers [who] provided them with food or clothing or gold or silver, sometimes too with horses or other gifts'. The 'second class' consisted of 'those young men in the various offices who, closely following their master, both honoured him and were honoured by him'. And the third class consisted of 'those young servants or vassals, whom both the greater and lesser officials zealously sought to have, to the extent that they were able to manage them and support them without sin, that is, without plunder or robbery'. Here we seem to be in a world of gift-giving and devotion to a lord which is very like the war-band of Tacitus's *On Germany*, and here too we have a clear echo of Tacitus's emphasis on the importance of plunder as a means of obtaining the wherewithal to make gifts. Without gifts, the 'young servants or vassals' (the terms had military connotations by the ninth century) would engage in just the sort of military activity which Tacitus envisaged.

At about the same time that Hincmar was writing, a compiler in the kingdom of Wessex was assembling and writing the annals of the *Anglo-Saxon Chronicle* in its original form. One of those annals, that for 755, bears directly on the importance of the war-band. It is a long annal which tells the story of how the king of Wessex, Cynewulf, wanted to drive out of the kingdom of Wessex an *ætheling*, that is, a prince, called Cyneheard. The *ætheling* presumably knew this and made a pre-emptive move. Learning that the king was 'in the company of a woman' at a place called Merton, Cyneheard rode there and surrounded the chamber in which the king and the woman were 'before the men who were with the king became aware of him'. Realising that he was surrounded, the king went to the door and fought his opponents, wounding the *ætheling* but in the end being killed himself.

The annal continues in a vein which would have done justice to Tacitus's view of the war-band. The woman's cries, it tells us, alerted the king's thegns, that is his faithful armed men, the members in other words of his war-band. When they 'became aware of the disturbance', they hurried to where the king had been killed.

> The *ætheling* offered each of them money and life, and not any of them wanted to accept it; but they were fighting continuously until they were all killed except for one British hostage, and he was very wounded.

Just as in Tacitus's *On Germany*, just as in the *Battle of Maldon*, it was clearly dishonourable for the members of the war-band to leave their lord even after his death.

The events of the next day, as the annal describes them, are even more interesting. Those of the dead king's thegns who had been left behind when he went to Merton to visit the woman now rode there, and found the *ætheling* and his men in the place where the dead king lay, with 'the gates locked against them'. There then followed an attempted negotiation, the failure of which may perhaps highlight the value-system according to which these men were acting. The *ætheling* not only offered the king's thegns 'their own choice of money and land' if they would agree to him becoming king, but he also impressed on them that 'relatives of theirs were with him who did not want to leave him'. In other words, he put it to them that to attack him would entail attacking kinsmen. But the king's thegns replied that 'no relative was dearer to them than their lord'. It is a clear affirmation of the bonds of the war-band as Tacitus had presented them, bonds which over-rode those of kinship. The same bonds clearly applied to the *ætheling*'s thegns, for when the king's thegns offered to allow those of their kinsmen who were amongst them to depart unharmed, they replied in a similar vein to that in which the king's thegns had replied to the *ætheling*'s offers. Then the king's thegns forced their way in and killed the *ætheling* and all the men who were with him except one who 'saved his life, although he was often wounded'. Although we should not treat this annal as an expression of any sort of legalistic principle that lordship bonds took priority over kinship bonds, the emphasis on the tension between family bonds and war-band bonds is striking.

Feasting, drinking, and the hall

That the war-band was intensely sociable emerges from Tacitus, who emphasises the importance of 'drinking bouts, lasting a day and a night', during which the barbarians discuss 'such serious affairs as the reconciliation of enemies, the forming of marriage alliances, the adoption of new chiefs, and even the choice of peace and war' (Tacitus, *On Germany*, ch. 22). Such activities seem clearly connected with the war-band.

Feasting and drinking as crucial aspects of the war-band take us back to one of the central motifs of *Beowulf*: the great hall of Heorot which King Hrothgar built and which Grendel so savagely attacked (lines 67–85). The term for hall frequently used in

Old English, including in *Beowulf*, was 'mead-hall' because its primary purpose was drinking, an activity which, you could argue, was as much a means of formalising and ritualising family-like bonds of the war-band as a purely social activity. It was over drink that the members of the war-band committed themselves to action and, as Tacitus observed, made decisions. In the *Battle of Maldon*, drink is what seals undertakings to act, for the warriors refer in the course of the battle to 'the words that we uttered many a time over the mead', that is to what, during drinking in the hall, they have undertaken to perform. Likewise in the Old Welsh poem, *The Gododdin*, the warriors are entertained before they set out to battle in the hall at Edinburgh, chiefly by being plied with mead. In *Beowulf*, halls almost seem to be a symbol for kingdoms, for of the early Danish king Scyld Scefing the poet writes:

> Was it not Scyld Scefing that shook the halls
> took mead-benches, taught encroaching
> foes to fear him?
>
> (*Beowulf*, lines 5–7)

These halls with their mead-benches were in effect the kingdoms which Scyld was conquering.

Great halls are not found just in literature, but are a consistent feature of royal sites across Europe. Traces of a sequence of great timber halls have been found at the seventh-century royal site of Yeavering on the edge of the Cheviot Hills in the kingdom of Northumbria. The remains of two enormous timber halls, one of the mid-sixth century, one of the mid-seventh, have been found at the Danish royal site of Lejre, which may well have been a centre of power for the very kings to whose dynasty King Hrothgar in *Beowulf* belonged, and may even have been the place where the story of the poem was set. Such halls were clearly of central importance to these royal sites; immense resources were evidently expended on them; and there seems little doubt that they were indeed the equivalent in real life of the hall of Heorot in *Beowulf*.

Halls were equally characteristic of Carolingian and Ottonian palaces. Charlemagne's principal palace at Aachen had a great stone-built hall, the *aula regia*, as also had the Carolingian palaces at Ingelheim (Fig. 8, above), Paderborn, and Frankfurt-am-Main (Germany). We could interpret these halls as imitations of the Roman basilicas, like the one that survives at Trier on the River Mosel (Germany), and no doubt in architectural terms they were. But their function may nevertheless have been that of mead-halls, and their prominence in these royal sites may point to the importance of the war-band even in parts of Europe where Roman forms were at least superficially very important.

The social pyramid

However we assess the evidence, we should probably not think of the war-band as a formal institution, and it certainly seems unlikely that it can have endured unchanged across the centuries between Tacitus and the barbarian kingdoms in the west. But it may nevertheless suggest that bonds of personal dependence were a very high priority in attitudes, and probably also in the reality of the way power and society worked. But if we are to understand how such dependence interrelated with the nature and exercise of power, we need to understand more about how society was structured. At the extremes, we have two possible hypotheses. The first would envisage it as a steep-sided pyramid, dominated by layer upon layer of the aristocratic elite, each layer bound to the next by ties of loyalty, and ultimately bound to the king, with only very lowly social layers of peasantry and slaves below it. The second would envisage it as a much flatter pyramid, made up principally of a wide group of freemen (with slaves beneath them, of course), and with only its point made up by the aristocratic elite around the king.

To argue for a steep-sided pyramid, we could point to the prominence of the aristocracy in Bede's *Ecclesiastical History of the English People*, where virtually everyone mentioned (or at least named) is of aristocratic status, one of the only exceptions being the cowherd Cædmon, who owes his appearance to his miraculous gift of song (Bede, *Eccl. History*, IV.24(22)). Much the same is true of other texts from England in the same period, notably Stephanus's *Life of Bishop Wilfrid* (chs 2, 13), which presents the future bishop as very much of aristocratic stock, able to equip himself and his followers to see the queen, and indeed to equip and man what was evidently by contemporary standards a substantial ship. The same picture emerges from Gregory of Tours's account of Frankish society in the sixth century. When officers of the king of the Franks arrived to confiscate Duke Rauching's property, for example, they 'discovered more things in his coffers than they could have expected to see in the public treasure of the king' (Gregory, *Hist. Franks*, IX.9). When Eberulf, the treasurer of King Childebert II (575–96), was toppled and his treasure confiscated, it proved to include gold, silver, precious objects, 'land granted him for life', herds of horses, pigs, beasts of burden, and a 'house inside the city walls . . . filled with corn, wine, fowls and all sorts of other things' (Gregory, *Hist. Franks*, VII.22). If we move to a later period of Frankish history we know that the Carolingian family, which took the throne of the kingdom in 751, was in origin just another family of great aristocrats, who first appear in the historical record around 600. Most bishops, in this time and later, were of aristocratic origin. A very notable exception was Archbishop Ebbo of Rheims in the ninth century, and he was criticised for his low social origin.

The archaeology of pagan graves, at any rate for the seventh century, and the grave-goods deposited in them, supports this interpretation. These graves point in the richness of the objects in them to a dominant aristocracy, in the weapons deposited in them to an aristocracy of predominantly military status, and in the drinking cups and horns in them to the importance of communal drinking in the mead-hall. Sutton Hoo Mound 1 is one of the wealthier examples from the early seventh century. From the sixth century are a number of chieftains' graves from the Frankish area, always with rich weapons, often with drinking vessels, sometimes with helmets which were clearly amongst the highest status of objects to be deposited in graves.

These graves point to the existence in the sixth and seventh centuries of a steep social pyramid. In the case of graves in Denmark, it has been possible to intepret them as showing chieftains with retinues of young warriors occupying subsidiary graves around them. The steepness of the social pyramid seems also to be suggested by the archaeology of settlement-sites, such as the lost village of Vorbasse (Denmark), which seem to show the bringing together and organisation of previously scattered settlements, presumably under the power of the aristocracy.

Strong as the evidence for a steep-sided social pyramid is, however, there is nevertheless a case to be made in favour of the existence of a much flatter social pyramid, in which the dominant group was a much broader one consisting of all freemen. It is possible to argue (below, pp. 178–9) that the sources which we have tend to over-emphasise the importance of the aristocracy, and that the land of Western Europe was much more in the hands of humbler freemen than it was in that of aristocrats. Thus we could emphasise the importance especially of the *ceorl* ('free yeoman') in England, and the *liber homo* ('free man') on the Continent. We could support an argument for the dominance of a wide group of freemen with reference to assemblies, which we could envisage as involving all the freemen of society, leaving out only the slaves. Against this, however, it is possible to argue that assemblies were the preserve of the dominant aristocracy and not of a wider community of freemen, and that the Latin word *populus* ('people') used for those who attended them meant 'the politically important people', that is the aristocratic elite.

The strongest evidence in favour of a flat pyramid, however, comes from what we know of early medieval military organisation. Charlemagne's 807 capitulary for the recruitment of freemen with particular levels of wealth (above, p. 112) could be used to argue that the king's army was made up of freemen rather than aristocrats. A similar conclusion could be drawn about the army in England raised by King Alfred of Wessex (871–99). This was called in Old English the *fyrd*, and it seems to have been recruited by a levy on those groups in society who would otherwise have been concerned with agriculture, for the king created (according to the *Anglo-Saxon Chronicle* for the year 894) a rotating system of service in the army fighting against the Viking invaders, presumably so that there should always be men at home to attend to the harvest.

The army may then have reflected a flat pyramid dominated by freemen, with the small upper point of aristocrats providing the leadership at most. Against this, however, the evidence of how armies fought – their mobility, suggesting that they were mounted, for example – and their hunger for rich booty – as when Charlemagne's army captured the treasures stored in the fortification (or 'ring') of their enemies the Avars (*Royal Frankish Annals* for the year 796) – points to the reality of the situation being that the army was aristocratic, whatever sources like the capitularies might suggest. Along these lines, it is possible to argue that the word *fyrd* had various meanings, and that the king's army in his campaigns was an aristocratic 'select *fyrd*'. As for the Carolingian armies, you could argue that, since the capitularies dealing with the recruitment of freemen belong to the early ninth century, when the Carolingian realms were threatened by attack from the Vikings, they related to the creation of a sort of home-guard on the land, rather than casting light on the make-up of the king's principal armies.

Aristocratic elites

If you accept such lines of argument (and you need not), you will probably conclude that the evidence is strongest for the steep-sided, rather than the flat, pyramid, although naturally the shape of the pyramid may have been different in different parts of Western Europe or in different sub-periods. But even where we are dealing with a steep-sided pyramid, we need to ask how complex and wide-ranging were the connections between the members of aristocratic elites. How cohesive, in other words, were the elites with which the kings had to deal? Some aristocratic families of the twelfth century and later have left us genealogies, showing the succession of generations across the preceding centuries in the form of 'a was the son of b, who was the son of c, who was the son of d', and so on. These genealogies, however, never go back beyond the ninth century. This creates a strong impression that before that period there were no firmly established aristocratic lineages or family groupings, so that the aristocracy can only have been a very loosely constituted and fluid elite. In addition, we do not find in Western Europe before the tenth century any but the most sporadic use of surnames or family names, which might be held to suggest the same thing, at any rate until the tenth and eleventh centuries when such names appear.

Another interpretation, however, is possible. We know that the Carolingian rulers, especially Charlemagne (768–814), enjoyed a very high reputation in the decades, and indeed centuries, following the break-up of their empire in the ninth century. Charlemagne was widely idolised as a ruler and, from the later twelfth century, as a saint-king. There was consequently a clear motive for aristocratic families of the twelfth and thirteenth centuries to associate themselves with him and his dynasty by representing their histories as beginning in his time. Their genealogies might, in other words, have been a fictional shaping of the past in the interests of the present, rather than a realistic picture of the origins of the Western European aristocracy.

As for the rarity of surnames, you can argue that the reason for this was not that the aristocracy did not have cohesive and lasting family structures, but that these structures were different from those which developed later involving succession of the first-born son, that is, primogeniture. Inheritance would instead have involved more members of the aristocratic family, so that family's relationships amongst its members were more complex, and it used a different system of names for representing this. That system was based not on surnames as we are familiar with, but rather on personal names, or, as we should say, Christian names. In Continental Germanic, Old English, and Old Norse, personal names took two forms: monothematic and dithematic – the first form had only one element, the second form had two. Monothematic names could be shortened (hypocoristic is the technical term) forms of longer names, as the Continental Germanic name Gozo is of a name beginning Gaut- or Goz-, such as

Gozbert; or they could be nicknames, such as the Old English name Eccha, possibly meaning 'war-horse'. Dithematic names on the other hand generally consisted of two entirely comprehensible elements placed together, as in the case of Ecgmund, meaning something like 'sword' and 'protector', or Continental Germanic Burghard, meaning 'fortress' and 'stern'. Monothematic names could clearly be used by all levels of society, including the peasants who are named in the Carolingian polyptychs and kings like Offa of Mercia, or indeed Carl the Great (Charlemagne). But the majority of the men who appear in documents and records associated with kings, and were therefore presumably high up the social scale, had dithematic names.

Now, a glance at the family-trees of early medieval royalty suggests that monothematic names could be used as markers of family relationships, as in the case of the use in Charlemagne's family of the name Carl (or, in its modern form, Charles), for himself, for his grandfather Charles Martel, for his son Charles the Younger, for his grandson Charles the Bald, for his great-grandson Charles the Simple, and so on. Royal families, however, show a comparable tendency to use dithematic names in such a way as to repeat in successive generations name-elements which were in effect family-markers. In England, for example, the West Saxon royal family made repeated use of the element Æthel-, as in King Æthelwulf (802–39), his sons Æthelbald, Æthelberht, and Æthelred, and his grandson Æthelstan. Similarly the royal family of Bernicia, the northern kingdom of Northumbria, made extensive use of the element Os-, as in the names of kings Oslac, Oswudu, and Oslaf around 600, or of King Oswald (634–42) and King Oswiu (642–70).

If such naming-patterns existed in royal families, they may have existed more widely in society, and may provide the key to reconstructing aristocratic families at periods before we have either genealogies or surnames for them. This offers the possibility of collecting all occurrences of names in early medieval records and considering whether enduring aristocratic family groups can be discerned in the pattern of the name-forms. For example, we may be able to see an aristocratic family group in the appearance of a duke called Wandalbert in a record of 642, in connection with a duke called Wandelmar (590–613), and an apparently younger man named Wandelmar. This family group may have included others with the name-element Wandal- (or Wandel-), including a whole series of bishops, that is Wandalenus of Saarland, Wandalmar of Troyes, Wandelius of Châlons, together with bishops bearing hypocoristic forms of the name-element, including Waldo of Nevers and Waldo of Basel. You may, however, have doubts. Were these name-elements really used in such a systematic way? Or are we just seeing the popularity right across society of particular elements?

Despite its use of such Germanic name-forms, it may be that the aristocracy, or at least a significant part of it, was of Roman senatorial origin, so that it had cohesive family-structures inherited from the past. In the Late Roman period in the west, senatorial families such as those of Symmachus and of Bishop Sidonius Apollinaris dominated the upper echelons of society. Gregory of Tours shows that they came to dominate appointment to bishoprics, not least his own family, which successively provided bishops of Tours and was, by his own account, of Roman senatorial origin (Gregory, *Hist. Franks*, X.31). Such families often had armed retainers, known as *bucellarii* or 'biscuit-eaters' – an allusion to their dependence on their lords – in much the same way as later aristocratic families in the barbarian kingdoms had armed retainers; and we know that they had fortified residences like later aristocrats, for these are described in Roman writings such as the poetry of the late Roman writer Ausonius, describing along the River Mosel residences which sound like fortifications:

> One, over there, is high on a cliff,
> that one on the edge of a jutting bank . . .
> This house is high in the clouds . . .
> Another lifts a tower in the clouds . . .
> Another glowers down on a river
> made more distant by the tumbling fog.
> (Isbell, 1971, p. 60)

The dominance of such families may also be shown by a man with the Latin name Mummolus, who was clearly very influential at the court of the sixth-century Frankish king (Gregory, *Hist. Franks*, IV.42). Similarly a man with the equally Latin name Florentinus appears as having two sons, one with the Latin name Nicetius becoming Bishop of Lyons, while the other, who was given the Continental Germanic name Gundulf became first *domesticus* (a high palace-official) and then *dux* (duke) under King Childebert I (575–95) (Werner, 1979, p. 154). Gregory describes him as 'of senatorial family' (Gregory, *Hist. Franks*, VI.11).

Naturally, the importance of aristocratic families of Roman origin must have varied across the different barbarian kingdoms. Such families can hardly have been of significance in areas like Ireland and Scandinavia which were outside the former Roman Empire, and readers of Bede's *Ecclesiastical History of the English People* will know that families with Latin names do not appear in his pages after the end of Roman Britain in the early fifth century, although it is possible that English aristocratic families were Romano-British in origin and had assumed English names.

The role of women

If then we are dealing with aristocratic elites occupying the summits of steep-sided social pyramids and with wide family connections, what was the role of women in those elites? The picture we began with of a society dominated by an aristocracy, defined by its military functions and its warlike ethos, points to an essentially male-dominated society. But was this the reality, or are we seeing a false image created by our sources, overwhelmingly written by men as they were?

In some respects the status of women looks to have been higher than that of the women in the centuries after the end of our period. Women's wergelds (the payments that had to be made by the family of one who had killed a woman to avert a bloodfeud being waged against them by her kin) could be higher than those for men. In the laws of the Bavarians and the Alamanns they were twice that of men, and for a woman of childbearing age they were three times as much as men's in the Salic Law.

Women's position in marriage was also not unfavourable to them. They were entitled to a dowry which they could control after their marriage, and also to gifts at their wedding. In Tacitus's account, these were 'gifts not chosen to please a woman's whim or gaily deck a young bride, but oxen, horse with reins, shield, spear and sword' (Tacitus, *On Germany*, ch. 18).

It is arguable that the position of women was improved by changes taking place in marriage itself, especially the increased importance of monogamy as opposed to the sort of polygyny (marriage with several women) which the Merovingian kings of the Franks are known from Gregory of Tours to have practised. Moreover, there was also a rise in primogeniture, that is the inheriting of land and titles by the eldest son in preference to other children, or other relatives, of the deceased. The consequent importance enjoyed by the eldest son reflected on the position of his mother, and tended to reinforce her position as the sole and legitimate wife of her husband. The importance of that wife is obvious in how in the ninth century Hincmar represents the queen as responsible for the management of the palace itself (Hincmar, *Organisation of the Palace*, sec. 22).

Nevertheless, the position of women appears to have been uncertain and fragile, as is shown by two famous sixth-century cases involving royal Frankish women. The first is that of the wives of King Chilperic I of the Franks (561–84), who initially married the Visigothic princess Galswinth. When there arrived at Chilperic's court a Frankish woman called Fredegund, who had apparently been a sexual partner of the king before his marriage, the old flame of affection was re-ignited. Chilperic, wishing to free himself of Galswinth but not wishing her to take back to the kingdom of the Visigoths the treasure she had brought with her, had her strangled, and took Fredegund as his new queen (Gregory, *Hist. Franks*, IV.28). When Chilperic himself was murdered, however, Fredegund's position was difficult. She had to put herself under the protection of the Bishop of Paris, but even so her brother-in-law Guntram sent her away to a residence suitable for a dowager-queen with no husband and no power. She was in the end able to get the regency for her son Chlothar, but by scheming and manoeuvring rather than by any exercise of power to which she was entitled. Her situation, in other words, was no better than Galswinth's, even if the outcome for her was better.

The second case is that of Brunhild, who acted as regent for her son King Childebert II (575–91), and her grandsons Kings Theudebert II of Austrasia (595–612) and Theoderic II of Burgundy (595–613). She managed her children and her own relationships, especially her marriage to the late King Chilperic I's son Merovech, which she suppressed by confining him to a monastery. After the death of Theoderic II in 613, however, she was betrayed and executed by being pulled apart by wild horses on the orders of Fredegund's son, King Chlothar II. It looks then as if, however ruthless and effective even royal women like these might have been, power for them was only possible in circumstances of royal minorities, where they could rule for their under-age children.

Whatever their importance, women did not bear arms, despite Tacitus's claim that the wedding-gift included arms, for where we have graves of women with grave-goods they never contain arms. A very good example is that of the high-status woman, poss-ibly a princess, found under Cologne Cathedral. She was equipped with jewellery and with an eating knife, but not with arms, unlike the high-status young man, possibly a prince, in the adjacent grave who was buried with arms, despite his youth.

It seems then that women's power derived from their position as wives, sexual partners, and mothers and grandmothers. Fredegund's displacement of Galswinth at Chilperic's court presumably resulted from her sexual attractiveness to the king (although admittedly nothing is known of her background); and the same must have been true of the mistress, and mother of his son, who displaced King Lothar's official wife, Theutberga. Lands and family-connections could also be sources of power to women, and it must be this that accounts for the position of the English queen Emma (or Ælfgifu as she was known in England) who was successively the queen of the English king Æthelred the Unready and then of the conqueror, King Cnut (1014–35). In this sort of role, women's position could be enhanced in circumstances of political instability when established frameworks were no longer strong. Thus the power in Germany of the Byzantine princess Theophanu, widow of Emperor Otto II (961–83), derived largely from the fact that her son Otto III was a minor, as had been the case with the son and grandsons of Brunhild. More striking still is the case of Æthelflæd, called by a contemporary writer the 'lady of Mercia', who organised Mercian campaigns in north-west England against the Vikings and, according to the twelfth-century writer William of Malmesbury, was 'a tower of strength for the men of her own side and such a terror to the rest' (Will. Malm. *Kings*, II, 125.4). Her position, however, derived from the fact that her husband was the ealdorman of Mercia, and that he was ill and then died, so that she was left filling a power vacuum. Her family position as the sister of the most powerful English ruler of the time, Edward the Elder, king of Wessex, certainly helped her to exercise power in the way that she did.

Nearness to the king

However complex and long-standing the Western European aristocracy was, there remains one crucial question if we are to understand the interrelationship between it and kings. How dependent on kings for its position was that aristocracy, or, looked at the other way, were kings faced with pre-existing aristocratic families, on whose support they were consequently dependent, and who were therefore able to constrain their power? If it was the kings, with their power and wealth, who had raised up families in close contact with them and so effectively shaped the Western European aristocracy through their moral, economic, and political support, this offers us a quite different picture of the nature of royal power and of society.

It is possible to argue that the aristocracy depended for its continuing status on nearness to the king (*Königsnähe* in German). In his history of the abbots of his own monastery, Monkwearmouth-Jarrow, Bede describes the origins of its founder, Benedict Biscop, as 'of noble English lineage' and being given by the king 'possession of the amount of land due to his rank' at the age of 'about twenty-five' when he was 'one of King Oswiu's thegns' (Bede, *History of the Abbots*, ch. 1). It is striking that such a person could apparently depend on the king for land, after a period of what was presumably war-band service as a thegn (or companion). You may think that this points to an aristocracy which, even if it was hereditary as Benedict Biscop's position evidently was, was nevertheless entirely dependent on the king. Such a career-pattern may underlie the distinction which Bede's use of Latin words seems to draw between those he describes as *milites* ('soldiers' or in Old English 'thegns', singular *miles*) or *ministri* ('ministers' or 'thegns', singular *minister*) on the one hand, and *comites* (singular *comes*, 'counts', or in Old English 'gesiths') on the other. Just as we suggested in the case of Benedict Biscop, *milites* or *ministri* were armed retainers in the palace of the king, while *comites* were settled, married men with land, like the *comes* whose church Bishop John of Beverley dedicated and whose wife he healed of sickness (Bede, *Eccl. History*, V.4). Bede then may have been envisaging the male members of English aristocratic society as beginning their careers as thegns in the palace of the king, who would later give them land and convert them into gesiths. Their position would in such a case have been dependent on the king. A similar distinction may appear in Continental documents which distinguish between *vassi* ('vassals' or 'military retainers') and *fideles* ('faithful men'). The former may be the equivalent of the English thegns, the latter of the English gesiths. If so, the pattern of royal control of the progress of aristocratic men may have been general.

At the heart of this, however, is a highly complex problem about the nature of land-holding in Western Europe, which is at its most acute as regards a letter written by Bede to his close associate, Bishop Ecgberht of York (soon to be Archbishop of York) in 734 (Bede, *Letter to Ecgberht*). Bede seems to have envisaged that laymen were obtaining hereditary rights to land by pretending that they were founding monasteries, which, as perpetual communities, would naturally have had permanent rights to the land granted to them. Such laymen would therefore have been using bogus monasteries to circumvent the process by which the king controlled aristocratic possession of land, so that this aspect of the Christian Church's role in society would have considerably advanced the aristocracy's independence of the king (see also below, pp. 272–3).

Even if we do not accept this interpretation, however, it still may have been the case that kings created the aristocracy, or at least enhanced its position, because they were in a position to make gifts of land from their own resources. Royal gifts of high-status objects, such as jewellery, may also have been important, especially if we accept that gift-giving was a very powerful way of creating dependence in society (below, p. 213). Appointment to royal offices may also have been a powerful way in which kings created, or at least shaped, the aristocracy. A classic case is Charlemagne's own family, members of which first appear at the end of the seventh century. The most senior of them were evidently involved in royal service, often as 'mayors of the palace', a key role which Charlemagne's grandfather, Charles Martel, used as his base to rule the kingdom of the Franks during the reign of the last, weak Merovingian kings. It may be significant too that the power-base of the Carolingian family was their landed wealth in the area between the rivers Meuse, Mosel, and Rhine, which was of great concern to the Merovingian kings, who were seeking to extend their power eastwards. We may reasonably conjecture that the usefulness of the Carolingian family to the Merovingian kings in that area lay at the base of their rise to prominence, and ultimately to the throne.

Naturally the dependence of the aristocracy on nearness to kings will have varied across Western Europe, depending on the power of the kings in different areas, and also from century to century, again depending on the power of the kings, for when they were weak (as in tenth-century western Frankia, for example) the aristocracy could naturally make themselves independent, and could make the royal offices they had received, like that of count, hereditary in their own families.

———————————————

In considering your view on the importance of personal power, you need to pursue an enquiry on a number of fronts. But you need to have very much in mind the nature of the evidence you are dealing with. Are you willing to take literary texts such as *Beowulf* seriously as historical sources, or do you think them fanciful fictions of no value for historical analysis? How do you rate the evidence of archaeology, of graves such as Sutton Hoo for example? You need also to think of the question of change through our period. Is it justifiable to use Tacitus's work, or do you think that there could really have been no continuity between his period and, say, the tenth and eleventh centuries? Do you think that there were changes in the course of our period, so that the structure of society, and so the scope for exercising personal power, was different immediately after the end of the Roman Empire in the west from what it was by, say, around 1000? These are questions that take our discussions to the heart of what power and society were like in our period.

Research and study

Broad research questions

How real an instrument of power was the war-band?

How valuable are literary texts for understanding the nature of power?

Was society dominated by aristocratic elites?

How much power and influence did women have?

Did kings depend on aristocrats or did aristocrats depend on kings?

Books and papers to begin with

In a very important, influential, and quite readable book, Althoff (2004) makes the case that power in society really depended on personal bonds rather than on bureaucratic machinery. He examines bonds of kinship and those of lords and men, but he also lays emphasis on bonds created by treaties of friendship and by sworn confederations.

The view that a proportion at least of the later aristocracy originated in the Roman period is developed by Werner (1979), drawing largely on the evidence of names. You should try to read alongside this the work of Le Jan (2002). For the Late Roman and the post-Roman aristocracy of Gaul, two old books by Dill (1933, 1926) are very readable and bring you close to the sources, although the more up-to-date work is by Matthews (1990), summarised by Wormald (1976). A summary of the development of the aristocracy across Europe in the post-Roman period is offered by Wickham (2005, ch. 4), in a chapter which, despite its length, is worth reading for some quite useful evidence, and an interpretation which you need to think critically about.

For social structure later in our period, a classic, and very stimulating, starting-point is Bloch (1961), originally published in 1939–40 but still very worthwhile. Airlie (1995, 2005, 2006) offers useful and concise discussions of the Carolingian aristocracy, and especially its relationship to kings, a theme also of Le Jan (2000). The structure of that aristocracy in relationship to kings, and the distinction between 'vassals', interpreted as specialist military retainers, and 'faithful men', interpreted as the top rank of the aristocracy, is the subject of very accessible work by Odegaard (1945, 1941), which really brings you face-to-face with the evidence. Where reasonably large archives of charters and other documents have survived, as in the case of the thousands of charters from the Rhineland monastery of Lorsch, it is possible to finesse a picture of the development of the aristocracy. Innes (2000) does this, arguing that the aristocracy was indeed dominated by a group at its top, but that group had wide connections lower down the scale of both blood-relationship and patronage.

The present chapter has looked at wide sweeps of time, but in fact there must have been differences between different parts of Western Europe and different sub-periods. The argument that there were major changes in the tenth and eleventh centuries which resulted in the appearance for the first time of a feudal aristocracy is summarised by Duby (1974, ch. 6), and powerfully made by Moore (2000, ch. 2). See also below, pp. 342–3.

A detailed survey of the aristocracy in the period 400–800 in different parts of Europe is given by Wickham (2005, pp. 153–258). Karl Leyser (1983, ch. 7) discusses the aristocracy in Ottonian Germany. Useful for this too is Fichtenau (1991, part 3). An extremely useful collection of papers translated mostly from the German is Reuter (1979), including the paper by Werner referred to above, but also papers by Irsigler,

'On the Aristocratic Character of Early Frankish Society', and Tellenbach, 'From the Carolingian Imperial Nobility to the German Estate of Imperial Princes'. The paper by Bosl, '"Noble Unfreedom": The Rise of the *Ministeriales* in Germany', discusses the extent to which kings actually created nobles from unfree men by making them their officials, or *ministeriales*. If you want to pursue the much earlier history of the Western European aristocracy, back into the Iron Age, you can consult Hedeager (1992).

Pursuing more specific aspects

War-bands

How close to reality in its representation of the war-band is literature in this period?

The importance of war-bands is the central theme of Enright (1996), which is open to all sorts of criticism (e.g. use of late and early sources together, reliance on literary texts, use of archaeological evidence of widely differing dates) but is extremely stimulating. You need to decide how seriously you are prepared to treat literary texts like *Beowulf* as historical evidence for social structure, even if their narratives are wholly or partly fictional. Another striking study which does accept this is Bazelmans (1999), although it is rather technical. White (1989) is a detailed discussion of the passage about Cyneheard and Cynewulf, and is well worth wrestling with, although you need not agree with its argument that there was no quasi-legal principle that lordship-bonds should take precedence over those of kinship-bonds, but that the annalist envisaged immediate political decisions being involved. A general discussion of the importance of kinship is Smith (2005, ch. 3).

A very useful introduction to cemeteries is Halsall (1995), and there are discussions in James (2009, 1988). It is well worth mastering the various graves at Sutton Hoo, which you can do with the aid of Carver (1998) and Carver and Evans (2005). An accessible introduction to Mound 1 is Evans (1986). A rich collection of papers on Sutton Hoo (Carver, 1992) also contains papers on Frankish royal burials by James, and on Norwegian and Danish burials by Hedeager and Myhre respectively.

Halls

How important were the social and political functions of royal halls?

It is not an easy book to use, but there is exciting material not only about the halls of Lejre and their possible relationship to *Beowulf* but also other north European halls in Niles (2007). Laing (1969) provides a survey of halls in Britain. To examine more closely the important hall-complex of Yeavering, you can look at Hope-Taylor (1977); more recent commentary is in Frodsham and O'Brien (2005). On Carolingian palaces, there is a summary by Lobbedey (2002). The use of halls is vividly, but often not very critically, reconstructed by Pollington (2003). It is well worth thinking about the role of alcoholic drink in social relations, with the help of Bullough (1991b), Haycock (1999), for whom 'mead in early Welsh poetry is the central symbol of sustenance of the war-band, its solidarity and community of purpose', and a very amusing article by Edwards (1980) on alcohol in *Beowulf*.

Assemblies

What light do the sites and character of assemblies throw on the nature of power?

Two collections of papers have been published, one edited by Pantos and Semple (2004), much concerned with the archaeological context of actual sites of assembly, the other by Barnwell and Mostert (2003), which is more concerned with the function of assemblies. Carolingian assemblies are discussed by Rosenthal (1964), and there is an old but interesting book on English assemblies by Oleson (1955). It is very worthwhile looking closely at Hincmar, *Organisation of the Palace*, secs 34–5.

Military recruitment

How important to the recruitment and maintenance of armies were plunder and tribute?

The fullest discussion is by Halsall (1998, chs 3–6), who adopts a chronological approach, arguing that there was a transition in our period from more public levies towards those based rather on the personal networks of aristocrats. The most stimulating discussion, however, is that of Reuter (1985), discussing the significance for understanding Carolingian armies of the importance of plunder and tribute. For England, there is a full study by Abels (1988), although you need to think critically about his argument that there was a select army (or *fyrd*) distinct from the general *fyrd* of freemen.

Women

How powerful were royal women?
What was the status of women in relation to men in society at large?

This is a subject in its own right and there are a number of studies. Most useful for this chapter is Wemple (1985) on Frankish women. More general surveys are by Bitel (2002) and Jewell (2006). For England, there are surveys by Jewell (1996), Henrietta Leyser (1996), and Fell (1984). On royal female saints, you can look at McNamara, Halborg, and Whatley (1992). On queens, the best study is Stafford (1998), although useful for Frankish queens is Nelson (1978). For royal women in Ottonian Germany, see Karl Leyser (1979, pp. 48–76). MacLean (2003) provides a clear and interesting discussion of the way in which widowed queens derived power from their role in nunneries, which is also relevant to Chapter 11.

Conclusion

We have in this part of the book been examining power in Western Europe in our period by seeing how far it conformed to the models, derived from Max Weber, of ideological, bureaucratic, and personal power. This approach arguably has its advantages in helping us to get at the nature and origins of power, but it has the drawback of placing less emphasis on changes in the nature of power over time. As you go on with your research and study, you need to have the question of change over time, and the relationship between what happened in our period and what happened before and after it, clearly in view.

In the case of ideological power associated with kingship (Chapter 4), you may think that we have been too impressed by the apparent continuities in the ideas underpinning that institution, and by the continuity of at least the underlying features of kingship back to the Roman period and even beyond. But you need to ask whether change was more important than continuity. Was the influence of Christianity on kingship so radical that what emerged was a quite different institution than had existed previously? Did the introduction of anointing kings with holy oil, for example, mark a real turning-point in the ideological basis of power? And was kingship radically different not only in different parts of our period, but also in different parts of Western Europe? Were the Irish kings, for example, who ruled over tiny areas and tiny populations, the same sort of rulers, as we have treated them, as a king of the Franks like Charlemagne, ruling over a very large part of Western Europe? Questions such as these are particularly exciting because on the one hand kingship really does appear consistent across long periods and wide areas, while on the other we need to be aware that the images of kingship we are receiving from the past may be very different from the reality. Widening your perspective, both chronologically and geographically, may provide you with some of the keys, and very helpful for this is a recent, wide-ranging, and thought-provoking discussion of kingship during and beyond our period and our geographical area by Francis Oakley (2006).

As regards bureaucratic power (Chapter 5), how far was there an uninterrupted development during our period? Were the institutions of Roman rule, notably the machinery of taxation, absorbed into the barbarian kingdoms and, if so, for how long did they endure? Was there a period following the end of the Roman Empire in the west when these and other mechanisms of power were much reduced in their efficacy, perhaps more so than in any other historical period? If that were the case, did the real development in bureaucratic power occur in the Carolingian period of the eighth and ninth centuries and later, or, if we were to conclude that it did, would we be being misled by the relative abundance of documents surviving compared with earlier centuries? As with kingship, we need to consider how different were the various parts of Western Europe. England in the tenth and eleventh centuries, for example, can be presented as having particularly precocious governmental institutions. How different was it from other Western European kingdoms?

Personal power (Chapter 6) poses us some of the most acute questions. Here too we have been treating the development of the structure and practices of the aristocracy as showing continuity across our period, even though we have identified some possibilities of change. But you need now to consider the extent to which there may have been much more radical changes than we have yet identified. Is it right to argue that the aristocracy of the barbarian kingdoms was much the same thing as that of the later Roman Empire, except with a general change in personal names to Germanic forms, or did a quite new social structure emerge in the post-Roman period? Was the development of ideological and bureaucratic power, especially in the Carolingian period, the turning-point for the European aristocracy, as aristocrats defined themselves by reference to their relationship to kings and their place in royal government? Or was the turning-point much later, perhaps not until the eleventh century, when the position of the aristocracy was arguably revolutionised by the rise of primogeniture (inheritance by the eldest son), more intensive exploitation of the peasantry, and more systematic use of Christianity as a means of reinforcing their position? Here, too, to deepen our ideas we need to widen our perspective. Useful for this are a collection of papers edited by Timothy Reuter (1979) and dealing with the period from the sixth to the twelfth centuries, a remarkable discussion of more ancient societies in Western Europe by Lotte Hedeager (1992), and a challenging discussion by R. I. Moore (2000, ch. 2) which forcefully makes the case that the real turning-point in the development of the power of the aristocracy, as compared with later centuries, was the very last part of our period.

Time-line: Part III

100 BC–44 BC	Julius Caesar, Roman general and writer
55–c.120	Tacitus, Roman writer
	97/8 Publication of *On Germany*
357	Battle of Strasbourg
c.457–81	Childeric, king of the Franks
476–93	Odoacer, ruler in Italy
471–526	Theoderic, king of the Ostrogoths, king in Italy 493–526
481–511	Clovis, Merovingian king of the Franks
	507 Victory over the Visigoths at Vouillé
524	Killing of King Sigismund of the Burgundians
527–65	Justinian I, emperor
561–84	Chilperic I, joint king of the Franks
575–95	Childebert I, king of the Franks
	Killing of Queen Galswinth
613	Killing of Brunhild, regent for Childebert II (575–91), Theudebert II (595–612), and Theoderic II (595–613)
c.616–633	Edwin, first Christian king of Northumbria
634–42	Oswald, king of Northumbria
655	Killing of King Oswine of the southern Northumbrians (Deira)
c.673–735	Bede
	731 *Ecclesiastical History of the English People*
	734 Letter to Bishop Ecgberht of York
716–57	Æthelbald, king of Mercia
751–68	Pippin III, king of the Franks
	751 Replacement of Childeric III, last Merovingian king of the Franks, by the first Carolingian king, Pippin III, and his anointing by Archbishop Boniface
	754 Anointing of King Pippin III by Pope Stephen
757–96	Offa, king of Mercia
	Construction of Offa's Dyke
	794 Killing of Æthelberht, king of the East Angles
768–814	Charlemagne, king of the Franks, and emperor
	778 Expedition to Zaragoza
	794 Coinage reform (Class III to Class IV)
	799 Deposition of Pope Leo III and his flight to Charlemagne's court at Paderborn

	800 Coronation of Charlemagne as emperor in Rome
	802 Reform of *missi dominici*
	805/6 Capitulary of Diedenhofen (Thionville)
	806 Capitulary of Nijmegen
814–40	Louis the Pious, king of the Franks and emperor
840–70	Charles the Bald, king of the Franks and emperor
	829 Jonas of Orléans writes *Royal Institution*
	848 Anointing as king of Aquitaine
	869 Anointing as king of Lotharingia
c.806–82	Hincmar, archbishop of Rheims, author of *On the Organisation of the Palace*
871–99	Alfred the Great, king of Wessex
918	Death of Æthelflæd, lady of Mercia
919–36	Henry I the Fowler, king of Germany
927–39	Æthelstan, king of England
936–73	Otto I, king of Germany
	936 Coronation at Aachen
	962 Crowned emperor in Rome
961–83	Otto II, king of Germany
	961 Crowned king
	967 Crowned emperor
	972 Married the Byzantine princess, Theophanu
	973 Came to power on Otto I's death
978–1016	Æthelred the Unready, king of England
	978 Murder of Edward the Martyr, king of England
983–1002	Otto III, king and emperor
	984 Crowned king at Aachen
	997 Crowned emperor in Rome by the pope
991	Battle of Maldon (Essex)
1002–24	Henry II, king of Germany
	1014 Crowned emperor
996–1031	Robert the Pious, king of France
1030	Death in battle of King Olaf of Norway
1016–35	Cnut, king of England, king of Denmark (c.1018–35)
1042–66	Edward the Confessor, king of England

PART IV

The economic foundation

Introduction

The aim of this part of the book is to discuss the extent to which there were fundamental changes in the economic basis of Western Europe across the early medieval period. The topic is an exciting one, partly because understanding how human societies were resourced is such a crucial aspect of appreciating how they were shaped and how they functioned, partly because of the exciting advances in research, especially in archaeological and numismatic research (research into coins) over recent decades.

To understand how the topic has developed, however, we need to go back to the work of one of the most influential scholars of the twentieth century, Henri Pirenne. His book, *Mahommed and Charlemagne*, was published in its original French version in 1937, while his *Medieval Cities: Their Origins and the Revival of Trade* was published in 1925 (Pirenne, 1939, 1925). They were not Pirenne's only publications, but taken together they set out an interpretation of the development of early medieval Western Europe which was so influential that it came to have its own label, the 'Pirenne Thesis'.

In essence, that thesis envisaged the history of our period as a succession of three stages. The first spanned the end of the Roman Empire in the west and extended up until the first half of the seventh century, thus covering in Gaul the first part of the period of the Merovingian kings of the Franks. According to Pirenne, this stage was characterised by continuity between the barbarian kingdoms and the Roman Empire in the west which had come before them. This continuity could be seen, he believed, in three ways. First, economic. The barbarian kingdoms (and his focus was primarily on Merovingian Gaul) continued to be dominated by a trading system which looked towards the Mediterranean and was concerned principally with the same trans-Mediterranean trade in luxuries from the Far East via the overland routes across Central Asia, just as it had flourished under the Roman Empire.

Secondly, cultural. The Mediterranean economic connection, the thesis maintained, ensured that Merovingian Gaul was a continuation of the late Roman cultural world, with art and architecture continuing in Roman fashion, late Roman senatorial families such as that of Gregory of Tours continuing to dominate Western European society, and the centres of scholarship and cultural influence remaining the old Roman ones in the south, at places such as Clermont, Tours, and Lyons.

Thirdly, political. The barbarian kingdoms, Pirenne thought (and here too he was largely discussing Merovingian Gaul although his comments could be extended to other barbarian kingdoms), still turned towards the Mediterranean and toward the east Roman Empire. This, in his view, was shown by the way in which barbarian kings, such as Clovis at Tours, as we saw earlier, acknowledged subjection to the east Roman emperor. It was also shown, he thought, by the policy of the Merovingian kings of the Franks to mount military campaigns southwards towards the Mediterranean, as Clovis did in Aquitaine in the early sixth century, and his sons did later in the century when they conquered Burgundy and Provence, giving them access to the Mediterranean coastline with its opportunities for contact with the eastern Mediterranean and with the Byzantine Empire. In short, the barbarian kingdoms were really a continuation of the Roman Empire in debased form (even if Pirenne was largely thinking of the kingdom of the Franks), and Pirenne was thus a precocious supporter of the view that the end of the Roman Empire in the west was a process of transformation, more to do with continuity than with cataclysm (above, Chapter 2).

The second stage of Pirenne's thesis was ushered in by the great military and political expansion of the Arabs which began in the early seventh century. Following the teaching of the prophet Mohammed (died 632) and the inauguration of the religion of Islam, Arab armies achieved spectacular conquests. Bursting out of Arabia, they advanced deep into the Middle East, capturing the Byzantine provinces of Syria, Mesopotamia, and Armenia, and capturing and destroying completely the great kingdom of Persia, which had for centuries been a formidable opponent of the Roman Empire. The control of the Arabs extended eastwards to the River Indus and the foothills of the Himalayan Mountains by the early eighth century (Map 8).

Westwards, the Arab armies moved remorselessly along the southern coast of the Mediterranean Sea, capturing the east Roman provinces of Egypt, Libya, and Tripoli in 639/41, and extending to the Atlantic Ocean with the conquest of the whole east Roman province of North Africa, including the city of Carthage, by the end of the century. Then in 711 Moslem armies, probably consisting chiefly of Berbers from North Africa, invaded Spain, destroying the kingdom of the Visigoths and the Byzantine exarchate in the south, and leaving the Iberian peninsula almost entirely a Moslem-dominated area.

This spectacular expansion led, in Pirenne's view, to the Mediterranean ceasing to be a great thoroughfare between east and west, and becoming instead a 'Moslem lake' as he put it, dominated by Moslem fleets and Moslem pirates hostile to the Christians of the Byzantine Empire and the surviving barbarian kingdoms in the west, and with its southern shores ruled by Moslems and controlled by Moslem merchants hostile to

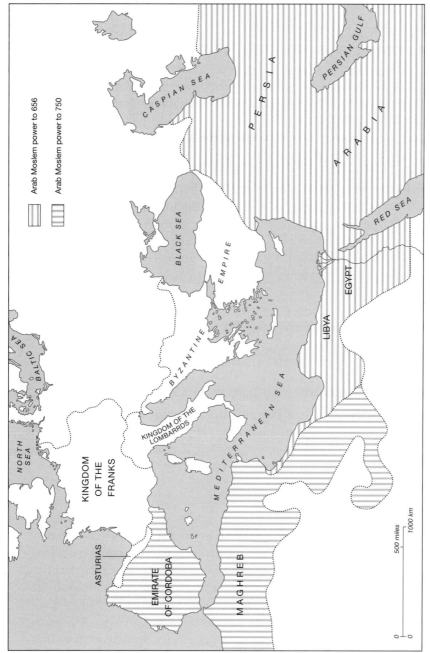

Map 8 Expansion of the Arab Moslems. The horizontal shading shows the expansion of Arab Moslem power down to 656, including the Byzantine provinces of the eastern and southern shores of the Mediterranean Sea and the kingdom of Persia. The vertical shading shows its expansion down to 750, including the kingdom of the Visigoths. Spain is now entirely under Moslem control, apart from the kingdom of Asturias in the north. The River Indus is almost the limit of Moslem power in the east, beyond the eastward extent of this map. Notice the rump to which the Byzantine Empire is reduced, consisting of Asia Minor and the Balkans, although the latter was fragmented by the incursions of Slavs.

contacts, including commercial contacts, with the Christians. Hence the links between east and west were severed, and the essentially Roman character of the barbarian kingdoms in the west was destroyed. This was a process accelerated, he thought, by the destruction of ancient centres of Roman culture in the south by Moslem pirates.

The results for Roman life and organisation in the west were, for Pirenne, dramatic. As regards economic development, the west came to be dominated by agriculture organised, he thought, on the basis of great landed estates, which formed 'closed' economies, producing everything they needed for themselves and their owners. There was therefore no significant trade, and certainly no long-distance trade as there had been in the immediately post-Roman period. As regards culture, Pirenne's view was that the closing of the Mediterranean meant that the barbarian kingdoms ceased to be an extension of the Roman world, since they were now cut off from the Byzantine Empire, and looked northwards for their cultural development towards the monasteries of the British Isles, places such as Monkwearmouth-Jarrow in Northumbria where Bede worked, and to the monasteries of north-eastern Europe which had largely been founded under English or Irish impetus.

Finally, Pirenne's thesis envisaged a similar shift in the centre of gravity of political power, which moved away, he believed, from the Mediterranean to the great northern rivers, such as the Rhine and the Meuse. Thus the Carolingian kings emerged as the most powerful rulers in Western Europe, and the great emperor Charlemagne established his principal palace at Aachen in the north. Also, the papacy, which had been dominated by the Byzantine Empire up to the early eighth century, turned away from accepting the authority of the Byzantine emperor, and towards the Frankish rulers, as was symbolised above all by Pope Leo III's crowning of Charlemagne as emperor – a definitive break, Pirenne thought,.

If the Arab invasions were thus the cause of the emergence of Western Europe from the Roman Empire, the third stage of Pirenne's thesis, set out in his *Medieval Cities*, was the commercial take-off of its closed economy. He dated this to the tenth and eleventh centuries, and saw it as involving the development of trade in the north on a considerable scale, and the growth of the cities which were the subject of his book. This development and growth was driven by new merchant classes which were to dominate European society for centuries to come.

Pirenne's thesis, in all its broad-brush imaginativeness, was highly influential, to the extent that it may be useful, even almost a century after its conception, to use its framework in our discussions in this part of the present book. Although it embraced much more than economic development, its underlying idea was that such development was the driving force of the whole character of Western Europe, and that is the aspect of it which we need now to consider. If we think in terms of using the framework of Pirenne's stages, they provide us with a useful series of questions. As regards commercial activity, which will be the subject of Chapter 7, we need to ask: first, how far is it true that trade continued in Western Europe as it had done under the Roman Empire through to the early seventh century? Secondly, what was the impact of the Arab expansion on the commerce of Western Europe? Thirdly, we need to enquire into the nature of exchange itself. Was trade really so important as Pirenne thought, even in the Roman period, or was it just a layer of frothy luxury benefiting only a tiny proportion of the population? And can what we are seeing in our period really be regarded as trade in the sense of commercial, profit-making activities familiar to us? Pirenne assumed that it could, as many scholars of the earlier twentieth century did, but it may be that what they regarded as trade was really state-controlled activity not aimed at profit, or the working of gift-exchange, or simply a thinly disguised aspect of plundering and tribute-taking.

As regards agriculture (which will be the subject of Chapter 8), was there a continuity of organisation across the end of the Roman Empire in the west, reflecting Pirenne's supposed continuity of commerce? And, from the period following the Arab expansion, was Western Europe really dominated by great landed estates and was its economy 'closed' in the way that Pirenne envisaged? In other words, was the rural economy of Western Europe stagnant and unaffected by commercial priorities and the demands of towns?

As regards Pirenne's view that there was an economic take-off in the tenth and eleventh centuries, we need to look above all at the development of towns, which will be the subject of Chapter 9. Here too, how far was there continuity across the period of the end of the Roman Empire in the west? Did Roman cities, in other words, continue at any rate up until the seventh century as Pirenne's thesis assumed? Secondly, can we locate a resurgence of urban and commercial activity in the tenth and eleventh centuries as Pirenne did? Thirdly, was Pirenne right to see the driving mechanism of commercial and urban expansion as being merchant communities and what was effectively a burgeoning middle class? Or was it rather the result of top-down activity by kings, nobles, and churchmen? Tied up with all this is the question of what were the principal functions of towns and cities across our period.

7

Trade as a driving force?

Pirenne and his critics

How far did trade continue in Western Europe as it had done under the Roman Empire through to the early seventh century? The evidence that Pirenne used to answer this question in the affirmative was of two types. First, there were the references in sixth- and seventh-century sources to 'Syrians' active in Western Europe after the end of the Roman Empire in the west. For Pirenne, the presence of these Syrians could be accounted for by the continuation of long-distance luxury trade in spices, silks, and ivory in particular. That trade was carried over the land-routes from the Far East across Central Asia and so down to the ports of the east Roman province of Syria on the coast of the eastern Mediterranean. From there, Pirenne supposed, Syrian merchants transported the luxury goods by sea to such western ports as Marseilles, and this accounted for the presence of Syrians in the west.

Pirenne's critics, however, emphasised the lack of evidence to establish that the Syrians found in our written sources really were engaged with trade. If you look in one of Pirenne's main sources, Gregory of Tours's late sixth-century *History of the Franks*, for example, they certainly appear and are evidently ethnically distinctive, as when Gregory describes (VIII.1) the welcome given to King Guntram of the Franks at the city of Orléans, when his welcomers included Syrians, whose speech 'contrasted sharply with that of those using Gallo-Roman and again with that of the Jews, as they each sang his praises in their own tongue'. The presence of these Jews, too, might be taken as evidence for continuing commercial contacts with the eastern Mediterranean. But for neither the Jews nor the Syrians is there any explicit indication that they were anything to do with trade. They could just have been exiles or immigrants. Gregory's other account of Syrians in the kingdom of the Franks (X.26) does, however, refer to a

Syrian in terms of trade, for it concerns Eusebius, 'who was a merchant and a Syrian by race'. He was elected as Bishop of Paris, and duly 'dismissed the entire household of his predecessor and replaced them by a number of other Syrians'. We might think that this passage is very good evidence for Pirenne's view, although equally it is disturbing that, if Eusebius was so much a merchant, he chose to make himself a bishop.

The second type of evidence used by Pirenne was the availability in the west of commodities which must have been obtained via the eastern Mediterranean: papyrus, spices, and silks. Papyrus was the writing material, a forerunner of paper, manufactured only in Egypt from a particular species of rush. It was what government documents were chiefly written on, until the late sixth century in the kingdom of the Franks, later in other areas, notably at the papal writing office in Rome. Its availability in the west was, for Pirenne, strong evidence in favour of the continued importance of trans-Mediterranean trading routes. As for spices and silks, Pirenne drew chiefly on casual references to them in sources of the late fifth and sixth centuries to show their availability in the west. They too must largely have come from the Far East via Central Asia. Spices were grown within the Roman Empire, but many could only be obtained from Arabia, East Africa, India, or the Far East – pepper, for example, of which 'long pepper' came from northern India and black pepper came from as far south in India as Malabar. Silk was originally the product of silk-worms raised in China and, for many centuries before the end of the Roman Empire in the west, it had been imported into the Mediterranean via the Central Asian routes which have consequently been popularly called the Silk Road. In the sixth century, silk-worms were introduced to Constantinople (supposedly by a group of monks who smuggled them through Chinese prohibitions on export by hiding them in the knobs of their walking-sticks). But still silk would have to have come from the eastern Mediterranean, and its occurrence in the west can therefore still be seen as evidence for the continued operation of the long-distance trade across the Mediterranean.

Pirenne's final type of evidence was coinage: the fact that the barbarian kingdoms used at first imperial Roman gold coins (*solidi*), and then, through to the early eighth century, their own imitations of such coins, the so-called *tremisses* of the Continent or the *thrymsas* of England. He interpreted this continued use of gold coinage to mean that the barbarian kingdoms were still deeply involved in trans-Mediterranean luxury trade, as it had existed under the Roman Empire in the west, and that the high value of the goods being traded required the use of gold coinage, rather than silver or bronze coinage.

The Roman economy

Since Pirenne's time, specialists in the Roman economy have developed an interpretation of it which is fundamentally hostile to Pirenne's view of the importance of long-distance trade and its continuation after the dissolution of the Roman Empire in the west. Written records for Roman trade, which consist chiefly of imperial edicts and other texts, emphasised the role of the Roman state in commercial activity. They encouraged scholars, such as A. H. M. Jones (1964), but most influentially the great classical specialist Moses Finley (1992) in a book first published in 1953, to envisage the Roman economy not as a commercial, free market of modern Western type, but rather as an economy directed and controlled by the state.

In this interpretation, it was dominated by the demands of the Roman imperial government for the supply of its armies in particular, and also for the delivery of the *annona*, the massive state-ordered, and state-funded grain shipments from Egypt to feed the city of Constantinople, and from North Africa to feed the city of Rome. In this interpretation, the economy was organised by the Roman state, which established state-controlled guilds for industrial production, created state-controlled industrial centres such as one at Pavia in Italy specialising in making shields for the army, and created state-funded dockyards such as the one at Ostia in Italy, the port of Rome. If this interpretation is correct, it must follow that the end of the Roman Empire in the west was disastrous for the Mediterranean economy, at least in the western Mediterranean where imperial government ceased. So the continued import of papyrus, spices, and silks, for which we have no information as to its volume since the evidence for it consists of passing references in literary texts, cannot have been more than a minor survival of trans-Mediterranean trade, once the centrally important state-controlled trade had come to an end with the collapse of the political structure which had created it.

Pottery manufacture and trade

This interpretation of the Roman economy, however, has itself been called into question by numerous archaeological excavations across Western Europe, which have undermined in their turn the picture which Pirenne drew. Archaeologists in Western Europe rarely find in their excavations papyrus, silk, or spices, which do not survive well in the conditions usually prevalent – papyrus, for example, needs very dry conditions such as those of the Syrian desert for it not to rot away. But archaeology is extremely effective at recovering pottery of all sorts, because ceramic material is nearly indestructible in the soil.

Many archaeological excavations have shown the use of high-quality, wheel-thrown pottery right across the Roman Empire, even at quite minor settlements. It is hard to believe that the supply of such pottery to such places was the result of an imperially organised and controlled system of manufacture and distribution such as Finley and Jones envisaged. One of the most easily recognisable of such wares is that known as Terra Sigillata, which is a lustrous, glazed ware of a deep red colour, usually with patterning on the surface. The frequency with which it is to be seen exhibited in museums attests to the scale and intensity of its distribution in the Roman period.

The evidence of such Roman pottery is impressive not just because of its abundance, but also because the consistency and style of particular types of fine ware make it possible to trace their place of manufacture, and this shows that they were made in

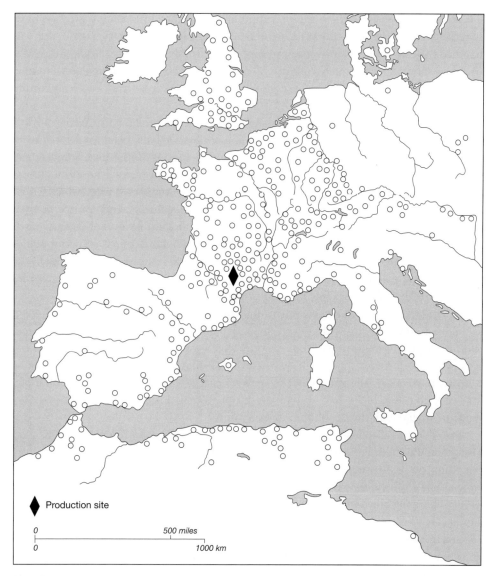

Map 9 Distribution of pottery (find-spots marked by white circles) produced in the Roman period at La Graufensque (marked by a black diamond) near Millau in the Languedoc of southern France. *Source*: Adapted from Ward-Perkins, B., *The Fall of Rome and the end of Civilisation* (Oxford University Press, 2005).

particular centres, in what was effectively a modern, centralised, industrial way. An example of such a centre of manufacture is La Graufensque near Millau in southern France. Map 9 shows the distribution of the pottery produced there across the Roman Empire as it has been recovered in archaeological excavations.

Its spread is extraordinary, reaching from the northern parts of Roman Britain southwards to North Africa and Sicily, and eastwards to the Rivers Rhine and Danube.

The distribution-system which this presupposes seems on common-sense grounds hard to reconcile with the notion that the production and supply of pottery such as this was handled by state-directed enterprises to supply governmental needs. It looks more as if we are dealing with a genuinely commercial economic system in which even quite humble consumers could, and did, purchase goods such as the wares from La Graufensque and other centres of manufacture.

The evidence of coins is capable of being interpreted in a similar way. Archaeological excavations have shown that coins, like the fine pottery we have been discussing, were widely distributed across the Roman Empire and in sites of quite minor importance. Moreover, the coins were not only minted from gold and silver, and therefore of high value, but also very extensively of bronze, and therefore of the sort of value which would make them suitable for day-to-day transactions in a monetarised and commercialised society. In other words, Roman citizens, even at the quite humble level of those living in such minor settlements as have been excavated, needed coins to purchase commodities in the way that we do in the modern world. If that is right, we are surely dealing in the Roman period with a genuinely monetary, commercial economy, rather than a series of state-directed enterprises for the supply of governmental needs.

Of course, you need not accept this interpretation of the Roman economy, for it is still open to you to argue that even the archaeological finds provide us with no real indications of the proportion of the economy which was functioning in this commercial way, whereas we know from reliable written records that government-directed economic activity, particularly the supply of the massive *annonae* to Rome and Constantinople, was very considerable – and in the case of the Roman Empire in the west certainly came to an end with the dissolution of the empire.

But, if you do accept it, it is potentially consistent with Pirenne's idea that the Roman commercial economy continued after that dissolution. Indeed, the evidence of pottery excavated on post-Roman sites in the west can be held to support just that. A potentially crucial piece of evidence is a type of pottery known as African Red Slip Ware. This is very characteristic and easily recognisable because it was coated with a layer of red, liquid clay (the 'slip') before it was fired; and its places of manufacture can definitely be located from archaeological evidence in North Africa. African Red Slip Ware was widely distributed in the Roman Empire in the west, and supporters of the Finley interpretation would connect that distribution with the government-directed importation of grain from North Africa to Italy to supply the *annona* to feed the city of Rome. Even if the parallel export from North Africa of African Red Slip Ware was not actually government-organised then, it can be argued, it must have benefited from the shipping organised by the government for transport of the *annona*. Many of the fragments of this pottery are from *amphorae*, great jars for the transport of wine or oil, so it seems likely that the trade was as much in the liquid produce of North Africa as in the pottery itself. Archaeological excavation, especially of sites in central Italy, has shown, however, that African Red Slip Ware continued to be imported into that area at least until well after the dissolution of the Roman Empire in the west, and that the real crisis affecting its supply came only in the seventh century. The correlation with Pirenne's own chronology for the cessation of a Roman-type commercial economy is striking. Another very important site for this case is the Crypta Balbi in the city of Rome itself, excavation of which has brought to light very substantial rubbish dumps. One of these dumps belongs to around the year 690 and, even at that late date, it contains African Red Slip Ware, although such pottery has disappeared from a somewhat later deposit dated around 720.

African Red Slip Ware was not, however, the only pottery to be moved around post-Roman Western Europe. Fine wares from the eastern Mediterranean and from southern Gaul are also found remarkably widely. This distribution includes, most dramatically, the western coasts of the British Isles, where fragments of such imported pottery have been found at a whole series of archaeological sites. These sites are the royal or ecclesiastical centres of the native British elite of the fifth, sixth, and early seventh centuries, including the rocky peninsula of Tintagel in Cornwall, the great refurbished Iron Age hill-fort of South Cadbury in Somerset, and the coastal fortress of Dinas Powys in Wales. We could argue that this evidence shows that long-distance sea-routes were still open even through the Bay of Biscay and into the Irish Sea as they had been in the Roman period. Indeed, there is specific support for this in the context of corn-imports and metal-exports to be had from a literary text, the *Life of John the Almsgiver* (died 619), which mentions (ch. 10) a merchant ship sailing from Alexandria in Egypt to the 'Isles of Britain' with a cargo of corn, and returning with a cargo of tin and gold, presumably from the metal-mines of Cornwall.

Striking as this evidence from the far north-west is, however, its significance is in itself open to doubt. In the first place, the volume of imported pottery discovered on these British Isles sites is very small, so that it must have come from only a tiny number of vessels. At the Crypta Balbi at Rome, we are dealing with far more vessels, but even so nothing very remarkable in terms of scale by the standards of the Roman period. We could, in short, be looking at just the last gasps of a commercial system now reduced to a tiny volume for the benefit of only a tiny elite (the Crypta Balbi deposits probably came from an elite monastery in Rome). We could of course interpret the history of coins in the same way. Whereas the kingdom of the Ostrogoths in Italy in the late fifth and early sixth centuries did produce some bronze coins, and it and other kingdoms produced silver coins, by and large post-Roman coins were imitations or adaptions of Roman gold *solidi*, of much too high value for day-to-day transactions and probably more to do with prestige, gifts, and tribute-payments than with trade.

Ward-Perkins (2005) has used these arguments to paint an entirely anti-Pirenne picture of the end of the Roman Empire in the west. In his view the contraction of the sort of commercialised exports he sees in the archaeology of the Roman period marks the definitive collapse of the Roman economic system (and indeed of the whole Roman lifestyle) from the late fifth century onwards. He notes that the reduction in volume and then disappearance of fine wares like African Red Slip Ware, which were wheel-thrown, are soon followed by the total dominance of crude, hand-made pottery of a standard much lower than that of the pottery used by inhabitants of the Roman Empire in the west. Whereas post-Roman Western Europe could and did produce high-standard metalwork, such as that made in seventh-century Britain and entombed in Mound 1 at Sutton Hoo, Ward-Perkins is struck by the fact that the native pottery in that grave, which was obviously of the very highest status, was not only hand-made but also poorly shaped and crude in its fabric. Clearly, he argues, the whole Roman system must have collapsed with a corresponding collapse in living standards, except in terms of jewellery and weaponry for the highest elite of western society.

How far then did trade continue in Western Europe as it had done under the Roman Empire through to the early seventh century? Your answer will depend, first, on whether the Roman economy was commercialised or government-directed. If you opt for the latter, you are effectively concluding that there was a significant cutting-off of Roman economic activity with the end of the Roman Empire in the west. If you opt for the former, you then need to resolve whether the archaeological and numismatic evidence for the continuation of that economy is sufficient to demonstrate continuing Roman-type trade, or whether (following Ward-Perkins) it points to a collapse of the Roman economic system.

The economic influence of the Arab caliphate

Pirenne's evidence for his view that Arab expansion had severed the Mediterranean and its trade-routes was the mirror-image of the evidence he used to support his view of the continuation of the Mediterranean as a thoroughfare, and the economic system deriving from that, up until the early seventh century.

Coins

Whereas Pirenne laid emphasis on the continued minting of gold coins as the primary currency of post-Roman Western Europe to demonstrate the survival of the Roman trade-system, he used the almost universal adoption in Western Europe from the late seventh and early eighth centuries of a silver coinage of *denarii* (*deniers* in French, pennies in English) in place of the Roman-derived gold coinage as evidence for the cessation of that Roman trade-system. Gold coinage, he believed, had been needed for the luxury long-distance trade which, in his view, dominated the Roman economic system. When that long-distance trade came to an end, such high-value coins were no longer required, so silver was substituted.

Pirenne's critics, however, noted that this change-over from gold to silver, although clear enough in England and in the kingdom of the Franks, was not universal in Western Europe, for gold coins continued to be minted, for example, in Lombardy beyond that kingdom's destruction by Charlemagne, king of the Franks, in the late eighth century. Moreover, it is possible to argue that the new silver *denarii* were also of high value, even if lower than the gold coins, and that, if they had commercial functions, these cannot have been very dissimilar to that of their gold predecessors.

Indeed it is possible to argue quite the opposite of Pirenne's view, that is that the introduction of silver coins signalled increased commercial vigour, since they appear to have been more numerous and the issues of them more regular and more controlled by the Carolingian rulers of the eighth and ninth centuries. Charlemagne, for example, produced four distinctive issues of coins in the course of his reign, with a significant change in 794 in weight (from 1.3 g to 1.7 g) and consequently of silver-content. Such effort, it can be argued, would not have been expended unless the coins had been of central importance, and that importance must have been a commercial one.

That argument, however, was one of the great bones of contention between two of the greatest numismatists of the twentieth century, Philip Grierson and Michael Metcalf. The former argued that coinage in our period was primarily minted to enhance the prestige of rulers, and for the payment of dues or fines, or for the giving of gifts, tribute, and ransoms. He maintained that the coinage showed little sign of use, which seemed to suggest that it was not in circulation, and that the size of the issues could only have been small in view of the relatively small number of coins which have survived. Metcalf attacked this view head-on. For him, the coins were used commercially and were numerous, each issue amounting to some millions of coins. These claims were based on two numismatic approaches to the coinage.

The first was analysis of the dies from which the coins had been struck. Medieval coinage was hammered coinage, that is to say that it was made by placing a disk (or flan) of metal over an obverse die which was fixed to a block of wood and had its upper face cut with the design that was to appear on the obverse face (head) of the coin. The moneyer then held over the flan the reverse die, which had on its lower face the design that was to appear on the reverse face (tail) of the coin. He then struck the reverse die with a heavy hammer and the coin was duly made or 'hammered'. Eventually the dies naturally became worn out, the reverse die first because it was most affected by the hammer-blow, and they had to be replaced. They were of course hand-cut so that, even for the same issue, they were never identical. By studying the surviving coins very closely, Metcalf was able to work out how many dies the surviving coins had been cut from. This provided him with a statistical means of calculating how many coins were likely to have been minted in particular issues. If Grierson had been right that there were very few, it should have been possible to see the same die or dies being used in a considerable proportion of the surviving coins. But this was not in fact the case. Metcalf had no figures for how many coins an early medieval die could produce, but there are figures for sixteenth-century dies from the Royal Mint in London. Using these, Metcalf developed a statistical formula for estimating from the surviving coins for a particular issue how many there would originally have been. That is how he arrived at his figure of millions.

If we accept the validity of his approach, which Grierson never did, for he believed that the sixteenth-century figures had no validity for our period, then the coins do indeed provide evidence for a resurgence of trade at any rate from the early eighth century when the silver *denarii* began to be minted. But were they used commercially? Metcalf's second method to attack Grierson consisted of studying hoards of coins which had been buried in the ground in Gaul in the ninth century. Although no one knows why these hoards were made, we can argue that if the coins in them represented those from issues which were all current together, then the hoards were more likely to represent coins which were being used for trading and were therefore circulating immediately prior to being put into the hoard, rather than coins which had been collected as prestige-trophies and set aside for many years. This is what he found in the case of the coins of Charles the Bald, king of the Franks (840–70); and he argued that the commercial use of coins which this suggested could also be seen in the regular re-issuing of coins, including changes of weight, by the tenth-century English kings. Commercial use would be even clearer if the mints from which the coins in particular hoards came seemed to define a plausible trading network, encompassing river-routes, for example. In the case of the coins of Charles the Bald, this is exactly what he found.

If you think (and you need not) that coins are thus acceptable evidence for commerce, then you can also follow Michael McCormick (2001), who argues that the appearance of Arab gold coins (dinars) in archaeological sites of the eighth century in Italy, and especially in Venice around 800, shows revived trans-Mediterranean commerce with a balance of trade favourable for western merchants. The distribution of Arab and Byzantine coins in locations stretching from Venice inland towards the area of modern Hungary can also be interpreted as evidence of commerce, in this case the supply of amber, the orange-coloured fossilised resin of trees, much prized as a semi-precious stone, which was harvested in that area. If the evidence of the coins is acceptable for proving the existence of such commerce, then the 'Amber trail' must have led overland to the Adriatic Sea, and so across the Mediterranean Sea to Byzantium and the Arab caliphate.

As regards the commodities imported into Western Europe via the eastern Mediterranean, which Pirenne believed to have been so important until the early seventh century, he claimed that they disappeared thereafter as a direct result of the disruption of the Mediterranean routes by Arab fleets and pirates. Pirenne's critics, however, have been able to undermine the significance of all these commodities, so that little of Pirenne's evidence can still be seen as valid.

Papyrus

Pirenne was certainly right that papyrus was used as a writing material by the writing-office of the kings of the Franks up until sometime between 659 and 677. At the latter date, the royal writing office began to use parchment made from animal-skins, and papyrus was abandoned for ever. Pirenne's critics pointed out, however, that papyrus was produced in Egypt as a government monopoly, and was thus the sort of economic production directed by the imperial government (in this case the Byzantine imperial government) posited by the interpretation of Jones and Finley. When Egypt was conquered by the Arabs around 640, the new Islamic government of the caliphs of Medina took over the production of papyrus as a state monopoly. It was therefore open to the caliph to prohibit the export of papyrus as an economic sanction against his enemies. This may have been done, Pirenne's critics conjectured, when the Arabs were at war with the Byzantine Empire, leading up to the siege of the Byzantine capital of

Constantinople, unsuccessfully as it turned out, in 678. Such a ban on the export of papyrus would have been aimed chiefly at the Byzantine Empire, but it would have affected Western Europe also. It may, it can be argued, have provided the motive for western writing-offices to adopt parchment, which was in many ways much more satisfactory for use in the generally damp climate of Western Europe, which preserves it rather well. Once the shift had been made, there was no advantage in returning to the use of papyrus, so there was no demand for it even if its export was resumed (as it clearly was in the Byzantine Empire). Indeed, the writing-office of the popes in Rome continued to use papyrus until much later; presumably the hotter, drier climate of Italy was more favourable to it.

Silks

Pirenne's view that silks had disappeared from Western Europe was based on his belief that there was a cessation of references to them in written sources. But it is now abundantly clear from the research into actual surviving silks in the church treasuries of Western Europe that, whatever picture the written sources may give, it is not a correct one, and silks continued to be available on a considerable scale. One of the finest examples is the great Nature Goddess Silk in the treasury of Durham Cathedral, which was placed in the shrine of St Cuthbert when the saint's relics were at Chester-le-Street, just to the north of Durham, and brought to Durham along with those relics at the end of the tenth century. It is now in a sad state, but if you look carefully at the surface of the remaining fragments in Durham Cathedral treasury, you can get a sense of the richness of colour and the wonderful pattern of fruit, ducks, and fish which it once had. The discovery, in 1987, of a Greek inscription woven into it establishes beyond doubt that it is a product of silk manufacture in the Byzantine Empire.

Spices

It is broadly true that there are fewer references to spices in literary texts after the seventh century. There is no real possibility of finding them in archaeological contexts, so there is no progress to be made there. But some of the written references are striking and suggest that Pirenne cannot have been right. One is in the letter written by a monk called Cuthbert about the death of his fellow monk, the scholar Bede, at the monastery of Monkwearmouth-Jarrow in Northumbria in 735. Just before his death, Cuthbert records Bede's desire to distribute his possessions:

> I have a few treasures in my box, some pepper, and napkins, and some incense. Run quickly and fetch the priests of the monastery, and I will share among them such little presents as God has given me.
>
> (Cuthbert, *Death of Bede*)

Here was not just pepper, which must have come from the Far East via the eastern Mediterranean, but also incense which must have come from southern Arabia, also via the eastern Mediterranean. These commodities were evidently regarded as treasures; but they were clearly available in some quantities to a Northumbrian monk; and we know that incense was widely used in church services.

Another reference is in a diploma of Chlotar III, king of the Franks (657–73), in which he granted the newly founded monastery of Corbie in northern Gaul the right to receive an annual rent in the form of a range of commodities from a royal warehouse which apparently existed at Fos near Marseilles in southern Gaul. These commodities included no less than 30 pounds of pepper, and 150 pounds of cumin, another spice probably imported from the East. We are dealing here with the highest level of the social scale, that of royalty, but clearly there were impressive quantities of spices being imported into Western Europe even at the end of the seventh century – and indeed the grant was confirmed by Chlotar III's successor, King Chilperic II, in 716. Interpreting the significance of these references is of course a matter of judgement, since they give us no indication, any more than does the archaeology of pottery, what the total quantities of Far Eastern goods such as spices were in Western Europe. Pirenne himself saw them as marking the final end of the trans-Mediterranean luxury trade; but the dates of the texts discussed above do seem rather late for this. And you may think that the continued availability of silks in Western Europe across our whole period suggests that spices too continued to be imported.

Ivory

You could also reinforce such a conclusion with reference to the continued availability of ivory, which must also have come to Western Europe via the eastern Mediterranean, either from Africa or India. It was widely used to make not only religious carvings throughout our period, but also ivory book-covers for luxury religious books from the ninth century onwards.

Saints' relics

We have a number of early lists of the great collections of saints' relics in Western European churches. These collections often included relics of saints from the eastern Mediterranean or relics associated with the life of Christ, such as fragments of the manger in which he was placed after his birth, or fragments of the True Cross on which he was crucified. If these were really what they were claimed to be, or even if they were not but nevertheless came from the Holy Land, they must have been brought to the West across the Mediterranean Sea. The most useful collections providing evidence in favour of the revival of trade after 700 are those of two Frankish churches, Sens a little to the south of Paris, and Chelles to the north-east of Paris. The importance of these collections lies in the fact that there have been preserved the little parchment labels which were attached to the relics when they were acquired by these churches in order to certify to which saint or which scene of the life of Christ they belonged. The handwriting on these labels can be dated quite precisely by palaeographers (specialists in the history of medieval handwriting), so that it is possible to build up a picture of the rate at which these relic-collections accumulated. In the case of Sens, there appears to have been a considerable growth in the number of relics from southern Italy, the Holy Land, and the Byzantine Empire in the eighth century, which can be interpreted as evidence for flourishing trans-Mediterranean trade. On the other hand, the relics may not have been authentic, given how difficult it was to prove the authenticity of, say, an alleged splinter from Christ's cross, or they may have been in the west for a long time and may only have been gathered into the collections of a church like Sens in the eighth century; or their arrival in the west may, at best, have been to do with pilgrims and gift-giving rather than with trade.

Nevertheless, there is clearly a case to be made that Pirenne's view that trans-European trade ceased with the Arab expansion was incorrect. You may, of course, wish to argue with Ward-Perkins that commerce as a widespread activity effectively collapsed with the Roman Empire in the west; but it is still open to you in view of the evidence we have just reviewed to maintain that a trans-Mediterranean luxury trade continued beyond the end of the Roman Empire in the west. Even if you do this, however, you need to consider the possibility that there really was a decline in trade perhaps in the sixth or early seventh centuries, followed by a revival which supplied the evidence we have been looking at.

Decline and revival of trade?

Trans-Mediterranean trade

McCormick (2001) focuses on written evidence showing, in his view, that routeways across or around the Mediterranean Sea or connected to it were disrupted from the sixth century onwards. These included land-routes such as the Via Egnatia, the crucially important road leading from the imperial capital of Constantinople across the northen Balkans to Dyrrachium (modern Split) on the coast of the Adriatic Sea, which was probably closed as the result of invasions by Slavs and Avars across the River Danube into the Balkans, where the latter established the kingdom of the Avars which was hostile to the Byzantine Empire. The Via Egnatia must certainly have been closed by 662 when Emperor Constans II launched a military expedition to the West. This took the immensely laborious route around the coast from Constantinople to Athens; clearly the Via Egnatia was not open or it would have offered a much faster route to the West. As for sea-routes, we have noted already the end of the imperial *annona* shipped to Rome after the later fifth century. In the early seventh century, the *annona* to Constantinople also ended, with disruption to shipping grain from Alexandria in Egypt by the capture of that great imperial port by the Persians in 617 and then by the Arabs a little later. River-routes and mountain-passes leading away from the Mediterranean Sea in the west also suffered considerable disruption. We know that the route up the River Rhone from the Mediterranean Sea at Marseilles, then overland to the River Rhine and so northwards, was a very important commercial route in the Roman period. But it was severely disrupted by Arab piracy and plundering in the Rhone Valley in the seventh century, so that the privileges granted to Corbie of obtaining commodities from Fos near Marseilles, which we looked at earlier, envisaged transportation from Fos to Corbie by wagon and not by river at all.

In McCormick's view, however, this decline in trans-Mediterranean communications was only temporary. In opposition to the Pirenne Thesis, he maintains that there was a considerable revival in Mediterranean commerce from around 700 onwards. One of the most interesting ways in which he has supported this interpretation is by compiling a prosopography, that is, a catalogue of biographies, of everyone who appears in written sources as having made a journey around or across the Mediterranean Sea between 700 and 900. No fewer than 669 travellers appear in this prosopography, and McCormick provides full accounts of their journeys. The prosopography is well worth close study, and a couple of examples will give a flavour of it. One of the travellers concerned is the English missionary, Willibald (c.700–c.787), one of whose journeys was a pilgrimage to the Holy Land. According to his contemporary biographer, he left England from the port of Hamwih (the predecessor of Southampton) and travelled by sea to Rouen on the River Seine in Normandy. From there he travelled overland to Italy across the Alps, reaching Rome and then Naples overland. From Naples, he took a ship on to Lebanon on the eastern coast of the Mediterranean Sea, and so overland to Jerusalem. A second example is the journey of Bernard the Frank, who travelled in 867 from his home in Champagne, overland to Rome and on to Taranto, and then by ship to Alexandria in Egypt, where he took a boat up the River Nile to Old Cairo, and so overland to Jerusalem. These two journeys are typical of many in the prosopography in that they were not to do with trade. Many of the journeys catalogued were, like these two examples, pilgrimages, and others consisted of diplomatic missions. But McCormick argues that such journeys would have been impossible if there had not existed an infrastructure capable of supporting them, an infrastructure that is of roads and wagons, ports and ships, hostelries and provisioning places; and that such an infrastructure is most likely to have come into existence to support trade, and to have been used incidentally by pilgrims and diplomats whose voyages must have been rarer and less regular than those of traders.

If we accept that argument, then McCormick's prosopography becomes a remarkable piece of evidence for the revival of trans-Mediterranean trade-routes after c.700. We can see, for example, the opening of the route through the Gulf of Corinth from the Aegean Sea, and then over the very short land-route to the Adriatic Sea; the first journey by that route appears in the prosopography under the years 831–2, and we know that c.900 a Byzantine official was placed there to supervise trade through the gulf and over the land-bridge. It looks as if the Danube Valley was being opened up as a thoroughfare overland to the west, to judge from the contacts between the Carolingian rulers of the Franks and the kings of the Bulgars, who had established their kingdom straddling the River Danube in the Balkans. And in the 860s envoys from the pope seem to have been able to cross the Balkans directly overland, suggesting that the Via Egnatia had reopened.

Trade in the northern seas

There is, then, a case to be made for the collapse of trans-Mediterranean commerce of any significance (if you follow Ward-Perkins), or for its decline perhaps around 600 with a resurgence beginning in the eighth century and continuing throughout our period to build into the great commercial activity of the high and late Middle Ages. In looking at this argument, however, we have been focusing on the Mediterranean Sea and routes leading to it. We need to go back to Pirenne and pursue for a moment his idea of a change in the centre of gravity of Western Europe towards the north. Was the northern part of Western Europe, the areas, that is, around the North Sea and the Baltic Sea, much more the dynamic commercial area than the Mediterranean Sea in our period?

Swedish Vikings

One of the most imaginative scholars of the twentieth century, Maurice Lombard, argued just this as a reaction to Pirenne's assigning to the Arabs the role of severing the Mediterranean trade-routes, cutting off Western Europe from commercial contacts. Lombard, who was a specialist in Moslem coins, assigned to the Arabs a role in the economic development of Western Europe which was constructive if indirect. He emphasised that the expansion of the Arabs created a state, the Arab caliphate, which was distinguished by its flourishing economy, especially its trade. Islam was a religion sympathetic to trade, which had originated in the Arabian merchant cities of Mecca and Medina. Moreover, their conquests gave the Arabs access to the gold-mines in Nubia, in the middle Nile Valley, from which the Romans had been cut off in the sixth century by incursions of nomads. By the early eighth century the Arabs' expansion had carried them eastwards to the foothills of the Himalayas, where they had access to immensely rich silver-mines. The Arab caliphate was bullion-rich, with the result (Lombard thought) that its commerce flourished. Now, unlike Pirenne, Lombard saw no reason to suppose that Moslem merchants were unwilling to trade with Christians. Indeed, Islam was distinguished as a religion which was tolerant of other faiths and felt no hostility towards contact with their devotees. For Lombard, then, there was every reason why the flourishing economy of the Arab caliphate should have stimulated rather than harmed that of Western Europe.

The route by which such stimulation was actually achieved was, in Lombard's view, not via the Mediterranean Sea at all, but through the activities of the Swedish Vikings in developing trade-routes from the Baltic Sea southward to the Black Sea, and above all south-eastwards to the Caspian Sea and the area of the caliphate (Map 10).

Map 10 Rivers between the Baltic Sea, the Black Sea and the Caspian Sea. Note how narrow is the watershed between rivers like the Dvina and the Neman flowing northwards into the Baltic Sea and rivers like the Dnieper and the Volga flowing southwards to the Black Sea and the Caspian Sea. These rivers were largely navigable, so that merchants could journey across what is now Russia largely by water, with only a relatively short overland section, over which boats were sometimes dragged. Note the position of the trading cities of Novgorod and Staraja Ladoga on Lake Ladoga, and of the Rus political centre of Kiev in the south.

Archaeological finds suggest that from as early as the sixth century these people had been active south of the Baltic Sea, in the area of the Gulf of Finland and Lake Ladoga (Ladozhskaye Ozero). For later periods, we know from a reference in the *Life* of Bishop Anskar of Hamburg that there was a successful Swedish military campaign in the area of Kurland (modern Estonia) shortly after 850. This evidence for Swedish expansion across the Baltic Sea is matched by dramatic evidence from much farther south. The text known as the *Russian Primary Chronicle* describes the foundation and early history of the state of Kiev, established on the River Dnieper north of the Black Sea in the second half of the ninth century – effectively the beginning of what was to become Russia. According to this, Kiev was founded by people called the Rus, who had reached Constantinople already in the 830s. These Rus (or *Rhos* in Greek) were certainly Swedish Vikings, for the *Annals of Saint-Bertin* records that in 839 Greek ambassadors came to the court of the Frankish ruler Louis the Pious in company with some people they called Rus. Louis duly questioned them closely and learned they were Swedish Vikings.

The evidence to show that such men traded with Arab merchants is twofold. First, the evidence of Arab writers. Writing in the early tenth century, but probably basing his work on an earlier account, Ibn Rusteh describes the Rus city of Novgorod east of the Baltic Sea:

> Concerning the Rus, they live on an island (or a peninsula) in a lake . . . Their only occupation is trading in sable and squirrel and other kinds of skins, which they sell to those who will buy them. They take coins as payment and fasten them into their belts.

The implication must be that the Rus traded furs with Arab merchants, and that they received money in exchange.

Another Arab writer, Ibn Fadlan, has left us an account of an embassy which he undertook in 921–2 from the Caliph of Baghdad to the king of the Bulgars who lived along the River Volga. He came across the people he called the Rus (*Rusiya*) as they came 'on their trading voyages and had encamped by the River Volga' (or Itil; Ibn Fadlan, *Journey*, pp. 63–71). The trading involved was evidently slave-trading, for Ibn Fadlan describes how each of the Rus 'has a couch whereupon he sits, and with them are fair maidens who are destined for sale to merchants' – although Ibn Fadlan was too shocked by their having sex with these girls in public to have space to offer more information about commercial activity. He does describe, however, how a Rus man would make a sacrifice to his pagan god with the words:

> I wish that Thou shouldst provide me with a merchant who has many dinars and dirhems, and who would buy from me at the price I desire, and will raise no objection to me to aught that I may say.

Dinars were gold coins of the caliphate, dirhems were silver coins. Ibn Fadlan, like Ibn Rusteh, conveys the clear impression that the Rus were trading with the Moslems, and that this was for the Rus a favourable balance of trade. They were exporting high-value commodities – our writers mention furs and slave-girls – and were being paid for them in money.

Secondly, the evidence of hoards, containing both fragments of silver (that is, hack-silver) and coins, chiefly silver dirhems, in the Baltic region. The Fittja hoard, found in Uppland in Sweden, for example, contained 136 coins from the early seventh century until the mid-ninth century, deriving from a wide area of the Arab caliphate, and extending into Central Asia: from Syria, from the area south of the Caspian Sea, from Baghdad, from Bokhara, from Merv, from Tashkent, and even from Samarkand. Some hoards contained objects in gold, and some gold dinars but many fewer than the dirhems – the hoard from Hon, for example, contained only nine dinars. These hoards were most numerous in Sweden, with a particular concentration on the Island of Gotland, and they belong to the period up to the tenth century. They unquestionably show considerable contact between the Baltic area, the Swedish Vikings or Rus in particular, and the Arab caliphate to the south-east. If this was commercial contact, then the hoards confirm the evidence of the Arab writers that the balance of trade between the Rus and the caliphate was a favourable one. Bullion, chiefly in the form of coins, was flowing into the Baltic region in return for the high-value commodities being exported to the caliphate by the Rus.

In Lombard's view, this inflow of bullion gave the Swedish Vikings the purchasing power to acquire high-value commodities from the areas around the North Sea, chiefly England and the kingdom of the Franks. Archaeological finds in Scandinavia suggest that English and Frankish swords, which were made to an especially high standard of metalwork, were sought after in Scandinavia, as were Frankish table glassware and fine pottery produced in the Rhine Valley. Thus, Lombard thought, the economy of north-west Europe as a whole was stimulated by the favourable balance of trade created by commerce between the Rus and the caliphate, and then between the Rus on the one side and the Franks and the English on the other. The inhabitants of the North Sea coastlands now had purchasing power in bullion as a result of selling their goods to the bullion-rich Swedish Vikings. Lombard thought that they proceeded to use that purchasing power to revive the trans-Mediterranean trade in luxuries, which they could now afford as their Roman predecessors had ceased to be able to do. This, in Lombard's view, was why the trading city of Venice at the head of the Adriatic Sea grew from the early ninth century onwards. It was handling, he thought, trans-Mediterranean trade with the Byzantine Empire and the ports on the east coast of the Mediterranean which gave access to the land-routes across Central Asia to the Far East. The eastern luxuries which it imported it then exported northwards to the kingdom of the Franks and England, in return for payments in coin, which in turn gave it the purchasing power to buy those luxuries from the east.

Thus a circulation of trade and currency was established, and the economy of Western Europe was revived by contact with the Arabs rather than harmed by it as Pirenne had supposed. Pirenne's book had been entitled *Mahommed and Charlemagne* to reflect its author's view that the Arab severing of the Mediterranean had made possible the creation of Charlemagne's empire as an independent but economically in-turned state. Without Mohammed and the Arab expansion resulting from the establishment of Islam, there could have been, Pirenne held, no Charlemagne. Lombard concurred. Without Mohammed, he thought, there could have been no Charlemagne; but for just the opposite reason. For him, it was the positive stimulus provided by the Arab economy, injecting bullion into Western Europe via the Russian river-routes, and through the activities of the Swedish Vikings or Rus, which had made possible the wealth and strength of Charlemagne's empire.

But was Lombard's thesis valid? In a very influential paper, Grierson (1959) attacked his interpretation of the hoards of coins in the Baltic, arguing that early medieval western society was not really monetarised or commercialised, and that the coins in the hoards were probably not the result of commerce at all, but rather of plunder, or the imposition of tribute, or the giving of gifts, or the paying of ransoms by Moslems for prisoners held by the Swedish Vikings. All that is possible, but the contents of the hoards in Scandinavia reflect the contents of hoards in Russia in terms of the issues of the dirhems they contain, suggesting that they were made in the commercial context of genuine circulation of money rather than in a situation of random raiding, gift-giving, and ransom-payments.

Another potential objection to the Lombard thesis is the absence of Islamic coins in the lands around the North Sea. Why should this have been the case if there had really been the favourable trade balance between the North Sea lands and the Baltic which Lombard envisaged? In answer to this question, it is possible to argue that the incoming Islamic coins were melted down at ports of entry and re-minted as English or Frankish coins. This could have been because it would have been objectionable to the Christians of the lands in question to have dealt with Moslem coins; but also because part of the function of early medieval minting was to certify the precious metal content of coins, so that re-minting incoming dirhems was an essential part of the commercial process. The Swedish numismatist Sture Bolin argued indeed that such was the interrelationship between Frankish *denarii* and Moslem coins that the former were increased in weight, for example by the king of the Franks, Charlemagne, in 794, so that they could be more readily related to dirhems coming in from the Baltic. His thesis faces the difficulty that, whereas Frankish coins were increased in weight, English coins were not; but the method he was proposing of using the precise weights of coins as a means of establishing the existence of commerce between areas even where the coins themselves had not passed from one area to another is well worth your consideration.

In fact there is one coin from the kingdom of Mercia in England which does seem to support the Lombard thesis. This is an imitation of a Moslem gold dinar issued in the name of King Offa of Mercia (757–96). The title *Offa rex* ('King Offa') appears in Latin script on the obverse face (head), while there is inscription which seems to be intended to represent an Arabic text from the Moslem holy book, the Koran, on the reverse face (tail). Such inscriptions were characteristic of Moslem coins from the late seventh century onwards. Offa's moneyer evidently did not understand Arabic, and the inscription is not in proper Arabic; but he was clearly trying to imitate a Moslem dinar. It is hard to believe that this coin was actually used in Mercian trade, but we might want to see its existence as strong evidence for familiarity with Moslem coins in England, and for exactly the contacts between the North Sea and the Arab caliphate, via the intermediary of the Swedish Vikings, which Lombard believed were so important to the development of Europe.

Since Lombard wrote in the early 1970s, however, archaeology has yielded evidence to suggest that the growth of commerce in the northern seas was more a matter of native development of the resources of those areas by traders who had been fostering commerce since at least the third century AD, rather than being dependent on external stimulus such as Lombard envisaged.

Frisians

First, the Frisians. Archaeological and written evidence suggests that this people originated around the Zuydezee (Ijsselmeer, Netherlands), but expanded eastwards to, and even beyond, the River Weser, and westwards to the delta of the rivers Rhine, Meuse, and Scheldt, establishing a kingdom of the Frisians which appears in written sources of the early eighth century. That the Frisians were very active and effective as traders from an early date is suggested, first, by the appearance of Frisians in that role in a number of sources, for example the story in Bede's *Ecclesiastical History of the English People* (IV.22) in which a Frisian merchant is planning to buy a Mercian prisoner to sell as a slave. Secondly, by the fact that the North Sea was known in a number of sources, for example Nennius's *History of the Britons* of the early ninth century, as the Frisian Sea. Thirdly, by the fact that 'Frisian' seems to have become synonymous in written texts with 'long-distance merchant'. That the Frisians were active traders from before the period of the Arab caliphate is shown by archaeological excavation of their *terpen*, or mounds. An example of these is that at Hessen on the North Sea coast which dates from the fifth or sixth centuries and had on it not only living accommodation, but also a slipway for launching a boat. That this was a trading vessel is shown by the survival on the site of a *firrer*, a side-rudder such as was used in the Frisian trading-ships in later periods. Clearly Frisian commerce had already begun, and was probably conducted through the beach-markets and beach trading-posts which have been increasingly recognised by archaeologists in recent years.

Ships

Secondly, ships. By the eighth century, these were of two types, which would develop in later periods into the cog and the *hulc* (Fig. 16).

The *hulc* consisted of a framework built on top of a hull hollowed out from a log. An example of such a boat was excavated at Utrecht dating to the eighth century. Measuring some 18 m long, it was evidently a substantial trading vessel. Such boats clearly originated very much earlier, for log-boats that are their ancestors are found in no less than forty graves at Slusegård on the Island of Bornholm in the Baltic Sea, dating from the second and third centuries AD, and similar log-boats of the same sort of date have been discovered at various sites in the southern part of the Jutland peninsula. Such boats were probably not themselves trading vessels, but they demonstrate that the technology and design behind the trading hulks was available at an early period.

Figure 16 Ships represented on coins. Those in the first row were minted at the port of Dorestad during the reigns of Charlemagne (768–814) and Louis the Pious (814–40). They seem to show early versions of the *hulc* (proto-*hulcs*). The representation of the hulls, notably that on the right, strongly suggests that they have been hollowed from logs. The second row shows coins from the Viking port of Haithabu. Despite the stylisation of the images, the clinker construction of the hulls of these ships is clearly represented by the lines along the hulls. Also evident are the stern and stem-posts. Most interestingly, the first two on the left are flat-bottomed, but the stems and sterns are angled up. This was to enable the ships to sail in shallow water between the dunes and the shore. When low tide grounded them, the high tide would float them off more easily thanks to this shaping of the hull.
Source: From *Frühmittelalterliche Handelsschiffahrt in Mittel und Nordeuropa* (Ellmers, D. 1972), p. 56, reproduced by permission of Prof. Dr Detlev Ellmers and the Council for British Archaeology.

The cog was clinker-built, that it is to say its hull was made of overlapping planks nailed together. This type of ship too had much earlier origins, for behind it lies the ship of the first century BC discovered in sacrificial deposits at Nydam in the bogs of southern Denmark, and now conserved at the museum at Schleswig in Germany. This ship was not a trading vessel but probably a troop-carrier, propelled by thirty oarsmen. But its clinker construction is striking, as is the *firrer* (side-rudder), and the great elegance of its design. It seems very likely that the technology of building ships like the cogs of the eighth century and later was very much earlier than the date of those vessels, and this may suggest that trading activity in the northern seas had much older and indigenous roots.

That there was a considerable increase in the speed of such vessels in the eighth century is suggested by the evidence first found in that period for the installation of sails in craft that seem previously to have been propelled by oars. The Nydam ship had no sail, nor did the ship interred in the early seventh century in Mound 1 at Sutton Hoo. But the ships represented on the coins in Fig. 16 clearly did, as did the Utrecht boat and other vessels found more recently in archaeological excavations, such as the tenth-century craft discovered at Graveney in Kent. Whatever the native origins of maritime trading in the northern seas may have been, there was clearly an increase in speed and therefore of volume being moved in the eighth century or thereabouts.

This evidence corresponds to the archaeological evidence obtained in recent decades from the excavation of trading centres. As we saw, the earliest such settlements were the Frisian *terpens* and the beach-markets of the northern seas. By the eighth century, however, much larger and more developed trading centres, the so-called *emporia* or *wics*, were appearing all around the North Sea and the Baltic. They are clearly evidence for the vigour and scale of northern trade, as well as for the history of urbanisation.

As you go forward with your research and reading, you need to keep in your mind the sorts of questions we have been trying to explore. What was the nature of trade? Was it genuinely commercial in our sense of the word, or was it driven by different forces, emanating perhaps from the process of gift-exchange? What levels of society did trade affect, and what was its significance for the organisation of society itself? How did it affect political organisation? You need also to go further than we have been able to do here in relating trade to other aspects of the economic foundation of Western Europe – to the nature of agricultural exploitation and to the functions of towns, which are the subjects of the next two chapters.

Research and study

Broad research questions

Did Roman-type Mediterranean trade continue and grow after the end of the Roman Empire in the west?

How far was trade only a matter for the elite (kings, nobles, churchmen) or how far did it penetrate all levels of society?

To what extent was trade based on monetary exchange for profit, or how far was it based on other mechanisms, such as state-control of supply, or forms of barter not involving money?

Was trading activity in the Baltic and northern seas more important for Western Europe as a whole than trading activity in the Mediterranean?

Books and papers to begin with

Because of its fundamental influence on subsequent research, it is still well worth reading Pirenne's work (1939), along with the work of his critics. Excerpts from early examples of the latter can be found in a compilation of papers edited by Havighurst (1969), and there is a very useful paper by Riising, especially on Pirenne's approach to silks, spices, and papyrus, in another collection of such papers edited by Hübinger (1968). The Pirenne thesis forms the starting-point of a revisionist (and quite accessible) re-interpretation by Hodges and Whitehouse (1983).

A more detailed development of the arguments dealt with in the last work is Hodges (1982), although this is rather marred by some very opaque discussion of archaeological theory, so that ch. 2 is best skipped. There has naturally been progress in archaeological research since 1982, and you should also consult Hodges (2000) to supplement his earlier work.

The argument for the state-directed nature of the Roman economy is classically expressed by Jones (1964, ch. 21) and, in a more developed form, by Finley (1992). The argument that the Roman economy really was commercial and reached deep into society so that the demise of the Roman Empire in the west spelled disaster for the economy and for living standards is presented in a very lucid and stimulating way by Ward-Perkins (2005, ch. 5).

There is a useful survey of the Mediterranean economy in the period 500–700 by Loseby (2005), who argues that Roman-type trade continued but came to an end before the period assigned to this by Pirenne, which is essentially the view taken by Hodges and Whitehouse (1983). Ward-Perkins (2005, ch. 5) presents a much more negative picture of this period throughout the Roman Empire in the west. Compare his comments on the Crypta Balbi with those of Loseby. A useful summary of the period 500–700 in the north is provided by Lebecq (2005), who argues for the importance of Baltic and North Sea trade, but treats it as a native development rather than the result of indirect Arab influence.

There is a useful summary of the argument that Roman trade came to an end and there was an 'early medieval depresssion' in Horden and Purcell (2000, pp. 153–60). The view that there was a serious decline in the Mediterranean economy from around the sixth century, but that trade later revived there to a considerable degree is expressed at great length and with rich evidence by McCormick (2001). This is a large and unwieldy book and you need to use it very selectively. The points from the book highlighted in the text of the present chapter are: the significance of saints' relics (ch. 10), the closing and reopening of routeways (chs 18–19 and maps 18.2, 19.2, 20.2–3); the prosopography of travellers (pp. 852–972); the 'Amber trail' (pp. 369–84); and the importance and scale of the early medieval slave-trade (pp. 733–58). For discussion of McCormick's ideas there is a useful group of papers in McCormick, James, Henning, et al. (2003).

On slavery, which McCormick regards as really important to the European economy, there is an earlier work relating chiefly to England by Pelteret (1995). There is also another discussion by McCormick (2002), which also provides a brief summary of that author's book (McCormick, 2001). Moreland (2000a) provides a stimulating, if quite difficult, discussion of ideas about the nature of the early medieval economy, and also a picture of the economy in England as one in which production was of central importance (Moreland, 2000b).

Wickham (2005, ch. 11) offers a rather involved discussion of 'systems of exchange', arguing that regional factors were the most important in the development of trade, and providing useful accounts of the evidence provided by pottery. Smith (2005, ch. 6) interestingly discusses trade in relation to treasure and gifts.

Pursuing more specific aspects

The role of money in trade

To what extent was coinage used for commerce?

A useful introduction to the complex but stimulating conclusions of numismatics is provided, with many illustrations of coins, by Grierson (1991), and there is a briefer summary for the Carolingian period by Blackburn (1995). But, for more detail, both the illustrations and the introductory chapters are extremely useful in Grierson and Blackburn (1986). Grierson's view that the function of coinage was not primarily commercial is expressed in a technical but very lucid paper (1965).

One of his principal disputes with Michael Metcalf over this issue is encapsulated in their respective treatment of the coins of the West Frankish ruler Charles the Bald. Metcalf (1990) developed his interpretation of hoards of coins in that king's reign as evidence for the genuinely commercial circulation of money, where Grierson (1990) had seen the coins as primarily intended to pay Danegeld to buy off the Vikings. The dispute is also evident in their encounter over the English coinage, with Metcalf (1965) arguing that it was very large, Grierson (1967) that it was small.

If you want to focus on Roman coins, there are useful surveys by Kent (1978) and Reece (1978). The use of Arab dinars in the west and their significance for the 'Amber route' is discussed by McCormick (2001, pp. 369–79). A dense but thought-provoking paper by Hendy (1988) argues for a basic distinction between Roman coinage, which was all to do with taxation, chiefly taxation of land, and Carolingian coinage, which was not for this purpose, although Hendy argues against the case that it was intended for use in trade.

The evidence of pottery, silks, and spices

How far is it possible to estimate the scale and importance of long-distance trade?

How important was manufacturing industry?

The evidence of pottery from archaeological sites is very important because it survives so well in the ground. To pursue it in more depth, there are useful handbooks to Roman pottery by Peacock (1982; see the general discussion in ch. 10) and Peacock and Williams (1991; see the general discussion in ch. 5). For African Red Slip Ware and the distribution of fine potteries in the Roman Empire in the west from 400 to 700, useful (for the British Isles at any rate) is Dark (1996), especially the editor's own paper making the case that the Late Roman economy was 'proto-industrial' (there is a very useful definition on p. 3), and the paper by Ewan Campbell (pp. 83–96) on imports into western Britain between 400 and 800. There is what is still a very useful survey of the importation of Mediterranean and Gaulish pottery into the western parts of Britain in the post-Roman period in Alcock (1971). This engaging book is particularly useful for its accounts of South Cadbury and Dinas Powys, with the excavations of which the author was directly involved.

It is not easy to pursue the importance of silks as a traded commodity, but it is a fascinating subject and there are ground-breaking, if rather technical, studies by Muthesius (2004, 1999). For the significance of the Durham Nature Goddess Silk, see Higgins (1989) and Granger-Taylor (1989).

Spices are even more difficult to pursue but there is a fascinating, if rather detailed study by Miller (1998) of the spices themselves and of the organisation of the spice trade down to 641.

The Swedish Vikings (the Rus), the Baltic and North Sea economy, and the Arabs

How important was the impact of the economy of the Arab caliphate on Western Europe?

Lombard's own discussion of the significance of a supposedly favourable balance of trade between the Baltic Sea and the Arab caliphate (1972) is available only in French, but there is a paper pursuing a parallel argument in English by Bolin (1953); an excerpt of the latter's work is in Havighurst (1969, pp. 72–84), and it is summarised by Hodges (1982, pp. 7–9). A clear and useful account of the penetration of the Vikings through Russia to the Byzantine Empire, but also to the caliphate, is given by Ellis Davidson (1976). There is a summary by Roesdahl (1987, pp. 277–92), and another, with more detail, in a book which is really about the origins of Russia by Franklin and Shepard (1996, ch. 1).

The hoards in the Baltic region are discussed with technical data by Sawyer (1971, appendices 1–2). Grierson's attack on the significance of these for commercial development is in his classic paper (1959).

To pursue the argument that North Sea and Baltic Sea trade was really a long-standing native development rather than one stimulated by indirect contact with the Arab economy, you should begin with the work of the great authority on the Frisians, Stéphane Lebecq, published usefully in English (2005, 1990, 1997). There is further interesting material about trade between London and the Continent in Gautier and Lebecq (2011). You can also consult the very useful paper by Ellmers (1990). As the title of this paper suggests, Ellmers's view is that the Frisians dominated trade from the Mediterranean via the North Sea and the Baltic until the Swedish Vikings opened up the routes across Russia.

The evidence provided by ships themselves is discussed by Lebecq (2005), but there is also a very useful discussion with drawings by Crumlin-Pedersen (1990). There is a classic general book by a great specialist in maritime archaeology, Seán McGrail (1987), although its arrangement under headings relating to the characteristics of ships across wide periods does not make it easy to use. There is a brief summary of the evidence for our period in Western Europe, treated chronologically, in McGrail (2001, pp. 207–23).

8

Cultivating the land: the basis of European society?

Agriculture was by far the most important economic activity in our period, so changes in the way it was practised and organised may have been crucial in driving the development of social, political, and commercial life. We can tackle two questions in connection with this. First, was there continuity in agriculture between the Roman Empire in the west and the barbarian kingdoms which succeeded it? Secondly, were there changes in agriculture during our period, which might have affected levels of productivity, and in turn other aspects of society?

The continuity of Roman agriculture

There is a *prima facie* case for the thesis that agriculture underwent a process of transformation and continuity after the end of the Roman Empire in the west. This is based, first, on what we know about the organisation of the Roman countryside. That knowledge comes from the work of writers such as Marcus Terentius Varro (died 27 BC) and Lucius Junius Moderatus Columella (died *c.* AD 70) who wrote manuals about agricultural management. Columella's was entitled 'On Agriculture', Varro's 'On the Affairs of the Countryside'. Secondly, from imperial edicts, which come from as late as the end of the fourth century. The picture that emerges is one of a countryside organised, at least in part, into large estates called villas.

Roman villa-estates

The term villa is often used in our day to mean the high-status stone-built residential house and attendant buildings at the centre of an estate. In the Roman period, however, the term villa really meant the landed estate which encompassed the buildings. Villas, in that sense, were organised in one of two ways, or in a combination of both. The classic Roman villa was worked by slaves who lived in one or more barrack-blocks, and who were maintained by the lord of the villa with food raised on the land and given to them for their consumption. They in turn undertook the agricultural work on the villa, raising food chiefly for their lord's consumption. In the later Roman period in the West, however, a second type of rural organisation had developed, in which those who did the agricultural work were supported, not by being given food-doles by the lord, but by being allocated a plot of land. One method of organising an estate in this way involved dividing the entire estate into peasant-tenements, the holders of which paid food-rents to the lord. A second method was to divide only part of the estate into peasant-tenements, with the rest devoted to providing produce directly for the lord. The holders of the peasant-tenements would support themselves and perhaps pay food-rents, but they would also be required to work on the part of the estate devoted to produce for the lord (that is, they paid labour-services).

This system of dividing estates wholly or partly into peasant-tenements may have arisen in one of two ways. First, it appears from the Roman writers that the use of slaves maintained in barracks was not always very satisfactory. In view of their circumstances, they were slow to reproduce, and their numbers had to be replenished from slaves purchased at slave-markets, the stock of which was provided as a result of successful Roman conquests and the ensuing enslavement of the conquered people. When Roman military expansion ceased, following the conquest of Dacia north of the River Danube by the emperor Trajan (AD 98–117), the supply of slaves may therefore have become less assured. In view of this, it was thought desirable to engage in the process known literally as 'hutting out' slaves – our sources refer to 'hutted-out slaves' (*servi casati*), who were slaves who had been established on their own tenements.

The second way in which peasant-tenements developed was through the process by which free peasants were 'tied to the land', so that their status came to resemble that of 'hutted-out slaves'. This may itself have been the result of two processes. The first was that by which free peasants, driven by the economic and political problems of the later Roman Empire, gave themselves and their land over to the protection of great lords. Thus tenements which had been the possessions of free peasants became effectively dependent on great estates, their holders reduced to the level of owing food-rents and labour-services to the lords. The second process was the work of the imperial government itself, which passed edicts forcing free peasants to be tied to the soil they worked, and to be under the protection of great lords. Peasants so tied were called *coloni*, and the process itself, the aim of which seems to have been to assure tax-income to the Roman government, is known to scholars as the creation of the colonate.

Carolingian polyptychs

The importance of the shape of these Roman estates for our question lies in comparing them with the estates which appear in the next detailed documents, after a long gap, in the time of the Carolingian kings, especially the ninth century. These documents,

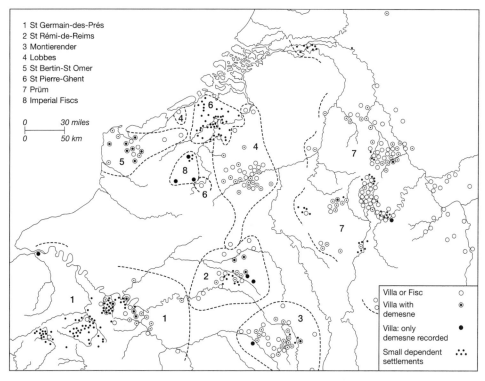

Map 11 Map of the principal Carolingian polyptychs for the northern part of the Carolingian empire. Villas with demesnes are marked as white circles with black centres. The churches to which the capitularies relate are listed in the top left-hand corner.
Source: Adapted from Pounds, N. J. G., *An Economic History of Medieval Europe* (Pearson Education Ltd, 1976).

known as polyptychs, are surveys of the enormous lands of a series of great churches, including the monastery of Saint-German-des-Prés in Paris, the monastery of Saint-Rémi at Reims, the monastery of Saint-Pierre at Ghent in what is now Belgium, and the monastery of Prüm in the hills just to the west of the River Rhine (Map 11). They not only record the structure and organisation of these estates, but they also name the peasants who worked them, sometimes naming also their wives and children, and specifying their status.

It is very striking that the pattern of rural organisation they present seems to reflect closely that of the Roman estates. Some of the estates which are surveyed in the polyptychs appear to have consisted only of land exploited directly for the lord, that is 'demesne'. If these estates were wholly made up of demesne, they must have been worked by slaves maintained in barracks as in our first type of Roman estate, for there cannot have been wage labour in a period with relatively restricted use of money.

The second type of estate appearing in the polyptychs, however, is 'bipartite', consisting of two parts, a demesne and peasant tenements, called in our sources *mansi* ('manses'). The holders of these manses were sometimes slaves (*servi*) and sometimes free peasants, the latter termed in the polyptychs *coloni*, with exactly the same sense of 'free peasants tied to the land' which we find in the Roman imperial edicts. In either case, they owed the lord (in the case of the polyptychs that was the ecclesiastical institution) food-rents or labour-services or some combination of the two. These estates, then, look very like our second type of Roman estate.

Free peasant communities

You may be sceptical, however, that this is really proof of continuity. There is after all a yawning void of several centuries between the Roman sources and the polyptychs. Could it not have been the case that the end of the Roman Empire in the west really had been followed by complete disruption of Roman rural organisation, and that what we see in the polyptychs is a quite new system, which only coincidentally resembled that of the Roman Empire? If you argue for very substantial migrations of barbarians bringing with them quite different social and political organisation, you will naturally favour this view, so that only with the Carolingian period did the rise of a new type of lordship, promoted by the power of the kings, succeed in subjugating some at least of these free peasant communities to lay and ecclesiastical lords, thus producing the pattern of estates we see in the polyptychs. So those estates would have been not at all Roman in origin. A similar view was fundamental to the outlook of the greatest specialist in early medieval English history in the mid-twentieth century, Frank Merry Stenton, whose highly influential book, *Anglo-Saxon England*, begins its discussion of the social structure of post-Roman England with a section headed in the contents-list, 'The basis of society was the free peasant' (Stenton, 1971, p. xix).

Stenton's prinicipal argument, that the peasants called in Old English documents *ceorls* were a dominant class of well-off free peasants in early medieval English society, has not stood up well to scrutiny of the documents. Nevertheless, it is still possible to argue that free peasants were more important in rural society than the impression the polyptychs would give us. As Map 11 above shows, the estates described in the polyptychs cover nothing like the whole area of Western Europe. In between them, there may of course have been others which were those of kings and great laymen, the records of which have generally not been preserved in the way that the polyptychs were, since ecclesiastical archives are generally so much better from our period. But it may be equally that those spaces were filled with the freeholdings of peasant proprietors, who had nothing in common either with Roman estates or with those of the polyptychs. Indeed, Map 11 shows that the polyptychs themselves record that, in the eastern and south-western parts of the area they collectively cover, there was a substantial number of rural settlements which consisted of what are called in Latin *vici*, that is settlements of peasants who owed dues to their lord (in this case the church in question), but which did not form part of slave-run or bipartite estates. You may want to argue that such settlements were the edge of the area in which lords were making progress towards establishing great estates, and that they represent what until relatively shortly before the time of the polyptych had been settlements of free peasants.

This possibility has been strengthened by research carried out where we have archives, always maintained by churches of course, of documents, charters, and so on, recording land-transactions. These archives have revealed that, in certain parts of Europe at least, many of the people buying, selling, or giving land were indeed small-scale freeholders, and so in effect free peasants not dependent on a great estate. Wendy Davies (1988), for example, has shown, from charters preserved in the archives of the monastery of Redon (near Nantes), the existence in eastern Brittany of villages in which most of the inhabitants were peasant freeholders, not dependent on a lord. They were organised collectively in a self-governing way, or they were under the governance of a leader called in Breton a *machtiern*. A similar picture can be derived from the archives of churches in Catalonia, such as Urgell Cathedral, suggesting that that part of Catalonia, mostly the eastern foothills of the Pyrenees Mountains, was comparable in the frequency of free peasant proprietors. Interesting as these results are, however, we might think that the areas in question were rather peripheral, either geographically or ecologically. Eastern Brittany was a deeply Celtic area, on the fringes of Roman imperial control, just as it was only imperfectly brought under the rule of the Carolingian kings. The area in Catalonia covered by the archives of Urgell Cathedral and other churches was not peripheral geographically to the Roman world, but its geography made it marginal for agriculture. Both areas, in other words, may never have been fully integrated into the Roman estate-system, so that the evidence from them has no real bearing on the continuity of that system into the Early Middle Ages.

An area much more central to the Carolingian world was the middle Rhine Valley, and numerous documents preserved by monasteries there sometimes show, as at the village of Dienheim (Germany), that the land was largely divided into small units. It may be that the holders of these were free peasants, so that this would be evidence of the importance of that class of person even in this area central to the power of the Carolingian kings. But the documents are not explicit about the status of the small land-holders in question, so the view that they were free peasants can be no more than an interpretation.

Evidence for the continuation of Roman estates

What then is the evidence that can be used to argue that Roman estates, or at least the system of Roman estates, really did continue into our period?

Written evidence

This consists chiefly of a series of wills of the bishops of Le Mans in western Gaul in the Merovingian period. These wills go a little way towards describing the estates which the bishops disposed of during their lifetimes, and it is very striking that these included tenements held by *coloni* just as we might have expected to see in the late Roman period. The evidence is not extensive, and it relates to only one part of Gaul, but it is suggestive.

Archaeological evidence

This derives from the excavation of Roman villas in the sense of the stone-built, high-status dwellings and other buildings at the heart of a Roman estate. The general pattern seems to be one of shrinkage of the inhabited area in the fifth century and onwards, with the end of sequences of coins and fine pottery found on the villas from earlier periods, and with decay of the buildings. On the face of it, this evidence seems pretty unequivocally to point to the collapse of the system of Roman estates.

Against that, however, two arguments can be advanced. The first is that the excavators of villas, especially those working before the Second World War period, were predisposed to find evidence for the 'Decline and Fall of the Roman Empire'. They were consequently not alert to what evidence there might have been on the sites they were excavating of continuing use of the villa, a use which might have left much more ephemeral remains than the Romans, consisting for example of the use of rubble or timber. Indeed, some excavations of Roman villas in the 1960s and later, for example, those of the villas at Latimer in Buckinghamshire and Shakenoak in Oxfordshire, did yield evidence of their continuing use after the end of the Roman Empire in the west, and comparable evidence was forthcoming from some excavated villas in Gaul. We may think, however, that this argument is only partially convincing, for the continued use was often quite different from the original use, where, for example, it consists of what are apparently post-Roman burials on villa-sites in Gaul and Spain.

The second argument which can be advanced is that the Roman villas which have been excavated were necessarily failed villas, and that is why they were available for excavation at all. Otherwise, they would have been submerged under buildings which were constructed in succession to the villa but which were responsible for managing the same sort of estate (or even the same estate with the same boundaries) as the villa was. The successful villas, in other words, had turned into medieval villages with medieval manor-houses and, since it has rarely been possible to excavate these, the archaeological evidence is hopelessly distorted as regards its bearing on the fate of Roman estate-structure. In support of this, it has been urged that when Gaulish writers like Sidonius Apollinaris (c.430–c.486), the senator who became bishop of the Auvergne, or the sixth-century Venantius Fortunatus, wrote descriptions of villas, these had begun to sound much more like medieval fortified sites. As the latter describes Bishop Nicetius's, for example, it was located on a high rock just as a later castle would have been, and defended by thirty turrets (Percival, 1976, p. 175; see also above, pp. 175–6). This, it can be argued, is what successful villas were turning into, while the classic Roman villas of the excavations had been left behind by the flow of time to wither.

Moreover, very occasionally, archaeologists have 'struck lucky' in finding the remains of a Roman villa under a later village or residence. The bishop of Trier is known to have had a palace at Pfalzel on the River Mosel (Germany) from the tenth century onwards, and this palace developed as the centre of a medieval village. There is no documentation to suggest that this was founded on an existing Roman villa, but when excavations were carried out in the area of the church, very clear remains of a Roman villa were discovered. The find does not prove continuity between early medieval Pfalzel and that Roman villa, but it suggests it. The same can be said of the famous Roman mosaic at Woodchester in Gloucester, which was found by chance at the heart of that Cotswold village. The mosaic belonged to a Roman villa and, as at Pfalzel, its topographical relationship to the later village suggests that it was the origin of that, although it cannot prove it.

Place-names

In the context of Roman and Frankish Gaul, this type of evidence hinges on the use of the suffix -*acum* or -*anus* in Latin names of villas. The suffix is usually attached to a personal name, so that the name as a whole means 'the villa of X'. Such suffixes certainly are found in the Carolingian polyptychs, for example in the case of the estate named *Waniaco* in the polyptych of Saint-Germain-des-Prés. Specialists in the development of place-names consider that this Latin suffix developed over the centuries into a series of suffixes in modern French place-names, such as -*at*, -*as*, -*y*, -*é*, and -*ay*. Names with these suffixes are very common in France, as any glance at a map shows. If they do provide evidence that the settlement to which they are now attached had grown out of a Roman villa which had continued to flourish and evolve, that would be very important evidence indeed. The difficulty lies in proving that that is really the case. The distribution of these names, in relation to Roman roads for example, is suggestive that it is; but against that is the fact that where villas have actually been excavated the places in question only sporadically have such names. It may be, of course, that the reason for that is that, while the villa estate has continued from the Roman period, its centre has moved away from its original site and has been given a new name. But, although it is clear from archaeological investigation that settlement sites did indeed move in the Middle Ages, it is only conjecture that this accounts for these discrepancies in the relationship between known villas and the place-names in question.

Aerial photography

This evidence has the potential to show that medieval settlements developed on the sites of, or at least in close relationship to, Roman villas. The technique of photographing the landscape from a slow-moving aeroplane, for preference a single-engine biplane which was steady in the air and lacked windows so that the photographer could lean out of it, was developed during the Second World War by the Cambridge archaeologist J. K. St Joseph, and later in France by specialists such as Roger Agache. Under appropriate light and at appropriate seasons of the year, previously unknown structures below ground level appear on aerial photographs, because the oblique light of the sun catches the line of shadow along where crops have grown taller over the richer soil of a foundation-trench, or conversely where they have grown more feebly over a buried stone wall, or in winter where such a buried wall has caused the soil above it to be of a paler colour (Wilson, 2000).

Roman
walls

Remains of rooms

Figure 17 The village of Chaussy-Épagny in the valley of the River Somme, photographed from
the air by Roger Agache. The later village is visible in the upper part of the photograph. Remains of
a substantial Roman building, probably a villa, appear in the field immediately adjacent to it in the
lower part of the photograph. They show up as white lines marking the walls and, on the left-hand
side of the field, what are clearly the walls of a row of rooms (Agache, 1978, plate 258). It seems very
likely that what we have is a typical courtyard-villa, with open space at the centre and corridors of
rooms on four sides.
Source: Courtesy of Roger Agache – DRAC de Picardie.

Agache's results for the valley of the River Somme in north-eastern Gaul are
particularly striking. A typical example of the sites which he discovered is the Roman
structure, probably a villa, immediately adjacent to the medieval village of Chaussy-
Épagny in the valley of the River Somme (Fig. 17). The number of times that such a
relationship between a Roman villa and a later village or hamlet was demonstrated
by aerial photography created a presumption at least that there may have been some
continuity between the two, and that the villa had transformed itself into its medieval
successor.

Archaeology and field-surveying of later villages

Long-term archaeological research on the village of Wharram Percy in East Yorkshire,
which was deserted in the later Middle Ages and so has been available for excavation,
has provided what is at least suggestive evidence of continuity between the Roman and
later periods there. Another project has been carried out at Shapwick in Somerset.
This is a flourishing village, not a deserted one like Wharram Percy, and the research

has taken the form of systematic sampling of pottery and other finds from cottage-gardens, as well as field-surveys around the village. This research too has not definitely established continuity between the Roman period and the later village, but the spreads of Roman pottery recovered from that settlement at least create a presumption that such continuity existed.

———————————

There is then a fair amount of evidence of various types pointing to the conclusion that there was some level of continuity in the Roman villa system and the basic framework of agricultural organisation across our period and beyond. It remains, needless to say, a matter of judgement as to how convincing this evidence is, and it is also a matter of judgement as to how far, even if we accept it, the results derived from it can be extended to Western Europe as a whole. As we have seen, it is possible to argue that the great estates surveyed in the polyptychs were not typical, and that the soil of Western Europe was exploited extensively by free peasants with no real connection with the Roman past. This interpretation itself, as we have discussed, involves assumptions about the general significance of evidence deriving from peripheral areas like Brittany, and particular readings of documents relating to more central areas like the Rhineland. You may think, then, that after all the really solid evidence is in favour of the idea of Roman agricultural continuity into the Early Middle Ages, even if that naturally involved shifts and changes over time.

An agricultural revolution?

That judgement, however, may be affected by how you want to address the second set of questions of this chapter. Are we to envisage the early medieval countryside as closed, unproductive, unprogressive, and unchanging? Or are we to envisage it as being founded on an agricultural economy and agricultural systems which were being driven forward, so that the countryside was an engine of change in society at large? And, if the latter, can we identify the forces which were driving the exploitation of the countryside onward?

Population-growth

If we could establish that there was population-growth in our period, then it seems likely that such growth would have been an instrument of change in the countryside, either because it resulted in an impoverishment of the peasantry with too little to feed their growing numbers; or because it provided additional manpower to increase and diversify production and was therefore a positive and not a negative force. But can we establish what the trend was in the population? We do not, needless to say, have anything remotely like the census-records of the modern period, or even the tax registers of later medieval Europe, so it is quite out of the question to produce population figures for Western Europe as a whole which are in any way precise. Every now and then, we do have a shaft of light. From the late eleventh century, the survey of much of England called the Domesday Book is detailed enough for us to have a go at estimating the population of King William the Conqueror's England. From the ninth century, some of the polyptychs make it possible to arrive at calculations of population for the estates in question. For the city of Rome, we have documents permitting similar calculations. But this is far too sketchy and sporadic for real numerical trends to be discerned.

There is, however, a possibility of discerning broad trends, even if we cannot put actual numbers on them. First, there are some very striking indications that the period of the later Roman Empire, through the sixth and seventh centuries, was a period of falling population. This is suggested, first, by the anxiety of Roman writers and Roman legislators over falling population. As we have seen, the latter referred frequently to 'deserted fields' (*agri deserti*), and they were preoccupied, as we have also seen, with tying the free peasants to the soil as *coloni*, presumably because the labour force was shrinking and it was necessary to tie down the peasants in this way, to avoid them moving on to better themselves, and (the most important thing from the legislators' point of view) leaving the land they had been tending deserted and so not liable for taxation.

If we accept that this evidence points to a decline in population in the Roman Empire, this must have been much accelerated by a dangerous pandemic of plague for which we have excellent evidence. The sixth-century Byzantine writer Procopius records the occurrence of plague in Byzantium in 543–6. It appears that this plague spread westwards, for the next reference to it is in the Auvergne (that is, the Massif Central area of modern France) in 563. In 570, it is recorded as having struck North Italy, Gaul, and Spain, and in 592 there is yet another reference to it in Tours on the River Loire and at Nantes in eastern Brittany. Nor did it stop with the Continent. One of the most vivid accounts of it is that of Bede in his *Ecclesiastical History of the English People*, which describes the plague's devastating impact on mid-seventh-century ecclesiastical communities in the newly Christianised kingdoms of England. At Bede's own monastery, the joint monastery of Monkwearmouth-Jarrow in the kingdom of Northumbria, all the monks died of plague, except the abbot, whose name was Ceolwulf, and one boy, usually thought to have been Bede himself, who together had to keep the liturgical services being celebrated in the stricken churches. Bede was reporting chiefly on the deaths of monks, nuns, and clergy, but it is reasonable to suppose that a considerable proportion of the lay population also died. This must be especially the case if we accept that, when Gregory of Tours in his late sixth-century *History of the Franks* describes the plague as having as one of its symptoms swellings (*bubones*), this shows that it was the same illness as the bubonic plague known as the Black Death, which had such devastating effects on European population in the fourteenth century.

It may be that, as in the fourteenth century, a decline in population actually provided a stimulus for growth and greater economic activity, so that the population recovered rapidly afterwards. For, there is evidence to suggest that by the end of the eighth century there had been significant population growth. This evidence consists in the first place of the information given in some at least of the polyptychs about peasant families. The polyptych of Saint-Germain-des-Prés, for example, gives information not only about the peasants who held the tenements (or manses), but also about their wives and children, living and deceased in childhood. A typical entry for a tenement on an estate called *Palatiolum* reads:

> Hairmund, a *colonus*, and his wife Haldrada, a *colona* [the feminine of *colonus*], people of Saint-Germain, have with them five children called Elisom, Hildegaud, + Eliseus, Teudhild, Hariveus.

The cross in front of the name Eliseus means that this child had not survived. It is therefore possible, at least for the area of the Paris basin in which the estates described in this polyptych lay, to have some indications as to the fecundity of the peasant population and the incidence of child mortality. Of course, the polyptych only provides a snapshot at a particular time – all Hairmund and Haldrada's children might have died the following year – but it is a clue at least. As such, it is a startling one. Calculations on the polyptych as a whole suggest that the estates surveyed had a density of population of between twenty-six and thirty-five persons per square kilometre, which was approaching the density of population in the same area in the early nineteenth century. Comparable figures of between twenty-five and forty people per square kilometre can be derived from the polyptych of the Flemish abbey of Saint-Bertin near Saint-Omer from 844–8. Moreover, further calculations based on the polyptych of Saint-Germain-des-Prés show that it lists 5,316 adults and 4,710 children, suggesting that the population was still growing. And this in turn tallies with royal legislation from the reign of Charlemagne's grandson, Charles the Bald, king of West Frankia (840–77), aimed at regulating the subdivision of manses. As we discussed earlier, a manse was defined as an area of land appropriate for the support of one family, and this appears to have been a very basic concept in European rural organisation. So to find in the course of the ninth century that a king was concerned that manses were being subdivided between more than one family is strongly suggestive of population pressure on the land. Of course, we could argue that all this can refer, at best, only to the great estates of the main heartlands of the Frankish kingdom; but there are parallel indications from other parts of Western Europe, notably a document of 913 concerning the repopulation of a valley in the Pyrenees around San Juan de las Abbadessas. This indicates that there were 160 households and fifty-six individuals occupying fifty-six square kilometres, which suggests a population density near to those calculated from the polyptychs. It may be, then, that there was a period of declining population from the late Roman Empire through to perhaps the seventh century, followed by a period of burgeoning population, with all the opportunities for economic expansion and the pressures which that entailed.

Climate change

Establishing the history of climate for a remote period is of course very difficult. But the case is not hopeless and there is a surprising amount of evidence available.

This consists on the one hand of the evidence of contemporary chronicles and writings, which describe the typical weather conditions in their own time. On the other hand, and more scientifically, it consists of data derived from a series of scientific procedures, some developed in quite recent years. These procedures involve, for example, identification under a microscope of the pollen grains from dated layers in archaeological sites. This is to discover what vegetation was present at the period when the layer was deposited, which can provide an indicator of climate. For example, pollen grains from excavations in the area of the Ardennes, between modern Germany and Belgium, show that beech trees, which require a warmer, drier climate than birch trees, made advances as a prominent element of the vegetation cover between the eighth and the twelfth centuries, suggesting a period then of drier, warmer climate.

Another scientific procedure involves drilling into the ice caps or glaciers in order to recover what the history of the ice has been. The ice shows dark and light layers which correspond to the years during which the ice has existed, and the pattern of these layers can cast light on the occurrence of warm or cold temperatures. The pattern of temperature change in these layers can be confirmed by the recovery from the ice of samples of oxygen isotopes, O-18 and O-16, since predominance of the former indicates that the climate was colder at the time when the layer in question was produced. The dating of the layers themselves can be established by means of measuring the radioactive output called thermoluminescence from the volcanic dust in each layer of ice. The length of time taken for thermoluminescence to decline can be calculated and calibrated scientifically, so that these measurements enable scientists to calculate the date of the dust and so the date of the layer of ice in which it was found. Similar sorts of results can be obtained by deep-sea drilling in the seabed, while another scientific procedure altogether involves examining the layered deposits of clay sediment (or varves) which have been deposited at the nose of a glacier. These sediments are deposited annually when the glacier retreats in the summer and melt-waters flow from under its sole. The thicker the varve, the warmer was the summer in which it was produced. Research of this sort at Fernau in the Austrian Tyrol has shown that there was advance of the glaciers in the Alps from the early fifth to the mid-eighth century, followed by a retreat (resulting from warmer climate) which persisted until the mid-twelfth century.

These scientific procedures do not produce very precise results in terms of chronology, and the evidence of chronicles and other writings is inevitably impressionistic, but it does seem possible in very broad terms to establish that the second half of our period, perhaps from the seventh century, perhaps from the eighth, was characterised by a warmer, drier climate – that it was in other words a climatic 'optimum' following the climatic 'pessimum' of the later Roman Empire and the immediately following centuries in Western Europe. If you accept that, it follows that the improvement in climate from an agricultural point of view could have been a major force in driving forward the exploitation of the land in our period. You may be struck by the correlation between this pattern and that proposed for population growth.

Technological advance and agricultural method

In a vivid and compelling, if rather extreme, book, Lynn W. White (1962) maintained that a series of dramatic innovations in technology and an equally dramatic innovation in agricultural method which (in his view) emerged in our period shaped the way that Western European society worked.

Mould-board plough

If we look back to the Roman period, the evidence we have for ploughing technology is mainly for the use of the so-called scratch-plough or ard. This can be seen represented in a model from Piercebridge (County Durham), and similarly in a model of a much earlier plough from Arezzo in Italy (Fig. 18), dating from the sixth century BC.

Like the plough in the Piercebridge model, this is yoked to two oxen, with the ploughman holding the handle. The crucial evidence in both models is provided by the representation of the ploughshare, which is the part of the plough actually digging into the ground. This appears on the model as nothing more than a point, which may have been tipped with iron, although we cannot of course tell that from the model. The important thing is that the ploughshare is just a point. It could have scratched the ground to make a furrow, but it had no means of actually turning over the soil behind

Figure 18 Model of a Roman plough in use from Arezzo (Italy).
Source: © The Art Gallery Collection/Alamy.

Figure 19 A mould-board plough represented in the margin of the Bayeux Tapestry.
Source: Detail from the Bayeux Tapestry, 11th century, by special permission of the City of Bayeux.

it. Such a scratch-plough was therefore not a very effective tool. It had to pass over the ground more than once in order to make it fit for sowing the crop. This was done by means of cross-ploughing, that is ploughing diagonally, with the result that Roman fields were characteristically square in shape (in British archaeology they are sometimes called 'Celtic' fields and can be seen still preserved in some upland landscapes).

With this scratch-plough in mind, we can turn to evidence from just after the end of our period, that is the representation of a plough in the border of the late eleventh-century embroidery known as the Bayeux Tapestry (Fig. 19).

This shows major differences from the plough represented in the Piercebridge model. Notice, first, that this is a heavier machine, requiring a set of wheels to support it. Behind the wheels is a sort of knife-like tool called a coulter, which cuts almost vertically into the ground to break it up ahead of the ploughshare which follows it and lies almost horizontal to the ground. But behind the ploughshare is the really crucial innovation in plough technology, the mould-board. This is a substantial wooden board, set at an angle in such a way that, as the ploughshare cuts the furrow, so the earth broken up by it is led along the side of the mould-board, and cast off to the side so that a really deep furrow can be created. This innovation meant that much heavier soils could be ploughed, and that the ploughing was much more efficient than with the scratch-plough since it was not necessary to cross-plough as it had been in the Roman period.

Even the two pieces of evidence we have just looked at suggest strongly that this innovation, which is still the basis of modern ploughing technology, appeared in the course of the Early Middle Ages, but greater precision as to the date and place of the innovation is hard, perhaps impossible, to obtain. Part of the difficulty is that survival of mould-boards on archaeological sites is very rare, because they were made of wood. Something can be done with ploughshares, which do tend to survive because they were more often made of iron, and which can be classified into symmetrical shares (which would have been for scratch-ploughs) and asymmetrical shares (which would have been for mould-board ploughs), but finds are rare and certainty of interpretation hard to achieve. Occasionally archaeology can help in a different way by uncovering remains of actual furrows, which from their depth and shape can reveal whether or not they were produced by a mould-board plough. There is also very obscure evidence from the use of Latin terms (some authorities have thought that the word *aratrum* referred to the scratch-plough and *carruca* to the mould-board plough), and unexpectedly from the richness of vocabulary for ploughing to be found in Slav languages to the east of the former Roman Empire. This, together with the observations of some Roman writers, has raised the possibility that the mould-board plough was invented in those eastern areas, and introduced into Western Europe as a result of barbarian influence after the end of the Roman Empire in the west. The uncertainty of all this, however, should not obscure the underlying importance of the development. At some time during the Early Middle Ages, possibly even before the end of the Roman Empire in the west, a really major innovation was made in ploughing technology in Western Europe, and we should not lose sight of that crucial, and reasonably certain, piece of information.

That innovation had other consequences for rural organisation and agriculture. Because the heavy plough turned the soil so much more effectively, it also required much greater power to pull it than the scratch-plough had done. But early medieval technology lacked, as Roman technology had also lacked, any means of harnessing animals other than by a collar round the neck. This meant that pulling constricted the animal's windpipe and reduced the amount of effort it could deliver. In the case of the heavy plough, this meant in turn that the only animals suitable for pulling it with such a collar were oxen, and that a team of eight oxen was required, which were harnessed in a row in front of the plough, as is shown in many medieval manuscript illuminations. This had two major implications for rural organisation. First, it meant that the shape of fields had to change, so that they could be made much larger and rectangular in order to accommodate this large team of oxen working, and at each end they had to have a 'headland' where the team could be turned. Such fields, with the characteristic 'ridge-and-furrow' produced by the mould-board plough, the ridges having an inverted S-shape showing where the plough began its turn at the ends of the fields, are still visible as earthworks in some parts of England, where modern deep ploughing has not destroyed them.

Secondly, the introduction of the mould-board plough meant that there had to be consolidation of resources for these eight-oxen teams to be assembled and maintained. This could have been done in one of two ways. Either the peasants themselves could have formed themselves into collectives, as independent farmers do today to give themselves access to combine harvesters; or the peasants could simply have been organised from above by their lords. In combination with the need to reorganise the whole pattern of fields, it might be thought that the hypothesis that it was the action of lords rather than the collaboration of peasants which produced the necessary changes may seem the more plausible. But much will depend on the view you take as to the relative importance of the great estates of lords to the independent tenements of free peasants in early medieval Western Europe.

Rigid-collar harness

The second technological innovation, seemingly in our period, was another affecting ploughing and animal traction. This harness transferred the weight of the pulling from an animal's neck to its shoulders (its withers, that is) so that the problem of partial asphyxiation was removed. This made it possible for horses rather than oxen to do heavy tasks such as pulling the mould-board plough, and it made the use of animal-power much more efficient. It is equally difficult to date this innovation precisely, but the earliest representation of it may be in a ninth-century manuscript of the Apocalypse in the city library at Trier in Germany. It was clearly in use in the plough represented in the Bayeux Tapestry (Fig. 19 above), where a horse (or possibly a mule) is being used to pull the plough rather than a team of oxen. It is not clear, however, how widely it was actually used in our period, for there is much evidence of the continuing use of oxen to pull ploughs into later centuries.

Water-mills

Water-mills, which replaced hand-milling by quern-stones with the hydraulically powered machine which was a familiar part of the countryside of Western Europe down to quite modern times, were known in the Roman period, but their real expansion may have been in the post-Roman period, when we have extensive evidence of them, not least in the Domesday Book which records no fewer than 5,624 water-mills in use in late eleventh-century England. Archaeological excavations have confirmed their sophistication, bringing to light, for example, an elaborate seventh-century mill with a vertical wheel from Old Windsor, and a mid-tenth-century mill with the more unusual horizontal wheel from Tamworth in Staffordshire. With the spread of water-mills as with field reorganisation, it is possible to argue about whether this could have been achieved by peasant collectives, or whether it suggests a rural society generally dominated by lords.

Three-field crop rotation

In the Roman period, two-field crop rotation was the norm. That is, the land was divided into two sets of fields, the first of which was ploughed and sown in the spring, while the second was left fallow for that growing season. The next year, the use of the two sets of fields was swapped round so that every field could have an alternate year of fallow to recuperate the goodness of the soil. Three-field rotation involved two periods of sowing, one in the spring and another in the autumn. So, in place of the two-way division, it was possible to have three sets of fields (or, in the case of one village using the mould-board plough, three very large fields). The first of these was sown in the spring, the second in the autumn, the third was left fallow for that growing season. The use of the fields was changed from year to year, so that each experienced in turn spring sowing, autumn sowing, and fallow. The potential increase in productivity is obvious, since a higher proportion of the land was growing crops at any one time; but there were other benefits too in terms of the range of crops which could be grown. This too, then, was a major breakthrough, which certainly occurred in our period.

As with the technological innovations, further precision is extremely difficult to achieve. It is possible to go back to the Carolingian polyptychs, especially that of the abbey of Saint-Amand. There the lists of crops grown include those suitable for spring sowing and those suitable for autumn sowing, which suggests that the three-field system of rotation was in use, and there are also indications that the settlements (or vills) were in fact organised around three great fields in this part of north-eastern Gaul in the ninth century. We can also detect signs of the existence of such 'open' fields in the law-code of the seventh-century king of Wessex, Ine. But the evidence is not at all satisfactory, and there is also evidence to suggest that two-field rotation continued far beyond the end of our period in Italy and the Mediterranean lands. As with ploughing, we should not lose sight of the fundamental importance of this innovation, but we probably have to accept that precision is impossible.

The motivation of lords

We have been considering the various forces which may have been driving forward early medieval rural organisation and agriculture. If we accept that there was increase in productivity and efficiency, we need to consider why such an increase was desired by contemporaries. What, in other words, was the motivation for transforming rural organisation and agriculture? You could argue that population growth itself pro-vided this, and that the need to feed more mouths lay behind it. But, if you accept the argument that rural society was dominated by great lords and their estates, this requires you to envisage a perhaps implausible wish on the part of these lords to improve the lot of their peasants.

You could argue, on the other hand, that improving the lot of their peasantry was much less important than increasing their own revenues. In the case of the great monastic houses, it is clear from the polyptychs that an enormous amount of food was produced for the support of quite small communities of monks or, in the case of cathedrals, canons. This is even clearer from another ninth-century document from Frankish Gaul, the *Customs of the Monastery of Corbie* (north-eastern France). These list the renders in food to be made to the monks of Corbie monastery. The scale of these was very considerable in terms, for example, of the number of chickens, so that it defies belief that all this food could have been consumed by the recipients. At any rate, it is hard to see that there was any motive in such a system for the lord (in this case the monastery) to promote increase in agricultural productivity, and we have no reason to think that large secular estates were any different.

If there was nevertheless an incentive for lords to increase agricultural productivity, it can only have lain in the potential for selling surplus food. Achieving this may have been all the more necessary for lords because the cessation of military expansion of Western European kingdoms, in the face of aggression from the invading Vikings and Magyars, meant that making money by selling surplus produce and using the income from this to buy luxury goods appropriate to their status was the only way they could obtain such goods which would previously have come to them as booty. High-status, very expensive luxury goods were just as important to churches as to secular lords, for the former needed silks for hangings, wrappings, and vestments, and precious metals for chalices and pyxes and the decorations of the church.

Accepting this, however, depends on having evidence that the rural economy in the Early Middle Ages was commercialised at a deep enough level for landowners to have had the opportunity to engage in commerce with their surplus produce, and this is very difficult to establish. We know from a mid-eighth-century capitulary that Pippin III, king of the Franks (751–68), regulated weekly rural markets, which is some evidence for their existence. We know that the monastery of Saint-Germain-des-Prés in Paris had regular connections with the port of Quentovic (north-eastern France), which shows that it at least was engaging in commerce, although it is not by any means clear that such commerce would have involved foodstuffs. We know too that there was a considerable amount of movement of commodities like wine, which could best be grown only in certain parts of Western Europe. But it is not clear whether the movement of these products was commercially based, or whether great estates simply had vills in areas which specialised in wine-growing, and these vills delivered wine to the centre of the estate more as a render than as a sale.

We have been exploring in this chapter the possibilities for there having been significant changes in agriculture and rural life across our period. The topic is one which is very difficult to pin down with precision. Our evidence is often too vague for precise dates to be assigned to the developments we have been discussing, even if you are willing to accept them, and in any case it is likely that what changes there were happened at different times and with different rhythms in different parts of Western Europe. As you go forward with your research and reading, you may want to develop arguments and collect evidence for the view that an area like northern France, say, was very different from a Mediterranean area such as the plain of northern Italy.

Nevertheless, you should keep open the possibility that there were fundamental changes in our period and that they affected wide areas. The modern period shows that it is not impossible for such changes in agriculture and rural life to happen extensively and in quite a short time, as was the case with the so-called Agricultural Revolution of the eighteenth century. So the question of whether we can establish that comparable changes happened in our period is a very real one.

We have also been exploring what might have been the forces driving such change. As you go forward and think further about this question, you need above all to keep in view the possible interrelations between agriculture and rural life on the one hand and the social and political structures of Western Europe on the other (above, Part III), as well as between agriculture and rural life and the growth of trade and towns (Chapters 7–9). However convenient it may be to separate out topics, we need always to remember that in reality they are all linked, and exploring those links may be one of the best ways of casting light on the individual topics themselves.

Research and study

Broad research questions

To what extent did Roman agricultural organisation influence early medieval agriculture?

How far did kings and elites shape the development of rural society and economy?

How important were free peasants in the rural society of the Early Middle Ages?

What were the forces driving agriculture to greater productivity?

Books and papers to begin with

Classic textbooks on agriculture and rural society in the Early Middle Ages and later, which are well worth having by you, are those of Slicher van Bath (1966), Duby (1968, 1974), and Latouche (1967). Much briefer but extremely lucid and worthwhile is Pounds (1994, ch. 2). An overview of Carolingian agriculture, reporting the results of recent research, especially in archaeology, is by Verhulst (2002, chs 3–4); and Smith (2005, pp. 151–73) also provides some useful discussion. Wickham (2005, ch. 4) provides a usefully documented summary of the history of great estates, arguing that there was no continuously evolutionary model for their development. To get a feel for what polyptychs are like, English translations of short extracts from that of Saint-Germain-des-Prés and that of the church of Marseilles in southern Gaul can be consulted in Dutton (2004, pp. 207–19). The clearest account of Roman agriculture and rural organisation remains that of Jones (1964, II, 767–823). There is another, more detailed account in the work of the Soviet historian Rostovtzeff (1957), and a succinct, up-to-date summary of research on Late Roman rural life by Whittaker and Garnsey (1998).

Pursuing more specific aspects

Continuity between Roman and early medieval agriculture and rural society?

The case that there was close similarity between the rural organisation described in the polyptychs and that known from Roman sources is presented most forcefully in two articles by Percival (1969, 1966). His is also the best book on all aspects of the evidence for the continuity of Roman villas to early medieval estates, and its difficulties (Percival, 1976). A discussion of the issues involved in this, informed by more recent archaeological research, is given by Christie (2004, pp. 1–38), and some of the papers in this volume, notably those of Scott (on late Roman villas in general), Arnau (on Spain), Poulter (on 'cataclysm' in the lower Danube), and Périn (on Gaul), are useful. Sarris (2004) supports the idea of continuity between Roman organisation and the Carolingian and later bipartite estates by drawing in the evidence of the Oxyrhynchi papyri from Late Roman Egypt and relating them to the west. The article is well worth mastering, although you need to be willing to cope with foreign-language terms. The counter-argument that such estates were a creation of the Carolingian period and do not prove continuity of estate-organisation with the Roman period is made by Verhulst (2002, pp. 33–7), although you should think hard about the evidence being presented for this. For Italy, Francovich and Hodges (2003) use archaeological evidence in some detail to argue that there was a 'dramatic shift in the settlement pattern' in the late sixth and early seventh centuries, leading to the establishment of hill-top villages in place of the Roman villas. Wickham (2005, chs 7–8) offers a rich, but rather involved, discussion of the status of the peasantry in various parts of Western Europe (there are also long sections on the eastern Mediterranean) and the nature of villages in relation to peasant society.

Free peasant society?

The view that early medieval agriculture, at least in England, was dominated by free peasants of characteristically 'German' or 'barbarian' type is evident in Stenton (1971, ch. 9). The case against this was made very forcefully in two works, which are not at all easy to read, by John (1964, 1966). For the Continent, Dopsch (1937, chs 4–5) is still well worth reading. Modern research on collections of charters showing, it is argued, the greater importance of free peasants in the Early Middle Ages is presented in a succinct and usefully documented account by Wickham (1995). In a later work, Wickham (2009, ch. 22) expounds the same view somewhat more fully but with less reference to documentation, and develops the idea that, even though some peasants were free down to the Carolingian period of the eighth and ninth centuries, lordly dominance increased after that and peasants were effectively subjected by the aristocracy. This view is matched by that of some specialists in English history, who maintain that the growth of what Norman records call the 'manor' was a product of the late Anglo-Saxon period. The key book is that of Faith (1997), who elsewhere gives useful summaries of her views (Faith, 1999).

An agricultural revolution?

A clear picture of the forces supposedly at work to produce such a revolution is offered by Duby (1974), and there is a much more negative assessment of the issue by Verhulst (1990). You can pursue several elements in more depth, or as subjects in their own right, including:

Population growth

The classic works are those of Russell (1958, 1969). The earlier of these is much the more rewarding, and contains really detailed and vivid discussion of the evidence and its limitations. Smith (2005, pp. 59–71) is a useful discussion with some insight into the use of evidence from excavated cemeteries. On the plague and its effects, a recent work is edited by Little (2007). It contains a very useful summary account by the editor of the evidence and its interpretation (pp. 3–32), as well as more detailed but quite accessible studies of plague in Spain by Michael Kulikowski (pp. 150–70), England by John Madicott (pp. 171–214), and Ireland by Ann Dooley (pp. 215–28). It is, of course, possible to be sceptical about the impact of plague on the grounds that texts like Gregory of Tours's *History of the Franks* were treating plague like a scourge of God and were therefore exaggerating its effects.

Climate change

One of the most recent surveys, which gives helpful technical notes on the most modern methods used to identify historic climate change, is Behringer (2010), but a classic study remains Lamb (1966, chs 9–10), although you need to be aware of the new scientific techniques discussed by Behringer.

Technology and agricultural method

The classic book, which is still absorbing and illuminating reading, is White (1962). Verhulst (1990) advances criticisms of White, although you need to think hard about whether the evidence being presented is really sufficient for definite conclusions to be drawn. For the development of the plough, there is a more recent survey by Brunner (1995). A very helpful little work with technical descriptions of ploughs and excellent illustrations is Rees (1981). The classic study of ploughing and the open fields at the Nottinghamshire village of Laxton, based in part on practical experience, is Orwin and Orwin (1967).

There is a very clear account of the evidence provided by the polyptychs for crop-rotation in Pounds (1994, pp. 56–77). A clause in the Laws of King Ine which has been regarded as referring to the open fields in early eighth-century England, which may have indicated crop-rotation in practice, was given a classic discussion by Thirsk (1966). It is a fascinating subject, and you can pursue it further with the help of Rowley (1981) and Aston (1958).

The evidence of archaeology

The archaeological study of settlements in England, north-western Gaul, Frisia, and Denmark has produced results suggestive of increases in agricultural productivity driven by lords, especially from the eighth century. This can be seen in the development of house-types, the organisation of village-plans, developments of crop and animal husbandry, and in the appearance of traded objects in rural villages. It is well worth wrestling with the lucid but detailed discussions in Hamerow (1994b, 2002), and getting to know particular sites such as Vorbasse in Denmark with Hamerow's help. In England, the archaeological investigation of the villages of Wharram Percy (Beresford and Hurst, 1991), Shapwick (Gerrard, Aston, Reynolds, et al., 2007), and Raunds (Audouy and Chapman, 2008, especially ch. 3 on village-formation) has been very important in understanding the way that villages were reshaped and developed, and it is well worth pursuing them.

The motivation of lords

The importance of this is an underlying theme of Duby (1974). It is developed in the light of more recent research by Wickham (2008), although you may want to think about the rather critical comments of Laiou (2008), and also how this relates to Wickham's views on free peasants (see above).

9

Towns and cities: the functions of urban life

One of the distinguishing features of the Roman Empire, as it had been of the social and political organisation of the eastern Mediterranean and the Middle East for many, many centuries, was its cities. These were numerous, even in Western Europe where urbanisation was less intense than in the east, and they were crucially important to the way the Roman Empire worked. Almost from its beginnings, it was organised around cities, which provided the foci of its political structure, as well as a civilised and cultured environment for the lives of its elites. To understand what happened to the fabric of Western European society after the end of the Roman Empire in the west, we need to think about what happened to those cities.

Pirenne (1925) presented a coherent and vivid interpretation of urban history in our period, according to which the cities of the later Roman Empire in the west were brought to an end by the collapse in the Roman trade-system which was effected by the Arab conquests of the seventh and early eighth centuries (although, as we saw in Chapter 7, it is possible to date this rather earlier). After this collapse of urban life, there ensued a period during which old Roman cities and any other urban centres that may have existed were of no importance. The economy was a 'closed' agricultural system, in which the great landed estates operated a sort of high-level subsistence farming, while royal government was largely conducted not from urban centres but from rural palaces. This was in turn followed by the revival of urban life, effectively from scratch, in the tenth and eleventh centuries, that is at the end of our period. The implication of this thesis was that town life as it revived had no continuity with what had come before because urban activity had been at a standstill in the preceding period, and because when towns grew again that was on quite different principles from Roman cities, and the towns themselves were quite outside the framework of society at large, dominated as it was by great estates and the landed military retainers of what Pirenne saw as the 'feudal system'.

The fate of Roman cities

How much continuity (and of what type) was there between Roman cities and their successors? The most impressive progress on this has been made since the Second World War by urban archaeologists, and it is very rewarding to consider their results as they relate to individual cities.

Winchester

Various archaeological sites in Winchester, which had been made available for excavation prior to urban redevelopment, were excavated in the 1960s and 1970s by a team led by Martin Biddle and the late Birthe Biddle. Winchester was in origin a Roman city, and the archaeological results gave a striking picture of its development from the late Roman period through to the eighth century. For the fourth century, results came from excavation of the Roman cemetery of Lank Hills, which lay like all Roman cemeteries outside the walls of the city. The number and chronology of the burials there suggested that in that period there had actually been an increase in the city's population, so that, rather than fading away, Winchester had in fact flourished towards the end of the Roman Empire in the west. This interpretation was reinforced by excavations along the line of the Roman city-walls, which showed that there had been substantial investment in those walls in the fourth century, when massive platforms had been constructed up against them. The purpose of these plat-forms seems to have been to serve as mounts for *ballistae*, the large Roman shooting engines which could have been used as part of the city's defences. Those *ballistae* must have required specialist operators who understood their quite complex mechanisms, and Martin Biddle connected them with fourth-century graves containing Germanic-type grave-goods in the form of pottery. These he interpeted as the graves of specialist barbarian mercenaries brought in by the Roman government to man the *ballistae*. Thus a picture emerged of fourth-century Winchester as a flourishing city, and a focus of military power with a significant barbarian presence. There was no indication that it was fading away.

The evidence from the fifth century and onwards suggested an entirely different picture. The sites excavated in the centre of the city produced an archaeological blank as far as urban life there was concerned, to the extent that timber houses of apparently agricultural type had been built over the line of the Roman streets. But, whereas this archaeological evidence pointed to a collapse of Winchester's urban life, other evid-ence suggested its continuing importance as a focus of activity. Archaeological study of cemeteries of around the year 500 in the Winchester region showed how they clustered round the city, giving the strongest of impressions that it remained a centre of import-ance which was drawing people, including those who were clearly important people, to be buried around it. Biddle connected this with what Bede tells us in his *Ecclesiastical History of the English People* of events involving Winchester in the seventh century. According to Bede, it was at Winchester that the Christian king of Wessex (Winchester lay in what emerged as the English kingdom of Wessex), Cenwalh, founded his church of SS Peter and Paul in 648, apparently as a royal church and as the church which was to become in 660 the church of the bishop of Wessex. The importance of Winchester is further underlined by Bede's account of how, in the 670s, the relics of the evangelist of Wessex, Birinus, were brought from his first resting-place at Dorchester-on-Thames near Oxford to Winchester, where he was enshrined in the church of SS Peter and Paul. The importance of Winchester is confirmed by the archaeological discovery in the city of four richly furnished graves of the late seventh or early eighth century. These were clearly the graves of aristocrats, possibly of royalty.

We have, then, a picture of Winchester enjoying continuity from the late Roman period into the Early Middle Ages, but that continuity was not one of urban life, but was rather to do with royal and perhaps aristocratic presence and activity in the city, and above all with the Church, although there is no indication that the bishopric of Wessex had any direct continuity with whatever Roman church existed in Winchester in the fourth century. Why then did Winchester continue to enjoy this importance after the end of Roman rule in the west? If we accept Martin Biddle's interpretation of the barbarian specialists brought in to man the *ballistae*, we might conjecture that it was precisely these barbarians who assumed power in the city after the withdrawal of Roman rule from Britain in the early fifth century, and it was they who fostered the political power which was to emerge as the kingdom of Wessex. This would explain the central importance of Winchester to that kingdom: it was because the barbarian military had originally been based in the city and continued to use it as the focus of their activities, even when they had changed their identity into that of West Saxons.

York

This conjecture is worth considering in the light of excavation at York. To understand this, it is important to have a grasp of the basic topography of the Roman and early medieval city. Although Map 12 shows the city as it was in the nineteenth century before modern redevelopment (you can see the railway station marked in the bottom left-hand corner), the components of the Roman city are still clearly visible.

Just as at Winchester, archaeological excavation has suggested that the late Roman city was a flourishing and important place, for it has shown the investment to create the new line of massive towers which appear clearly on the map along the south-west wall of the legionary fortress. One of these, the so-called Multangular Tower, survives and can be seen in the Museum Gardens. A further investment was made in the late Roman period in the construction of the legionary baths, the impressive remains of which can be seen in the Roman Baths Inn in St Sampson's Square. In addition, written sources emphasise the importance of York, telling us that it was the place where Constantine was made emperor in 306, and giving a fair indication that it was the headquarters of the principal military commander of late Roman Britain, the Duke of the Britains. As at Winchester, there is archaeological evidence from the cemeteries around the city of a barbarian presence, presumably indicating a barbarian garrison.

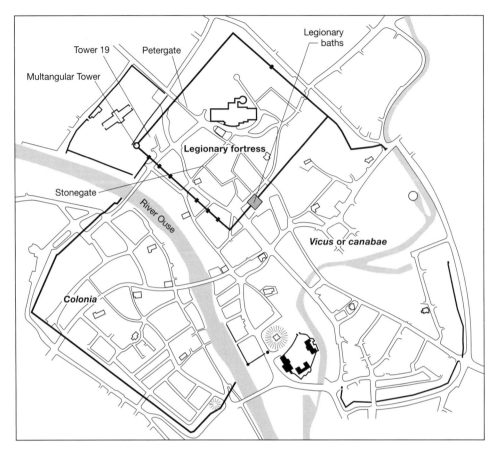

Map 12 York, showing the components of the Roman settlement. These were: first, the legionary fortress. This was a standard Roman fort, such as those that can be seen in ruins along Hadrian's Wall, but it was very large as it was the headquarters for a legion, the largest Roman military unit, and it was probably the military headquarters of the Roman Empire in northern Britain. The fort's north-east and north-west walls are buried under the later fortifications of the city; the south-west and south-east walls were removed at some point (probably the tenth century) and are known only from excavations and from the surviving Multangular Tower which is marked at the western extremity of the fortress. The second component of the Roman city was the *vicus* or *canabae*, which was the area of civil settlement which grew up around the gate of the fort, in origin to provide services for the soldiers in it. The third was the *colonia*, which was originally intended as a settlement of retired soldiers (which is what the word meant), but which developed into a substantial and wealthy Roman city.
Source: Adapted from *An Inventory of the Historical Documents of the City of York, 2: The Defences*. Stationery Office books (Royal Commission on Historical Monuments (England), 1973).

Indeed, we are told that it was a barbarian member of the Roman army who was responsible for the elevation of Constantine.

As at Winchester, the evidence from the fifth century and, in the case of York, through to the late ninth century indicates a hiatus in urban life. A glance at Map 12 makes this clear in the almost complete lack of survival of the Roman street-pattern, which was rectilinear in layout. Only Petergate, running from Bootham Bar past the south side of York Minster, and Stonegate, running at right angles to it to the River Ouse, reflect the Roman pattern. Elsewhere the streets have a rambling layout which is not at all Roman, and points to a discontinuity from the fifth century onwards such as we saw at Winchester.

Yet, just as at Winchester, there is evidence to suggest that York nevertheless remained an important place which enjoyed continuity of a type with the Roman city. Bede tells us in his *Ecclesiastical History of the English People* that it was at York that the first Christian king of Northumbria, Edwin, built his church and there he was baptised in 627, so clearly York was focal in some way to the kingdom of Northumbria as Winchester was to the kingdom of Wessex. As with the four rich graves at Winchester, archaeological finds – and casual finds – at York have shown that rich people, aristocrats or royalty we may suppose, were active in the city. Those finds, which can be seen in the Yorkshire Museum in the city, include a richly decorated hanging bowl, and, most importantly, the Coppergate Helmet (Fig. 37 below), dating from the early ninth century. This is not only a richly decorated and finely made object, suggestive of great wealth, but such helmets are relatively rare in early medieval sites across Europe, and were clearly objects of great prestige. Moreover this one has an inscription naming its owner, Oshere. The first element, Os-, of this name is characteristic of the Northumbrian royal family, occurring for example in names such as that of King Oswald. So the discovery of the helmet further suggests the importance of York to the Northumbrian kings.

But the most striking evidence for the importance of York at the highest level in the post-Roman period was provided by two excavations in the area of York Minster. The first was that of the Roman wall which was buried under a ninth-century earthen bank, and then under the thirteenth-century city walls, in the area of Tower 19 (marked on Map 12 just to the north-east of the Multangular Tower). Tower 19 (the 'Anglian Tower'), which was exposed by these excavations, can be interpreted as a repair of the Roman wall made perhaps in the seventh or eighth centuries, suggesting that York continued to be a centre of importance for the kings of Northumbria who thought such a repair worthwhile (Fig. 20).

The second excavation was that made under the south transept of York Minster in the 1960s in the course of engineering work to support the fabric of the building. This revealed what was obvious already from what was known of the layout of Roman forts, that is that the Minster was built over the headquarters building of the legionary fortress. Like all Roman headquarters buildings, it consisted of a courtyard with behind it a hall, called a basilica or sometimes a cross-hall. In the case of the York legionary fortress, this basilica was massive and, to judge from the surviving columns from it, extremely imposing.

But the unexpected thing revealed by the excavation was that there were spreads of pottery inside the basilica which suggested the possibility that it had continued in use until the ninth century. If so, the most likely interpretation would be that it had functioned as the royal palace of the kings who ruled what became the kingdom of

Figure 20 Tower 19 (the 'Anglian Tower') in the fortifications of York. The Roman wall here is that of the legionary fortress, robbed of its outer skin in later times so that only the rubble core is preserved. This was covered by the ninth-century defensive bank, on top of which the medieval city walls were constructed. The bank is visible behind the 'Anglian Tower' but it has been stripped away by archaeologists to reveal the Roman wall. The 'Anglian Tower' seems to plug what was a breach in the Roman wall. Its masonry was clearly quite different from the Roman masonry, which would have been of large square blocks called ashlar, and the voussoirs (i.e. the radiating stones) around its doorway suggest the possibility that it is of seventh- or eighth-century date.

Northumbria after the end of Roman Britain. This would also explain the location of York Minster in the middle of the legionary fortress rather than in the remains of the *colonia*, since, if the basilica had indeed been the palace of the first Christian king of Northumbria, Edwin, he may well have built his church in its courtyard. The present Minster, which is probably on a slightly different site, would have been its successor in broadly the same position. Just as at Winchester, then, we have the possibility that the continued importance of the city was due to the barbarian garrison, which may have taken over government from the Roman authorities, and have continued to use the basilica as a palace, just as the headquarters building had been the centre of their activities in the Roman period.

The evidence from Winchester and York thus points towards a sort of continuity between Roman cities and what came after them which was not based on urban life as we would recognise it. These cities were not characterised by, for example, dense populations, let alone populations pursuing economic activities within the cities as we see in later medieval cities. Rather they were foci for royal, ecclesiastical, and aristocratic presence. How general was this? There are striking parallels between, for example, these two British cities and the great Roman city of Cologne on the River Rhine (Germany).

Cologne

Like York, Cologne was a military base, and, also like York, there was founded there a *colonia* for military veterans which developed into a major city. Like Winchester in the late Roman period, Cologne was clearly flourishing: additions were being made to the walls, and the great Christian church of St Gereo, which still largely survives and has been lovingly restored after war damage, was being built. Yet archaeological excavation on sites cleared of buildings by bombing and shelling in the later stages of the Second World War has shown that, as at Winchester and York, the city ceased to have real urban life between the fifth century and the ninth, for there are clear indications of agricultural production taking place within the city walls. But, as did Winchester and York, the city remained a centre of importance for the Church and the kings of the Franks. It was a centre for Sigibert, king of the Ripuarian Franks, whom Gregory of Tours describes as leaving the city to walk in the forest on the other side of the River Rhine, where he was murdered by assassins sent by his son (Gregory, *Hist. Franks*, II.40). We know too that in Cologne there was buried Plectrude, wife of the first Carolingian king, Pippin III (751–68). The archaeological evidence confirms Cologne's importance as a royal, ecclesiastical, and aristocratic centre, for the excavations on the site of Cologne Cathedral showed a sequence of earlier churches reaching back to a Merovingian complex of buildings in which were found two graves so richly furnished that they are assumed to have been the graves of nobles or royalty. Still more strikingly in comparison with York, excavations of the headquarters building showed that it too had probably been used as a royal palace, in its case by the kings of the Franks.

Trier

Nor is Cologne the only city where this pattern of interruption of urban life accompanied by these very special forms of continuity is perceptible. We might argue that such a pattern must explain why at the Roman imperial city of Trier on the River Mosel (Germany) so little of the actual Roman layout survived into the Middle Ages, whereas massive buildings like the cathedral and the great hall or basilica which had been the emperor's meeting-hall survived and can be seen today (Fig. 31 below). The most likely explanation for these survivals may well be that barbarian rulers had simply taken over the Roman centre of rule and the ecclesiastical buildings in the city, while other aspects of Roman urban life faded away.

Canterbury

Equally striking is the case of Canterbury (Kent), a Roman city where archaeological evidence has shown no real sign of urban life continuing after the end of Roman Britain. But it has shown that the Roman amphitheatre, which could have been used for gatherings and general assemblies, continued as a focus of some sort. Moreover, Bede tells us in his *Ecclesiastical History of the English People* that the Roman structure of the cathedral had survived into the early seventh century, albeit ruined by that time so that the Christian missionary Augustine had to restore it; and more significantly still he describes the city as the 'metropolis' of the English kingdom of Kent. As with York, Winchester, and Cologne, something important was happening there even if urban life had effectively ceased.

Functions of cities and towns

We obviously need to explore more widely, but the cities we have looked at suggest strongly that, while urban life of Roman type failed to survive and there was no real continuity of that sort between Roman cities and what came after, there was a very important sort of continuity which concerned the continuing status of Roman cities. Barbarians clearly did not shun cities, as old textbooks used to maintain, and there are at least suggestions in the material discussed above that the process by which political power was transferred from Roman authorities to barbarian rulers may have been focused on the cities, where the barbarians were already ensconced as garrisons to protect them.

Urban archaeology is, of course, always adding to the data at our disposal, and there is now a certain amount of evidence pointing to craft-workshops functioning in the old Roman cities of Western Europe. It may of course be that this craft production was doing no more than supplying the kings, churchmen, and aristocrats who lived in the cities or visited them periodically, but it is also possible that it was producing for export or sale out of the cities, which would thus have been real centres of economic productivity. Such a picture would be quite different from that given by the excavations at Winchester, York, and Cologne, but it is possible that further excavation will confirm it. If so, it raises a further question about the nature of continuity between Roman cities and the form in which they may have existed in the post-Roman period.

To understand this, we need to think for a moment about the buildings which dominated a Roman city. These can still be seen in many ruins of such cities around Europe, but the most spectacular remains are those of the forum in Rome itself (Fig. 21).

Figure 21 The forum at Rome. A series of temples and other public structures, such as the imperial rostra in the centre of the photograph, stretch away towards the Triumphal Arch of the Emperor Titus, visible in the distance. Beyond that the walls of the Coliseum can be clearly seen, with a glimpse of the New Basilica of Constantine just to the left of them.

Here we can see the classic monumental core of a Roman city, consisting of the great public square, the forum, with regularly laid-out buildings round it, and containing a series of temples, public buildings, and triumphal archways for processions involving the emperor. Also in the core were Roman baths, the great bathing complexes that we can see, for example, in the two enormous sets of baths surviving at the Roman city of Trier. Then, around this monumental core, there were the luxuriously laid-out residences of the urban elite with their courtyards and splashing water-features called in Latin *impluvia*. There is little sign that the Roman city lived by specifically urban activities, such as commerce or industry carried on within it. To be sure, it had craftsmen and artisans, but their role may have been to provide for the wealthier residents who lived in the luxury residences. If we follow this argument, the city was a 'consumption city', or a parasite-city, the principal inhabitants of which drew their income from rural estates. They lived in the town or city for social reasons, because it offered the lifestyle and the possibilities for public life which they desired. They used their income from the land to be consumers in the town or city, to buy the wares of the craftsmen and artisans, for example, but they did not produce wealth in the city, which did not live off its own, but was simply a consumption centre. By contrast, we might think of the towns of the end of our period and later in the Middle Ages. Whereas the Roman city was dominated by the forum with its temples and triumphal arches, the later medieval town was dominated by market-halls, guild-halls where the merchant and craft guilds had their headquarters, and town-halls where the merchants who dominated such towns ran their affairs. The names of streets reflected the essentially industrial and commercial activities of these towns – Cheapside in London meaning the street of the market, or Coppergate in York meaning the street of the coopers or barrel-makers. The later medieval town lived off its commercial and industrial activities. It was only secondarily a residential and social centre as the Roman city had been.

It is possible, of course, to attack this interpretation, arguing that not all Roman cities were as monumental and grand as imperial centres like Rome and Trier, and that there were smaller Roman urban centres where industry and commerce were more prominent activities in the urban economy, apparently producing goods for sale outside the town rather than just providing them for the urban elite. Roman cities, in other words, were far from being all 'consumption' cities, although the evidence of great political centres like Rome may have misled us into thinking that they were. If that is the case, then the discovery of evidence for craft-production in them after the end of the Roman Empire in the west may point to continuity with their Roman existence rather than discontinuity.

Growth of cities and towns

Whatever you may decide about that issue, archaeological and documentary evidence shows convincingly that there was considerable growth in the number and size of cities and towns at some point towards the end of our period. Because of his influence on historical and archaeological thinking, it is worth going back to Pirenne's treatment of this. His answer to the question of why it occurred is clear enough from the title of his book, *Medieval Cities: Their Origins and the Revival of Trade* (1925). For him, cities grew naturally out of a revival in commerce. Trade was the cause of urban growth, and this was why the cities of the high Middle Ages and after were dominated by commercial and industrial activities.

At first glance, Pirenne's view seems to be supported by the distribution of the places where by the end of our period former Roman cities had grown or quite new towns had emerged, for this growth is focused above all on the great river-systems of Western Europe. Some of the earliest revivals or creations of urban centres that we can see from the latter part of our period are places like Ghent, Ypres, Lille, Douai, Arras, and Tournai, which lie in the areas of Frisia, Flanders, and the lower Rhineland, extremely well placed for access to rivers like the Rhine, Meuse, and Scheldt, which in turn gave access to the seaways of the northern seas; or Italian cities like Genoa, Bari, Taranto, Naples, and Amalfi, with their excellent access to seaways in the Mediterranean Sea, or Venice with its access not only to the Adriatic Sea but to over-land routes leading across the Alps and north-eastwards into Central Europe.

Pirenne could nevertheless see two serious problems for his view that trade led naturally to urban growth. The first was how to account for where the urban class which populated the revived and newly founded towns came from. For Pirenne regarded Western European society in our period as a highly rigid society, in which peasants were tied to the land on the great estates, and members of higher levels of the social scale were in their turn locked into relations of loyalty or vassalage to their lords. In such a society, so it seemed to him, the sort of social mobility which would have been required to fuel the spontaneous growth of towns in response to commercial growth was difficult to envisage. In addition, Pirenne knew that the Church was opposed to commercial activity since it prohibited usury and promoted the concept of a 'fair price' rather than a profit-making tariff. Yet, somehow, a specifically urban class with primarily mercantile functions emerged. How was this possible?

Pirenne's answer was that the urban class came from levels of Western European society so low down the scale that they were not locked into the rigid structures of society which were so antipathetic to social mobility. The evidence he cited for this was a *Life* of a late eleventh-century hermit called Godric, who lived in a hermitage at Finchale on the River Wear just below the city of Durham, and who was venerated as a saint by the Durham monks. One of those monks, Reginald of Durham, was the author of his *Life*, and in it he described Godric's career before he became a hermit. It seems that he had been born in Lincolnshire of such poor peasant stock that, far from being tied to any land on a great estate, he had no land at all, and so had to make his living as a beachcomber, gathering objects washed up on the shore and selling them. So successful was he in this activity that he graduated to become a pedlar, and from there he joined a band of merchants travelling from town to town, from fair to fair. Eventually he made enough money to enable him and his associates to invest in load-ing a ship coasting the North Sea. But, Reginald tells us, as his wealth increased, so he remembered the Bible's teaching that it is harder for a rich man to enter the Kingdom of Heaven than for a camel to pass through the eye of a needle, and he gave up all his wealth and became a hermit at Finchale. Setting aside this religiously motivated renunciation of commerce, Pirenne argued that his career as a rising, socially mobile merchant was in fact typical of how the lowest classes of society rose to form the new mercantile and industrial class of the towns, and that, because of Godric's change to a religious life and his veneration as a saint, we happen to have this insight into his life because Reginald of Durham wrote about him.

Even if we accept Pirenne's reasoning, however, this immediately leads us on to the second problem for his view of the relationship between commerce and urban growth. If we accept his interpretation of the origins of merchants like Godric before he became a hermit, why should this new merchant-class have lived in towns at all? Godric after all appears in Reginald's *Life* not as based in a town, but rather as moving from market to market, from fair to fair. Why should the new merchants that Pirenne envisaged not continue to have done this rather than settling in towns and cities? Pirenne proposed three explanations. First, that towns grew up spontaneously and organically around fairs and markets. Whereas at first these may have involved only temporary booths for merchants arriving to sell their wares, it became more convenient, he thought, for these to be made permanent, and so towns were formed. This is possible, of course, and – as

Pirenne argued – of the twenty-nine new markets created by the Ottonian rulers of Germany in the tenth century, many became flourishing high medieval towns, such as Wurzburg, Magdeburg, Bremen, Erfurt, and Dortmund. But equally there were many new or newly flourishing towns which did not develop around existing fairs and markets, such as Worms, Speyer, and Mainz.

Secondly, that new or newly flourishing towns developed around places which our written sources call *portus* (the Latin plural is the same as the singular, *portus*), and which appear to have been warehousing and transfer-points along the great rivers. As with fairs and markets, it simply became more convenient, he argued, for permanent towns to be established in place of intermittently used concentrations of warehouses. Now, as with fairs and markets, some towns do seem to have begun as *portus*, especially in Flanders, with towns such as Dinant, Huy, Valenciennes, Cambrai, Bruges, Ghent, and Ypres, and it is true that the Dutch word for town is *poort*, a linguistic use suggesting a link with Latin *portus*, and thus tending to strengthen the argument that urban origins lay in warehousing *portus*. But here too there is very far from being a universal link, and the linguistic point is far from being compelling, given how often the meaning of words changes in the course of their development.

Thirdly, that merchants clustered around fortified points for their own protection, and that these fortified points consequently formed the nuclei of urban growth. Pirenne here cited written sources describing the existence of an 'enclosure of the merchants' attached to the walls of Verdun in Flanders (France) in the tenth century, and suggested that the merchants had created such an 'enclosure' so that they could benefit from the protection of the walls in times of danger. Such a relationship between fortifications and urban development during and after the end of our period is indeed frequently found, and cities like Lincoln and Durham demonstrate it clearly enough. But it is not common to all urban centres, nor is it clear whether the existence of fortications was the cause of urban growth of a commercial and industrial type, or whether some other force was at work.

New towns

It seemed, then, that a radically different explanation of the revival of urban life in the latter part of our period was needed, and this emerged in a remarkable book by Maurice Beresford (1967). This was concerned with late medieval towns, and it begins with a gripping account of the foundation of the new town of Berwick-on-Tweed on the Scottish border by King Edward I at the end of the thirteenth century, but its general thesis is of considerable relevance to our period. That thesis was that the overwhelming majority of towns – Beresford was concerned with English and Gascon towns but his conclusions had implications for Western Europe at large – were deliberate foundations, made 'top-down' by kings, lords, or churchmen, whose aims in founding them were to benefit from ready access to the commodities available from the merchants who lived in them, but above all to reap the proceeds of tolls and dues levied on the

Figure 22 Aerial view of Burford (Oxfordshire).
Source: © English Heritage (NMR) Wingham Collection.

commercial activities taking place in them. Such new foundations were documented in writing, as in the case of Berwick-on-Tweed, but Beresford's evidence for *de novo*, top-down foundation of the majority of towns came not from documentary evidence but from topographical evidence.

His method was to study the layout of towns, in relation to archaeological evidence, to show that they could only have come into existence through a process of systematic planning, which seemed most likely to have been undertaken by a lord founding a new town. So he was impressed by the grid-like layout of towns such as Bury St Edmunds, and he was impressed also by the layout of a town like Burford in the Cotswolds (Fig. 22).

There, the parish-church stands awkwardly away from the town itself, suggesting that it was older than the town, which had been founded as a block at some point in time without reference to it. As for the town itself, the wide, straight central street seemed clearly to have been laid out as a market-place, and the regular, rectangular tenements, each consisting of a house or shop with a plot of land behind it, seemed equally clearly to have been laid out deliberately and as part of a coordinated process of town-planning. Towns displaying such types of feature were, Beresford maintained, typical and not exceptional, so that the basic process of town foundation and development in the Middle Ages was, in his view, top-down planning directed by the social and political elite.

If we were to adopt the view that town-growth was directed from above, the problems which Pirenne faced would evaporate. To be sure, flourishing commerce would be a precondition of urban growth or towns based on it could hardly have succeeded. But there would be no problem in explaining how the new urban class broke free from the constraints of a rigid social structure, if their move into urban life was stimulated by the strategy of the very elite which controlled that structure.

But does evidence for such top-down planning of towns exist for our period? Archaeological evidence, which has only become available since Pirenne's time, can be seen as suggesting that it does, and most clearly in the case of two types of town: first the eighth-century towns often called by modern scholars *emporia*, and, secondly, towns appearing from the late ninth century onwards, towns which are known to specialists in English history as *burhs*.

Emporia

Archaeological evidence, sometimes in combination with much more limited written evidence, has permitted the identification of a series of trading towns around the coasts of the North Sea and the Baltic Sea and dating from roughly 750 to 850. Some of these were urban settlements which had not apparently existed at all at earlier periods, for example Dorestad in the delta of the River Rhine, Haithabu (or Hedeby) on the south-eastern coast of the Danish peninsula, and Hamwih near to the later medieval and modern site of Southampton. Some were in effect annexes to existing towns or cities, usually Roman cities, as in the case of London, where archaeology has shown that from the eighth to the tenth centuries commercial and specifically urban activity was taking place not in the City of London, which was the fortified Roman area, but rather to the west of it along the modern Strand and in the area of what is now Aldwych, although the name is probably a very ancient one, meaning 'old trading centre'. Writers such as Bede occasionally use the word *emporia* (singular *emporium*) of such urban commercial centres, and modern scholars have generalised its use to this whole class of newly emerged trading centres of the eighth and ninth centuries.

The proof that these *emporia* were deliberate top-down foundations can be derived, first, from the evidence of their layouts, just as for Burford and the towns studied by Beresford. One of the clearest cases is that of Hamwih, which was at the height of its prosperity in the eighth century and had disappeared to be replaced by Southampton by the mid-tenth century. Nineteenth-century quarrying and modern excavation has brought to light streets of the appropriate date, some running parallel to and some at right-angles to the River Itchen, suggesting that the *emporium* had a layout in the form of a rectilinear grid (Fig. 23) and was consequently a town laid out in a planned way like Beresford's new towns of the later Middle Ages.

Such planned layouts are not demonstrable for all the *emporia*, but the archaeological excavations of Haithabu, which was founded in 808 (although there are indications

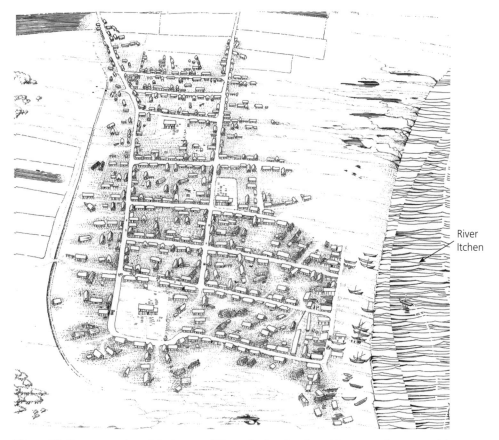
River Itchen

Figure 23 Reconstruction of the layout of Hamwih showing the grid pattern of streets at right angles to the River Itchen.
Source: Courtesy of John Hodgson.

that the first building activity dates from 737) and abandoned in 1050, are strongly suggestive (in the grid-like lines of postholes marking buildings) of a similarly planned layout (Map 13).

At Dorestad (Netherlands), in the delta of the River Rhine, it is not so clear that the town itself had a planned layout, but excavation has recovered an impressive series of jetties, progressively extended into the water for the use of ships, which strongly suggests that there was a planning authority behind their development.

Other types of evidence can be adduced to suggest that these *emporia* were not only planned but actually under lordly, generally royal, control. This evidence consists, first, of written sources showing the presence in the *emporia* of royal officials who, it can be conjectured, were responsible for their management. Thus the laws of the seventh-century kings of Kent in England, Hlothhere and Eadric, refer to an official called a port-reeve in a place called *Lundenwic*, which is assumed to be the trading centre of London in the area of the modern street, The Strand. A document issued by the

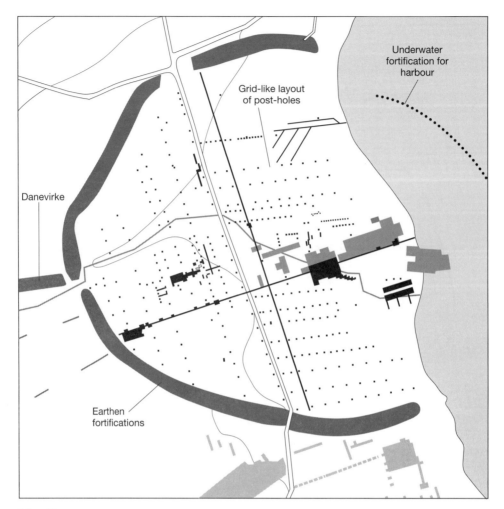

Map 13 Archaeological remains at Haithabu (Hedeby). Notice the fortifications, linked to the linear fortification called the Danevirke running from the left; and notice too the evidence for underwater fortifications protecting the harbour on the right of the map. Within the land-fortifications the arrangement of the roadway and the lines of post-holes, marking where timber structures stood, suggest a rectangular layout. This would be consistent with the town having been deliberately planned as a new creation.
Source: Adapted from Elsner, H., *Wikinger Museum Haithabu: Schaufenster einer frühen Stadt* (Literaturhaus Schleswig-Holstein, 1989).

Carolingian ruler, Louis the Pious (814–40), known as the 'Instructions to the Merchants', refers to the presence at Dorestad of the main customs office of the Carolingian kings, and we know from this and other documents that there were royal 'officers' and 'procurators of the kingdom' there. We do not, of course, have such evidence for the *emporia* in the lands around the Baltic Sea, for the societies in which they were based were not literate in this period and so they produced no written records.

Secondly, it has been argued that the proximity of *emporia* to known royal centres, cities and palaces, is evidence for the dependence of *emporia* on royal direction. The *emporium* of Birka (Sweden), for example, is very close to the royal centre of Uppsala, where the first Christian king of Sweden and his father were buried in great mounds. The *emporium* of Ipswich (Suffolk), which is well known archaeologically, is relatively close to the place called Rendlesham, which Bede in his *Ecclesiastical History of the English People* identifies as the royal centre of the English kings of the East Angles. Dorestad is likewise relatively close to the royal centre of Nijmegen, which was (according to his biographer Einhard) one of Charlemagne's favourite palaces.

The most suggestive case, however, is Hamwih. This *emporium* was twenty-two miles from Winchester by a direct route following the old Roman roads, and the archaeological and written evidence from both urban settlements suggested that they had a differentiation of functions. Winchester was characterised by the presence of the king and the bishop and by those aristocratic or royal graves which we noted earlier in this chapter. But, before the late ninth century, it had no regular layout of streets, or evidence for long-distance trade, industrial activity, or dense population. These aspects, however, were characteristic of Hamwih, which was not visited or lived in by kings, bishops, or nobles. This apparent difference of function led Biddle to suggest that Hamwih was the specialist *emporium* for the royal and ecclesiastical centre of Winchester. If that were the case, it would seem entirely plausible that Hamwih should have been founded by the king to fulfil that role.

Modern interpretations of *emporia*, however, have taken a further step in proposing that such urban settlements were not just founded by kings, but that they played a key role in the maintenance of royal power. According to this, a very important foundation of authority in early medieval society was the giving of gifts, and the reciprocal obligations which such giving created. This is derived from the work of the mid-twentieth-century French anthropologist, Marcel Mauss, whose famous – and very stimulating – book *The Gift* (2002) used evidence derived from practices he studied in British Columbia and Papua New Guinea to create this picture of the importance of gift-giving. Noting the prevalence of gift-giving by kings in early medieval texts such as the Old English epic poem, *Beowulf*, you can argue that the same applied in the case of early medieval kings. Gift-giving would then have been crucial to their authority, and therefore they needed a monopolistic supply of high-status, luxury goods which they could use as gifts to their principal subjects, thus creating bonds of obligation in them which could be repaid by obedience to the king. In this interpretation, the role of *emporia* was to act as monopolistic entrepôts for such high-status objects destined to function as gifts. Kings founded the *emporia* close to their own royal centres, controlled them, and used them in this crucial aspect of the maintenance of their authority.

It is an exciting idea which should prompt you to consider the nature of commerce in early medieval society, but if you wish to interpret *emporia* in this way there are objections you will have to be prepared to counter. First, the geographical relationship between *emporia* and royal centres is by no means always close enough for us to assume the sort of relationship postulated by this interpretation. Twenty-two miles, in the case of Hamwih and Winchester, is not an insignificant distance, and the distance between Dorestad and Nijmegen is even greater. Secondly, archaeological finds from the *emporia* suggest that trade in luxury goods was far from being their exclusive function. At Dorestad, for example, there have been found considerable quantities of leather goods, as well as evidence of working in antler and bone, which do not look like luxury produce. Thirdly, the prevalence of minting of coins in *emporia*, principally around the Christian lands of the North Sea, suggests that these *emporia* at least were involved in monetary transactions of a commercial type rather than engaged in monopolistic supply of luxury goods to the kings. The mint at Dorestad, for example, was one of the most active in the Carolingian realms, and Dorestad coins are found very frequently. Fourthly, finds made in recent years by amateur users of metal detectors have shown, for England at least, that *emporia* were far from having a monopoly of luxury goods. These finds have demonstrated the presence of numerous so-called 'productive' sites, where luxury objects occur, in the hinterlands of the *emporia*, suggesting that the latter were as much engaged in trade with their hinterlands as in monopolistic supply to the king of objects for gifts. Moreover, a combination of metal-detecting and archaeological investigation has suggested that there are far more sites that could be termed *emporia* than was previously thought, so that the theory that all *emporia* were royal foundations under royal control seems less plausible.

In the light of these objections, you may want to develop a quite different interpretation, that is that the *emporia* were created by merchants working independently of political authority, and that their connection with kings was the result of the latter seeking to dominate them in order to profit from toll-payments on goods being moved in or out of the *emporia* as well as from other profits associated with royal minting of coins. It is very striking in this connection that archaeological evidence suggests that Dorestad originated in the seventh century, when the Rhine delta, where it lies, was a sort of no-man's-land between what was then the kingdom of Frisia and the kingdom of the Franks. This may have been, we could argue, an ideal situation for merchants to develop a trading town free from royal control. But in the early eighth century, the Franks under Pippin III conquered Frisia, and so Dorestad became part of the kingdom of the Franks, the kings of which were then able to exploit and control it, as our documentary sources suggest that they did.

It is also striking that our very best piece of written evidence for royal foundation of an *emporium* is an annal in the *Royal Frankish Annals* for the year 808. According to this, King Godefrid of the Danes:

> destroyed the trading place on the sea-coast, which was called Reric in Danish, and conferred great benefit on his kingdom through the payment of tolls. He transported the merchants from there, had his fleet set sail and arrived with his entire army at the port called Schleswig.

Since modern Schleswig is very close to Haithabu, and Reric has been identified with Groß Strömkendorf, which was a Slav town on the shores of the Baltic Sea, this annal has been interpreted as meaning that King Godefrid founded Haithabu by forcibly relocating the trading centre of Reric which was in the hands of his Slav enemies (although the annal suggests that it was already paying him tolls) into his own kingdom. This would thus be clear evidence of a king's role in the foundation of an *emporium*. The annal is not, however, very clear, and in any case you could argue that this was just an extreme example of a king profiting from an existing *emporium*. The annal does not say that Godefrid or any other king had founded Reric. It may well have been created originally by merchants independently of kings, but Godefrid had apparently begun to levy tolls on it, presumably because he had subjugated the Slav lands in which it lay, and his removal of it to Haithabu (if that is indeed what the annal describes) would have facilitated his exploitation of an existing community of merchants in a situation which was easier to dominate.

Still stronger evidence for the origin of *emporia* independent of kings would be provided by the case of Venice, if we were to regard that southern trading centre as as much an *emporium* as the North Sea and Baltic centres which have more usually been regarded as such. We first have evidence for its development as a trading centre in the second half of the eighth century, when northern Italy was being contested between the kingdom of the Lombards, which had only recently gained formal control of the area at the head of the Adriatic Sea where Venice lay, and the kingdom of the Franks which conquered and absorbed the kingdom of the Lombards under Charlemagne in the 770s. Venice thus developed as a trading centre in just the same circumstances of political instability that saw the emergence of Dorestad in the north. Its position in the marshy ground noted for lagoons may have further protected it from royal intervention, at any rate until it was well established as a trading centre. Then rulers did attempt to control it, as the Franks did in the early ninth century, but with little success – so that Venice emerged as one of the great independent city-states of Italy.

If you decide to reject the intepretation of *emporia* as royal creations, you are still left with Pirenne's problem of where the merchants and craftsmen to populate them came from. In the case of Venice, however, it can be argued that it was originally created at the time of the end of the Roman Empire in the west by refugees, perhaps from the nearby Roman city of Aquileia, who were seeking refuge in the marshes and lagoons of the region in which Venice was founded. If that is so, and it is little more than a conjecture, you might argue (as Pirenne also did) that urban populations were in general refugees, people who fell outside the framework of post-Roman society as Godric of Finchale did. But your assessment of all this will also depend on what view you have taken of the structure of rural society (above, Chapter 8). If you follow Pirenne and his successors in emphasising the dominance of great estates with dependent workers, then the problem is there to be solved. But if, rather, you lean towards the dominance of free peasants, then the problem no longer exists and you are free to argue that towns developed in the context of a population that was to a large extent free, the members of which were well able to set themselves up as merchants or urban craftsmen without having to break free of royal or lordly control. If this is what happened, then you would have to interpret planned layouts of streets as the creations of independent, self-governing, urban communities rather than of kings and lords, and you will need to consider whether you find that convincing, there being no evidence for it.

The development of *burhs*

The northern sites which scholars have called *emporia*, however, came to an end at some point between the later ninth century (in the case of Dorestad, for example) and the mid-eleventh (in the case of Haithabu). The evidence for a creative royal or lordly role in the phase of town-development which succeeded their demise from the late ninth century onwards is much stronger. As with the earlier period, some of the most important advances have been made by urban archaeologists in England. The Biddles' excavations at Winchester, which were so productive for the post-Roman centuries, were even more revealing for the development of that city from the late ninth century onwards. Map 14 shows its layout in that period based on the evidence of their excavations.

The Roman walls still served as the fortifications of the city, while the area given over to the royal palace and the royally founded churches of the Old Minster, the New Minster, and the Nunnaminster emphasises how royal a city this was. But the really striking thing is the regular, rectilinear street-plan, which looks for all the world like a Roman layout. The excavations, however, showed that it was not in fact Roman, since it sat over the layers of soil showing how agricultural activity had obliterated the Roman streets in the post-Roman period. Instead, the excavations established, the street-pattern belonged to the late ninth century, leading Martin Biddle to postulate – entirely plausibly – that it was the work of Alfred the Great, king of Wessex (871–99).

This was especially striking because Winchester was one of the *burhs* (the Old English word means fortified place) listed in a West Saxon document of the late ninth or early tenth centuries known as the Burghal Hidage. This is simply a list of *burhs* in the kingdom of Wessex. Outside the kingdom of Wessex, we know from the *Anglo-Saxon Chronicle* that Alfred's successors, especially his son King Edward the Elder, established such *burhs* as they extended the lands they were reconquering from the Danes northwards into what had formerly been the kingdom of Mercia. The extent to which the creation and organisation of these *burhs* was undertaken 'top-down' by the king was underlined by two features of the Burghal Hidage. First, in it the *burhs* are arranged in a clockwise order around the kingdom of Wessex suggestive of a means of facilitating tours of inspection of them by royal officials. Secondly, the Burghal Hidage contains figures showing the number of land-units (hides) assigned to each *burh*. Presumably this means that the service of so many men would have been levied from these hides for the maintenance and manning of the fortifications of each *burh*. The striking thing is that, where the fortifications survive so that it is possible to measure their length, and these measurements are compared with the number of hides assigned to the same *burhs* in the Burghal Hidage, it becomes clear that there was a standard ratio of length of wall to number of hides, and this suggests that some centrally organised system was in place for their maintenance and manning.

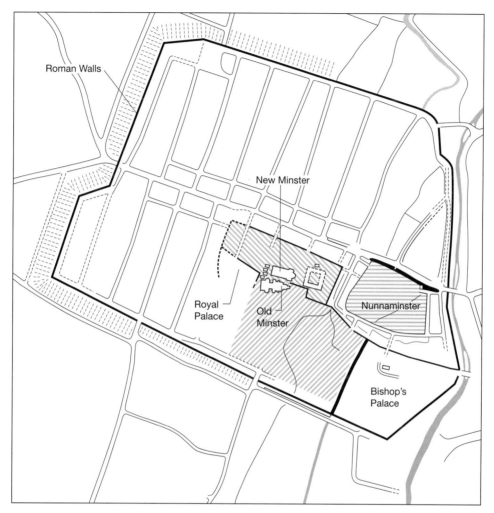

Map 14 Winchester in the period 993 to 1066. Notice how the streets, which seem on archaeological grounds to date from the late ninth century, are arranged at right-angles to the Roman walls, which were evidently in use as defences. The streets form a rectangular pattern, with a central street running from left to right between the old Roman gates. The bottom right-hand area of the map shows the quarter of the city which was given over to royally founded monasteries and to the royal palace. The influence of the king on the development of this city is clear.
Source: Adapted from Parsons, D. (ed.), 'Felix Urbs Wintonia: Winchester in the Age of Monastic Reform', in *Tenth-Century Studies: Essays in Commemoration of the Millennium Council of Winchester and Regularis Concordia* (Phillimore & Co, 1975), courtesy of Professor Martin Biddle.

It used to be assumed that *burhs* were mostly just empty fortifications, places of refuge to which the surrounding population could flee when there was a threat of Viking attack. The fortifications could be either former Roman city-walls, like those at Winchester, or former Iron Age forts of a much earlier period pressed back into service, or newly constructed earthen banks such as can still be seen at Wallingford on the River Thames

Figure 24 Aerial view of Wallingford, Oxfordshire. Notice the line of the surviving earthen ramparts of the *burh* visible in the top-left corner of the town's plan and running left-to-right across the top of the photograph, where they are interrupted by the earthworks of the castle, which is a Norman structure and so of the late eleventh century. Urban development does not, even today, occupy the whole of the area within the *burh*'s fortifications, but what is striking is that the street-plan seems to have just the sort of regular, rectangular appearance that we have seen at Burford, with just the same sort of wide market-street at the centre. This could, of course, be a later piece of planning as it presumably was at Burford. But the fact that the earthworks of the Norman castle seem to break into it strongly suggests that it is in fact pre-eleventh-century, and the layout may well have been an aspect of the original establishment of the *burh* by the West Saxon kings.
Source: © English Heritage NMR.

near Oxford. The Biddles' excavations at Winchester, however, suggested strongly that they were not just fortifications, but also planned towns, intended to be self-sustaining and to extend and consolidate royal control and (through tolls and other dues) royal income. Nowhere except at Winchester is this so clearly demonstrable from archaeological evidence. But Fig. 24 shows that in the case of a much less thoroughly excavated *burh* such as Wallingford, there is nevertheless a strong presumption that it was established as a planned town.

We have been focusing on England, but there is clear evidence that Continental rulers, kings, counts, and bishops, were similarly undertaking town-foundation in the latter part of our period. The Ottonian rulers of Germany are recorded as having pursued a policy parallel to that of the *burh*-building of the kings of Wessex, and the first of them, Henry I the Fowler (919–36), a contemporary of King Edward the Elder, is especially noted for this. The tenth-century chronicler Widukind of Corvey wrote of how this ruler chose one man of nine from the free peasants subject to military service in his kingdom, and ordered them to move to fortified places and to construct buildings there. He goes on:

> The king also commanded all courts and meetings and celebrations to be held in these places, that during a time of peace the inhabitants might accustom themselves to meeting together in them, as he wished them to do in time of invasion.
>
> (Kowaleski, 2006, pp. 22–3)

The fortified places mentioned in this passage were evidently intended as places of refuge for the population at large, but it seems clear that they were also being regarded as towns constructed by the king's orders and manned by the king's orders.

Earlier on, it appears that Charlemagne's grandson, King Charles the Bald (840–77), constructed the Frankish equivalent of *burhs*, notably one at a place called Pont l'Arche on the River Seine downstream from Paris. Like certain of the West Saxon kings' *burhs*, notably the one at Nottingham, this appears to have been a double fortification, covering both sides of the river and so impeding Viking ships from passing up it. It is not clear that Pont l'Arche was a planned town rather than a fortification, but in the light of the evidence from England it does not seem an unreasonable supposition.

If you were to accept the thesis that kingship and lordship played the dominant role in urban development in our period, the problems which confronted Pirenne would evaporate. Thus you could plausibly argue that the urban class developed because the kings and lords encouraged it to do so (or in Henry the Fowler's case ordered it to do so); and that merchants chose to live in towns because of the incentives offered by kings and lords or by their coercive strategies. In this way, you could regard urban life not as something spontaneous and organic, emerging from the base of the social spectrum, as Pirenne wished to see it, but rather as one of the most striking demonstrations of the hierarchical and authoritarian character of Western European society.

The fact that that character was hard to maintain in the case of towns may provide the clue to why Pirenne and his generation before the coming of urban archaeology could not perceive the mechanisms we have been examining. From the middle of the eleventh century, and especially in the twelfth, the urban class began to assert independence from kings and lords. In 1057, the population of Milan (Italy) set itself up as an independent commune, and in 1080 the populace established independent consuls at Lucca (Italy). The same process of setting towns up as independent communes was also evident in Flanders, with the formation in 1077 of the commune of Cambrai (France), and it was found also in England in the case of London. It was often bitterly opposed by the rulers, and often repressed, especially in England. But its partial success, and more complete success in Italy where the cities became increasingly independent, meant that myths of urban origins were created which certainly did not embody accounts of foundation by kings and lords, and it is this, we may think, which for so long masked the possibility we have been exploring here.

The case, however, is not impregnable, and you might want to argue quite differently. As with the *emporia* of the eighth century and onwards, you may think that the role of kings was one of capitalising on urban growth by using places which had developed spontaneously as towns as the basis of fortified places. And you may think that sites like Winchester should be regarded as atypical since they were so closely associated with the kings as their principal places of residence. As with the *emporia*, you may think that town-planning was not the monopoly of kings and lords and may equally well have been undertaken by self-governing urban communities, such as later emerged as communes. The history of the Italian towns is highly instructive here, for they largely developed outside the reach of royal or lordly power, and would repay close attention as to how far they demonstrate the same features as we have been identifying in towns like the English *burhs*.

So we are left with a series of issues which demand your attention, and which are fundamental to understanding the development of urban life. First, what was the contribution of Roman city-life to later developments, and how different were Roman cities in their function from what came after them? Secondly, was the revival of urban life from the eighth century a tool in the hands of ambitious kings, or was it a spontaneous development from below, which kings and lords sought (sometimes unsuccessfully, as in the case of the Italian communes) to control and exploit? Thirdly, did the developing monarchies of the late ninth century onwards stimulate town-foundation as part of their military strategy of fortification and control, or were their objectives purely military, and did they perceive what were in fact spontaneously developing towns as no more than suitable places of refuge? There is much exploration to be done, and much to understand, but the importance of the issues is not in doubt.

Research and study

Broad research questions

How different from Roman cities were the towns and cities that developed in the barbarian kingdoms?

What was the role of trade in the development of towns and cities?

What was the relationship between towns and cities on the one hand, and kings and secular and ecclesiastical lords on the other?

Books and papers to begin with

There is no free-standing survey of the history of towns and cities in Western Europe in our period. The nearest to it is provided by Nicholas (1997, part I). Verhulst (1999) is very helpful for north-west Europe, as are Clarke and Ambrosiani (1991) for the same area, and also Scandinavia, in the tenth and eleventh centuries. A very helpful collection of papers is Hodges and Hobley (1988). There is a survey of recent research across Western Europe and beyond in Wickham (2005, ch. 10). For research across England, very useful and accessible is Biddle (1976b) and, for more recent work across Britain, Ottaway (1992, chs 4–5) and Palliser (2000, part II, especially chs 3, 4, 7, 10–11). For Pirenne's ideas, which have been so influential, it really is worth going back to his lucid work (1925), although you need to read it alongside the criticism of Verhulst (1985).

Pursuing more specific aspects

Towns and cities as parasites

How much were towns and cities genuine centres of production, rather than residential, social, political, and religious centres drawing their income from the land or from taxes and tributes?

For Roman cities in the time of the later Roman Empire, the classic account is Jones (1964, ch. 19). The idea of 'consumer cities' was taken from the work of the German sociologist Max Weber, and applied to Roman cities by Finley (1992, ch. 5), whose work is very attractive and illuminating reading. His conclusions are largely defended in a very lucid paper by Whittaker (1990), who questions, however, the relevance of distinguishing between city and country, and defended also by Parkins (1997), who modifies them somewhat by giving more importance to production of goods in and for the city. Whittaker also stresses the different character of Roman 'small towns' or *vici*, which you can pursue for Roman Britain in Rodwell and Rowley (1975). The question of whether, in at least some parts of our period, post-Roman towns were also parasitical can be pursued with Henning (2007) and Loseby (1998), both of whom stress the productive functions of towns. This is also emphasised for early Scandinavian towns by Skre (2007).

Continuity between Roman towns and cities and later towns

How much continuity was there between Roman urban centres and post-Roman urban centres?

In addition to the work of Verhulst (1999), which stresses this aspect, useful is Ward-Perkins (1996). Rather more specialised, but very thought-provoking, is Brühl (1988). Much the best approach, however, is to focus on particular cities. Collins (1983, pp. 87–104) provides a very striking discussion of the Spanish city of Merida in the Visigothic period, and Verhulst (1999) offers a series of case-studies with plans. It is, however, easiest to consider English examples, especially the rich and exciting work of Biddle (1973b) on Winchester and Hall (1996), Ottaway (1993), and Tweddle, Moulden, and Logan (1999) on York. (Archaeology never stays still and current work being carried out by the York Archaeological Trust has led to the tree-ring (dendrochronological) dating of timbers from the base of the Multangular Tower to the second century, so this part of the fortifications may represent much earlier investment than used to be thought.) This last work contains a very interesting analysis of the evidence of the street-layout in the city, and also some general chapters, including one by the present author. The bulk of the book, however, is a catalogue of finds from the 'Anglian' period, that is, between the end of the Roman Empire in Britain and the Viking period beginning in the late ninth century. This catalogue is itself worth pondering, as to whether the sheer number of finds in existence undermines the idea that York was no more than a ceremonial and ecclesiastical centre in this period. For a technical, but stimulating, discussion of the interpretation of the fortress basilica, see Carver (1995). Brooks (1984, ch. 2) very interestingly discusses Canterbury with a useful map of the Roman and later remains in the city.

The significance of *emporia*

Were emporia created by kings to consolidate their control of trade for purposes of gift-exchange, or did they develop spontaneously to be exploited by kings for tolls and taxes?

The fullest statement of the view that *emporia* were top-down foundations, created for the purpose of obtaining prestige objects for gift-exchange, is Hodges (1982, ch. 3, 2000). A cogent attack on Hodges's position is made by Coupland (2003) in the light of the chronological development of Quentovic and Dorestad.

You really need to get to grips with the evidence for particular *emporia*. Hodges (1982, ch. 4) provides a very useful gazetteer giving access to archaeological evidence as it was in 1982, and this can be updated with the gazetteer in Hill and Cowie (2001, pp. 85–94). More specialised, but quite readable, works on individual *emporia* include: on London (Vince, 1990, Blackmore, 2002), on Hamwih (Addyman, 1973, Biddle, 1973a, Stoodley, 2002), on Dorestad (Verwers, 1988), on Ipswich (Wade, 1988, Scull, 2002); and – a place not always treated as an *emporium* – Venice (McCormick, 2007). Further studies of individual sites can be found in collections of papers edited by Hodges and Hobley (1988), Anderton (1999), Hill and Cowie (2001), Hårdt and Larsson (2002), and Prestell and Ulmschneider (2003). These works also present new interpretations of *emporia*, influenced by the results of metal-detecting and by recent archaeological investigations.

Planned towns from the late ninth century

Were towns the deliberate, planned creations of kings and lords?

It is easiest to pursue this for English towns, for which there has been archaeological and topographical research. The beginnings of this are very clear in an exciting and influential paper by Biddle and Hill (1971), setting out ideas further developed by Biddle (1976a, b). It is well worth the effort of grasping the results of his and his late wife Birthe's extremely significant excavations at Winchester (Biddle, 1973b, 1975). For a range of relevant southern English towns, including Wallingford, Wareham, London, and Southampton, there is a useful collection of papers edited by Haslam (1984), by whom there is also a useful short guide (Haslam, 1985).

The best way to appreciate the significance of the Burghal Hidage is to ponder the maps, chart showing the figures derived from the document, and informative notes in Hill (1981, pp. 85–6). There are more detailed studies in Hill and Rumble (1996).

For Continental towns, Verhulst (1999, chs 4–5) provides some case-studies, for example of Arras and Ghent, and some plans, but there is nothing as rich or as detailed as in the English material.

Towns and religious sites

Why were towns and markets sited by pagan cult-sites or Christian churches?

This question is sometimes tied up with that of the relationship between kings and towns, because religious sites were frequently royal in character. The evidence for pagan Scandinavia is very interestingly discussed by Skre (2007), who argues that the coincidence in site was owing to the protection which the cult-site and the royal presence there offered to merchants. This is in opposition to Hedeager (2001), arguing that it was directly the result of religious ideas. There is an interesting discussion of a market-site linked to a pagan cult-site at Tissø in Scandinavia (Jørgensen, 2003). In a Christian context in England, the relationship between churches and towns is explored by Blair (2005, ch. 5). For the Continent there is a thoughtful article by Theuws (2004b), who argues that religious symbolism and cultural interchange, for example between the Christian and pagan world, was an important function of *emporia*. If you want to pursue this, there are discussion-papers by Hodges (2004) and Moreland (2004), with a reply by Theuws (2004a), in the same journal. You need to think about whether you find the applications of anthropological ideas in these papers convincing.

Conclusion

You may think it a drawback that we have, in this part of the book, handled the economy of Western Europe separately from its political and social history in particular, and, within our discussions, we have dealt separately, and in separate chapters, with the development of agriculture, trade, and towns. Analysing topics out in this way is a helpful tool, because it makes it easier for us to marshal the evidence and to focus on the issues; but it does sometimes inhibit us from seeing the full range of inter-connections between the various aspects of life in the past. As you go forward with your research and study, you need to be more open to this than it has always been possible for us to be in these chapters. How far was the development of towns, for example, dependent on the development of agriculture, both to feed the urban populations and to provide surpluses for sale in urban markets? Was trade concerned only with foreign luxury goods or was it handling also home-grown, agricultural produce – and if so what was the connection between its growth and the progress of rural productivity and technology?

We have in these chapters touched on the question of how the economic foundation related to the political and social structure, but you need to push that question further. If you accept that towns were in large part created by the powerful, what role did they themselves play in the structures of power? At what stage, for example, did towns begin to emerge as capital cities? To what extent did towns grow up around centres of royal government, as perhaps at Aachen and at Winchester? Was the growth of trade just an aspect of the ways in which the powerful harnessed wealth? And, if so, can we see trade growing at the same pace as we can see mechanisms of power becoming more effective, suggesting a relationship between the two? Or are we wrong to adopt such 'top-down' approaches to economic development, and are we rather seeing a 'bottom-up' mechanism of economic growth, by which it was small traders, townsmen forming their own urban communities on their own initiative, and peasants organising themselves to increase their own wealth who were the real drivers of the economy? In that case, are we seeing the powerful seeking merely to draw the wealth so created to themselves, rather than creating it by their own actions? And how great was the role of the Church in economic development? Were monasteries hubs of economic growth? How much did towns owe to churches of all sorts functioning as nodes of urban growth? You need to be on the look-out for ways in which you can prove, or disprove, such connections and relationships. Here, as in other areas of this book, you may find it helpful to place your discussions in a wider chronological context, for which the range and clarity of N. J. G. Pounds's textbook on medieval economic history are very helpful (Pounds, 1994).

There are also chronological questions which we need to have in mind as we go forward. We have in our chapters been able to consider the question of continuity or discontinuity between the Roman Empire and what came after it, and in the case of towns and trade we have made some progress in discussing developments of the second half of our period. But you need to assess more thoroughly the case for and against there having been continuity in the economic foundations across our period and beyond it. In particular, was there a change of such importance near the end of our period that it can be described as a revolution? Did slavery, as the Romans understood it, persist into the tenth and eleventh centuries, to be swept away and replaced by a system of serfdom with peasants tied to their manors, which was different from the Roman system and was to characterise rural life for centuries to come? Was the pattern of villages and fields that existed in later centuries an inheritance from the Roman world, or did it too emerge as the aristocracy sought to extract more and more from the peasantry from the last part of our period onwards? The case for that being part of a revolution in European history is powerfully made by R. I. Moore (2000, ch. 2). You can see it argued for the history of the peasantry by Pierre Bonnassie (1991, ch. 1), although you need to be aware that this is part of a fierce debate. One of Bonnassie's most vocal opponents is Dominique Barthélemy (2009), who argues for much more continuity in the history of the peasantry.

Time-line: Part IV

27 BC	Death of Marcus Terentius Varro, author of *On the Affairs of the Countryside*
70	Death of Lucius Junius Columella, author of *On Agriculture*
543–late 7th century	Plague
	543–6 in the Byzantine Empire
	563 in the Auvergne (France)
	570 in North Italy, Gaul, and Spain
	592 at Tours and Nantes
	Mid to late 7th century: in England
561–92	Reign of Guntram, joint king of the Franks (welcomed by Syrians)
	591 Eusebius the Syrian becomes bishop of Paris
619	*Life* of John the Almsgiver
627	Edwin, first Christian king of Northumbria, baptised at York
635–c.750	Arab military and political expansion
648	Cenwalh, king of Wessex, founds church at Winchester
657–73	Reign of Chlotar III, king of the Franks
662	Emperor Constans II uses the coast-road from Constantinople to Athens
670s	Relics of St Birinus translated to Winchester
690/720	Dumps at the Crypta Balbi, Rome
	690 First dump
	720 Second dump
c.673–735	Bede, monk of Monkwearmouth-Jarrow, author of the *Ecclesiastical History of the English People*
Early 8th century	Pippin (from 751 King Pippin III) conquers Frisia
Late 8th century	Venice emerges as a trading centre
c.700–c.787	Willibald, English missionary and pilgrim to the Holy Land
751–68	Pippin III, king of the Franks
753–96	Offa, king of Mercia
768–814	Charlemagne, king of the Franks and emperor
	770s Conquest of Lombardy
	794 Reform of coins from 1.3 g to 1.4 g
	c.800 Polyptych of St Germain-des-Prés
Early 9th century	Coppergate Helmet, York
808	King Godefrid of the Danes moves the merchants from Reric to Haithabu

814–40	Louis the Pious, emperor
	839 Greek ambassadors come to Louis the Pious in company with Rus
831–2	First journey recorded via the Gulf of Corinth
840–70	Charles the Bald, king of the Franks and emperor
	844–8 Polyptych of Saint-Bertin
	Mid-9th century Dorestad ceases to function
c.850	Swedish campaign in Kurland, south of Baltic Sea
860s	Papal envoys cross the Balkans overland
867	Bernard the Frank's journey to Jerusalem
871–99	Alfred, the Great, king of Wessex
	Winchester street-plan laid out
c.900	Compilation of the Burghal Hidage
913	Repopulation of San Juan de las Abbadessas (Spain)
921–2	Embassy of Ibn Fadlan from the caliph of Baghdad to the king of the Bulgars
Mid-10th century	Southampton replaces Hamwih
1050	Haithabu abandoned
1086	Domesday Book
1170	Death of St Godric of Finchale

PART V

The Church's triumph

Introduction

The rise of Christianity to a position of absolute dominance in Western Europe is one of the most striking developments of our period. So successful was that rise that, by 1050, the Christian Church was probably the largest landowner and the most powerful single institution in Western Europe, the extent of which was effectively defined as 'Christendom', with the pagan lands of the Slavs, Balts, and Finns away to the east (although by 1000 important Slav-speaking regions such as Poland and Bohemia had already been converted to Christianity) and the lands conquered by Moslems to the south-west in Spain, where they had destroyed the Christian kingdom of the Visigoths at the beginning of the eighth century. Europe had come to mean Christendom. How had this come about?

First, how was Western Europe converted to Christianity and why was that conversion a success? The answers to these questions will no doubt depend on the area we are considering – for example, the Roman Empire, which had known Christianity from its very beginning, as opposed to the Viking kingdoms, which lay beyond the former frontiers of that empire, which had been relatively immune to its influence, and where Christianity was introduced relatively late in our period. Nevertheless, we need models, however crude and however in need of refinement they may be, if we are to make sense of the evidence we have. There are arguably two such models which can, and have been, applied to our questions. We can call them the 'top-down' model and the 'bottom-up' model.

The 'top-down' model

This shorthand label is intended to convey the idea that, if this model applies, Christianity was imposed from above on a people who received it by virtue of the power and authority of the persons or the institutions transmitting it to them. We could envisage this having taken a variety of forms.

(i)   Conversion of the ruler of a people may have led to the imposition on that people of Christianity. The ruler, naturally in association with the Church, used the types of power we explored in Part III to bring about the conversion of the people subject to them. This may have involved the linking of their ideological power with Christianity, as, for example, in the ceremonies surrounding their inauguration, the use of legislation and other aspects of bureaucratic power to impose Christianity as a legal requirement on their subjects, or the transmission of Christianity to their faithful men through the mechanisms of personal power.

(ii) The Church may have organised missionaries to impose Christianity on non-Christian peoples, and devoted its structures of organisation to the instruction and supervision of the converts, and thus to the maintenance of Christian beliefs and practices once they had been delivered.

The 'bottom-up' model

This shorthand label is intended to convey the idea that, if this model applies, Christianity gained its position in Western Europe not because of the political or cultural dominance of those promoting it, but rather because it was so inherently attractive to people at large that they embraced it in large numbers. Eventually this rising tide of Christianity engulfed even the rulers and the political structures of the states of Western Europe, so that the religion came to be a part of their fabric, even if it had in origin come from the people below rather than from the rulers above. We could envisage this working in a number of ways.

(i)   Christianity may have had a particular relevance to the social developments and problems of the time of conversion. Its adherents, for example, may have belonged to groups which were rising within their societies, so that the increase in the number of converts was the result of social forces. Alternatively, such changes may have produced changes in people's lives, which were sufficiently radical to shake their old religious allegiances and to make them open to accepting Christianity as a new religion. Or, the people being converted felt themselves inferior to a dominant culture and society in which Christianity had previously been embraced. We might, for example, consider this type of conversion in the context of the barbarians who accepted Christianity within a Roman Empire which was already largely Christian.

(ii) The teachings of Christianity may have provided the key to people's acceptance of the religion, perhaps because of their inherent value, but perhaps also because they had a particular relevance to the problems and tensions of the period of conversion. In particular, Christianity may have adopted not only into its beliefs, but also into its practices and the buildings and objects which it used, elements from the pagan beliefs of the people it was converting, thus making its acceptance easier for them.

Crude as they are, these models may also be useful when we consider one of the most important developments of our period, which is the rise of monasticism as a form of religious life. Why were so many people drawn to become monks and nuns? And why were kings and members of the elite so willing to patronise monasteries so generously with, at any rate from the sixth century onwards, enormous tracts of land? Was the development of monasticism a 'bottom-up' process, in which the way of life exercised a profound appeal for contemporaries for its religious and spiritual attractions, or perhaps because it offered particular solutions to the social tensions of their time – offering, for example, an escape from the demands of an oppressive lay society? If one or both of these was the case, did monasticism rise on a tide of popularity which eventually embedded it in the fabric of Western Europe? Or was it a 'top-down' process in which rulers and the powerful created monasteries, partly for their own spiritual benefit in the form, perhaps, of the prayers of the monks saving their souls from hell, but partly because monasteries offered considerable social, economic, and political attractions, as means to obtain particular rights over land, as centres of trade and industry, and as institutions which could assist rulers in the exercise of bureaucratic power?

We have not only, however, to explain the conversion of Western Europe to Christianity, and the rise of monasticism. We need also to explore how, in the long term, the Church was able to sustain a position of such dominance, in the practical world of Western Europe as well as in the world of beliefs and ideas. What forms of organisation in the hands of its leaders made the Church so effective? What resources did they draw on, and what means did they use to establish their authority?

In testing out these models and asking these questions, we need to be realistic about the extent to which we can expect results. They touch, after all, on the inner world of minds and beliefs, on which our sources only cast the most flickering of lights. And these sources are almost always the products of writers prominent within the Christian Church, so that we may well wonder how realistic and impartial is the evidence they are giving us. Nonetheless, the issues are of such importance that we must attempt to tackle them, even if we have to recognise that we shall only ever see in a glass darkly.

10

Conversion to Christianity

The difference in the circumstances of the conversions of the Roman Empire in the fourth century and before, the barbarians within the Roman Empire from the fifth century onwards, and the conversion of peoples outside the former Roman Empire from the eighth century onwards seems to make it necessary to treat them separately, which is what this chapter attempts to do. But, as we think about each, we need to have in our minds the 'top-down' and 'bottom-up' models which we sketched in the introduction to this part of the book.

The Roman Empire

'Top-down' model

Constantine's conversion

How far is the 'top-down' model for the conversion of the Roman Empire supported by the role of the emperors? We need to begin with the conversion of the first Christian emperor, Constantine (306–37). He had been made emperor at York in 306, but had been faced by rivals for the imperial throne of the western Roman Empire, first and foremost Maxentius, against whom he was victorious outside Rome at the Battle of Milvian Bridge (312). It is in the context of Constantine's march towards Rome prior to that battle that two writers, Lactantius and Eusebius, wrote accounts of dreams and visions experienced by the emperor, the former writing at his court soon afterwards, the latter much later in his life. According to Lactantius,

> Constantine was directed in a dream to mark the heavenly sign of God on the shields of his soldiers and thus to join battle.
>
> (Stevenson and Frend, 1987, p. 283)

According to Eusebius,

> He said that about noon, when the day was already beginning to decline, he saw with his own eyes the trophy of a cross of light in the heavens above the sun, and an inscription *conquer by this* attached to it.

Then, during the night,

> the Christ of God appeared to him with the sign which he had seen in the heavens, and commanded him to make a likeness of that sign which he had seen in the heavens, and to use it as a safeguard in all engagements with his enemies.
>
> (Stevenson and Frend, 1987, pp. 283–4)

Eusebius goes on to relate how Constantine did this, and how he also led his army under a banner of Christ in the form of what he had seen across the sun in the vision that preceded the dream. This banner, which was called the *labarum*, is known from various sources and representations as well as from Eusebius's account, and it took the form not of the cross itself but of the *Chi-Rho*, the monogram formed of the first two letters of Christ's name in Greek. Thus equipped, his army defeated Maxentius, who on his side used magic arts and pagan soothsayers to promote his army, but to no avail. Shortly after this victory, Constantine issued the Edict of Milan (313), in which he put an end to the persecution of the Christians and restored property to the Church which had been confiscated during those persecutions. The edict can therefore be seen as the immediate consequence of Constantine's conversion.

It may be that Constantine's conversion was the crucial factor in the rise of Christianity, since with it came the imperial support necessary for Christianity to establish itself as the dominant, ultimately the only, religion of the empire. After Constantine, all the emperors were Christian, with the exception of Julian (360–3), who tried unsuccessfully to re-establish paganism. Constantine conferred benefits on the Church, such as the right for bishops to use the imperial post-system, for rapid travel. He summoned the Council of Arles (314) to deal with the Donatists, North African Christians who sought to expel from the Church those who had collaborated with the persecutors, and the Council of Nicaea (325), which ruled on the doctrines of Arianism, which maintained that Christ was not really the Son of God, but rather a creation of God, created at a point in time rather than co-eternal with God. Theodosius I the Great (397–405) even prohibited paganism throughout the Roman Empire.

You might, of course, want to argue that neither Lactantius nor Eusebius is credible, since both were Christian and might have been expected to exaggerate Constantine's change of faith, and Eusebius was writing many years after the supposed conversion. Whatever you think of the significance of the vision and the dream, however, it is not easy to reject the assertion that, for whatever reason, Constantine was converted to Christianity. For one thing, Eusebius's *Life of Constantine* contains many documents and letters which seem really to have been written by the emperor himself, and these suggest very strongly that Constantine took Christianity seriously. Indeed, he himself is credited with the composition of a Christian *Oration to the Saints*.

Moreover, there is circumstantial evidence for Constantine's conversion. His father and predecessor, Constantius Chlorus, was also supportive of Christians even though he was not said to have been a convert, so there may have been a family background for his son's conversion, and this is further suggested by the fact that Constantine's sister was called Anastasia, a name of distinctively Christian character meaning 'resurrection'.

There is a further piece of evidence suggesting, albeit indirectly, that Constantine was a genuine convert at the time of the Edict of Milan. This consists of the triumphal arch which the senate of Rome erected by the Coliseum in Rome, where it still stands, following Constantine's victory over Maxentius (Fig. 25).

Figure 25 Arch of Constantine, Rome. The form of this arch is entirely classical, although its details, with the three openings and the attached columns, are characteristic of Constantine's period. The sculpture decorating it has been reused from earlier, pagan monuments. The inscription is visible above the central opening.

A triumphal arch like this was very much part of the pagan tradition of the Roman Empire, and it would have been used in the context of the emperor's victory celebrations. Moreover, the senate was an especially pagan body, for later in the fourth century it fiercely resisted the emperor Theodosius when, as part of his promotion of Christianity, he had the pagan Altar of Victory removed from the senate house (although Ambrose, bishop of Milan, may have exaggerated the case for this resistance made at the time by the pagan senator Symmachus). The senate's paganism makes the text of the inscription on the arch all the more striking, for it accounts for Constantine winning his victory as being:

> by the greatness of his mind and
> the instinct of divinity.

'Divinity' is in the singular, and so refers to a monotheistic deity as the Christian God is. It is possible that the god in question was in fact pagan, perhaps a supreme god guiding the emperor; but you may think that a purely pagan text would nevertheless have put 'divinity' in the plural as a reference to the multifarious Roman gods. The explanation may be that the senators were unwilling to acknowledge that they were dealing with an emperor who was a Christian convert, and yet dared not offend him by referring to pagan gods. The formula 'instinct of divinity', you might argue, was the closest they could force themselves to come to acknowledging Constantine's Christianity.

'Bottom-up' model

The growth of Christianity

The importance of Constantine's conversion, and of his and his successors' policies to the Church, is a strong card in favour of a 'top-down' model for the conversion of the Roman Empire. How then could you support the 'bottom-up' model, that Christianity was growing relentlessly and that the emperors were merely a part of that process? We have already noted that Christianity was by no means strong among the Roman senators. They appear to have been staunchly pagan throughout the fourth century, although in the course of that century Christian senators do appear in our sources, though not in Rome, such as Paulinus of Pella, a Christian at any rate of senatorial status, living chiefly in south-west Gaul. It looks, nevertheless, as if the emperor's conversion to Christianity would have been unlikely to have won significant political support for him from the senatorial aristocracy. Indeed, the senate even supported a pagan usurper, Eugenius, who invaded Italy to try to seize the imperial throne, but was defeated by Emperor Theodosius I at the Battle of the Frigidus (394).

As for the Roman army, it is striking that, amongst the innumerable Christian martyrs produced by the various persecutions of Christians down to c.300, there are relatively few soldiers. There are some, notably St Maurice (a saint now commemorated at Saint-Maurice in Switzerland) and the detachment of soldiers called in their 'passion' (that is, the account of their martyrdom) the Theban Legion. This latter was a case where a whole legion is supposed to have been martyred in the persecutions. But the accounts of them and of St Maurice are particularly implausible even by the standards of martyrs' *passions*, and they are probably of relatively late date, maybe later inventions. This lack of martyrs in the Roman army suggests strongly that its soldiers were generally pagan, since it would have been very hard for a Christian to opt out of the various pagan rituals of the pre-Constantine Roman army, so that they would have been likely to be martyred if they had existed.

There is one other 'straw in the wind' regarding the army. After his victory over Maxentius at the Battle of Milvian Bridge, Constantine went on to defeat the rival emperor in the east Roman Empire, Licinius, in *c.* 324. We are told by the Roman chronicler that after that victory the army hailed Constantine with the words 'Hail, august Constantine, the gods will serve you through us' (Momigliano, 1963, p. 24). Here we can see the opposite of what happened in the case of the triumphal arch of Constantine in Rome, since the 'gods' are referred to in the plural, and the allusion was therefore unquestionably to pagan deities rather than to the Christian God. The account may therefore suggest that the army was essentially pagan, even twelve years after the Edict of Milan, and was therefore unlikely to have been politically influenced in the emperor's favour by his Christianity.

It would seem, then, that the position of paganism was a dominant one, all the more so if we consider that classical paganism was at the time of Constantine's conversion an essential and integral part of the very fabric of the Roman world. The education of the elite proceeded on the basis of pagan texts, with their accounts of gods and heroes. The life of the Roman cities revolved around pagan ceremonies and rituals, all involving pagan sacrifice and devotion to the shrines of the gods. And the position of the emperor itself was embedded in paganism, so that, in parts of the Roman Empire at least, the emperor was himself regarded as a god.

It may be, however, that Christianity was in a much stronger position at the beginning of the fourth century than this evidence would suggest. In organisation, it had developed to the extent that there was a system of bishops and bishoprics throughout the empire, although admittedly more concentrated in the eastern than the western empire. It had produced a series of important thinkers and writers, the so-called 'fathers' of the Church, such as Origen and Clement of Alexandria, and these had given the religion considerable momentum in intellectual terms. Christian communities had shown considerable resilience and resource, as in the case of the Christians of the city of Lyons in the face of persecution, or indeed the Christians of the city of Rome itself, who have left behind the extraordinary and beautifully decorated series of underground burial chambers, the catacombs. Clearly, Christianity was not restricted to the lower classes and the downtrodden.

As for the number of Christians in the empire, it is possible to argue, on the basis of what figures we have, combined with studies of modern cults, that this must have been increasing exponentially by the late third century. It can also be argued that this number was being increased by the fact that Christians forbade the murder of unwanted baby girls, abortion, and sexual intercourse without possibility of conception, all of which appear to have been common in the Roman world. So Christians were increasing in number faster than the population at large, a process helped in the context of the many epidemics of disease, for example those of 165 and c.250, by the Christians' commitment (as an integral part of their religion) to charity and care for the sick and afflicted. The disruption of these epidemics may also have favoured the dominance of Christianity, partly because they disrupted existing pagan networks, partly because the Christians' behaviour during them put them in a very good light.

Conversion and change

It can be argued in addition that change in general in the later Roman Empire was an important factor in promoting Christianity, precisely because paganism was embedded in the whole fabric of the Roman world.

The civil service

The growth in size and complexity of the imperial civil service from the time of the emperor Diocletian must have been at the expense of the power and influence of the old senatorial aristocracy, so that the paganism of that class ceased to be a real political consideration for the emperors. The senate may have been bothersome in the city of Rome itself, as it was in the case of the Altar of Victory; but the senatorial aristocrats increasingly lacked real power. The emperor could ignore them, and he could also patronise Christians by giving them places in the civil service, access to which he could control.

Cities

Roman cities may have been flourishing at the end of the Roman Empire, at least in terms of imperial investment in their fortifications (above, Chapter 9). But, even if that is correct, there is still considerable evidence that the elite members of Roman society were no longer so intent on living in cities, and were instead developing luxurious country villas in which to reside. This 'flight to the countryside', as it is sometimes called, meant that the governing councils of cities were difficult to sustain, and indeed we find the Emperor Julian urgently seeking to prop them up. Thus we could argue that the change afflicting cities meant that the old pagan rituals on which they were focused were less important than they had been earlier in the history of the Roman Empire because the cities themselves were less important, and so the way was more open for the establishment of Christianity.

Recruitment of barbarians

Recruitment of barbarians into the Roman army, either as regular auxiliary troops or as federates, bound by treaty to military service to the empire, was a process which had been going on since at least the second century, but it appears to have increased in the later Roman period, so that the Roman army was increasingly dominated by barbarians who were not adherents of classical paganism, but rather had their own Germanic cults. You could argue that the importance of classical paganism was consequently reduced, and that there would have been a potential advantage to the emperors in embracing Christianity, which would have replaced both classical and barbarian pagan cults and would thus have cemented the Roman army together.

However you assess these suggestions, you probably need also to consider the possibility that change across society at large promoted conversion to Christianity because it unsettled the framework within which the previous religions had been established. Such changes may have been matched by changes in the underlying pattern of religious beliefs, as may be suggested by the penetration into the Roman Empire of mostly eastern pagan cults in the period before Constantine's conversion.

Religious beliefs

From as early as the first century AD onwards, the cult of Mithras became increasingly prominent in the Roman Empire, especially among the Roman army, for we find temples of Mithras particularly on military sites, for example along Hadrian's Wall. Mithras was a figure in the mythology of ancient Persia, credited with the creation of the world. According to his myth, he was born from a rock, or in some versions a tree, and after a life of hardship he captured and brought back to his cave the primeval bull, being the first living thing created by the chief of the gods, Ormazd. Mithras there slew it, and from its blood came the vine, from its body herbs and plants, and from its semen all useful animals. This sacrifice of the bull, the 'tauroctony', was thus the act of creation of things useful to mankind, and it was what was celebrated in the liturgical services of Mithraism, with the words 'you have saved men by the spilling of the eternal blood'. Mithraism was only one of a series of new cults emerging in pagan worship, which included veneration of the Great Mother of Pessinus, and also the cult of the Unconquered Sun, imagery of which was prominent in imperial art in the Late Roman period.

Like Christianity, these cults generally came from the eastern Mediterranean and the Middle East, and may therefore bear witness to currents of religious influence flowing from that part of the world which would have been favourable to the establishment of Christianity. Moreover, they tended towards a monotheistic view of the deity, and may therefore have prepared the way for Christianity, even if they were not so wholeheartedly monotheistic as Christianity itself. Finally, especially in the case of Mithraism, these cults required adherents to make a binding commitment. This was castration of male devotees in the case of the Great Mother of Pessinus, and in the case of Mithraism it was a process of initiation in the temples which had some resemblances to Christian initiation through baptism. This distinguished these cults from classical pagan cults which simply required sacrifice at particular altars, without any role for a conversion experience. So we could argue that their emergence demonstrated that changing perceptions of man's relationship to the supernatural were preparing the way for Christianity, and that this must in part account for its dominance from the time of Constantine onwards.

If so, Christianity may have capitalised on such advantages by showing itself well able to adapt to both the pagan heritage and to these new trends. Its doctrines were in some ways very rigid, especially regarding the oneness of God and the need for an absolute commitment to Christian beliefs on the part of its adherents. But it was also able to absorb into itself some of the symbols and even the ideas of its pagan rivals (a process called syncretism). Particularly notable in terms of the former was the use of imagery deriving, it would seem, from the cult of the Unconquered Sun in Christian contexts. For example, what is certainly a Christian tomb discovered under the basilica of St Peter in the Vatican at Rome is decorated with a mosaic showing Christ with a flaming halo, as the Unconquered Sun is represented in contemporary art, and driving a chariot in just the way that the Sun was represented in classical pagan art traversing the sky. The same process of adopting and adapting pagan symbolism may explain why Constantine's coins continued to have pagan symbols on them, and there was a statue of Constantine in Constantinople, described by Eusebius, representing the emperor as if he were the Sun.

Christianity's flexibility extended beyond symbols. St John's Gospel (1.1) reads:

In the beginning was the Word and the Word was with God, and the Word was God.

This Bible passage referring to Christ as the Word lent itself to adaptation within a system of originally pagan philosophy rooted in the teachings of the Greek philosopher Plato. He had taught the existence of fundamental essences or principles in the universe, and his ideas had been particularly developed in the late Roman period by the so-called Neo-Platonists, one of the most influential of whom was Porphyry (*c*.232–*c*.303). This philosopher had been an opponent of Christianity, and had written a now lost work 'Against the Christians', but it may nevertheless be that Christianity was in a very good position through passages like that quoted from St John's Gospel to absorb into itself the thinking of the Neo-Platonist school and to draw strength from it.

Christianity may have possessed the advantage that its emphasis on sacrifice as a fundamental aspect of religious practice and belief fitted with the outlook of previously pagan converts, to whom sacrifice would also have been fundamental before their conversion. Christianity's concept of sacrifice was focused on the mass, the commemoration of Christ's Last Supper which was also a ritual sacrifice of him, his body represented by the bread and his blood by the wine. But Christian sacrifice could also be seen in the practice of making gifts to God or to saints, such as lands or money or even possessions, in order to create an obligation on the part of God or the saint. Because God or the saint had received the gift made by way of a sacrifice, so they were obliged to answer the giver's prayers. The possibility to create such a reciprocal relationship must have been a powerful source of attraction to Christianity; but it also reflected pagan practices and so made adherence to Christianity easier for former pagans. Pagan altars, after all, also required sacrifices to be made in return for benefits. But, in the case of the Christian cult of saints, the practice of gift-giving created another link with Roman society. For the reciprocal obligation created made the saint very like the great men, or patrons, of late Roman society who protected those who submitted to them. The parallelism between that secular concept and Christianity's concept of the saint may provide us with another line of thought to explain the religion's success.

The barbarians within the Roman Empire

You can then make a strong case for the operation of the 'bottom-up' model in the Roman Empire, although the role of the Christian emperors may nevertheless point towards elements of the 'top-down' model. What then of the conversion of the barbarian peoples within the former Roman Empire? How similar was this to the conversion of the Roman Empire itself?

'Top-down' model

Conversions of kings

Just as Eusebius and Lactantius focus on the conversion of the emperor Constantine, so Gregory of Tours focuses his account of the conversion of the Franks on King Clovis, which was, according to Gregory, initiated by the influence of his Christian queen, Clotilda, a princess of the Burgundians who had been converted somewhat earlier. Clovis's conversion went hand-in-hand in Gregory's account with the conversion of his Frankish followers, promoted by the preaching of the bishop Remigius:

> Like some new Constantine [Clovis] stepped forward to the baptismal pool, ready to wash away the sores of his old leprosy and to be cleansed in the flowing water from the sordid stains which he had borne for so long. . . . More than three thousand of his army were baptised at the same time.
>
> (Gregory, *Hist. Franks*, II.31)

Here it is the king who is leading the process of conversion, although the reference to Constantine may make us suspicious that Gregory of Tours was creating a literary picture aimed at making Clovis resemble the great Roman emperor. Indeed, you can argue that a reference to the baptism of a king in a letter of a bishop of Vienne called Avitus at the beginning of the sixth century in fact refers to Clovis, and shows that the baptism took place much later than Gregory maintains.

Bede's accounts of the conversions of the English kingdoms are generally similar to Gregory's. The account of the conversion of Kent, for example, is focused on the decision to listen to the missionary Augustine taken by the king of Kent, Æthelberht, who may have been influenced by his earlier marriage to a Frankish Christian princess, Bertha. The first conversion of the kingdom of Northumbria is presented by Bede as having been initiated by the marriage of the pagan king Edwin to a Christian Kentish princess, Æthelburg, and to have been decided on in the king's council which was held in one of his royal halls. After Edwin's death and the apostasy of Northumbria to paganism, its restoration to Christianity was achieved, in Bede's account, by the personal intervention of Oswald, the king who gained control of the kingdom through a victory at a place called Heavenfield. Oswald had been converted to Christianity while he was in exile at the Irish monastery of Iona, and it was he who invited into Northumbria the bishop and missionary Aidan, who founded the monastery of Lindisfarne on what is now called Holy Island, off the coast of Northumberland.

Christianity as a success-religion

Just as Eusebius and Lactantius present Constantine's victory over his rival Maxentius at Milvian Bridge as the result of his conversion and the consequent support of God, so Bede and Gregory of Tours similarly present Christianity as a military success-religion for kings. King Clovis's conversion was, in Gregory's account, the result of his having appealed to the Christian God in the course of a battle with the Alamanns, and his having (as a consequence in Gregory's view) won a victory over them. Likewise, King Edwin of Northumbria's conversion is presented by Bede as partly the result of his having miraculously survived an assassination attempt on him, and having won a victory over Wessex with God's help. As for King Oswald of Northumbria, Bede presents his victory at Heavenfield, through which he gained his kingdom, as the result of God's intervention, invoked by Oswald himself having erected a wooden cross at the beginning of the battle. Christianity, in other words, was presented as the means of promoting kings' military victories.

The extent to which Christianity was viewed as a success-religion in other matters as well as military victories is apparent from two passages from England. The first is Bede's account of the speech made by the pagan priest Coifi at the council when it was decided that Edwin should seek his own and his kingdom's conversion to Christianity. In this, Coifi lamented the lack of worldly success which his adherence to paganism had brought him:

> I frankly admit that, for my part, I have found that the religion which we have hitherto held has no virtue or profit in it. None of your followers has devoted himself more earnestly than I have to the worship of the gods, but nevertheless there are many who receive greater benefits and greater honour from you than I do and are more successful in their undertakings. If the gods had any power, they would have helped me more readily, seeing that I have always served them with greater zeal. So it follows that if, on examination, these new doctrines which have now been explained to us are found to be better and more effectual, let us accept them at once without delay.
>
> (Bede, *Eccl. History*, II.13)

It seems, of course, utterly unlikely that these were really Coifi's words, but it is striking that Bede, who presumably composed them, should have presented Christianity as so patently a success-religion.

One of Bede's contemporaries, Bishop Daniel of Winchester, gave an even starker picture of Christianity's efficacy in a letter he wrote to the English missionary on the Continent, Boniface. In this, he advised Boniface on how best to achieve the conversion of the pagan Saxons. He advised him to argue to them that:

> If the gods are almighty and beneficent and just, they not only reward worshippers, but also punish those who scorn them. If they do both in the temporal world, why then do they spare the Christians who are turning almost the whole globe away from their worship and overthrowing the idols? And while they, that is, the Christians, possess fertile lands, and provinces fruitful in wine and oil and abounding in other riches, they have left to them, the pagans that is, with their gods, lands always frozen with cold, in which these, now driven from the whole globe, are falsely thought to reign.
>
> (Whitelock, 1979, no. 167)

Christianity's appeal to rulers may have been increased, in a warlike age, by the extent to which it was capable of being presented as a warrior-religion, especially when emphasis was laid on the martial stories of the Old Testament. A good example is the scene of the boy David fighting the giant Goliath as the Bible describes, which illustrated the Frankish manuscript know as the Stuttgart Psalter.

It is clearly open to you to argue that the presentation of Christianity as a success-religion suggests that it was to rulers that it appealed first and foremost, and therefore that the 'top-down' model best explains the nature of conversion. But, on the other hand, you may want to question the validity of the evidence we are using. It consists, after all, entirely of the writings of churchmen themselves. It represents what they themselves thought – or at least wanted to be believed – rather than how the kings themselves saw their conversions. Not until we get to the ninth century and the reign of King Alfred the Great of Wessex (871–99) do we find a writer-king, who does indeed seem to accept the link between Christianity and the military success of his kingdom – but, we might argue, that was long after the conversions of the sixth and seventh centuries, by which time Christianity must surely have strengthened its hold over the minds of kings.

Missionary activity

Visigoths

We could interpret the conversion of the Visigoths as one produced by Christian missionaries, a 'top-down' conversion in other words, if we were to accept that they were converted while they were still living north of the River Danube, that is, outside what was then the Roman Empire. The evidence for this is a surviving *Passion of St Saba*, who was martyred in that area, showing that there were Christians among the

Visigoths at that time; and sources relating to the missionary activities of a Visigoth called Ulfilas, who had been converted to Christianity while he was a captive of the Romans. Now, there is no doubt that Ulfilas did teach Christianity amongst the Visigoths north of the Danube, and we have his translation of the Bible into the Gothic language. But against the notion that his work was successful in actually converting the Visigoths is the very authoritative testimony of the contemporary Christian scholar, Jerome, who maintained that the conversion of that people as a whole took place only at the end of the fourth century – that is, after they had been admitted into the Roman Empire in the 370s. We need not dismiss either the St Saba or the Ulfilas evidence as showing that there were some Christian converts among the Visigoths before this, but that is not inconsistent with Jerome's evidence that the real conversion took place after the Visigoths were as a people within the Roman Empire. Here too, then, it looks as if conversion went hand-in-hand with what must have been a momentous change, the removal of whatever a barbarian people consisted of into the Roman Empire.

English

A much likelier example of 'top-down' conversion through missionary activity may be that of the English. They moved into Roman Britain either in the fifth or the sixth century, but were not converted to Christianity until the very end of the sixth and into the seventh century, as Bede describes in his *Ecclesiastical History of the English People*. Clearly, it was not the process of movement into Roman Britain which produced their conversion, nor was it triggered by the influence of Roman Christianity within Britain. The explanation may be that Roman Christianity, culture, and society were largely destroyed within Britain perhaps soon after the early fifth century, either by the arrival of the English, or as a result of the precocious withdrawal of Roman governance at the beginning of the fifth century. Most telling is the fact that none of the bishoprics, which we know existed in the Roman period, can be shown definitely to have survived into the period of the conversion of the English. It is possible to assemble some evidence to suggest that Christianity remained in existence throughout Britain after the withdrawal of Roman rule, for example, Bede's fleeting reference to the continuing functioning of the shrine of the British martyr Alban at the Roman city of Verulamium (St Albans) into his own time (Bede, *Eccl. History*, I.7), and the occurrence of the place-name 'Eccles', which seems to derive from the Welsh word for 'church' (*eglws* itself derived from Latin *ecclesia*), which suggests the possibility that places so named were the sites of churches existing before the English came, and continuing to exist after their arrival. But this evidence is not voluminous ('Eccles' names are found, for example, only in any numbers in the wild uplands of the Peak District), and, set against the evidence of the discontinuity of the bishoprics, it is hard to think that it indicates anything more than very patchy and sporadic survival of Christian communities of the native Britons. So the long delay in the conversion of the English to Christianity would have been due to the absence of effective Christian influence from the former Roman population. The Britons of the western kingdoms of Wales and Cornwall, and of the northern kingdoms of what is now lowland Scotland, had remained Christian from the Roman period, but their failure to bring about the conversion of the English was the thing that Bede held so vehemently against them.

The explanation for the conversion of the English in the seventh century may thus be much more to do with the 'top-down' model, specifically with Christian missionary activity, than with the absorption of a pagan people into a Christian society, as we seem to see on the Continent. This missionary activity was initiated by Pope Gregory the Great who sent to the kingdom of Kent a mission led by Augustine, which arrived in 597 and was successful in converting Kent and the neighbouring kingdom of Essex, and in sending a further mission to the kingdom of Northumbria, which was also converted under its king, Edwin. None of these conversions was permanent, for all three kingdoms apostasised (reverted to paganism) shortly after their conversion. But new missionaries were brought into the kingdom of Northumbria, this time led by Bishop Aidan from the Irish monastery of Iona in the Hebrides, and they definitively converted the kingdom of Northumbria as well as Mercia and surrounding kingdoms. Meanwhile, an Italian missionary called Birinus arrived in the kingdom of Wessex and achieved its definitive conversion to Christianity.

Machinery of power

Conversion in depth, and the maintenance of Christianity among a converted people, must have required machinery for organising preaching, teaching, and pastoral care. On the Continent, such machinery was already in existence as a result of the survival of the structures of Roman Christianity, with a framework of bishoprics and below them a hierarchy of mother-churches and daughter-churches. Kings nevertheless promoted Christianity, as Roman emperors had done, by making grants to churches, sometimes of land, sometimes of immunities, that is, privileges exempting the church in question from paying taxes or being subject to the operations of royal officials; and sometimes by establishing and endowing new churches, especially monasteries. By the Carolingian period, kings also used their authority to develop the machinery of the Church, as Charlemagne did by legislating for the organisation and development of a structure of parishes independent of secular landlords. Just as Roman emperors had done, kings were closely involved in councils, sometimes purely church councils like the Council of Orléans in 522, sometimes combined ecclesiastical and secular councils, such as the Synod of Frankfurt which Charlemagne presided over in 794.

In England, where, we have suggested, little trace of Roman Christianity survived, the role of kings in creating and promoting ecclesiastical structures may have been more important. Bede tells us that it was King Æthelberht of Kent who gave the ruined Roman church of Christ Church to the missionary Augustine for the establishment of his cathedral; and that it was King Oswald of Northumbria who, with the Irish missionary Aidan, founded the bishopric of Northumbria on the island of Lindisfarne, handing over the requisite land to the Church. Missionaries such as Aidan made use of royal residences for their preaching, for Bede tells us that Aidan died at such a place in the course of his work. You can argue that the whole framework for developing

Christianity in England, and indeed elsewhere in Western Europe as well, was focused on royal centres, which formed the sites of so-called minster churches, responsible for the pastoral care of territories around those royal centres. It is not easy to establish that such an organisation of the Church existed shortly after the period of conversion to Christianity, but there is evidence in favour of it – notably the existence in later records of churches which were apparently ancient and which had wide responsibilities for surrounding churches, for example, responsibilities for baptism, burial, and for the distribution of chrism or holy oil. Such churches, it can be argued, represented the earliest form of Church organisation, and were linked to royal centres, as can, for example, be shown – tentatively at least – in the case of Kentish minster churches such as Lyminge and Folkestone.

'Bottom-up' model

The cultural dominance of the Roman Empire

The conversion of the barbarians within the Roman Empire may provide us with a good example of conversion resulting from changes in society. Many barbarian peoples were converted to Christianity at what was presumably for them the point of maximum change, that is, shortly after their entry into the Roman Empire, as we have suggested for the Visigoths. This was also the case for the Ostrogoths, who were converted to Christianity after they entered the Roman province of Pannonia in modern Hungary and Croatia at the end of the fifth century, and equally for the Burgundians, who seem to have been converted after the Roman authorities had settled them in the province of Germania Prima. The Franks had been living partly within Roman territory in the area of the lower and middle Rhine since the third century, but their conversion to Christianity, which began with the baptism of their king Clovis either in the late fifth or the early sixth century, occurred after their military expansion into what had been Roman Gaul brought them into contact with Roman structures more than had been the case in the past, and effectively settled them within one of the key provinces of the Roman Empire in the west. Such change may have severed connections with pagan sites and sanctuaries, such as the sacred groves which Tacitus refers to in his *On Germany*, and the experience of the incoming barbarians of working for Romans who were by then Christians, notably in the Roman army, may have further disturbed their adherence to paganism.

Conversion may not only have been the result of change of circumstance, but also of the influence of Christianity on barbarians within the Roman Empire. By 400, Christianity was the official and exclusive religion of the Roman Empire, so that it would naturally have appeared a desirable religion to be converted to in the eyes of barbarians seeking to establish positions of power and influence within it. So it may be that the real motor of conversion was not so much change in itself, although this may have provided an opportunity for conversion, as the influence and pressure of established Roman Christianity.

Nonetheless, it is striking that the first conversions of barbarians were not to Catholic Christianity but rather to Arianism, a form of Christianity which was condemned as heretical by the Council of Nicaea in 325, but went on to be the dominant form of Christianity in the Roman Empire until the Council of Constantinople in 381 restored Catholic Christianity. If the conversion of the Visigoths had been the result of Ulfilas's missionary work, it would have taken place at a point when the Roman Empire was Arian; but if the Visigoths were not converted as a people, as we suggested, until the end of the fourth century, their adoption of Arianism must have been a choice they made. We could argue that it represented a desire on their part to emulate the Romans without being very closely associated with them.

Nor were they alone, for all the other barbarian peoples, with the exception of the English, and possibly the Franks, were initially converted to Arianism rather than to Catholic Christianity. In the case of the English, their conversion was much later than that of the other peoples, so the option of Arianism was presumably no longer open. In the case of the Franks, however, it is of course Gregory of Tours who tells us that they were converted directly from paganism to Catholic Christianity. On the basis of various hints in his writings about Arianism in the family of their first Christian king, Clovis, it is possible to argue that Gregory's hatred of Arianism, by his time a condemned heresy, caused him to distort the record.

We could support the 'bottom-up' model further if we could show either that the religious beliefs of the barbarians were no match for Christianity, or that Christianity was able to adapt itself in ways which were particularly appealing to barbarian converts.

Barbarian paganism

Most of what we know about barbarian paganism comes from Scandinavia in texts written in the twelfth century and later. This is because Scandinavia was converted very late to Christianity compared with other areas of Europe, only beginning in the ninth century and only really being established in the eleventh, so that paganism was relatively recent history when the increase of writing which affected Europe in the course of the twelfth century reached Scandinavia. The result is that we have quite detailed accounts of Scandinavian (or Norse) paganism. But we cannot be sure how far these accounts apply to the paganism of the barbarians who created the barbarian kingdoms within the former Roman Empire; and, since the Scandinavian texts were all written by Christian writers, we cannot be sure how accurate they were. So it is probably impossible to reconstruct what the paganism of the barbarians in the period of the end of the Roman Empire in the west was like.

If we fall back on brief references to it in more contemporary sources, we may be struck by the extent to which, in Bede's account of the conversion of the English, the kingdoms apostasised after their initial conversion, which might suggest that paganism was strong. On the other hand, we may be struck rather by the small amount of evidence for pagan worship from England in this period. Apart from a possible pagan temple excavated at the Northumbrian royal palace of Yeavering and identified as such by evidence of animal sacrifice from within it, there are no sites of English pagan temples known at all. There are a few place-names surviving referring to pagan gods, such as Wednesfield (meaning 'field of the pagan barbarian god Woden') and Thurstable (meaning 'pillar of the pagan barbarian god Thor'), but these are often peripheral to the English kingdoms and are in any case very limited survivals. We cannot, in other words, really tell from this whether paganism was weak or strong.

Three particular pieces of archaeological evidence may be germane to this discussion. First, the grave of the pagan king of the Franks, Childeric, Clovis's father, now under Tournai Cathedral (France), but not originally connected with a church. This burial had grave-goods with the body, which is not necessarily a sign of paganism. But it also appears to have had the remains of a horse, or at least a horse's head, which suggests some sacrificial practice and was certainly not Christian. Nearby, and probably connected with the grave, was a pit containing a number of sacrificed horses, which may point to the strength of paganism at any rate amongst the kings of the Franks just before their conversion.

Secondly, the early seventh-century Sutton Hoo burial-mounds in Suffolk, near the East Anglian royal centre of Rendlesham. These are probably royal burials, in view of the richness of the objects recovered from them, and they seem at first sight to be pagan in character, since they are associated with sacrificed animals, and since the use of a ship as the container for the body (as in the famous Mound 1) is suggestive of pagan belief, the ship having continued in use as a container for burials in pagan Scandinavia until a much later period.

Yet, in this case, there are signs of a coexistence between paganism and Christianity, which may have made the latter more acceptable to potential converts. Amongst the treasures recovered from Mound 1 were very Christian objects in the shape of a pair of spoons, one inscribed 'Saul' and the other 'Paul'. These inscriptions are a reference to the story of Paul the Apostle, who was originally called Saul but changed his name to Paul after his vision and conversion on the road to Damascus, as described in the New Testament in the Acts of the Apostles. Of course, they may have had no significance for those who made the burial, and perhaps regarded them as just another piece of treasure alongside the other magnificent objects in the ship-burial. But you may want to argue that their occurrence in what was the overwhelmingly pagan context of the ship-burial in Mound 1 in fact underlines the power of Christianity in early seventh-century England to infiltrate even such a site as that.

The third piece of evidence is the eighth-century whalebone casket from Northumbria, now in the British Museum in London, and known as the Franks Casket after the man called Franks who added it to his collection of antiquities in the nineteenth century. One of the two scenes on the front of the casket is not labelled, but the narrative represented is well known from the Old Norse writings as part of the story of Weyland the Smith (Fig. 26).

Figure 26 Franks Casket, left side of the front. On the left, the scene shows a blacksmith, marked out by the pincers he holds and the hammer in front of him. His right leg is bent at an awkward angle. This figure must be Weyland, a blacksmith who was captured by a king who wanted to use his near-magical skills, and to retain him hamstrung him (that is, he cut the tendons of his leg). To wreak his revenge, Weyland killed the king's sons and made a drinking cup from one of their skulls. The headless corpse of one of them appears at Weyland's feet, while he offers a cup to the first of two ladies. According to the Old Norse writings, this was the king's daughter (presumably with her attendant), whom Weyland would drug with the drink in the cup made from her brother's skull, and would then rape. He would then make good his escape with a magical flying cloak made by his brother from the feathers of birds. The brother is evidently the person on the right of the scene who is strangling birds in preparation for making that cloak.

This was a story from the pagan world, so we might at first sight regard this carving as evidence for the strength of paganism. But it may be evidence for quite the opposite, for on the Franks Casket it is next to another scene, that of the three wise men presenting their gifts to the infant Jesus. There is no doubt about the identification of this scene, which includes the Star of Bethlehem as well as the Virgin Mary with Jesus on her knee, and for good measure the inscription 'Magi' in runes. You could argue that the fact that the carver of the Franks Casket should have seen no objection to juxtaposing this very Christian scene with that of Weyland the Smith suggests that paganism had disappeared so completely in the face of the Christian conversion that there could have been no objection to such a juxtaposition.

Christian syncretism

We may also be seeing in this one of the strengths of Christianity, which we noted in the conversion of the Roman Empire, that is, its adaptability and openness to syncretistic borrowing. A particularly striking example of this comes from a stone cross of the tenth century which has always been in the churchyard of the church of Gosforth near the coast of Cumbria. This was an area settled by pagan Vikings in the ninth and tenth centuries, and the carving of the cross was probably part of the process of their conversion to Christianity. It has on it a carving of the Crucifixion, but this is accompanied by a series of scenes from pagan mythology as it is known from those later Scandinavian sources. One of the most striking of these (Fig. 27) represents an incident from Scandinavian pagan mythology, and particularly from the story of Loki.

This pagan god was responsible for the death through trickery of another god, Baldr, so that the chief of the gods, Odin, had him bound under the head of a serpent which would drip venom into his face. But his wife devotedly stayed by him and caught the venom in a bowl, thus sparing him from the worst of this trial. When she was unable to do this, however, Loki took the full force of the venom, broke free, and initiated the Ragnarok, the version of the end of the world as it is found in Scandinavian pagan mythology. Loki's punishment is clearly what is shown in the panel, and other scenes on the cross correspond to the progress of the Ragnarok. In other words, we find here, as on the Franks Casket, a juxtaposition of pagan and Christian scenes. In this case, you may want to argue that this is evidence for Christian missionaries promoting the conversion of the Vikings by associating the Bible's account of the Crucifixion and its prophecies of the end of the world with the pagan mythology of Ragnarok as a means of making Christianity more acceptable to the Vikings. This is not exactly syncretism such as we may be seeing in the Roman period, but it does suggest that Christianity was strong enough to use the images and stories of paganism in promoting itself. In a way, it echoes a letter which at the beginning of the seventh century Pope Gregory the Great addressed to Mellitus, one of the missionaries he had sent to the kingdom of Kent. In this Gregory advises Mellitus simply to take over pagan temples and, where there had previously been pagan rituals of cattle-sacrifice, there should now be feasts with beef in celebration of Christianity (Bede, *Eccl. History*, I.30).

Conversion outside the former Roman Empire

In the case of the conversions of both the Roman Empire and the barbarian kingdoms which succeeded it, we may then be seeing a combination of the 'top-down' and 'bottom-up' model, or at least a case can be made for both. For the former, the case

Figure 27 The Gosforth Cross, Gosforth churchyard (Cumbria), detail showing the punishment of the god Loki. Loki's body is carved at the bottom of the roundel with his head to the left and his limbs apparently bound in knotted cords appearing above his body. His wife, recognisable as a woman by her pointed plait projecting to the right, kneels and places her arm between his head and that of the snake above him. The inverted head of a rider above belongs to a different scene interpreted as part of the Ragnarok.

can be based on the conversions and role of rulers, the actions of missionaries, and the use of machinery of power to sustain conversion; for the latter, the case seems to rest on the effects of change, the importance of the support of rulers, the influence of Christianity itself, and its flexibility and adaptability. Some of the conversions we have been looking at so far were difficult to achieve, as is shown by the apostasies in seventh-century England, where – interestingly – the 'top-down' model may have been more important than the 'bottom-up'. But there is a considerable contrast between them and the conversions of some of the peoples whose territories were outside the former Roman Empire. This was least so in the case of the Irish, whose conversion seems to have proceeded peacefully and early, as the result of the activity of the missionary Patrick, a Romano-British Christian who had been enslaved by the Irish, and returned to Ireland after his release to evangelise the country, and/or to minister to the Christians already there.

Saxony

Very different was the conversion of Saxony, which lay east of the River Rhine and west of the River Elbe, well to the east of the former Roman Empire. The Saxons of this area had seemingly been unaffected by Roman influence. There is no evidence of Christianity amongst them during or immediately after the Roman period, and, according to Bede, their political institutions remained inchoate, for they lacked kings, having (Bede says) only potentates called 'satraps' to rule over them. From the early ninth century, they appear as enemies of the Franks, who were then Christians, for they conducted raids into Frankish territory, and were in their turn invaded by Frankish armies, which sometimes imposed tribute on them. In the time of Charlemagne, however, a consistent strategy of conquest began, and a series of almost annual campaigns aimed at the Frankish conquest of Saxony. After great difficulties, bloodshed including mass executions of Saxons, transportations of others, and false victories undermined by Saxon revolts, this was finally achieved in the early ninth century. The conquest was explicitly a matter of the imposition of Christianity. As Charlemagne's biographer Einhard wrote, the Saxons were to 'give up their devil worship . . . and, once they had adopted the sacraments of the Christian faith and religion, they were to be united with the Franks and to become one people with them' (Einhard, *Life Charl.*, II.7). That, following defeat, conversion was imposed with great harshness is evident from Charlemagne's first Saxon capitulary, issued in 782. This laid down death as the punishment for a range of actions, including eating meat during Lent and cremating the dead; and very substantial fines for other pagan practices, such as 'offering prayers to springs or trees or groves' (*Capitularies*, no. 3). We can argue, then, that the conversion of Saxony was a particularly stark example of the 'top-down' model in action. Royal power seems to have produced the conversion, and it was, you could argue, a political act.

Scandinavia

The conversion of the Scandinavian countries was late in coming and evidently faced considerable pagan resistance. Limited as our evidence is, it does suggest that the process was essentially top-down. Missionary activity began in the late seventh century when the Anglo-Saxon Willibrord attempted unsuccessfully to convert a Danish king, Onegundus, and there was further missionary activity conducted or directed in the early ninth century by Anskar, archbishop of Hamburg (831–65), and others. Even so, Anskar's first mission was connected with the conversion of the Danish king (or at least Danish royal claimant) Harald, who was baptised amid great ceremony at the court of the Frankish ruler Louis the Pious at Ingelheim. He took back to Denmark with him books and vestments for Christian services, and also missionaries, including Anskar. But pagan resistance was too great, or at least Harald's position in Denmark was too insecure, and this development came to nothing; nor was Anskar's second mission to Birka (Sweden) in 829, itself in response to the request of a Swedish legation, much more successful. The real establishment of Christianity in Denmark was the work of King Harald Bluetooth (*c.*958–*c.*987). According to Widukind of Corvey, writing almost at the time, this was brought about as the result of an ordeal of hot iron performed for the king by the priest Poppo to prove that Christ was the greatest of gods. 'After this trial the king was converted, decided to worship Christ as sole God, commanded his pagan subjects to reject the idols and accorded from then on due honour to the priests and servants of God' (Roesdahl, 1987, pp. 161–2). Harald seems to have proceeded with the Christianisation of Denmark, and in particular he modified the great pagan burial-site of his father, Gorm, at Jelling. This was in origin an enormous series of stones in the shape of a ship with two great burial mounds at either end, in one of which Gorm was probably buried. Harald built a Christian church between the mounds, and seems to have re-interred Gorm in it. He also erected a magnificent stone with a figure of Christ, below which was an inscription in runes:

> King Harald commanded this monument to be made in memory of Gorm, his father, and in memory of Thorvi, his mother – that Harald who won the whole of Denmark for himself, and Norway and made the Danes Christian.
>
> (Roesdahl, 1987, p. 67)

There can be few more explicit statements of 'top-down' conversion.

In Norway, King Olaf Tryggvason (995–9) pursued a similarly 'top-down' approach. He himself was baptised in England with the king there as his sponsor. On his return he brought the wherewithal for the conversion of his country, which he implemented systematically and ruthlessly. His successor, Olaf Haraldsson (1015–28), destroyed pagan shrines and made Christianity compulsory at a Thing (or assembly) in 1024. Less is known of the conversion of Sweden, but it too seems to have been the work of its king, Olof Skötkonung (*c.*995–1022). As for Iceland, conversion to Christianity was the result of a decision of the Althing (the Icelandic assembly) in 999, in response to a message, admittedly brought by a group of Christian Icelanders, from the king of Norway, Olaf Tryggvason, threatening the population of Iceland with death unless it accepted Christianity. In the face of the threat of violence at the Althing as a result of controversy over responding to this threat, the pagan lawspeaker declared a com-promise, by which all should be Christian, but the exposure of newborn children, the eating of horse-flesh, and sacrifices in secret should continue to be permitted. Although it was the decision of the assembly to accept this, the 'top-down' character of the introduction of Christianity nevertheless seems clear.

The contrast between the conversions of Saxony, Frisia, and the Scandinavian countries on the one side, and the Roman Empire and the barbarian kingdoms which succeeded it on the other, is striking. In the former areas, there was not the same change produced by the movements of whatever constituted barbarian peoples; nor was there any pre-existing Christianity to advance the process of conversion; nor were there always firmly established and powerful kings. In Saxony there were none at all, although in Denmark there was a period in the late eighth and early ninth century when a strong king ruled in the shape of Godefred, at any rate for a time. The contrast, then, may enable us the better to bring into focus and assess the relative importance of 'top-down' and 'bottom-up' processes in conversion within the former Roman Empire and outside it.

Research and study

Broad research questions

To what extent were the processes of conversion 'top-down' or 'bottom-up'?

Why did rulers adopt and foster Christianity? Were they carried along by the growth of the religion or did they themselves produce that growth?

How important were underlying social and political processes in the growth of Christianity?

How far did Christianity adapt or accommodate itself to paganism?

Books and papers to begin with

The clearest and most wide-ranging discussion, dealing with the period from 387, is Fletcher (1997). There are many interesting ideas to be derived from Brown (2002, chs 2–5, 14–16, 18–19, 20). A much shorter, but quite thought-provoking, discussion is Smith (2005, pp. 217–39). For the rise of Christianity in the Roman Empire, the thesis that the increase in the number of Christians was following an exponential curve from the late third century, and that Christian prohibition of infanticide, abortion, and non-procreative intercourse, and Christian emphasis on social support were major factors in this, is made very excitingly by Stark (1996, 2007). There is a summary in Stephenson (2009, pp. 39–42; for other views, see p. 323), which is in its own right an absorbing and thought-provoking discussion, arguing that Constantine was carried along by the religion's growth, including that of a substantial presence of Christians in the Roman armies; and that his conversion was in fact a slow process, beginning from a general pagan belief in a single, supreme god. You could also look at Clark (2004). A classic treatment of the social context of Christianity's emergence, but focusing rather on the eastern Mediterranean, is Brown (1978).

Still a very important book about the nature of conversion, treated in the Roman context, is Nock (1998); and still very helpful too, although it needs to be read in conjunction with more recent work, is Momigliano (1963, especially a paper by A. H. M. Jones). Markus (1990) offers a thought-provoking discussion about what conversion meant in the earlier part of our period, and how it was seen as affecting life as a whole. For Constantine's conversion, an engaging and still very helpful work is Jones (1962). There is a helpful summary of discussions of that conversion in Liebeschuetz (1979, pp. 277–91), and useful too are Grant (1998) and Pohlsander (1996). Very clear for Constantine's policy towards the Church is Lane Fox (1988, ch. 13).

Elsner (1998, especially ch. 8) provides a lucid and brilliantly illustrated discussion of the evidence of art and architecture for both pagan cults and the rise of Christianity.

Informed by archaeological research for the English conversion is Yorke (2006). Illuminating and absorbing discussions based mostly on written sources are those of Mayr-Harting (1991a) and Campbell (1973). A lucid paper arguing for 'top-down' conversion in England, and emphasising the importance in conversion of younger sons of kings, royal god-parenting, and control of archbishoprics, is Angenendt (1986). If you want to argue that the English really were converted through the influence of the Britons, the most extreme statement of the survival of Roman Christianity is Thomas (1981).

For the Franks, you can look at Wallace-Hadrill (1983, ch. 2) and Pearce (2003); for the Irish, Ó Cróinín (1995, ch. 1) and Charles-Edwards (2000, ch. 5); for the Goths, Thompson (1966). For the various Scandinavian kingdoms, there are good summaries in Sawyer and Sawyer (1993, ch. 5) and Roesdahl (1987, pp. 147–67), and there are useful papers in Berend (2007). Very clear and interesting on the conversion of Iceland is Strömbäck (1975).

Pursuing more specific aspects

The nature of conversion

How useful are the theoretical approaches of social sciences such as anthropology in explaining conversion to Christianity?

On the conversion of the barbarians, two wide-ranging books by Cusack (1998, 1999) make extensive use of the evidence of archaeology, especially that for burial-practices, as evidence for the nature of conversion, and they also try to apply anthropological and psychological research to our period. For individual peoples, a similar sort of approach, dealing with the Anglo-Saxon conversion, is that of Dunn (2008). She and Berend (2007) use 'Christianisation' rather than 'conversion', since they do not regard the latter term as doing justice to the complexity of the processes involved. You can pursue such approaches further with Russell (1994), who brings anthropology and psychology to bear on early medieval conversion to argue that Christianity was 'Germanised' by that process. Cusack has a similar approach, but is critical of Russell. Urbańcyk (2003) presents comparable general ideas, although he is chiefly concerned with north-west Europe.

Christianity's interaction with other religions and practices

How far did Christianity benefit from the popularity of other, comparable religions?

On Christianity's relationship to Roman pagan cults such as those of Mithras and the Unconquered Sun, see Stephenson (2009, chs 1, 3). To pursue particular pieces of evidence pointing in this direction across our period, you can consult, for the Arch of Constantine, Holloway (2004, ch. 2, with excellent illustrations); for the Franks Casket, Webster (1999); for Sutton Hoo, Carver and Evans (2005); and for Viking period sculpture, the very lucid and exciting discussion in Bailey (1980, ch. 6). For the significance of the evidence of charms in England, there is a very interesting book by Jolly (1996).

Paganism

How strong was paganism relative to Christianity?

Bearing in mind that paganism was not a religion like Christianity, and that the term itself was condescendingly applied by Christians to non-Christians, it is well worth exploring what is known of it. For an overview which is also advancing a thesis, see Dowden (2000). For Roman paganism, there is a lucid and succinct discussion in Stephenson (2009, ch. 1); for more detail, you can consult Ando (2008) and useful too is Alföldi (1948, ch. 1). The experience of pagans in the Christian Roman Empire is discussed by McLynn (2009). For more depth and detail on Mithras, see Beck (2006), and to explore the remains of this cult on Hadrian's Wall, Daniels (1962) or, more readily available, Bruce and Breeze (2006). It is well worth mastering what is known, admittedly often from late sources, of Scandinavian paganism, for which there are absorbing and lucid guides in Davidson (1964, 1993) and Turville-Petre (1964). These mostly draw on literary sources, but there is a very useful discussion of the value of more factual sources for northern paganism in Bartlett (2007). Bearing in mind that English paganism may or may not be closely related to that of Scandinavia, two very useful (and quite different) books for the former are Owen (1981) and Wilson (1992). For paganism in Saxony and neighbouring areas, see Wood (1995).

Missionaries

How great was the role of missionaries in conversion to Christianity?

The classic book on the English missionaries on the Continent is Levison (1946); there is more modern discussion in Wood (1994a, ch. 18). You can also consult Talbot (1954) for the lives of the missionaries in English translation. For the strategies which missionaries employed as a means of conversion, there are very useful discussions of Carolingian mission-activity by Sullivan (1953, 1956). A classic paper emphasising the political context of mission is Wallace-Hadrill (1971a). For St Augustine's mission to the English, see Wood (1994b). Wood (1999, 2001) uses accounts of the lives of missionary saints (i.e. hagiography) which can at least show us something of their attitudes and values.

11

The success of monasticism

Why were monasteries so important and numerous in early medieval Western Europe? Why did so many people want to become monks or nuns and, perhaps more importantly, why were kings, queens, princes, princesses, and nobles so enthusiastic about founding them, often transferring enormous amounts of land and wealth to them? These questions are all the more intriguing because the origins of monasticism lay in areas very different from Western Europe, that is Palestine and especially the valley of the River Nile in Egypt, an irrigated strip of fertile land, studded with cities, and hemmed in by desert. The first monk for whom we have a *Life* (by a contemporary, the bishop Athanasius) was Anthony of Egypt, born around 251 at Queman on the River Nile. According to Athanasius, he came of a good family and, after the death of his parents, he placed himself under the direction of an old man leading a holy life. Eventually he moved to live in a tomb, and then to a ruined fortress on the edge of the desert, where he struggled with demons who appeared to him in various forms, such as those of animals or beautiful women. Overcoming the temptations which these apparitions placed before him, he attracted a considerable following of persons who venerated him for his holiness and, wishing to escape their presence and to be alone in his spiritual struggles, he moved to an even more remote place, the Outer Desert, where he died in 356. Anthony was thus essentially a hermit, and he represents a strand in monasticism which is termed eremitic (hermit-like). The hermits who followed him nevertheless functioned for part of the time at least in communities, so that their monasticism was not as distinct as has sometimes been maintained from an alternative form, cenobitic monasticism. This was based on communities of monks living together, and it is associated with another Egyptian, Pachomius, who founded such a community at Tabennisi in the Nile valley in 323, and went on to establish further such monasteries, often very large in size and occupied by monks living under a monastic rule.

Monasticism was thus a phenomenon of the very beginning of our period and particularly of the very special environment of Egypt, which makes it the more remarkable that it spread throughout the Roman Empire and its successor kingdoms in the West with considerable speed. Already in 357–8, a certain Basil had travelled from Asia Minor to Palestine and Egypt to learn from the monks there, and he returned home to write a rule for monks and to found monasteries in Asia Minor. From the western Roman Empire, Jerome, the scholar responsible for the Vulgate translation of the Bible into Latin, visited Egypt likewise to study the life of the monks, and he settled in 386 in Bethlehem as abbot of a new monastery there. Monasticism was already penetrating the west. In around 360, the Christian convert and missionary Martin of Tours established a hermitage at Ligugé in the valley of the River Loire, and in 372 a colony of hermits at nearby Marmoûtier. A major monastic centre was established by Honoratus around 410 on the island of Lérins, just off the delta of the River Rhône.

Outside the Roman Empire, monasticism was an important part of Christianity from the time of the conversion of Ireland in the fifth century, and Irish monks spread their way of life far afield: to what is now Scotland, where Columba established the monastery of Iona in the Hebrides in the late sixth century; to England, where Aidan, himself coming from Iona, established the monastery of Lindisfarne in 635; and to the Continent, where from the late sixth century the Irish monk Columbanus established a series of monasteries, including Luxeuil in what is now eastern France, and Bobbio in what is now northern Italy. Meanwhile, around 540, Benedict of Nursia, founder of the southern Italian monastery of Monte Cassino, had written the *Rule of St Benedict* for monks. This was in its time one of a series of rules, including the earlier *Rule of the Master* and the later *Rule of Columbanus*; but it was to become in later centuries the most important monastic rule in Western Europe, being heavily promoted by the Carolingian kings and their churchmen in the ninth century.

What, then, was the attractiveness to Western Europe of an essentially Egyptian and Palestinian institution? As we noted in the introduction to this part of the book, there may be advantages in treating this question also in terms of the 'top-down' and 'bottom-up' models which we have applied to explaining conversion to Christianity (Chapter 10).

'Bottom-up' model

Just as in the case of conversion, we can think of this model in terms both of the religious and spiritual attractions of monasticism to potential monks on the one hand, and its social and economic attractions on the other.

Religious and spiritual attractions

Monasticism as part of Christianity

Was monasticism attractive because it was an essential and integral element of Christianity itself? We can identify, as medieval monks themselves did, possible models for monasticism in the New Testament, in the account of how John the Baptist lived in the desert, like monks such as Anthony would do, eating locusts and honey, and also in the account of Christ's period of temptation in the wilderness, that is, the desert, when – again like Anthony would do – he wrestled with the temptations of the Devil. Important as these accounts are in the Bible, however, they do not seem to provide a basis for representing monasticism as central to the original teachings of Christianity, and indeed the delay of two to three centuries between Christ's lifetime and the emergence of monasticism would seem to confirm this.

Monasticism and martyrdom

A second possibility is that the self-denial which the ascetic practices of monasticism required, such as living in the desert, eating only very little food of limited type, chastising the body, and avoiding contact with the opposite sex, were attractive because they responded to the same impulses which had driven early Christians to seek martyrdom at the hands of the authorities during the persecutions of Christians in the Roman Empire. Following the cessation of these persecutions, Christian saints came to include amongst their number monks and nuns notable for their ascetic practices, whereas previously sainthood had been limited to martyrs. We could argue that the self-denial of monastic life was a substitute for martyrdom, and that monks and nuns were in effect driven by a thirst for bloodless martyrdom, and for the benefits to their souls which they believed would stem from this. It is hard to prove such a possibility, rooted as it is in the world of beliefs, but we may note that Jerome regarded monastic life as comparable to martyrdom, and St Patrick in Ireland mentions that those dedicated to virginity suffer just like the martyrs, as if a parallel was being drawn between martyrdom and monastic life (see below, p. 282).

The reputation of the Egyptian monks

A third possibility is that the Egyptian monks came to acquire such a reputation for sanctity that this reputation was in itself the reason why monasticism spread so quickly. We have already seen monastic founders such as Basil and Jerome travelling to Egypt in the course of the fourth century specifically to study the way of life of the monks there. To these we could add John Cassian (*c.*360–after 430), who also studied monasticism in Egypt, and was subsequently responsible for founding monasteries in southern Gaul and for writing the *Institutes* and the *Conferences* devoted to the way of life of monks. The prestige of the Egyptian monks is equally apparent in another fourth-century figure, in this case not a founder of monasteries in the west, but a lady pilgrim from the west. Her name was Egeria, and the account of her pilgrimage to the eastern Mediterranean treats the monks of Egypt as every bit as holy as the Holy Places proper of Palestine, such as Nazareth and Bethlehem.

That monasticism in the west was shaped to a large extent by Egyptian monasticism is clear enough. The strong emphasis in western monasticism on eremitic and ascetic life is clearly derived from Egyptian models such as St Anthony. The *Rule of St Benedict* was directed by its author to cenobitic monks (i.e. those who lived in communities under a rule and an abbot), but it nevertheless envisaged that 'after long probation in the monastery' the most successful monks would graduate to become hermits just like Anthony (*Rule of St Benedict*, ch. 1). There was, of course, no exact Western European parallel to the Egyptian desert, but its equivalent was found in wild and desolate places. Sometimes these could be inland sites, such as the site in southern Northumbria chosen by its founder for the monastery of Lastingham (North Yorkshire), which lay (Bede tells us) 'amid some steep and remote hills which seemed better fitted for the haunts of robbers and the dens of wild beasts than for human habitation' (Bede, *Eccl. History*, III.23). It was, we may think, a substitute for the Egyptian desert, and we may reach the same conclusion about the monastery and bishopric of Lindisfarne, established in 635 in northern Northumbria on what is now Holy Island (Northumberland), a knob of volcanic rock, surrounded by sand-dunes and great sweeps of beach, accessible only at low tide. A very desert place in many respects! When its bishop Cuthbert (died 687), who was himself a monk, aspired to a higher level of monastic life, he withdrew – just like Anthony withdrawing to the Outer Desert – to the smaller and even more desolate island of the Inner Farne, where he lived as a hermit, eating in his last days nothing but onions. We find the inaccessible island used as a substitute for a desert hermitage in Gaul too, where (as we have seen) the monastery founded by Honoratus was on the island of Lérins, but even more so in Ireland. The sea around that country was full of islands, many of them used as hermitages. The most famous is Skellig Michael, a spectacular rock in the Atlantic, with the cells of the hermits still preserved on it, and accessible even today only in calm weather. To have lived so remotely and in such a state of self-denial in the midst of the ocean no doubt replicated quite closely what was believed to have been the experience of the Egyptian monks in the desert.

The *Life of Anthony* demonstrably influenced those who wrote about Western European monks, not generally in the original Greek version of the *Life* but in the Latin translation of it by Evagrius. We find Bede using it in his *Life of St Cuthbert*, and it is the model for another eighth-century *Life* of a hermit, that of St Guthlac of Crowland by a writer called Felix. Guthlac began as a monk but, as the *Rule of St Benedict* envisaged, he progressed to be a hermit, in his case in the middle of the fens at Crowland, where he struggled with demons in much the same way as St Anthony had done in the desert.

The *Life of Guthlac* introduces the possibility that the really important religious and spiritual attraction of monasticism, in the west as elsewhere, was the fear of hell and the belief that a place in heaven could be secured by asceticism and the neglect of bodily comforts, as were practised by monks and nuns, and before them by the Egyptian hermits. According to his *Life*, Guthlac was an aristocrat of the English kingdom of Mercia in the eighth century, and in his youth he led the violent lifestyle of the young of his class, although, as Felix explained, he nevertheless showed some symptoms of his predilection for a religious life, for, having 'devastated the towns and residences of his foes . . . he would return to the owners a third part of the treasure collected'. After he had been doing this for nine years, he had a 'revelation' concerning 'the wretched deaths and the shameful ends of the ancient kings of his race . . . the fleeting riches of this world and the contemptible glory of this temporal life, [and] . . . the form of his own death'. Then, 'trembling with anxiety at the inevitable finish of this brief life . . . he became first a monk and then a hermit at Crowland' (*Life of Guthlac*, chs 17–18).

The adoption of monastic life, and its culmination in hermit life, is here presented as motivated by fear of what would happen after death. A life of prayer, of resisting the temptations of the Devil, of depriving the body of pleasures – and indeed of punishing it – was perceived as pleasing to God and as a route to heaven. That was why monks such as Cuthbert of Lindisfarne undertook such rigorous ascetic practices. Bede tells us, in his *Life of St Cuthbert* (ch. 10), that at night Cuthbert left the monastery of Coldingham and 'went down to the sea . . . going into the deep water until the swelling waves rose as far as his neck and arms, and he spent the dark hours of the night watching and singing praises to the sound of the waves'. The point was to chastise the body to make it more acceptable to God.

The link between this and the afterlife is made explicit in Bede's account of an ordinary Northumbrian head of a family called Drihthelm. This man, he tells us, appeared to be dead, but was in fact taken by an angel to be shown a terrible vision of the extreme cold and extreme heat of hell. When, to the amazement of those who believed him to be dead, he came back to life, he promptly became a monk at Melrose (Borders), where he often 'used to enter the river to chastise his body, frequently immersing himself beneath the water . . . When he came out of the water, he would never trouble to take off his cold, wet garments until the warmth of his body had dried them. When in wintertime the broken pieces of ice were floating round him, people would say to him, "Brother Drihthelm, however can you bear such bitter cold?" He answered them simply, for he was a man of simple wit and few words, "I have known it colder"' (Bede, *Eccl. History*, V.12). He was referring, of course, to his vision of hell.

In later centuries, probably the twelfth, there developed in Christianity the concept of purgatory, a sort of holding area in which the souls of the dead would be tormented for the sins committed by the deceased, as a means of preparing them for entry into heaven. The torments of purgatory could be lessened by the prayers of the living for the souls of the dead named in their prayers. The full doctrine of purgatory had not developed in our period, but the broad idea that the living could ease the pains of hell for the dead clearly did exist. What the soul of the dead person needed to promote its progress to heaven was prayer, and above all the liturgical service of the mass performed repeatedly for him or her. A ninth-century text, for example, describes a vision experienced by a poor woman of Laon in modern France, in which she saw the soul of Charlemagne 'placed in torment' and was told by the person guiding her in the vision that he would be able to enter heaven 'if the Emperor Louis, his son, fully provides for seven memorial services on his behalf' (Dutton, 2004, no. 29). Another ninth-century account of a vision, that of Wetti, finishes with the visionary asking ten of his friends to offer for him 'a hundred masses and a hundred psalms' so that he will not be oppressed in death with 'a heavy weight of punishments' (McLaughlin, 1994, p. 240).

Becoming the friend of a monastery, by founding one or endowing an existing one with land, was seen as a particularly efficacious way to obtain in perpetuity the prayers and masses needed to escape the punishments of hell. Suitably endowed with lands and wealth, subject to a regular rule of life like that of St Benedict which set out a routine cycle of prayer and service of God, monasteries were in part machines for promoting the welfare of the souls of the dead. This was all the more so as our period progressed, and from the tenth century, for example, monasteries connected with the great community of Cluny in Burgundy mounted an enormous cycle of services, many aimed at the relief of the dead. Because monasteries were in principle perpetual communities, founders and benefactors could expect promotion of their souls to go on for ever. And their gifts to monasteries were often cast in the form of contracts: a symbol of the gift, for example, a rod, was placed on the altar of the church receiving it as a sign that the expectation of the donor was that the church, usually a monastery, would deliver a quota of prayers and masses for the salvation of their soul.

The monastery's duty of prayer is expressed in the great lists of names of persons to be prayed for which are the Books of Life (*Libri vitae*) of the Early Middle Ages, such as those of Salzburg, Fulda, Winchester, Reichenau, and Durham. A Book of Life, often containing thousands of names, some of monks and nuns, some of clergy, but many of lay-people, would probably be placed on the high altar of a monastery-church. It would serve like a Tibetan prayer-wheel; as the monks said mass or went through other services, so names of those in the book would benefit on their road to heaven.

An indication of the number of masses which could be said in a monastery-church is provided by a document now preserved in the library of St Gall in Switzerland. This is a very detailed plan of a monastic layout, drawn up in the early ninth century, and not only showing the features of the buildings, but also having quite extensive captions to explain their functions. It has a contemporary note on it, which can be interpreted as meaning either that it was intended as a blueprint for the design of monasteries, or that it was just for pondering. Either way, the layout represented, which was closely based on the *Rule of St Benedict*, became extremely important, even if it was never as such built; and later monastic layouts resembled it very closely. Its features are therefore of importance to us, and for the present discussion it is striking that the monastery-church in the plan is full of altars: each bay of each aisle of the nave has such an altar carefully screened off to form a series of side-chapels. Clearly a major function of the monks was to say masses, and these are likely to have been for the dead.

As for lay founders and patrons, another means by which they could derive benefits for their souls from their support of monasticism was to become members of a monastery as lay-brothers (*confratres*) or lay-sisters (*consorores*). This enabled them to continue with their lives, but as death approached they could withdraw to the monastery and there die in the monastic habit, with all the benefits to the progress of their souls which that was believed to bring.

Lay-people could also be buried in or close to the monastery's church, which is presumably why monasteries often served as mausolea of the great, as Saint-Denis did for the Frankish kings, and the Old Minster Winchester, and later the abbey of

Westminster, for the English. For one's body to rest close to the prayer-machine of the monks, and also to the relics of saints which their churches usually contained, offered some hope that at the Last Judgment one would be favourably placed for enjoying the monks' support, and that of the saints.

Social, economic, and political pressures

Did pressures of life encourage the development of monasticism along the lines of the 'bottom-up' model? A case can be made for this in the context of the later Roman Empire, when such pressures were those to do with the burdens imposed by the imperial government – heavy taxation, widespread conscription into the army, and the rigidity of imperial control, not least over where people could live. Fragmentary as our evidence is, it does suggest that these pressures, especially taxation, were especially acute in Egypt, which raises the possibility that this may in some way have been connected with the rise of monasticism there, in effect as an escape route from those pressures. This is hard to prove, but it is a possibility and it may apply to the west as well as to Egypt. When Augustine tells us in his own words of his establishment of a quasi-monastic community at Cassiciacum in Italy, he presents it as a means of escape from the pressures of his day, not only those of the imperial government but also those created by barbarian disruption. This may be what underlies the history of a Roman aristocrat, Paulinus of Nola (353/5–431), who left lands and office in Gaul and Italy to lead a monastic life at Nola in southern Italy. And it is evidently the basis rather later on of the history of Cassiodorus (485/90–*c*.580), who withdrew from public office when the kingdom of the Ostrogoths was disrupted in Italy by the invasion of the east Roman emperor Justinian, and who eventually founded the monastery of Vivarium near Naples. It may be that the sixth-century *Rule of St Benedict* promoted this function of monasticism as a defensive retreat for the cultured elites of the Roman and post-Roman world, for it was, as described by its author, intended to be for 'the beginnings of the monastic life' (ch. 73), so it may have been a rule suitable for those withdrawing from the pressures of upper-class lay life, rather than seeking the farther limits of self-denial and spiritual discipline.

'Top-down' model

There is, then, a case to be made for the 'bottom-up' development of monasticism, as a result of its inherent attractiveness to potential monks. After its first beginnings, however, when monasteries were established in the desert with little in the way of resources being required, monks needed the support of the powerful. They needed land, which in the barbarian kingdoms was generally only available as gifts from the powerful, whether kings, aristocrats, or bishops. Why were such people apparently so eager to found and endow monasteries? It may be, of course, that they were themselves swept along by the 'bottom-up' popularity of monasticism. But it is hard to prove – and still harder to envisage – that such enormous gifts of land which were often made to monasteries were really prompted by pious enthusiasm for the monastic way of life. Another possible explanation, which you need to consider, is that they were establishing monasteries in a 'top-down' way for purposes of their own, notably their wish to use monasteries as tools in the development of their positions and the exercise of their power.

Monasteries as tools of the Church

In areas where urban development was minimal or non-existent, monasteries may have functioned as substitute towns, providing centres of activity which the Church would otherwise have lacked. Christianity had from its inception been a religion based on cities, with bishoprics in the Roman Empire always centred on them, so that there was in the non-urban parts of Western Europe a serious need for a substitute. It is in this connection striking that in Ireland, but also in England and in the areas east of the former Roman Empire, bishoprics were often centred in monasteries, with the abbot of the monastery sometimes (although not always) functioning as the bishop. Lindisfarne in Northumbria, as Bede describes it, was such a monastery-bishopric, as were Fulda and Lobbes in the Carolingian Empire, and also various centres in Ireland where monk-bishops were the normal governors of the Church. Moreover, monasteries were units out of which larger structures could be built, so that certain monasteries could be placed over a network of lesser monasteries. Thus were created monastic 'families' (*familiae*), such as that of Columba, ruled over by his monastery on the island of Iona (Scotland), or that of Columbanus, ruled over by his monastery of Luxeuil (France).

The extent to which monasteries could sometimes look like towns in their extent and the density of their population is apparent at sites in Ireland such as Clonmacnoise, where the scale of the buildings is suggestive of an urban centre, or Nendrum, on Strangford Lough in Northern Ireland, where the excavator interpreted the layout as being a series of three enclosures, with the church and the monks' dwellings in the central one, and a series of facilities and buildings for others, including laity, in the outer enclosures, so that the whole site looked very much like a town. At Jarrow in Northumbria, it is still possible to see the remains of the workshops down by the River Don (then a navigable tributary of the River Tyne) where industrial production was carried out. The excavations of the sites of Brandon in Suffolk and Flixborough in Lincolnshire have produced so much evidence for industrial production that it has been uncertain whether these sites were or were not monasteries, although the discovery of objects inscribed in Latin has created a strong presumption that they were. Craft-buildings and elaborate accommodation for distinguished guests were also to be found in the ninth century at the monastery of San Vincenzo al Volturno in Italy, as archaeological excavations have shown.

The Plan of St Gall is important here also, since it presumably shows what was required of a monastic plan, even if it was not translated into an actual monastic layout until later. It shows the monastery-church with its cloister and buildings such as the monks' refectory and dormitory at the core of the site, carefully segregated from an array of buildings for guests and pilgrims, and agricultural and industrial production around that core such as to give the impression of really quite a densely settled site that in many ways resembled a town. Some of the service-buildings have labels showing that they were spaces for shoemakers, saddlers, grinders, sword-polishers, woodworkers, curriers (preparing leather), goldsmiths, coopers making barrels, and wheelwrights (Horn and Born, 1979, II, 189–201).

In another respect too, we could see monasteries as substitutes for towns. In the Roman period, education had largely been carried out in schools based in cities, and it was there that bishops and other churchmen had been educated. Monasteries seem increasingly to have provided a substitute for urban schools, and to have become training-grounds for bishops in particular. Thus the influential archbishop of Arles, Caesarius (c.470–542), who was particularly known for his preaching, had been educated at the monastery of Lérins (France), and Bede relates how the monastery of Whitby in Northumbria had trained a whole series of bishops, including Bishop John of Beverley.

If monasteries could function as towns, they could also function as mission-centres, for preaching, converting, and providing pastoral care (especially baptism, and burial rites) to the people living around them. We have already seen that monasteries such as Lindisfarne and Iona served as the centres of bishoprics, as was the case in later periods with English monasteries such as Norwich and Durham, and it is clear that missionaries often did establish monasteries as bases, as was the case with Fulda in Germany, founded in 744 by the missionary Sturm, who was concerned to convert the nearby pagans. It is possible, however, to go further than this, and to argue that in large parts of Western Europe the original framework for missionary work and pastoral care was provided by monasteries, long before the development of parishes and parish-churches took over the role of pastoral care.

This has been particularly argued for England by John Blair (2005, 1988), who has advanced the thesis that from the conversion of the country in the seventh and early eighth centuries monasteries (which he prefers to call by the Old English-derived term 'minsters') were responsible for the pastoral care of wide territories (*paruchiae*), which formed a network of support for Christianity. A monastery was, of course, a community, and Blair's view is that those of the monks of that community who were priests were responsible not only for prayers, services, and masses in the monastery-church, but also for going out into the surrounding territory to preach and conduct services. Although especially important in England, where the organisation of the Roman Church had largely not survived the period of Anglo-Saxon settlement, this system of pastoral care based on monasteries or 'minsters' is argued to have been widespread across the British Isles and indeed on the Continent.

If that was the case, it provides a good reason why monasticism was so attractive in Western Europe, at any rate to the Church. But there are difficulties. The evidence for reconstructing the monastic territories (*paruchiae*) is usually much later in date, and the reconstruction depends on accepting that the pattern of later parishes shows that they had split apart from early territories of monasteries (or minsters). The evidence for the role of monks in pastoral care can of course be shown in the case of monastic bishoprics, like Lindisfarne, or in the case of monasteries founded in areas of missionary work such as Fulda, but it is not at all clear that pastoral care was a function of monks in general, who were committed to prayer, services especially masses, scholarship, and manual work, as well as being tied to a vow of 'stability' requiring them to remain in the monastery. It can be argued that these last objections only have force after the *Rule of St Benedict* had been made widespread in Western Europe, that is in the ninth century, or the tenth in England. We should have to accept that earlier monasteries were sometimes quite different from later monasteries, much more informally organised, so that their monks would have been able to go out and deal with the laity. It is not, however, easy to show that this was really the case. Moreover, throughout our period, the role of the bishop seems to have been crucial in the working of the Church. Only the bishop, for example, could supply the holy oil (or chrism) required for baptism and for the last rites for the dying, and only the bishop could ordain a priest. Important as monasteries no doubt were, the view that they were a key element in the Church's system of pastoral care needs your close and critical attention.

Monasteries as tools of kings

The function of monasteries as centres of literacy and learning may have been an attraction for kings, since monasteries could act as the writing offices of royal government in periods when literacy amongst the laity was at best restricted. A classic case is that of the royal chancery of pre-Norman Conquest England, which was staffed by churchmen (principally monks). Indeed, it may not have existed as an institution in its own right, but may have consisted of monks in various monasteries close to the English king who undertook the writing of documents. Monasteries could also act as archives of royal documents as was the case with Winchcombe (Gloucestershire), since a document of 825 orders that names of estates now given to the Archbishop of Canterbury but claimed by the royal princess, Cwoenthryth, who was abbess of Minster-in-Thanet in Kent, should be 'erased from the ancient documents which are at Winchcombe' (Levison, 1946, p. 252). That monastery had evidently been used as a royal archive.

It may be that the abbey of Saint-Wandrille in the valley of the River Seine near Rouen (France) had even more important functions as an archive for the Carolingian kings. Many of the capitularies of those rulers, that is, the documents which were most often the records of their councils containing governmental edicts and directions, have been preserved in a collection made in the ninth century by Ansegisus, abbot of Saint-Wandrille. It is possible that he made this collection in an entirely private capacity, but it seems more likely that he was acting as a royal archivist and that the monastery of Saint-Wandrille had been chosen to fulfil the function of royal archive in this respect.

The literary capabilities of monasteries also offered kings the possibility that they could be used to write history under royal patronage and in a way which would promote royal reputations. The *Anglo-Saxon Chronicle*, which was begun as a historical record in the time of King Alfred of Wessex in the late ninth century, was in large part a celebration of the king's family and achievements. It is not certain that it was produced in a monastery at first, but from the early tenth century it was continued in a series of monasteries, including Abingdon and New Minster Winchester, which produced parallel but somewhat different versions. This potential function of monasteries in writing history on behalf of kings, or at least in their favour, is evident also in the way in which the abbey of Fleury (Saint-Benoît-sur-Loire, France) produced in the early eleventh century the *Life of King Robert the Pious* by Helgaud, and the abbey of Saint-Denis in the twelfth century produced also a version of the *Great Chronicles of France*. These crucially underpinned the legitimacy of the new Capetian dynasty of western Frankia, which had come to power in 987, by presenting it as descended from the dynasty of its Carolingian predecessors.

Monasteries, however, had the potential to act even more practically on behalf of kings. In parts of Western Europe, they may have acted as the governmental centres of royal administrative units. In Northumbria, the monastery of Coldingham sat at the centre of what was known later as Coldinghamshire, which seems to have been an early administrative unit. Similarly the monastery of Hexham sat at the centre of Hexhamshire, while in the kingdom of Kent it looks as if there were close associations between the early administrative units which appear in the Domesday Book as 'lathes' and monasteries such as Lyminge, Folkestone, and Minster-in-Thanet.

The value of monasteries as centres of government would naturally have lain in the kings' ability to control and supervise them, and this may have been an important reason why when kings moved about (on the royal 'itinerary', that is) monasteries were often places where they and their courts stayed (see also above, p. 105). There may be architectural evidence of this at the monastery of Lorsch in the Rhineland, where the lavishly decorated chamber above the 'triumphal arch' in the monastic precinct has been interpreted as having been assigned for the use of the king – indeed, the arch itself may have been intended to function in the processions of the king at his arrival (*adventus*) at the monastery (Fig. 28).

The great west gallery above the nave of the monastery-church at Corvey on the River Weser (Germany) has in its west wall a raised niche which has been interpreted as the place where the king's throne would have been located for him on his visits to the monastery in the course of his itinerary.

It is extremely frustrating that, although the Plan of St Gall shows a large building just to the west of the monastery-church which may have been intended to receive the king on his itinerary, there has been damage to the parchment at this point so that the inscription which would have confirmed this has been erased. Nevertheless, the same pattern of monasteries being used on the royal itinerary seems evident in England, where Bede's own monastery of Jarrow is also known in our sources as 'the port of King Ecgfrith', while Bede himself describes the visits of King Oswald to the monastery

Figure 28 'Triumphal Arch' at Lorsch (Germany). The surviving parts of the monastery-church are behind us as we look at this free-standing arch, which is dated on the grounds of its style to the eighth or ninth centuries. Notice particularly the geometrical patterning with coloured stones (polychrome work), in conjunction with the Corinthian capitals at the top of each attached column. The first-floor room, which is magnificently decorated with wall-paintings imitating marble cladding, is reached by the spiral staircases in the turrets on either side. This may have been a room for the emperor when he stayed in this royally patronised abbey. The triple arches have been compared with the Arch of Constantine in Rome (Fig. 25), which the architect of this arch may have been imitating.

of Lindisfarne (Bede, *Eccl. History*, III. 26). His descriptions suggest that these visits were solely for pious purposes, but in fact the island of Lindisfarne was well provided with a natural harbour, in which we can easily imagine the king's war-fleet at anchor, and it is entirely possible that the monastery functioned also as a royal gaol, if Lindisfarne is the same place as *In-broninis* ('on the isle'), where Bishop Wilfrid was imprisoned by the king of Northumbria in the late seventh century (*Life of Wilfrid*, ch. 36).

In terms of economic power, we have seen already in our consideration of the Carolingian polyptychs the enormous scale of the landed estates which monasteries held, and the wealth which could be derived from these, as is clearly set out in the *Customs of the Monastery of Corbie*. Impressive as it was, land was not the only source of monasteries' wealth. The monastery of Saint-Denis near Paris had from an early date supervised, and probably promoted, the great fair of Saint-Denis, which took place annually, drew in traders from right across Europe, and was evidently a considerable means of wealth-generation, as well as of revenue for the monastery. Monasteries could also be involved more directly in commercial activities and indeed in industrial production. A series of English charters from the eighth century record the king of Kent granting to monasteries such as Minster-in-Thanet remission from paying tolls on trading ships moving, apparently, between Kent and the port of London. Monasteries like Jarrow and Whitby, well-placed in coastal locations with good natural harbours, seem very likely to have been directly involved in trade, and, as we have seen, it is certain that they were involved in the production of commodities.

The economic functions of monasteries may have offered benefits to kings in other ways. In areas like Saxony, conquered by Charlemagne in the late eighth and early ninth centuries and converted to Christianity as a result, it may also have been advantageous to rulers to make them more part of their own realms by introducing them to the commercial and monetary practices of their own kingdoms. Certainly, we often find kings granting to monasteries rights to hold markets and to mint coins, as they did, for example, with Fulda in the recently converted area of Hessen in what is now Germany. In the tenth century, the monastery of Saint-Maurice which the German ruler Otto I founded in Magdeburg seems to have overseen the development of wide-ranging trade in slaves, honey, beeswax, and luxury goods. It also derived considerable wealth from the lands granted to it, including new clearings in the forests, woodland pasture for pigs, and, in one case at least, iron mines. There were, of course, profits likely to accrue directly to the monasteries from the overheads they would take from these activities, but it may be that the kings were also envisaging benefiting through the cultural changes to the areas in question which would result from the introduction of commerce and the use of coins.

Aside from wealth, however, land was more directly a source of power in the Early Middle Ages, because it could be used to reward followers and to sustain military vassals. The vast landed estates in the hands of monasteries were thus potentially of great importance to kings if they could control them, and we could argue that these estates were actually easier to control because they were monastic, and that this was another attraction which monasteries offered to kings. The Carolingian rulers, beginning with the mayor of the palace Charles Martel in the early eighth century, who effectively ruled the kingdom of the Franks on behalf of an ineffective king, simply took control of monastic estates (and indeed other ecclesiastical estates) in order to grant them to military retainers (vassals). This was evidently a crucial source of landed power for the ruler, and it created a running conflict with the Church, which sought to recover the lands in question. A solution was eventually worked out by which the Church was entitled to an additional duty (a 'ninth') payable to it from its lands which had been granted to the king's vassals, but the balance of benefit seems to have remained on the side of the kings.

There were, however, more direct means by which kings could control and exploit the lands of monasteries. Crucial to these was the kings' ability to control the choice of abbots and abbesses. By the end of our period, they could unquestionably do this, but it is not so clear when this *de facto* power developed. The *Rule of St Benedict* may indirectly have promoted it by insisting that the abbot of a monastery should be elected by the monks. Paradoxically, this may have made it easier for the king to control the abbot's appointment by influencing the election, which would have been a means of wresting control over the abbacy from the hands of local aristocratic families which might otherwise have had the preponderant influence over it. There seems clear evidence that Charles Martel gained control of monasteries in this way as part of his campaign to absorb the area of south-west Gaul called Aquitaine into the kingdom of the Franks.

Kings could, however, exert control over monasteries and their lands even more directly if they could supply the abbots from their own families. The island-monastery of Iona, founded as we have seen by Columba in the late sixth century, was closely connected with the Ui-Neill kings of northern Ireland, of whose family Columba was himself a member. So this was in a very real sense a royal monastery – and the dominance of the kings must have continued when no fewer than fourteen generations of abbots were all members of the Ui-Neill royal family. In England, we have already seen the Mercian princess Cwoenthryth as abbess of Minster-in-Thanet in Kent, at the time a formerly independent kingdom which the kings of Mercia were absorbing into their own. And we could add to this the presence at the monastery of Whitby of a series of royal abbesses, beginning with the foundress, Hild, and the presence as abbess of Coldingham (which we have already seen as being at the head of what was probably a royal administrative unit) of the king's sister Æbbe. On the Continent, Charlemagne's cousins, Adalhard and Wala, were likewise abbots of important monasteries, themselves closely associated with the kings. On the Continent too, the institution of the lay abbot, by which a layman could effectively function as the protector and manager of a monastery and its lands, offered further possibilities. Charlemagne's grandson, King Charles the Bald, was lay abbot of the important monastery of Saint-Denis, which he effectively used as a royal palace.

In all or any of these ways, monasteries offered considerable potential to kings as centres or islands of power used in the royal interest. A particularly striking example which may illustrate this is the patronage by the tenth-century kings of Wessex of reform of monasteries according to the *Rule of St Benedict*. These monasteries often represented refoundations of ancient communities, as in the case of the monastery of Ely. They were located in various parts of England, including the kingdom of Wessex itself; but the important thing for us is that there was a concentration of them in eastern England, especially in the area of the Fens, including Peterborough, Ely, Ramsey, and Thorney. This was one of the areas which had been most affected by the Viking incursions of the ninth century, and which it was most urgent for the kings of Wessex to assert control of in their campaign to expand their kingdom to embrace all England. We may think that their close links with reformed monasteries in those areas was part of this campaign.

Monasteries as tools of aristocratic families

Much of what we have been discussing in this respect with regard to kings might also have applied to the interests of aristocratic families, who were also founders and patrons of monasteries. They too could have used them as sources of wealth and power in the same sorts of way. But in their case the implications of monasteries for the way in which they could hold and accumulate land may have had even greater attractions than they did for kings. In 734, the last year of his life, Bede wrote to Bishop Ecgberht of York, lamenting the state of society and the Church in his day, his mind being chiefly on the kingdom of Northumbria in which he himself lived. One of the principal problems, as he saw it, was the fact that there was 'nowhere that the sons of the nobles or retired warriors can take possession of', so that they either left the kingdom or gave themselves up to shameful lives of self-indulgence, and 'wandering without a spouse' they were 'not even abstaining from virgins consecrated to God'. There was, in other words, a shortage of land on which these men could settle, and the reason for this, Bede writes, was that there were many places which 'go by the name of monasteries' but 'have been taken under the control of men who have no knowledge of true monastic life'. Bede goes on:

> There are others, laymen who have no love for the monastic life nor for military service, who commit a graver crime by giving money to the kings and obtaining lands under the pretext of building monasteries, in which they can give freer rein to their libidinous tastes; these lands they have assigned to them in hereditary right through written royal edicts, and these charters, as if to make them really worthy in the sight of God, they arrange to be witnessed in writing by bishops, abbots, and the most powerful laymen. Thus they have gained unjust rights over fields and villages, free from both divine and human legal obligations. . . . Also with equal shamelessness they obtain places where their wives may construct monasteries.
>
> (Bede, *Letter to Ecgberht*)

In other words, Bede's view was that one of the great problems of the kingdom of Northumbria was that laymen were founding what he saw as bogus monasteries, with the result that there was a shortage of land to grant to military vassals.

The question is: why should laymen have wished to found bogus monasteries and why should such foundations necessarily have produced this shortage of land? The explanation seems to lie in the history of land-holding. In the Roman Empire, land had been held on more or less the same basis as freehold land is held today. That is, it was simply possessed by its landlords in perpetuity, with the right to give it away and above all to bequeath it at will. In barbarian society, however, the evidence of law-codes and above all of the documents called charters or diplomas which recorded the grant of land, suggests that land-holding, especially in less Romanised parts of Western Europe such as England, was more complex and, at the beginning of our period at least, was certainly not freehold in the Roman and modern sense. Instead, land may have been held in one of two ways. First, there is evidence from Frankia and also from Ireland that it was held in such a way that it still belonged in some sense to the extended family – the kindred – of its holder, so that on his or her death it had to be divided between all the children, if not amongst a wider circle of kin. This was a form of what later legal historians have called partible inheritance. Secondly, there is evidence from English charters to suggest that the holding of land was normally what is called in Old English 'folkland'. The meaning of this may be land which was not held in hereditary right, but had to be returned to the people (the 'folk') on the death of its holder, the people being represented by the king.

Setting aside the complex scholarly discussions which have attempted to distinguish these types of land-holding, the key point must be that land held under either type was not strictly freehold in the Roman and modern sense; it was not capable of being bequeathed at will as a block. This may explain what the motive of the lay founders of bogus monasteries referred to by Bede's letter was. A monastery was a perpetual and indivisible body. Land granted to it was, as Bede himself states and as is explicit in the early English charters (to which Bede is evidently referring when he writes about 'edicts' and charters with written lists of witnesses), made over 'in perpetual right' or 'in hereditary right'. As the head of a monastery, even if a bogus monastery, a layman would therefore be able to evade the customs of barbarian land-holding. He could indeed bequeath the monastery and its lands as an undivided entity to whomsoever he wished. And on the basis of this he could begin the process of building up a great block of land in the hands of his family, undivided at each bequest without reference to the systems of partible inheritance or folkland. By the late eighth and ninth centuries, in England at any rate, perpetual or hereditary tenure of this sort was available to laymen in any case, but before that it seems that only churches, chiefly monasteries, or (in Bede's view) bogus monasteries, were eligible for it.

It may be that Bede's condemnation of monasteries as bogus was the result of an exceptionally purist, not to say puritanical, viewpoint. These monasteries may simply have been ones which did not conform to the *Rule of St Benedict*, or an equivalent rule, to the standards that Bede expected. Or Bede may have been writing a polemic aimed at denigrating communities other than his own, although it is hard to explain why he should have wanted to do this, when he was so committed to the spread of Christianity, unless there was truth in his criticisms. In any case, the point seems clear that founding a monastery was the principal way in the early part of our period by which laymen could obtain what was effectively freehold tenure, and this may well have been one of the great attractions of monasticism to them.

Another may have been the extent to which monasteries could be made to fit in with the values and lifestyle of barbarian society. In Bede's time, at any rate, most monks seem to have been of the aristocratic class, and his account of the double monastery for men and women at Coldingham (Borders) suggests that the same was true of nuns, who spent their time 'weaving elaborate garments with which to adorn themselves as if they were brides' (Bede, *Eccl. History*, IV.25). The lifestyle of an early monastery could clearly be very aristocratic in character. Feasting was important, for example, as is shown by Cuthbert of Lindisfarne's participation at a dinner in a monastery by the River Tyne where, like Christ himself had done, he made water taste like wine (Bede, *Life of St Cuthbert*, ch. 35); and the abbot of Bede's monastery at Monkwearmouth-Jarrow was at one time seeking a harpist, presumably to play at his feasts (Whitelock, 1979, no. 185).

But there was a deeper sense in which monasteries entered into aristocratic values. When Oswine, the king of Deira (the southern part of the kingdom of Northumbria), was murdered in 655 at the behest of his co-ruler, Oswiu, the latter built a monastery at Gilling where Oswine had died, and this was 'to atone for his crime', prayers being offered in it 'for the redemption of the souls of both kings, the murdered king and the one who ordered the murder' (Bede, *Eccl. History*, III.14). In one sense this looks like merely a Christian act of organising through a monastery prayers for the soul. But later in his work Bede explains that it was 'Queen Eanflæd, King Oswine's kinswoman' who had 'asked King Oswiu to expiate Oswine's unjust death by granting God's servant Trumhere, also a near relative of the murdered king, a site at Gilling to build a monastery' (Bede, *Eccl. History*, III.24). Here, monastic foundation was seen as a sort of compensation payment (*wergild* in Old English) which we find in barbarian laws. This was made to the kindred of the murdered man by the kindred of the killer in order to avert the vendetta or bloodfeud being waged against them. So deeply had monasteries entered into barbarian society that they could be regarded as suitable *wergilds*.

They could also be regarded as *wergilds* paid not to man but to God himself. According to a series of English texts, the earliest of which was probably composed in the eighth century, the monastery of Minster-in-Thanet was founded as just such a *wergild*. The circumstances were that the king of Kent, Ecgberht, was made suspicious of the possible ambitions to the throne of his cousins, the princes Æthelberht and Æthelred, by the counsels of his wicked counsellor, Thunor. The latter eventually killed the two princes and buried them secretly under the royal throne. When the king went out, however, he saw a column of divine light over their burial-place, and the killing was revealed. Fearing God's vengeance, the king called a council which recommended that the princes' sister, Domne Eafe, should be summoned and offered compensation for the killing. The compensation (or in effect *wergild*) which she chose was as much land on the Isle of Thanet as her tame hind would run round. She and the king and his courtiers duly crossed to the isle and set the hind running. Thunor, fearing that it would grant too much land to Domne Eafe, tried to head it off, but he was miraculously swallowed by the earth. The hind completed its course, and the land it had delineated was granted to Domne Eafe, who founded on it the monastery of Minster-in-Thanet. That this *wergild* was envisaged as paid to her acting on behalf of God himself is suggested by our sources' emphasis on the secret nature of the killing of the princes. To contemporaries, this would have made it a 'murder' (a *morðweorc* in Old English) rather than a public killing which would have been subject to the rules of bloodfeud and *wergild*-payment. But it was the divine column of light which revealed that it had happened, and so the kinship of the princes, who came to be regarded as saints, was being claimed by God, to whom the *wergild* was in effect paid (Rollason, 1982).

All this can be seen as a testimony to the depth with which monasteries had penetrated Western European mentality and outlook, and it underlines the challenge of explaining the popularity of monasticism in Western Europe in our period. Was it to do with the spiritual attractions of that way of life? Or the political, economic, and social advantages which it gave? Or was it do with the ways in which monasticism as an aspect of Christianity had changed to adapt itself to the outlook and lifestyle of Western Europe?

Research and study

Broad research questions

What were the mechanisms by which monasticism spread from Egypt and the Holy Land to Western Europe?

Why was monasticism so attractive to recruits in Western Europe?

Were the practical benefits offered by monasteries more or less important than the spiritual benefits they were believed to confer?

How far did monasteries fit into the social and political structure of Western Europe?

How far had monasticism come to fit in with the ideas and outlook of early medieval Western Europe?

Books and papers to begin with

A clear and authoritative account of the history of monasticism throughout our period is Lawrence (2001, chs 1–6). The later chapters are really concerned with the later Middle Ages, during which monasticism was in some respects rather different. Chapters 1–4 of the classic book by Knowles (1963) are well worth reading. A longer and more recent discussion, which considers a range of religious aspects of monasticism, is Dunn (2000). There is insightful discussion, particularly of changes in monasticism in relation to religious beliefs, in Brown (2002, chs 9–11). Brown (1989, especially chs 11–12) and Markus (1990, ch. 11) are classic studies of the earliest period of monasticism. Yorke (2002) discusses the importance of nunneries, principally in England.

The early period of monasticism in Egypt and the eastern Mediterranean is dealt with in very clear books by Chitty (1966) and Chadwick (1968, ch. 1). For more up-to-date research, you can consult Hedstrom (2006). There is a very helpful map of the spread of monasticism 300–700 in Van der Meer (1966, no. 32).

For Frankish Gaul, there are accounts of the Merovingian period and the influence of the Irish monk Columbanus in Wallace-Hadrill (1983, ch. 4), and Wood (1994a, ch. 11). There are important papers in Clarke and Brennan (1981), including those by Wood, Riché, and Prinz – the last two especially useful as being English-language versions of scholarship published in French and German. For the Carolingians, there is a thoughtful summary in De Jong (1995).

For England, there is a brilliant treatment of Northumbrian monasteries by Mayr-Harting (1991a, ch. 10). There is a comprehensive discussion of the period 600–900 in Foot (2006), but more wide-ranging and interesting is Blair (2005), which also tackles the economic and other practical implications of monastic foundations, as well as archaeological evidence which is also covered by Cramp (1976).

For Irish monasticism, see Charles-Edwards (2000, chs 6–8), but useful too is Hughes and Hamlin (1977). There are summaries of archaeological excavations in Edwards (1990, ch. 6), and fuller treatment in Herity (1995). An excellent introduction to Irish island-hermitages is Herity (1989). On the question of monasticism and martyrdom, see Stancliffe (1982).

For Ottonian Germany, useful is Fichtenau (1991, chs 12–13); on the church of Magdeburg, there is a brilliant and very clear paper by Mayr-Harting (1992). For France and the influence of the monastery of Cluny, see Evans (1931).

Pursuing more specific aspects

Archaeological evidence and the Plan of St Gall

How far do the results of excavations and the plan of a monastery in the Plan of St Gall reflect written sources, especially the Rule of St Benedict?

How far do they illuminate the economic and political functions of monasteries?

What light do they cast on their religious functions, especially in the detailed layout of the monastic church?

It is very well worthwhile getting to know the Plan of St Gall, which you can do very easily with Horn and Born (1979). This provides reproductions of sections of the plan together with a commentary on individual buildings. It is possible to argue that the plan is not the early ninth-century blueprint for monasteries which the authors envisaged (e.g. Hodges, 1997, pp. 11–13), but its importance for the subject is not in doubt. It is very instructive to consider it alongside the excavations of the eighth-century Italian monastery of San Vincenzo al Volturno, rebuilt in the ninth century (Hodges, 1997 is very clear, or for more detail see Hodges and Mitchell, 1985, or you can look at the full excavation reports in Hodges and Coutts, 1993–), and the excavated monasteries of Monkwearmouth and Jarrow in Northumbria (Cramp, Bettess, Bettess, et al., 2005–6; there are shorter summaries, for example in Cramp, 1994). As noted above, for other sites see for England Cramp (1976) and Blair (2005), for Ireland Edwards (1990, ch. 6) and Herity (1995). For Gaul, there is a paper by James (1981). For monasteries as towns and economic centres, see Doherty (1985) and the very thought-provoking discussion in Blair (2005, ch. 5).

Prayers and masses for the dead

How far were gifts to monasteries (and the foundation of monasteries) specifically intended to obtain prayers and masses for the dead?

How far were such gifts and foundations more to do with creating networks of friendship with monasteries?

McLaughlin (1994) is not easy to read but presents a very full account and a thought-provoking discussion, including clear and full references to the sources. For *libri vitae* there are papers in English by Angenendt and Geuenich in Rollason et al. (2004).

Monasteries and pastoral care

How far did monasteries provide pastoral care?

What was the relationship between monasteries and bishops in doing this?

The discussion is most easily accessible largely, but not exclusively, focused on England in Blair (1988, 2005) and Blair and Sharpe (1992). It is worthwhile following a debate on the pastoral role of monasteries, in which Blair was attacked (in a friendly way) by Rollason and Cambridge (1995) and replied (Blair, 1995). The papers contain succinct statements of the case for monasteries' pastoral care and criticisms of it. The debate has been continued, most recently in the context of the early medieval Spanish Church, by Davies (2011).

12

The power of bishops and popes

The 'top-down' model for explaining the conversion of Western Europe to Christianity, and the subsequent maintenance of the religion amongst the population, may involve the power of secular rulers, as we have seen, but it surely must involve also the power of the Church as an organisation. If we are to argue for the 'top-down' model, we need to explore how developed that power was in our period. The purpose of this chapter is to attempt that, focusing on bishops, including the bishop of Rome, or the pope, who appear in the sources for our period as men of great power and influence in the world as well as in the Church itself. How extensive was this power, what was its nature, and on what did it depend? How far did the bishops occupy a position at the head of a hierarchy of power, which in the case of the pope embraced the whole of Western Christendom? How far did they have a machinery enabling them to reach down to the lowest levels of Christian society?

Bishops and popes in the Church hierarchy

Rituals

From at least the time of the Council of Carthage in 390, only bishops had the right to consecrate the holy oil or chrism (in fact, a mixture of olive oil and balsam) which was an essential ingredient of baptism and the ordination of new clergy to their offices, being used to anoint the new entrant to the Christian community in the former, and to anoint the new priest in the latter. So only the bishop's church could distribute chrism, which was normally done just before Easter, and elaborate systems were set up for this distribution, which naturally confirmed the bishop's position of authority over the

Church at large. When the ritual for inaugurating a king or emperor came to involve the use of holy oil, in the Visigothic kingdom in the seventh century, in the Frankish in the mid-eighth (above, p. 85), bishops and popes naturally had a monopoly over this ritual too, since only they had the right to use holy oil.

In addition, the bishop had a monopoly over the dedication of churches in his diocese, an elaborate ceremony (at any rate by the end of our period) involving sprinkling the walls of the church with holy water in the course of a solemn procession around the inside and outside of the church, culminating in the installation of relics of saints in the altar, and the marking of dedication crosses on the altar itself and on the walls (these can sometimes still be seen as, for example, at the early church of Escomb in County Durham). We could argue that the effect of the bishop's monopoly over this ritual was likewise to confirm his authority.

Church hierarchy

Since the second century, bishops had been the leaders of the Christian communities of their dioceses, superior to priests and deacons in the clerical hierarchy. The bishop had charge of his own court, the competence of which was extended after the conversion of the emperor Constantine at the beginning of the fourth century to judge all cases involving the clergy.

Over and above individual dioceses, bishops' power depended crucially on the hierarchical organisation of all bishops, which in turn reflected the government structure of the later Roman Empire. This consisted of administrative units which were the cities and their territories (*civitates*, singular *civitas*), which formed the components of an overarching administrative unit called a province (*provincia*), governed from a city which was known as a *metropolis*. The organisation of the Church followed this, with individual dioceses normally corresponding to cities and their territories, with their bishops subject to the bishop of the *metropolis* of their province, who came to be known from the time of the Council of Nicaea in 325 as a 'metropolitan'. This bishop was in charge of a provincial synod or council to which the bishops of the province would be summoned, as well as for inspecting those bishops, managing their dioceses when the office of bishop was vacant, and disciplining them when necessary.

A further development in this hierarchy followed on from the emperor Diocletian's organisation of provinces under overarching units called, rather confusingly, civil dioceses. The Church followed suit, so that metropolitans were themselves subject to the bishops of these new civil dioceses, who came to be known in the eastern part of the Roman Empire as patriarchs. In the West, the equivalent was the Bishop of Rome, the pope, who became responsible for summoning councils of bishops and metropolitans for the whole of the West, for the doctrine and discipline of the western Church, and for the appointment of metropolitans. It came to be accepted, at any rate from the ninth century for Western Europe as a whole, earlier in the case of the English Church, that the latter could only take up their offices if they had received from the pope the pallium, a distinctive white woollen shawl worn on the shoulders.

The system of holding Church councils or synods at the different levels of the organisation was a major element in the authority of the bishops as a group, because it gave them a sense of group identity and group authority, based on communication between themselves, and collective decision-making. Soon after the conversion of the emperor Constantine, there were held two councils for the whole Church, the Council of Arles (314), attended by bishops from as far away as York, and the Council of Nicaea (325), which was probably attended by as many as 250 bishops, and was opened by the emperor himself. These councils were held to consider divergences within Christian doctrine, that of Arles being concerned with Donatism (the teaching that those who had collaborated with the persecutors in any way should be excluded from the Church), that of Nicaea being concerned with Arianism (the teaching that Christ was created by God the Father rather than being genuinely his son and so made of the same substance as He was). Nevertheless, the effect of these councils was to give a sense of unity and authority to the bishops as a group, even if the councils were still a source of controversy. This was especially the case with the Council of Nicaea, which promulgated the Nicene Creed as a statement of Christian belief which has remained valid through all the history of the Church. Councils were equally important after the conversion of the Frankish king Clovis around 500, with the holding, for example, of the important Council of Orléans in 522, and again with the so-called Carolingian reforms of the Church in the late eighth and ninth centuries, when a series of councils was held.

The rise of the papacy

The development of the hierarchy of bishops, metropolitans, and popes was not, however, a smooth or an uncontested process, especially as it concerned the position of the pope in Western Europe. An observer of the pope's position in the fourth century, for example, might have been excused for failing to anticipate the eventual rise of the papal office to dominance in Western Europe. In the latter part of the century, for example, dominance over the Church of the western Roman Empire might seem rather to have belonged to the bishopric of Milan, which was one of the principal cities where the imperial court resided at that period. Its bishop, Ambrose, convened the Council of Aquileia in 381. This considered the problem of Arianism which had already been considered by the pope, and in 391/2 the Council of Capua was held without the pope even being present. On the face of it, the pope's position was not a strong one. The city of Rome had long ceased to be an imperial residence, and when Milan lost this role in the late fourth century the court transferred itself to Ravenna at the head of the Adriatic Sea rather than to Rome. Our sources show that the latter was a city in chronic decline, its population falling from possibly as much as 1.5 millions in the second century to as little as half a million by the mid-fifth century, and to as low as 100,000 by 500, by when there had developed the malarial swamps which plagued the city until the time of the twentieth-century dictator Mussolini. The rise of the papacy to dominance over the western Church can be explained in two ways, which are not necessarily mutually exclusive.

We could argue that the popes pursued a consistent policy of raising their office to a position of dominance, partly in response to the claims to dominance of the patriarch of Constantinople. As early as the second century, they made the claim that, as bishops of Rome, they were the successors of Christ's own apostle, St Peter (i.e. the 'Petrine succession'). This claim was completely unfounded, since there is no evidence in the Acts of the Apostles in the New Testament, or in other early Christian writings, that Peter had been bishop of Rome. Nevertheless, the popes asserted it with such vigour that it came to be generally accepted, and was an important element in the popes' assertion of their authority. Peter had certainly been martyred in Rome, and one of the pope's principal churches, that of St Peter in the Vatican, was built over a tomb believed to be Peter's – a belief that modern excavation under the church has shown to be entirely plausible, possibly even correct. The connection between the popes and this saint became an important element in papal authority. Before the pallium was sent out from Rome to confirm the appointment of a metropolitan, for example, it was kept for a night in contact with St Peter's tomb as if to emphasise what the source of the pope's authority was.

Peter's importance to Christians was considerable, so the papal claim of succession to him was very significant. According to St Matthew's Gospel (16.18–19), Christ had said to Peter: 'You are Peter [the Latin is *petrus*], and on this rock [the Latin is *petra*] I shall build my Church.' The play on words in the Latin version made this memorable, and the claim that Peter was the foundation of the Church was a crucially important card in the pope's hands. Moreover, Christ stated further that he had given Peter the keys to the Kingdom of Heaven, which is why Peter is normally represented in Christian art with a key. The importance of this emerges very clearly from Bede's account of the synod held at Whitby in Northumbria in 664 to consider whether the English Church should accept what was believed to be the Church of Rome's method of fixing the date of Easter (a complex matter since Easter was tied to the Hebrew festival of Passover, which was dated according to the lunar rather than the solar calendar; see below, p. 316). The proponent of the method believed to be that of Rome was Bishop Wilfrid, who quoted St Matthew's Gospel in summarising his case: 'You are Peter and upon this rock I shall build my Church, and the gates of hell shall not prevail against it, and I will give you the keys of the kingdom of heaven.' King Oswiu of Northumbria, who was presiding, was (according to Bede) completely swayed in Wilfrid's favour by this argument, concluding: 'Then, I tell you, since he [Peter] is the doorkeeper I will not contradict him; but I intend to obey his commands in everything to the best of my knowledge and ability, otherwise when I come to the gates of the kingdom of heaven, there may be no one to open them because the one who . . . holds the keys has turned his back on me' (Bede, *Eccl. History*, III.25). There could be no more vivid demonstration of the resonance of the claim to the Petrine succession.

The popes repeatedly asserted their authority, especially in the case of Pope Leo I (440–61) and of Pope Gelasius (492–6). The popes of the early ninth century continued this, as well as seeking to establish Rome itself and its territory as independent polit-ically as well as ecclesiastically, creating in effect a 'republic of St Peter'. The growth of papal authority over the Church was not continuous, but it reached a climax in the late eleventh century, especially under the leadership of Pope Gregory VII (1073–85), in the so-called Gregorian Reform, which sought to give the pope and the ecclesiastical hierarchy under him absolute control over the appointment of clergy, a process which had been in part taken over by laymen. The results were dramatic, involving war between the pope and the emperor of Germany, Henry IV, and the result was a compromise, but one which confirmed the pope's authority over the western Church.

Against this, however, you could argue that statements of papal authority made by popes were less the result of a coherent papal policy to dominate the western Church, and more responses to particular rival claims from other churches, especially the patriarchate of Constantinople, or claims from kings to dominate Rome. The statements of Pope Gelasius about papal superiority, for example, seem to have been made in response to claims to supremacy made by the Patriarch of Constantinople in the context of a controversy in the Church called the Acacian Schism.

The resources of popes and bishops

The cult of saints

The popes' claim to succession to St Peter was only part of a wider process by which bishops and popes associated themselves with saints and their relics, and (you could argue) sought to use belief in them as tools of power. The cult of saints had originated in the time of the persecutions. Those who had been martyred in the course of those were regarded by the Christians as a special category of the dead, who merited great veneration, and great attention to their mortal remains. This is documented earliest in the *Passion* of the second-century martyr Polycarp of the city of Smyrna in the eastern Mediterranean. After his death at the hands of the persecutors, the authorities, clearly aware of the importance of his mortal remains to the Christians, tried to destroy his body by burning it and throwing the ashes into the river. But the Christians were able to recover them and to enshrine and venerate them as more precious than gold. Although the *Passion of St Polycarp* is the earliest account of such veneration of a martyr, it is only one of a considerable number of *Passions* of varying dates, bearing witness to the widespread veneration by Christian communities of martyrs. Following the cessation of the persecutions, however, the supply of such martyrs largely dried up, aside from the occasional missionary martyred by heathens, and in the course of the fourth century veneration developed of particularly holy Christians who had not been martyred, but who had led especially saintly lives as bishops, abbots, monks, hermits, or virgins. Indeed, the concept developed of 'bloodless martyrdom', by which it was possible to be regarded as a martyr as a result of the sufferings caused by self-denial in the role of a hermit or a virgin, for example (see also above, p. 260). The growth in the number of saints and the scale of veneration of them was exponential, so that by the end of the fourth century Christianity was largely identified with the cult of saints.

The underlying belief-structure of this was that the saint received special treatment from God in recognition of his or her sufferings and virtues. This special treatment meant that the saint was taken to heaven immediately after death, and was already with God, even before the Last Judgment had come. But that was not all. The saint was not only with God in heaven, but was also present in his or her mortal remains on earth, as is clear from the inscription on the tomb of St Martin of Tours:

> Here lies buried Martin the bishop of holy memory, whose soul is in the hand of God, but who is here completely present and made manifest by all the grace of miracles.
>
> (Brown, 1981, p. 4)

The saint's simultaneous presence in heaven and in his or her earthly remains meant that there was, to express it crudely, a sort of hot line between the saint's remains and the saint in heaven. The saint could be contacted in heaven by the believer's prayers at the saint's remains, and the saint would then intercede with God to grant those prayers – hence the miracles referred to in the inscription on St Martin's tomb. Moreover, the saint's earthly remains, the corporeal 'relics', could be fragmented and distributed, with each fragment providing the same sort of hot line, or their power could be transferred by mere contact to non-corporeal or secondary relics, that is, objects or materials which had merely been in contact with the saint's remains.

The importance of the cult of saints is perhaps most evident in the change which it produced in attitudes to the dead. In the pagan Roman Empire, the dead were regarded as a source of spiritual pollution. Contact with them necessitated ritual cleansing, cemeteries were required by law to be outside the walls, and disturbance of the bodies of the dead was forbidden. There was admittedly a ceremony of holding a meal over the tomb of the deceased on the anniversary of their death, the so-called *refrigerium*, but nothing in pagan practice prepared the way for Christianity's attention to the bodies of saints. It was this aspect of the religion which impressed contemporary critics, and the emperor Julian the Apostate accused the Christians of having 'filled the whole world with tombs and sepulchres'.

This change of attitude in its turn had important effects on the shape of cities. Because Roman law forbade burial inside the walls of a city, tombs of martyrs – and later of saints – were naturally outside the walls of cities, as for example the tomb of St Peter on the Vatican Hill outside the city of Rome. Churches were erected over them, so that the saints' shrines were principally extramural, and to them pilgrims flocked, and around them the lives of Christian communities gravitated. This had a major impact on the topography of late Roman cities, disrupting their classical layout and drawing their foci away from their old centres. Tours on the River Loire is a good example, where, although the city remained important with its cathedral within the walls, another centre of gravity was created around the extramural shrine of St Martin, where the abbey of St Martin was subsequently founded. The city of Xanten on the River Rhine grew up around the shrines of martyrs, so that the original Roman city was deserted, and indeed the name Xanten means 'Ad Sanctos', that is, 'At the

Saints'. Much the same may have happened at St Albans in Hertfordshire, where the Roman city of Verulamium became deserted, and the settlement transferred to the area of St Alban's Abbey, probable site of the burial of the early Christian martyr St Alban. This disruption of the ancient topography of Roman cities may itself have contributed to the success of Christianity by lessening the importance of paganism's hold on the old civic cores.

The cult of saints was certainly not a monopoly of bishops, but bishops sought to regulate it and to dominate it. On the one hand, they increasingly came to associate their churches with the tombs of saints. This was what the popes themselves did with their church of St Peter's in the Vatican, and what the bishops of Tours did with the church of St Martin, located outside the Roman city of Tours. In the centuries after the end of the Roman Empire in the west, Roman funerary customs weakened and it became acceptable to translate (that is, ceremonially to remove) saints' bodies into the heart of cities, where they could be placed in even closer contact with the bishop's cathedral-church, and with his throne. Pope Paschal I (817–24) did this with the translation of the relics of St Cecilia to the new church which he had built within the city of Rome.

They could also be translated across wider distances. A classic case is that of St Cuthbert, the monk, hermit, and bishop of Lindisfarne, whose body was believed to be so holy that it had never decayed. After his death in 687, the saint was buried in the cemetery of the church of Lindisfarne, but under his successor, Bishop Eadberht, it was translated to a raised tomb (or shrine) in the interior of the church. When the religious community which served the church was threatened by Viking attacks in the late ninth century, it was removed by a circuitous route to the Roman fort at Chester-le-Street some fifty miles to the south. There it established the bishop's church for over a century, until in 995 it was finally transferred to Durham, where it still is. At each move, the body of St Cuthbert was carried with the community, and the choice of Durham as a final site for his church was credited to the saint's intervention, since he was believed to have become too heavy to move when the community was in the region of the great rock-girt peninsula in the River Wear which was to be the site of Durham Cathedral. The claim of the church of Durham that it was the successor to the ancient church of Lindisfarne was crucially based on the belief that the bishops had in their church the undecayed body of their predecessor, Cuthbert, whose holiness was revealed through the working of miracles.

Not all bishops leaned so heavily on association with saints and possession of their relics as a source of authority, but many did. The bishopric of St Andrews (Fife), for example, claimed from the ninth century to have the relics of Christ's apostle, St Andrew, which had been miraculously translated to that far northern shore, and similarly the bishops of Santiago de Compostella in the north-western corner of Spain laid claim to close association with another apostle, St James (*Sant Iago* in Spanish), whose relics were likewise believed to have been miraculously translated to Spain. In the case of Santiago de Compostella, the position of the bishops was immeasurably enhanced by the development of a Europe-wide pilgrimage to the shrine of St James, for which a detailed guide-book to the routes from France across the Pyrenees, and the sacred sites to be visited on the way, was compiled in the early twelfth century.

To no church, however, was the cult of relics more important than it was to that of the popes in Rome. We have already examined their close association with St Peter. The importance of his cult and relics to them is clear from their architectural development of the church of St Peter in the Vatican. In the time of Pope Gregory the Great (590–604), the east end of that church was remodelled in such a way as to give easier access to pilgrims to the tomb of the saint (Fig. 29).

The importance of St Peter, and of the other saints whose remains were also believed to be in Rome, including another apostle of Christ, St Paul, derived not only from what the popes were doing to promote their cults, but also from the enthusiasm of the Western European Church to be associated with them. Rome emerged very early on as a centre of pilgrimage, for we have from as early as the eighth century accounts of hospices being built in the city providing board and lodging for pilgrims and others from various peoples of Western Europe. One of the most prominent was the 'school of the English' (*schola Saxonum*), which was not really a school in our sense, but rather a hospice. Some came to Rome to spend their last days 'at the threshold of the apostles' as contemporary sources express it. Bede records a number of English kings who visited Rome, or wanted to visit Rome, in order to pray at the shrines of the saints, and in some cases to die there so that their access to heaven might be more surely guaranteed. Carloman, the brother of King Pippin III of the Franks, similarly retired to Rome and ended his life there.

There was also a considerable demand across Western Europe for relics from Rome, which were clearly believed to be very holy indeed. The popes seem for a long time to have adhered to the old Roman prohibitions on disturbing or fragmenting the remains of the dead, and they consequently forbade the removal from Rome of saints' bodies or fragments of saints' bodies. Instead, they offered Western European churches secondary relics, inanimate objects which had been in contact with the bodies of saints and so had absorbed some of their holiness and miracle-working power. In particular, the popes distributed what were called *brandea*, cloths which had been in contact with the relics of St Peter. According to the earliest *Life of Gregory the Great*, written in the eighth century by a monk, or perhaps a nun, of the Northumbrian monastery of Whitby, Gregory on one occasion gave such *brandea* to messengers to Rome asking for relics of St Peter, but he gave them in sealed containers so that the messengers did not know what they were receiving. On their journey home, they opened the containers and, horrified to find only the pieces of cloth in them, they returned to Rome to complain to the pope. Gregory, however, instructed them to cut the cloths, with the result that they bled, showing that they really were every bit as holy as actual portions of St Peter's body. Indeed, Gregory of Tours describes in the sixth century how pilgrims visiting St Peter's in the Vatican would make their own *brandea* by lowering cloths through the grill above St Peter's tomb to bring them into contact with the saint's remains. They would weigh the cloths before they did this and, on hauling them up, they would be found to weigh more than they had done previously because of the miraculous power transferred into them.

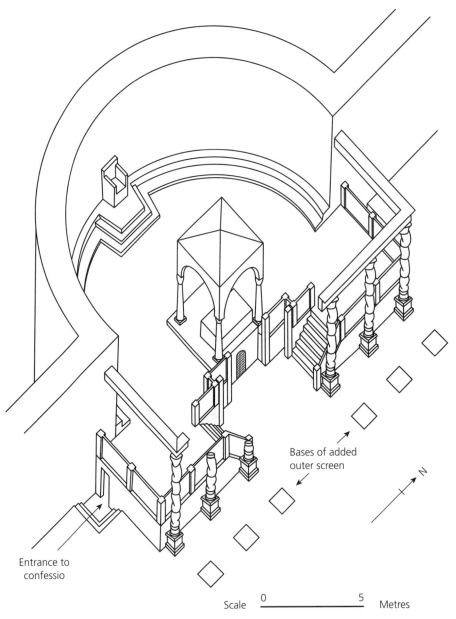

Bases of added
outer screen

N

Entrance to
confessio

Scale 0 5 Metres

Figure 29 The east end of St Peter's in the Vatican, reshaped by Pope Gregory the Great. The pope's throne stands at the apex of the apse (the rounded east end). On the raised floor stands the high altar with a canopy over it. The tomb of St Peter lay directly below the high altar. It could be glimpsed, and cloths could be lowered on to it to collect its miraculous power, through the metal grill of the door which appears in the wall immediately below the high altar. A corridor allowed pilgrims to circulate close to the tomb itself. The entrance is marked 'entrance to confessio' on the drawing; the exit was in the same place on the opposite side of the apse.

Source: Adapted from The shrine of St Peter and its twelve spiral columns, *Journal of Roman Studies*, xlii (Ward-Perkins, J. 1952), Cambridge University Press.

The sheer scale and intensity of the demand for saints' relics from Rome is shown by the account given by Charlemagne's biographer, Einhard, of how he obtained from Rome the relics of two martyrs, SS Marcellinus and Petrus for the church he had founded at Seligenstadt near Frankfurt-am-Main (Germany). He tells us that he sent an agent who made contact with what was in effect a relic-smuggling ring, led by a deacon called Deusdona, and aiming to circumvent the pope's prohibition on the export of relics from the city. Deusdona took Einhard's agent under cover of darkness to find the relics, which seem to have been enshrined in one of the ancient underground burial-places of the city, the catacombs. They were duly removed from Rome, despite pursuit by the Roman populace, and despite the fact that Einhard's agent came up against another party sent by the abbot of Saint-Denis near Paris to obtain the self-same relics. Nevertheless, the prestige of Roman relics is clear from this, as it is from the number of churches in Western Europe dedicated to St Peter and St Paul, the most important saints of the city of Rome.

The importance of the cult of saints to the authority of bishops and popes lay not only in their possession of relics, but also in their claim to arbitrate as to whether a person being venerated really was a saint or not. By the end of the thirteenth century, this had developed into a full process of canonisation, which was the monopoly of the pope and required submission of evidence establishing the holiness of the person's life and the performance of miracles after their death. In the course of our period, the process of recognising saints was much less formal, but it was increasingly claimed as the responsibility first of bishops, but increasingly of popes, and this too must have enhanced the authority of these leaders.

Scholarship and expertise

Whereas monasteries were often the seats of libraries and of learning based on them, these activities could also be part of the basis for the authority of bishops' churches. The cathedral of Canterbury had a particularly renowned school, proficient in both Greek and Latin, in the time of Archbishop Theodore, as also did the cathedral of York in the eighth century. The best-known representative of the latter school was Alcuin, whom Charlemagne 'head-hunted' as a prominent member of the school at his own palace at Aachen. The cathedral of Chartres, in north-west Gaul, had developed a particularly distinguished school by the early eleventh century, and it was that school which later on made possible the creation of the sophisticated programme of stone sculpture and painted glass which is so miraculously preserved in the twelfth-century cathedral. Back in the ninth century, the church of Rheims was a centre of scholarship under its archbishop, Hincmar, and in the sixth century so too had been the church of Seville under its bishop Isidore.

As with the cult of saints, however, Rome emerged as a key centre of expertise for the western Church. It was partly the scholars who had worked there: in the fourth century Jerome, who translated the Bible into Latin to produce the version known as the Vulgate and used throughout the western Church in the Middle Ages, worked there as secretary to the pope; and in the sixth century so did the Scythian canon lawyer and mathematician Dionysius Exiguus, whose work on astronomy and mathematics made possible Bede's great breakthrough in resolving the problems of correlating the lunar and solar calendars in order to fix the appropriate date for the festival of Easter, and those Church festivals which were connected to it.

The status of the church of Rome as a source of authority was considerably enhanced, however, by a combination of churches throughout Western Europe appealing to the popes for decisions on questions of doctrine, organisation, and discipline. The impetus for them to do this presumably arose from the perception of Rome as the church established by St Peter, and from the claims to superiority made by popes like Leo I and Gelasius I. It seems that the popes archived their decisions in the form of documents known as decretals, which made it possible for them to issue authoritative answers to problems brought to them on the basis of past decisions, and to build up a body of expertise which must considerably have enhanced their authority. By the twelfth century, these archives had taken the form of important collections of papal decretals, such as those of Gratian. The popes' practice of keeping a record of their activities in the compilation known as the 'Day Book' (*Liber Diurnus*) must also have contributed to their authority, as must the compilation over some centuries of a collection of Lives of the popes, the 'Book of the Popes' (*Liber Pontificalis*).

Missions

The authority of some bishops, and of the popes in particular, could evidently be increased by their leadership of missionary work, since areas which had received Christianity from a particular church naturally looked up to that church. Missionary work was undertaken in particular by the archbishopric of Mainz in what is now Germany, the archbishop of which in the first half of the eighth century, Boniface, was very active in organising and leading the conversion of the still pagan areas to the east and north of his episcopal church, chiefly Thuringia and Frisia. Similarly, the bishops of Hamburg in what is now northern Germany were actively involved in the conversion to Christianity of pagan Scandinavia.

But the most significant missionary work for the development of a church's authority was arguably that of Pope Gregory the Great in the conversion of the pagan English. The story is known from Bede and from the *Life of Gregory the Great*, written probably in the mid-eighth century. Inspired by seeing pagan English boys for sale in Rome as slaves, the pope despatched Augustine and a group of companions to England. They arrived in the kingdom of Kent in 597, and the king, Æthelberht, received them encouragingly and was in due course converted to Christianity, while the activities of the missionaries led, directly or indirectly, to the conversion of the neighbouring kingdoms of the East Saxons and the East Angles, as well as the more distant kingdom of Northumbria. In the longer term, however, Augustine's mission was not very successful. Æthelberht's successor as king of Kent reverted for a time at least to paganism, as did the kings of the other kingdoms converted. The definitive conversion of the kingdom of Northumbria, and of other kingdoms including that of Mercia, was much more the work of Irish missionaries who came into the kingdom of Northumbria in connection with the monastery of Lindisfarne in 635, and spread their influence from there. The conversion of the kingdom of Wessex was the work of another missionary altogether, Birinus. Yet, although the efficacy of Augustine's mission was not great, by the eighth century it had come to be regarded in England as the principal cause of the conversion of the country, and the responsibility for its launch was clearly recognised as Pope Gregory's. Alcuin, in producing a verse account of the conversion, presented it in this way, and the Whitby author of the *Life of Gregory the Great* was explicit about the pope's role and the importance which attached to him as a result. For this writer, the pope was for the English 'our teacher', 'that wonderful man St Gregory', who would lead the English before the Lord on the Day of Judgment (*Life of Gregory the Great*, prologue, chs 4, 6).

One of the consequences of this attitude was that the English Church was particularly committed to the papacy. Already in the late seventh and early eighth centuries, Bishop Wilfrid was making a series of appeals to Rome, while the English Church itself was distinguished by paying a special tax to the papacy, a sort of pious render known as 'Peter's pence'.

The importance of this for the authority of the papacy must itself have been considerable, but it was increased by the extent to which English missionaries such as Willibrord and Boniface were active on the Continent in the late seventh and the first half of the eighth centuries. That activity not only involved the conversion of pagan areas, which were as a result imbued with the same respect for the papacy which the missionaries had by virtue of their perceived debt to Gregory the Great; but, in Boniface's case, they were also very much involved with the reform of the Frankish Church, which consequently came under the same influence, an influence that was continued when Alcuin transferred from York to the court of Charlemagne at Aachen. This may explain why the Frankish Church of Charlemagne's time and before was so intent on seeking guidance from Rome. Already in Pippin III's time, it had sought from the pope a collection of church services, known as the 'Gelasian of the Eighth Century'; and Charlemagne sought another such book, which was expanded into the standard liturgical book for the Frankish Church, the Hadrianum. He sought in addition a collection of canon (i.e. Church) law which was edited by his scholars to create the highly influential compilation of canon law, the Dionysio-Hadriana. It is arguable, then, that the missionary activities of Gregory the Great in England had a really major impact on the authority of the papacy even beyond the shores of England.

Bishops and popes in the world

As governors

Gregory of Tours relates in his *History of the Franks* a story set in the middle of the fifth century in the city of Orléans, at the point when it was being threatened by Attila, king of the invading Huns, who was doing 'all he could to capture it by launching a fierce assault with his battering-rams'. The bishop of Orléans, Gregory tells us, was Anianus, and the citizens now begged him to tell them what to do. The account of what followed is such a brilliant example of Gregory of Tours's power as a story-teller that it is worth quoting in full:

> Putting his trust in God, he [Anianus] advised them [the citizens] to prostrate themselves in prayer and with tears to implore the help of the Lord, which is always present in time of need. As they carried out his orders and prayed to the Almighty, the bishop said: 'Keep a watch from the city wall, to see if God in his pity is sending us help.' His hope was that, through God's compassion, Aetius might be advancing, for Anianus had gone to interview that leader in Arles when he foresaw what was going to happen. They watched out from the wall, but they saw no one. 'Pray in all faith,' said Anianus, 'for this day the Lord will deliver you.' They continued their prayers. 'Look out for a second time,' said the bishop. They peered out, but they saw no one bringing help. The bishop said a third time: 'If you continue to pray in faith, God will come quickly.' With much weeping and lamentation, they begged for God's succour. When their prayer was finished, they were ordered by the old man to look out a third time. Far away they saw what looked like a cloud of dust rising from the ground. This they reported to the bishop. 'It is the help sent by God,' said he. The walls were already rocking under the shock of the battering rams and about to collapse when Aetius arrived, and with him Theoderic, the king of the Goths, and his son Thorismond. They hastened forward to the city with their armies and drove off the enemy and forced them to retreat. Orléans was thus saved by the prayers of its saintly bishop.
>
> (Gregory, *Hist. Franks*, II.7)

As the last sentence makes clear, this is a sort of miracle-story, with the bishop as the miracle-worker through his prayers, and we need not accept it as literally true. But the idea underlying it is that, following the effective collapse of Roman rule in Gaul, the bishop was the person responsible for the city. He was filling the power-vacuum and assuming roles which the imperial government would formerly have done. For Gregory of Tours is clear that, however important the bishop's prayers may have been, Anianus had in fact taken the practical steps of ensuring the safety of his city by consulting with the commander of what was left of Roman military capabilities in Gaul, Aetius.

This theme of the responsibility of bishops for their cities occurs more than once in the *History of the Franks*. When in the late sixth century the Frankish king Chilperic imposed a new series of what Gregory describes as very heavy taxes, the people of the city of Limoges were so incensed that they called a meeting and resolved to take the most direct action, that of killing the king's tax-collector, whose name was Mark. It was the bishop of Limoges, Ferreolus, who intervened to save Mark, although he was apparently unable to prevent the people from burning Mark's demand-books, or to prevent the king from carrying out reprisals, some directed at abbots and priests (Gregory, *Hist. Franks*, V.28). Nevertheless, the underlying idea of this story too is that the bishop was the person responsible for the city.

It is possible to argue that Gregory of Tours, being himself a bishop, over-emphasised the importance of bishops to cities, and underestimated that of the counts, the secular officials of the king. The theme of bishops and popes filling the power-vacuum left by the weakness or disappearance of secular government, however, is not found only in Frankish Gaul. It can be clearly seen in the case of the popes, for, just like Bishop Anianus at Orléans, Pope Leo I was responsible for leading the defence of the city of Rome against the Huns, and for negotiating with them. Gregory the Great assumed a similar role when Rome was threatened by the Lombards in the late sixth century.

The classic case, however, is that of Gaul, especially southern and central Gaul, in the late tenth and eleventh centuries. The disintegration of royal power in the western kingdom of the Franks had left Gaul a mosaic of small political units, often hostile to each other, so that the maintenance of any sort of peace and order was a difficult task. In these circumstances, a movement arose, largely although not exclusively led by bishops, known as the Peace and the Truce of God. This movement, which was set in motion by a series of Church councils, notably the Council of Charroux of 991, had as its goal the establishment of a prohibition on violence (a 'peace', that is) on particularly vulnerable categories of people, namely the peasantry, the clergy, and women, and also the establishment of a prohibition on violence on particular days (a 'truce', that is). This movement was heavily promoted by lay potentates, such as the dukes of Aquitaine, and it is possible to interpret it as being as much in their interests as anyone else's; but the fact remains that bishops – and abbots of monasteries – were in principle the initiators of it, and it does provide an excellent example of churchmen's secular authority growing to fill a power-vacuum.

Legal powers sometimes came into the hands of bishops through the kings granting them immunities often embracing much wider areas than just areas within their cities, as we see in the case of Trier (Map 15). Some of these immunities were intended to free their holders from paying taxes, to make them 'immune' from royal tax-collectors in other words, and we find these being granted from the fifth century, at Lyons for example, and in the sixth century at Clermont-Ferrand and Tours. But some immunities were intended to make the holder 'immune' from royal jurisdiction too, and so effectively to give the bishop rights over justice comparable to those of the king himself. We can discuss whether the granting of such immunities resulted from the weakness of kings who had no alternative, or whether it was rather a sign of strong kings effectively using the bishops as their provincial agents and delegating to them the powers to do this job.

It may be also that judicial immunities developed not so much out of royal grants as out of churches' right to offer sanctuary, that is temporary protection, to fugitives from enemies, or fugitives from the working out of a bloodfeud, or fugitives from royal justice. It had been a principle from a very early date that such a fugitive who had taken refuge in a church could not be seized there by his pursuers for a defined period, during which he enjoyed the church's protection. In origin, this had applied to any church, but increasingly the greater churches came to offer more extensive protection in the context of this right of sanctuary, and many of these greater churches were

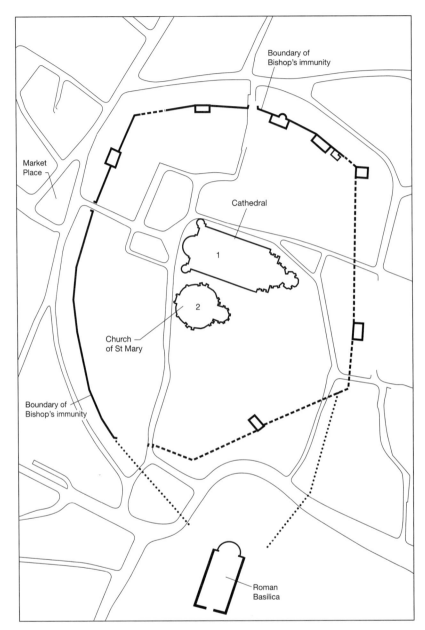

Map 15 The city of Trier in the Early Middle Ages. Nos 1 and 2 are the two churches which together formed the bishop's cathedral complex. Where the medieval walls of the bishop's immunity survive, they are marked by a continuous black line; where they no longer exist but their site is known, the line is broken, where conjectured it is dotted. Notice how the market-place (the triangular space on the top left of the map) has grown up around the entrance to the immunity, suggesting the role of the bishop in the formation and development of the city. We could draw similar maps for cities like York and Mainz, and indeed by the end of our period some cities were emerging as the cities of 'prince-bishops', of which that of Durham is an especially well-known example, in English history at least. *Source*: Adapted from *Führer zu vor-und frühgeschichtlichen Denkmälern*: Vol 32: Trier, Philipp von Zabern (Römisch-Germanischen Zentralmuseum Mainz, 1980).

those of bishops. Sanctuary did not in itself confer judicial rights, but it seems likely that it did promote the bishops' claim to such rights, since by granting sanctuary to a fugitive from royal justice the church was effectively intervening in the judicial process, and it can only have been a small step for the bishop to assume the right to take that justice into his own hands.

Social status

Not all bishops were men of noble families, as in the case of the early ninth-century archbishop Ebo of Rheims, who was criticised for being a commoner; but it is clear that very many were. In the last years of the Roman Empire and the period immediately after it ended in the west, the bishop of the Auvergne in what is now central France was a very influential figure, Sidonius Appollinaris (c.430–c.486). He was a member of a great family of senatorial aristocrats, and his surviving letter-collection shows that he was a man of great wealth, deeply imbued in classical Roman culture. His becoming bishop may make us think that the episcopate was becoming a career-track for an aristocrat such as senatorial office or imperial governmental office would have been in an earlier period. The same impression that scions of Roman aristocratic families were becoming bishops because this had become a natural route to power can be derived from Gregory of Tours's *History of the Franks*, which specifies that a bishop such as Francilo of Tours had previously been a senator, and which gives an account of Gregory's predecessors at Tours showing that they were all members of an aristocratic family (Gregory, *Hist. Franks*, III.17, X.31).

In areas like England, where Roman influence had largely disappeared before the conversion to Christianity, there was no question of Roman senatorial aristocrats diverting their careers into the episcopate, because no such aristocrats were there. But it is abundantly clear from the writings of Bede and others in the eighth century that bishops were often men of considerable wealth. In his *Life of Bishop Wilfrid*, the monk of Ripon, Stephanus, presents an account of Wilfrid which suggests that, long before he became a bishop, he was wealthy enough to equip himself and his followers to meet the queen of Northumbria, and wealthy enough too to equip and arm a ship with his evidently numerous followers. That his family was aristocratic is suggested by Stephanus's account of how in his youth he would serve in his father's house, where he attended to the king's retainers.

It is sometimes argued that Bishop Cuthbert of Lindisfarne, destined to become St Cuthbert after his death in 687, was of much humbler stock, because the early eighth-century *Lives* of him (one by an anonymous monk of Lindisfarne and one by Bede) present him as watching over his master's sheep when he saw the soul of St Aidan being taken to heaven by angels and became a monk (Colgrave, 1940). It seems very unlikely, however, that this is evidence of his low social status, for it seems to be showing him imitating the shepherds at the Nativity of Christ, who were also watching over sheep when they saw an angel. It is, in other words, a miracle-story focused on Cuthbert's holiness rather than the reality of his social status. Moreover, the anonymous *Life* presents him as having served in the king's army, which probably means he was noble, and as arriving to join the monastery of Melrose mounted on a horse, carrying a spear, and accompanied by a servant, which certainly does.

Wealth

In addition to the wealth which a man possessed before becoming a bishop, once he had done so he had access to the very considerable wealth which normally belonged to the bishopric. The scale of this wealth is apparent from Stephanus's account of how Bishop Wilfrid managed his resources. Just before his death, 'he bade the treasurer open the diocesan coffers and set out all the gold, silver, and precious stones in four separate piles', and these he allocated one to churches in Rome, one 'so that the abbots of Hexham and Ripon might have something in hand wherewith to secure the favour of the kings and bishops', and one for 'those who laboured with me in my long exile and whom I have not already rewarded with lands and estates' (Stephanus, *Life of Bishop Wilfrid*, ch. 63). The passage shows not only the scale of a bishop's wealth but also some of the ways in which it could generate power – bribing kings and other bishops, and rewarding what was in effect the bishop's 'war-band' who had, in this case, accompanied him into the exile which the king of Northumbria had for a time imposed on him.

The church of Rome clearly had an immense income, managed by a large staff of bureaucrats, and the church of St Peter's in the Vatican alone had the equivalent of 3,700 *solidi* per annum. It is possible to reconstruct the landed wealth of the popes on the basis of surviving records, including important records left from the pontificate of Gregory the Great. These estates stretched right across central Italy, amounting to some 1,360 square miles, and forming the Patrimony of St Peter – the nucleus of what was much later the Papal States. Papal ambitions for land went beyond this, for in the mid-eighth century there appeared a document which scholars call the Donation of Constantine. This was certainly a forgery of that period, which represented the Emperor Constantine as having granted to his pope, Sylvester I, very wide lands in northern Italy, including the city of Ravenna.

Building

Wealth made it possible for popes and bishops to construct a range of buildings, including cathedrals and related churches, which (we could argue) contributed to their power through the prestige which they brought and the impression they made. In Rome, the emperor Constantine had patronised the building of St Peter's in the Vatican and St John's in the Lateran, but the popes themselves built many churches which survive today, sometimes with their rich decoration of mosaics and wall-paintings, as most spectacularly at the church of San Prassede and its attached chapel of San Zeno, glowing with early ninth-century mosaics. The popes also took over and converted Roman classical buildings. A basilica which was attached to the pagan Temple of Peace in the Forum of Peace became in 527 the church of SS Cosmas and

Damian; by 565–78 a Roman ceremonial hall had had installed in it the church of Santa Maria Antiqua; and in 630 the assembly hall of the Roman senate became the church of San Adriano. Most impressive of all, in 608 the immense domed pagan temple that was the Roman Pantheon became the church of Santa Maria dei Martiri. Bishops were no less active in their cities elsewhere. In the sixth century, the bishop of Ravenna decorated the church of San Vitale with mosaics showing his important position in the court of the Byzantine emperor Justinian, who had recently conquered Italy. In Cologne, the archbishops constructed an immense church with an apse (or rounded projection) at each end, the details of which are well known since the church was excavated following wartime destruction of buildings around the surviving Gothic cathedral. In Winchester, the Old Minster was massively extended in the tenth century to provide a spectacular setting for the tomb of the late ninth-century bishop of Winchester, Swithun.

Relationship with kings

An important source of bishops' authority must have been their relationship with kings and emperors, and the power they were able to derive from the relationship. It was arguably very important to the position of bishops that the emperor Constantine's policy to the Church included giving them access to the imperial court, and such access was clearly very important also to bishops in the barbarian kingdoms. In late seventh-century England, we read, for example, of Cuthbert of Lindisfarne meeting with the abbess who was the king's sister on Coquet Island off the Northumbrian coast, and prophesying to her who would be the next king after the present king, Ecgfrith's, death. At the time of that death, which occurred in battle against the Picts, we read of Cuthbert comforting the queen at Carlisle and arranging for her escape from the king's enemies. As for Wilfrid, Stephanus presents him as always in close contact with kings, even if not always on good terms with them; and this was not limited to England, for Stephanus claims that Wilfrid was instrumental in restoring Dagobert II to the throne of Austrasia (the eastern part of Frankia) after he had been in exile in Ireland. Likewise, Gregory of Tours presents himself as very close to the king of the Franks, Chilperic, even if he did not always approve of his actions.

In the Carolingian realms, bishops (in common with abbots) were prominent in the king's palace, as was the case with Archbishop Hincmar of Rheims, who was a close adviser and guide of the king of western Frankia, Charlemagne's grandson, Charles the Bald. In the tenth century in Ottonian Germany, bishops were so important in government that it used to be thought by scholars that there existed what they called an 'imperial church system' for ruling through the agency of the Church. Otto I's brother, Bruno, archbishop of Cologne, was particularly prominent in the government of the realm.

Before the Gregorian Reform of the eleventh century, bishops (in common with abbots) could have military functions, supplying men to serve in the king's army, and sometimes fighting themselves. In Northumbria in the tenth century, the archbishop of York, Wulfstan I, appears in the *Anglo-Saxon Chronicle* fighting alongside the pagan king of York against the army of the Christian king of Wessex. In this case, independence from a southern power, and his alliance with the Viking king of York, clearly meant more to the bishop than religious orientation.

Holiness

Church writers make it clear that, from an early date in the history of Christianity, the authority of bishops was viewed as deriving from God, conferred when the bishop was ordained to his office with holy oil. It was this which made it possible for the bishop to readmit sinners to the Church through the laying-on of hands, which passed on to the sinner the Holy Spirit which the bishop had himself received.

Bishops could also derive 'ascetic authority' from living like monks, or indeed as monks. St Martin, bishop of Tours, had begun as a monk, and continued as bishop to live as one. His biographer, Sulpicius Severus, writes that 'he kept up the position of bishop properly, yet in such a way as not to lay aside the objects and virtues of the monk' (Rapp, 2005, p. 151). Cuthbert appears similarly in Bede's *Life* of him as wishing to be a hermit even when he was a bishop, and subjecting himself to all sorts of deprivations. In the tenth century, the archbishop of Cologne, Bruno, who had very considerable political power, wore a hair shirt under his outer garments to afflict his flesh. It is naturally difficult to evaluate evidence such as this, since much of it comes from biographies of the bishops in the form of saints' *Lives*. But it is certain that bishops and popes did often live in monastic or quasi-monastic communities which formed their households. Jerome describes the household of unmarried clergy around Bishop Valerian of Aquileia, constituting a sort of monastic community, 'a choir of angels' as Jerome called it (Rapp, 2005, p. 151). Gregory the Great was a monk before he became pope, and his household as pope was monastic, as was the case with Augustine, the first archbishop of Canterbury. In the Carolingian period, the communities of priests providing services for cathedrals were increasingly organised on monastic lines, many according to the Rule of St Chrodegang. So it may be that the bishop's authority rested, to some extent at least, on the holiness of his life, and belief in the closeness to God which this procured for him.

Authority may also have come from the holy actions which the bishop performed, for example feeding the poor and succouring prisoners (as Christ had commanded). Such duties would originally have belonged to the Roman government, so there is ambiguity as to how they may have been regarded. When Pope Gregory the Great relieved a famine in the city of Rome, he was both acting as a Christian leader, and as the imperial government would have done had it still been in charge of the city. It is easy to see how such activities could be extended to include building hospices in the city, ransoming captives, building dykes to inhibit flooding (as Bishop Felix of Nantes is described as doing), or rebuilding the fortifications of the city (as Bishop Desiderius of Cahors is described as doing). Nevertheless, these activities too could be seen as manifestations of holiness (as we have seen with Bishop Anianus's role at the siege of Orléans), and it may be that it is wrong to distinguish between their secular and religious aspects. They may have been part and parcel of bishops' relationship to God, as well as of their role as successors to the imperial government.

How powerful, then, was the Church as an organisation by 1050? There is a strong case to be made that it was powerful from an early date in our period, and we have tried to set out some of the possible arguments in this chapter. But, as with so many of the topics in this book, you may find it helpful as you go forward with your research and reading to broaden your chronological perspective so that you can more accurately evaluate the significance of what we are seeing in our period. In the case of this chapter, you could, for example, pursue an argument that the organisation of the Church only became really effective as a result of the reform of the Church, beginning in the earlier eleventh century but reaching a climax under Pope Gregory VII (1073–85), whom we mentioned above. That reform ushered in a period when the popes were much more clearly the heads of a hierarchical structure, when they were responsible much more explicitly for Church law (or canon law), and when they acquired rights of taxation to boost their finances (Lynch, 1992, Tellenbach, 1993). You could argue that, by comparison with this, what we have been examining is much less significant. But it is a matter of judgement, and you may well think that there is a case to be made that the effects of the eleventh-century reforms have been exaggerated, and that we are seeing already in our period a Church, headed by bishops and the pope, which was every bit powerful enough to be the motor-force of a 'top-down' model of conversion to Christianity (Chapter 10) and the spread of monasticism (Chapter 11).

Research and study

Broad research questions

Is it useful to distinguish between the secular and religious power of popes and bishops?

How much of their power did bishops owe to filling the power-vacuum left by the disappearance of Roman government?

How far did the power of popes and bishops derive from their social status and wealth?

How much of their power did bishops and popes owe to secular rulers?

Books and papers to begin with

Rapp (2005) is concerned with only the early part of our period, but she provides a very thought-provoking discussion, centred around her thesis that it is wrong to separate secular and religious authority. Her analysis of the authority of bishops into 'spiritual authority', 'ascetic authority', and 'pragmatic authority' (i.e. authority deriving from actions) is the basis for the last section of this chapter and is very worthwhile wrestling with. For the bishops in the kingdom of the Merovingian Franks, there is a succinct discussion in Wood (1994a, ch. 5). Much can be derived from Wallace-Hadrill (1983), and James (1982, pp. 49–62). There is an exciting discussion about Ottonian bishops in Fichtenau (1991, ch. 9); and there is a very clear and critical discussion of the 'imperial church system' (*Reichskirchensystem*) by Reuter (1982). For early Anglo-Saxon England, there are stimulating articles by Coates (1996a, b), and much to be derived from Mayr-Harting (1991a).

Still worth reading is Ullmann (1955), which sketches in very broad terms the development of papal politics and political ideas. There is an excellent survey by Barraclough (1968), and a more detailed book which argues against the idea of a consistent papal policy to promote the popes' position by Richards (1979; chs 4–5 are the most useful for us). Partner (1972) is a clearly organised account of the papacy's development.

Pursuing more specific aspects

The popes

How far were the popes pursuing a strategy to dominate the Church?

How much did the popes owe to the resources and reputation of the city of Rome?

How exceptional was the papacy of Gregory the Great?

The city of Rome and its resources are the subject of Llewellyn (1971), which is very vivid on the saints' relics of Rome. There is excellent writing on Gregory the Great by Richards (1980), Markus (1997), and Straw (1988), although the last is chiefly about his religious thought and writings. Paschal I is the subject of Goodson (2010), although this deals chiefly with the pope's buildings (see below).

The cult of saints

In what ways was the cult of saints a source of power for bishops and popes?

The fundamental book is Brown (1981); for later comment on it, including an essay by Brown himself, you can look at Howard-Johnston and Hayward (2000). There is material about relics at Rome in Llewellyn (1971). Much can be derived from Van Dam (1993) for Gaul, Rollason (1989) for Anglo-Saxon England, and Boardman, Davies, and Williamson (2009) for the Celtic lands.

Building in cities

How effectively did bishops and popes shape their cities?

How far were they envisaging their buildings as demonstrations, and sources, of their power?

There are excellent books dealing with Rome, beginning with the great work of Krautheimer (1980), which is eminently worth reading. It is criticised in detail by Goodson (2010), who discusses the building activities of Pope Pascal I. Superb illustrations of the churches of Rome in our period can be found in Brandenburg (2004). More specialised discussion can be found in the papers in Julia Smith (2000) and Ó Carragáin and Neuman de Vegvar (2008). Very stimulating is Ó Carragáin (1995).

Episcopal building at Winchester is discussed succinctly by Biddle (1975), Ravenna by Paolucci (1978), Von Simson (1987), and Deliyannis (2009). For other episcopal building, much can be derived from Conant (1959).

Conclusion

We have, for convenience, separated out in these three chapters three different aspects of the history of the establishment of the Christian Church in Western Europe. But, as you go forward with your research and reading, you need to keep in mind the questions and issues which these aspects have in common, and which relate also to other aspects of Church history, such as the Church's role in scholarship and literature (Chapter 13).

How fluid and adaptable was Christianity in its relationship with Roman paganism and classical philosophy on the one hand, and with barbarian paganism on the other? Was it a religion which was genuinely capable of absorbing and making its own other beliefs and attitudes, as we have argued here, or was it rather a religion shaped by its writings, and driven by churchmen and scholars intent on the establishment of a rigid orthodoxy? Here, as elsewhere, it may be helpful to look ahead to later periods, and to compare our period with the High Middle Ages, when the persecution of heretics became common (Moore, 1987).

How creative and innovative was Christianity when compared with other faiths? We have considered in these chapters the way in which it developed practices for the commemoration of the dead which, we argued, formed a significant element in its attractiveness to believers; and we have examined too the development of the cult of saints, which represented a major departure from previous beliefs and practices. Was Christianity then a religion driven by new attitudes to the afterlife and the supernatural, or was it rather just an extension of trends which were already in operation?

And, finally, the question that we have used to shape these chapters, but which has a more wide-reaching importance as you go further: did Christianity work in a 'top-down' way, in which the Church depended for its success on a powerful organisational structure to impose its beliefs, a structure as powerful as, if not more powerful than, states themselves? If so, was the Church simply taking as its own existing governmental structures, such as the Roman provinces and dioceses, or the kingdoms and subdivisions of kingdoms of the post-Roman period in the west? And did the Church's success depend on the opportunity it offered to the powerful to extend their power through using its organisational capabilities? Or, on the contrary, did Christianity's success depend much more on a 'bottom-up' process, in which its devotees were driving it forward across Western Europe, even absorbing into their number emperors and kings? We might argue in that case that the development of the Church's organisation was a reaction to the surging growth and diversity of belief, which necessitated a system of Church organisation capable of restraining and controlling its devotees and preserving some unity in Christian teaching.

Time-line: Part V

c.100	Mithraism appears as a cult in the Roman Empire
c.155	Martyrdom of Polycarp of Smyrna
c.232–c.303	Porphyry, Neoplatonic philosopher
245–305	Reign of Emperor Diocletian
306–37	Reign of Emperor Constantine
	312 Battle of Milvian Bridge
	313 Edict of Milan
	314 Council of Arles on Donatism
	c.324 Victory over the eastern emperor Licinius
	325 Council of Nicaea on Arianism
360–3	Reign of Emperor Julian the Apostate
c.311–83	Ulfilas, missionary to the Goths, translator of the Bible into Gothic
c.315/c.336–397	St Martin, bishop of Tours
	360 Founds monastery of Ligugé
	372 Founds monastery of Marmoûtiers
353/5–431	Paulinus, founder of the monastery of Nola (southern Italy)
379–95	Reign of Emperor Theodosius I the Great
	391 Prohibits paganism
	394 Battle of the Frigidus and defeat of the usurper, Eugenius
354–430	Augustine of Hippo
c.330–79	St Basil 'the Great'
	357–8 Visits monks in Egypt and the Holy Land
	358–9 Rule of St Basil
c.339–97	St Ambrose, bishop of Milan
	381 Council of Aquileia
	391/2 Council of Capua
c.345–420	St Jerome, translator of the Bible into Latin (the Vulgate)
	382–5 Secretary to Pope Damasus
	386 Settled as abbot in Bethlehem
c.410	Honoratus founds a monastery on the island of Lérins near Marseilles (France)
c.360–after 430	John Cassian, monk, author of the *Institutes* and the *Conferences*
Mid-/late 5th century	St Patrick evangelises Ireland
440–61	Leo I, pope
492–6	Gelasius I, pope

481–511	Clovis, first Christian king of the Franks
	496 or 503, 506, 508 Baptised
c.470–542	Caesarius, bishop of Arles
522	Council of Orléans
480–524	Boethius, author of the *Consolation of Philosophy*
c.480–c.550	St Benedict of Nursia
	c.540 Rule of St Benedict
485/90–c.580	Cassiodorus, founder of the monastery of Vivarium
527–65	Justinian I, emperor
c.540–604	Gregory the Great, pope
	597 Pope Gregory the Great's missionary Augustine arrives in Kent
?–615	St Columbanus, abbot, founder of monasteries of Luxeuil and Annegray (France) and Bobbio (Italy)
c.560–636	Isidore of Seville, author of the *Etymologies*, bishop of Seville
c.616–633	Edwin, king of Northumbria
	Marriage to Æthelburg of Kent
	627 Baptism
c.620–30	Burial mounds at Sutton Hoo, Suffolk, England
634–42	Oswald, king of Northumbria
	634 Battle of Heavenfield
	635 Foundation of the island monastery of Lindisfarne (Holy Island) as the bishopric for Northumbria by the missionary Aidan and King Oswald
642–70	Oswiu, king of Northumbria
	664 Synod of Whitby
687	St Cuthbert, bishop of Lindisfarne, dies as a hermit on the Inner Farne (England)
634–709	St Wilfrid, bishop and abbot
8th century	The Franks Casket, Northumbria
c.705–44	Daniel, bishop of Winchester, author of a letter of advice on conversion to the missionary Boniface
744	Sturm founds the monastery of Fulda (Germany)
754	Martyrdom in Frisia of the English missionary Boniface, archbishop of Mainz
768–814	Reign of Charlemagne, king of the Franks and emperor
	782 First Saxon capitulary
	794 Synod of Frankfurt

817–24	Paschal I, pope
c.801–65	Anskar
	829 Mission to Birka (Sweden)
	831 Archbishop of Hamburg
10th century	Gosforth Cross, Cumbria, England
c.958–c.987	Reign of Harald Bluetooth, king of Denmark and Norway
	Establishes Christianity in Denmark
c.987–1014	Swein Forkbeard, king of Denmark (c.987–1014), king of England (1013–14)
995	Foundation of Durham
995–9	Olaf Tryggvason, king of Norway
	Establishes Christianity in Norway
	999 Initiates conversion of Iceland
c.995–1022	Olof Skötkonung, king of Sweden
	Establishes Christianity in Sweden
1014–35	Cnut the Great, son of Swein Forkbeard, king of England, king of Denmark (c.1018–35)
1015–28	Olaf Haraldsson, saint, king of Norway
	1024 Makes Christianity compulsory
	1028 Expelled from Norway
1030	St Olaf killed in battle
1073–85	Gregory VII, pope

PART VI

Scholarship and art

Introduction

We have looked in several of the preceding chapters at two related questions: first, how far there was a continuation of Roman organisation and Roman society after the end of the Roman Empire in the west, and how far something quite new and more barbarian emerged; and, secondly, how great the dominance of the Christian Church in Western Europe was, especially from the fourth century onwards, and what forms that dominance took. In this final part, we shall ask those questions of what, for want of a better word, we shall call the culture of early medieval Western Europe, as represented in the forms of it which we can most readily approach with the evidence available to us, that is, scholarship, literature, art, and architecture. This is not a peripheral area of study, but rather one which can be regarded as central to our concerns. For culture in this sense gives us at least the possibility of penetrating the ways in which contemporaries, or at least those groups of contemporaries who produced it or benefited from it, actually thought and felt. How far did they think of themselves as heirs of the Roman Empire? How far did they see the world in essentially Christian terms?

We need hardly remind ourselves of the difficulties we face in pursuing such lines of enquiry. We have no hope of examining the culture or the attitudes of anyone below the level of the aristocracy, aside from the culture of the various strata of the Church – but we have only rare opportunities to do this in later centuries, at any rate before the advent of mass publication and mass communications in the nineteenth century provides us with a quite different scale and type of source-material. Moreover, for the Early Middle Ages, and even for the medieval centuries thereafter, our evidence is hopelessly skewed towards the Church, since it was churchmen who wrote most of the texts and documents of the period, and so dominate the picture that has come down to us. Within these limitations, however, we possess remarkably rich source-materials, some written, some consisting of the monuments of art and architecture themselves.

Such culture is obviously that of the elite, but that does not necessarily make it less important to understanding early medieval Western Europe. To understand the influence and heritage of the Roman Empire, we need to ask how this culture related to that of Rome. To understand how far it was a part of an emerging Western European identity, we need to ask how coherent it was across Western Europe.

The first of these enquiries is subject to another type of difficulty, which is that of defining Roman culture so that we can perceive the influences which it exerted on subsequent culture. Naturally, Roman culture was itself changing, especially in the period after the conversion of the Roman Empire to Christianity in the fourth century, for the impact of that religion on it was very great from an early period. Roman scholarship was itself increasingly dominated by Christian learning, as can be seen from the importance in the late fourth and early fifth centuries of Jerome, the translator (although not the first translator) of the Bible into Latin, and of Augustine of Hippo, author of the most important early commentary on the history and moral status of the Roman Empire, *The City of God*, a work inspired by the sack of the city of Rome by the Gothic leader Alaric in 410. Similarly, in art and architecture Roman culture was changing to accommodate great churches such as St Peter's in the Vatican built by the emperor Constantine in the early fourth century, and Christian imagery in sculpture such as the image of Christ as the Good Shepherd with his lamb on his shoulders, as appears on many late Roman sarcophagi.

Moreover, this Christian development of culture and art continued in the Byzantine Empire with, for example, the construction of the great domed church of Haghia Sophia in Constantinople by the emperor Justinian, and the writing of accounts of the wars of Justinian by the court-historian Procopius. When we consider the scholarship, literature, art, and architecture of Western Europe, we cannot always be sure whether what we are seeing was an inheritance of the culture of the Roman Empire in the west, or whether it was the result of subsequent influence exerted on Western Europe by the culture of the Byzantine Empire as it developed after the end of the Roman Empire in the west. We may be helped as concerns scholarship, though, by the fact that Byzantine written culture was essentially in the Greek language whereas, as we shall see, that of the West was either in Latin or, to a lesser extent, in vernacular languages, and hardly at all in Greek, which was a language virtually unknown there. With all these limitations in view and all these problems in mind, let us turn to consider the culture of early medieval Western Europe, however elite and however ecclesiastically dominated what we are looking at may be.

13

Scholarship and literature

How far were scholarship and literature in the post-Roman barbarian kingdoms dominated by the Roman heritage, how far by the Christian Church?

Scholars

A strong case can be made, on the basis of the identity and careers of the scholars of the post-Roman period, that scholarship and literature were dominated by the Roman heritage. The writings that we have from the late fifth and sixth centuries are mostly the work of men who came from the Roman senatorial aristocracy, and had been shaped by Roman classical education. In the kingdom of the Ostrogoths in Italy, two of the most notable scholars were Cassiodorus (485/90–*c*.580) and Boethius (480–524). Cassiodorus, the author of a compilation of the official correspondence of the Ostrogothic kings called the *Variae*, of the *Divine and Human Institution*, and of a chronicle on which Jordanes based his *History of the Goths*, was the scion of a senatorial family. Boethius, chiefly known for his *The Consolation of Philosophy*, a masterpiece of philosophy which came to be important to later Christian scholars, was also a senator, and in his case he was accused by the Ostrogothic king, Theoderic, of collaborating with the east Roman government against the kingdom of the Ostrogoths, and he was imprisoned and executed. Indeed, the consolation of philosophy which he sought in the book of that title was needed during his prior imprisonment. Somewhat later, but also in Italy, another man of senatorial extraction, who was the son of a senator and prefect of the city of Rome in 573, was Gregory the Great, pope from 590 to 604, and the author of a series of Christian works: the *Dialogues* (a work on the lives of Italian saints, including the author of the *Rule of St Benedict* composed in the form of dialogues between Gregory and his deacon Peter); *The Pastoral Care* (a book about how rulers, including bishops, should act, later to be thought to be especially applicable to secular rulers); and *The Moralia on Job* (a book seeking to convey the teachings of Christianity through a commentary on the Old Testament book of Job, who was notable for patiently suffering God's retribution sitting on a dung-hill)

We can see a similar pattern in the kingdom of the Visigoths in Spain, where one of the most prominent scholars was Isidore of Seville (*c.*560–636), who came from a noble Roman family in the province of Cartagena, his father having fled to Seville from the incursions of the Visigoths. He was a prolific author, and his works include a sort of encyclopaedia called the *Etymologies*, and a *Great Chronicle* from the creation of the world, as described in the Bible, to the year 636. Likewise in Gaul, prominent scholars included Gregory of Tours (*c.*540–94), who came from a Gallo-Roman senatorial family and was the author not only of the *History of the Franks*, which we have had frequent occasions to consult, but also of eight books of miracles of saints. Finally, Venantius Fortunatus (*c.*535–*c.*610), the author of eleven books of poems, a *Life of St Martin* in verse, and lives of other saints of Gaul, was born in Italy and educated at the Roman schools of Ravenna, before his career in Gaul.

These men seem to show us the continuation of Roman scholarship into the barbarian kingdoms; they seem to be a tangible indication of the heritage of Rome in the culture of the post-Roman period. But we may nevertheless want to argue that more important was the growing momentum of the ecclesiastical influence on their scholarship and their careers. Just as Jerome and Augustine had been Christian scholars in the fourth and early fifth centuries, so these men were notable not just for the Christian character of their writings (even Boethius's book, which was not explicitly Christian and may have been pagan, was used in a Christian way) but for the eventual pursuit of their careers in the Church. Boethius, executed by Theoderic, was the exception. But, of the others, Cassiodorus turned from work in the Ostrogothic government to found the monastery of Vivarium (now Squillace in Calabria) where he became a resident if not a monk. Gregory the Great entered a monastery in the city of Rome around 574, and was eventually compelled by the Christian community there to become pope in 590. Isidore, who had been educated in a monastery, entered one around 589, and succeeded his brother as bishop of Seville. Gregory of Tours was elected bishop of Tours in 573, and Venantius Fortunatus became first the secretary to the Frankish queen and abbess Radegund in her monastery at Poitiers in western Gaul, and was elected bishop of Poitiers around 600. Just as we have seen (in Chapter 12) ecclesiastical careers sucking in the members and descendants of the Roman senatorial aristocracy, so the scholarship inherited from the Roman Empire seems to have become increasingly Christian in character, pursued by men prominent in the Church rather than in secular life.

The longer-term trends in scholarship also point in the direction of a comprehensive takeover of intellectual life by the Church. The scholarly heirs of these immediately post-Roman Empire luminaries were churchmen. When the founder of Bede's monasteries, Benedict Biscop, wanted to establish a library, it was to Rome that he turned, and there obtained books of ancient learning, such as Pliny's *On the Nature of Things*, as well as books of Christian learning like Augustine's *City of God*.

But his library was in a very real sense the heir to Cassiodorus's library at his monastery at Vivarium, for it is almost certain that it was from there that he obtained a copy of the Bible called the *Codex Grandior* ('Greater Book'), on which were based the three magnificent, and magnificently illuminated, copies of the complete Bible (pandects) produced at Monkwearmouth-Jarrow by his successor, Bede's own abbot, Ceolfrith (688–716). Astonishingly, fragments of two of these pandects have been found in modern times, one in a second-hand bookshop in Newcastle-upon-Tyne, one in the thatched roof of a cottage in Dorset; and one has survived in complete form as the *Codex Amiatinus*, now preserved in Florence. The reason for thinking that this book was based on Cassiodorus's *Codex Grandior* is that that author describes the latter in some detail in his work *The Institutions*, and the *Codex Amiatinus* matches the content and above all the illumination of it. What is especially striking is that the *Codex Amiatinus* was executed, as were its two companions, in a northern English monastery, in an area where Christianity had been definitively established for less than a century, on so precisely the lines of Cassiodorus's book. The similarity extends not only to the content and the illumination, but also to the script and manner of writing. The script is one derived from that used on Roman inscriptions and stone, and is known as uncial (Fig. 30), while the writing is laid out in

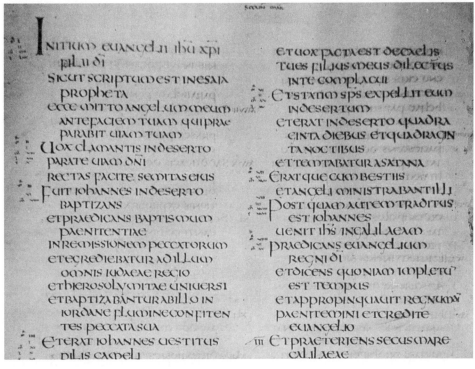

Figure 30 *Codex Amiatinus*, detail of the text of the Gospel according to St Mark. Notice the capital-letter forms of the letters in uncial script, and especially the very characteristic form of the letter 'A', for example the thirteenth letter from the right in the first line of the left column. Notice too the variable lengths of the lines in the columns, which is the method of punctuation *per cola et commata*. The numbers in small script to the left of each column are cross-references to the other Gospels. *Source*: Courtesy of Walton Sound and Film Services, Adrian Beney.

two columns, with no punctuation but with necessary pauses in reading indicated by the length of lines – a Roman technique of writing known as *per cola et commata*.

The language of scholarship

The connections between Monkwearmouth-Jarrow and the world of Roman scholarship can thus be demonstrated in a specific way. But we can argue that, in wider terms across Western Europe, Roman influence is apparent. At the most basic level, the principal language of scholarship was Latin, which was also the language of the Church in its services and ceremonies, and of the Bible in Jerome's Latin translation called the Vulgate. The Roman guides to Latin grammar, especially the one called the *Ars Maior* ('The Greater Art') by Donatus, were widely studied across Western Europe by churchmen who needed mastery of the language as an essential skill. Indeed, they made use in some respects of a more formal version of the language than was actually used in the period of the later Roman Empire in the west. Irish churchmen explored the more arcane reaches of Latin vocabulary in their grammars, which provided obscure synonyms for Latin words, and in some cases quite new words. And the scholars who gathered around the emperor Charlemagne (768–814), and formed the basis of the so-called Carolingian Renaissance, purified and refined Latin style so that it came more to resemble that of the great classical orator Cicero in the first century.

Against this, it can be argued that in some contexts, however, churchmen did make use of Germanic, vernacular languages, such as Old English and the various forms of Continental Germanic. Already in the fourth century, the missionary to the Goths living north of the River Danube, Ulfilas, had translated the Bible into the language of that people. On his deathbed, Bede was translating the Gospel according to St John into Old English, and we know that the English Church of his day treasured the Old English poetry of an inspired cow-herd called Cædmon, whose poem on the Creation was copied into one of the earliest manuscripts of Bede's *Ecclesiastical History of the English People*. A little later on the Continent, a free account of the narrative of the Gospels was written in Continental Germanic as the *Heliand* ('The Saviour').

But, for reasons which are by no means clear, it is above all in England that the use of the vernacular in writings flourished, for we have a remarkable corpus of Old English poetry, including the poems of the Mercian poet Cynewulf, as well as the epic poem *Beowulf*, the anonymous laments *The Seafarer* and *The Wanderer*, and the narrative of the Crucifixion from the viewpoint of the cross itself, *The Dream of the Rood*, the earliest text of which was carved in runes on the eighth-century Northumbrian Ruthwell Cross (Fig. 33 below). The use of Old English was especially promoted from the time of King Alfred of Wessex (871–99), who was himself responsible for translating Latin texts including Gregory the Great's *The Pastoral Care* and the histories by the Roman writer Orosius (born 380) into Old English. In later generations, the use of Old English was promoted by writers such as Ælfric of Eynsham (*c*.950–*c*.1010), who produced a whole series of homilies (sermons) and *Lives* of saints in that language.

Impressive as this move away from the Roman use of Latin was, however, we can argue that the intention was not to transfer scholarship to the vernacular, but rather to make Christian learning more accessible to the laity. Ælfric continued to write in Latin, as for example his *Life of St Æthelwold* and his letters of instruction to other monasteries were in that language, and tellingly he composed a grammar of Latin written in Old English, presumably so that the more learned laity could aspire to mastering the language of Rome.

Moreover, even those Old English writings which were not just translations from Latin sometimes show clear signs of the dominance of Roman scholarship. We have already had occasion to consider *Beowulf* as a story of pagan Scandinavian kings and princes in their struggles with mythical creatures. It is tempting to see it as the voice of a barbarian, Germanic tradition of literature challenging the dominance of Roman scholarship, and to an extent it was, because it has a clear relationship with widely diffused stories known rather later in Continental Germanic and Scandinavian languages. But in many respects its closest parallels are the great Greek epics of Homer, the *Iliad* and the *Odyssey*. These were not known in the west, but what was known was their Latin imitation, the *Aeneid* by Virgil, telling of the journey of the refugee Trojan called Aeneas from the siege of Troy to found Rome. Its style, and indeed its vocabulary, were used in Latin poetry of our period, such as the poems written by the scholars at the court of Charlemagne. This, and other Latin poems, may well have influenced the form of *Beowulf*, as is particularly apparent in the poet's description of the desolate mere from which the monster Grendel emerged to attack the hall of Heorot, and which bears a strong resemblance to the description of such deserts by classical writers.

Through all this, however, runs the dominance of the Church and of Christianity. *Beowulf* itself, set as it is in the pagan period of Scandinavian history, is infused with Christianity, not least when the monster Grendel roams outside the hall of Heorot and is infuriated to hear within it a minstrel singing of the Creation, and how:

> the Lord formed Earth,
> a plain bright to look on, locked in ocean,
> exulting established the sun and the moon
> as lights to illumine the land-dwellers
> and furnished forth the face of Earth
> with limbs and leaves. Life He then granted
> to each kind of creature that creeps and moves.
> (lines 92–8)

This was clearly the biblical story of the Creation. The fact that the poet envisaged it having been sung in a mead-hall just as it might have been in the refectory of a monastery suggests that *Beowulf* was at a deep level a Christian poem, perhaps even written for an ecclesiastical community. The same may be true of *The Wanderer* and *The Seafarer*. These describe at a superficial level the sufferings of two men as they forlornly roam the world, the Seafarer battered by the ocean, the Wanderer deprived of the support and generosity of a lord; but it may be that these poems are really concerned with the perceived horrors of not being under the protection of God, rather than being reflections on secular life at all, and so are just as much Christian works as *Lives* of saints.

Scripts

Just as we can argue that language in scholarship showed Roman influence on the one hand and the influence of the Church on the other, so it is open to us to interpret the scripts used in writing the manuscripts in which scholarship was published and copied, in this age before the invention of printing, in a similar way. We have already seen the use of Roman-derived uncial script in the *Codex Amiatinus*, and this was used in a range of manuscripts and, in England at least, in some of the documents called charters which granted land or privilege. It was, however, slow and laborious to write since it was essentially a script based on capital letters, and therefore not capable of being written rapidly. In the course of the seventh and eighth centuries, more rapid scripts were developed in England and Ireland on the one hand, and on the Continent on the other, which are called 'minuscule' scripts because they are based on what we would call 'lower-case' letters. In England, the script known as Insular Minuscule was used, for example, to copy the works of Bede at Monkwearmouth-Jarrow and it is found in the earliest copies of his *Ecclesiastical History of the English People*. There is no doubt that its development took place in monasteries, first in Ireland, and then in England. On the Continent, the equivalent script, which came to dominate writing across Europe, is called Carolingian Minuscule, and it too was developed at monasteries, probably first at the monastery of Corbie in northern Gaul. These scripts were thus new ones, but their style was strongly reminiscent of Roman predecessors and the inventors of printing in the fifteenth century were so convinced that Carolingian minuscule was a Roman script that they adopted it as the basis of the font which eventually became Times New Roman. Once again we can argue that we are seeing the dominance of the Roman tradition being taken over and modified by the Church.

Just as vernacular languages were used in some contexts, so we find the runic alphabet, a non-Roman system of writing, as an alternative to these Roman-derived scripts, usually for rendering Old Norse and Old English in inscriptions on wood, stone, or metal, for it is a 'straight-line' script eminently suitable for carving or inscribing on such materials. It was in use throughout most of our period in pagan Scandinavia, where there have been preserved a number of runestones with inscriptions using it; and it was also used in England, sometimes for very short inscriptions on objects such as combs or daggers. But, however much it was a script of the pagan period, as it certainly was in Scandinavia, it too was thoroughly taken over for use in Christian, and specifically ecclesiastical, contexts. We have already noticed its use to inscribe the Christian poem *The Dream of the Rood* on the stone Ruthwell Cross (Dumfriesshire; Fig. 33 below), and we find it also in use to inscribe the names of apostles and angels on the wooden coffin of St Cuthbert from the late seventh century, now in Durham Cathedral Treasury.

Syllabus

We can also argue that the takeover of Roman forms by the Church is apparent in the scholarly syllabus which was pursued. The syllabus as it was taught in the Roman period in the west had been described by a fifth-century scholar called Martianus Capella, who set it out in the pattern of the Seven Liberal Arts. These were divided into two sections. The more elementary was the Trivium (the three subjects – our word 'trivial' derives from this) and this consisted of grammar, rhetoric (the art of public speaking), and dialectic (or logic, the art of arguing a case). After the Trivium, students progressed to the Quadrivium (four subjects) which comprised arithmetic, geometry, music, and astronomy. These subjects were not envisaged as being practical, but rather as preparation for philosophy, which was the ultimate goal of the syllabus. They constituted approaches to the nature of the universe, its mathematical and geometrical interrelationships, the harmony of music which was thought to reflect the harmony of the universe, and the links between the heavenly bodies and human life which we today would regard rather as astrology.

The influence of this syllabus on early medieval scholarship is apparent, first, in references to it – as when the Visigothic scholar at the court of Charlemagne, Theodulf of Orléans, described a table decorated with the Seven Liberal Arts, or when the Irish poet Dungal wrote a poem on them. The syllabus was clearly regarded as of continuing importance, although philosophy as the ultimate goal was replaced by what we would regard as theology, since scholarship was proceeding in an essentially ecclesiastical context.

The works written or copied on the subjects of the Trivium seem to have been more important than those on subjects of the Quadrivium. As to the former, we have seen already the copying of the Roman scholar Donatus's work on Latin grammar, and many new textbooks on grammar were written, for example *The Art of Grammar* by Clement the Irishman (*Clemens Scotus*). The English scholar at the court of Charlemagne, Alcuin, wrote a book entitled *On Rhetoric*, which made much use of the first-century Roman orator Cicero, and he also wrote a treatise on dialectic. The Quadrivium, however, was much more poorly represented, even by copying of Roman texts. Geometry, for example, was represented only by the writings of an Irish scholar in the Carolingian realm called John the Irishman (*John Scotus Eriugena*), whose interest in this area seems to have been exceptional. There was some copying of astronomical texts, but a work on music had to wait until the writings of a scholar in Ottonian Germany called Hoger of Werden (died 902).

We can argue, however, that this Roman syllabus, while being retained in principle, had in reality been drastically modified by the needs of the Church. The study of grammar in particular was of immense importance to the Church because grammar was crucial to understanding the Vulgate Bible and other Christian writings in Latin. But some of the subjects of the Quadrivium may have been handled by early medieval scholarship in quite different ways. Whereas the Roman syllabus had envisaged music as an essentially theoretical subject, surviving manuscripts of music from the

Carolingian period of the early ninth century suggest that it was in fact developed in much more practical ways in the interests of church services. For it is in that period that we have the first evidence of the emergence of the type of church music which we call Gregorian Chant.

As for arithmetic and astronomy, this too was arguably developed in the interests of the Church as what early medieval scholars knew as 'compute'. The focus of this was the calculation of the dates of Church festivals, especially Easter. The difficulty of doing this in the case of Easter arose from the fact that, unlike Christmas which had a fixed date in the solar calendar which we still use today, Easter, then as now, had no such fixed date but was a movable feast, since it was a festival in the lunar calendar. This was because Christ's crucifixion and consequently his resurrection, which is what Easter is celebrating, took place according to the Bible at the Jewish feast of the Passover, for the Last Supper held immediately prior to the crucifixion was that feast. Since Passover was naturally a feast in the Jewish lunar calendar, fixing the date of Easter necessitated correlating the lunar with the solar calendar in relation to the motions of the moon and the sun. This was a highly complex astronomical and mathematical problem, which had occupied mathematicians at Alexandria in Egypt since at least the first century BC, and it was made more complicated by the need to predict the date of Easter well in advance so that churches everywhere could celebrate it on the same date, with other Church festivals (notably Lent, which had to begin forty days before it) correctly related to it. This then was another area in which the Early Middle Ages continued classical scholarship, in this case that of Alexandria, but we could argue that it took it forward not for pure science as the Alexandrian mathematicians had done, but in the quite practical interests of the Church. The most influential exponent of it was none other than Bede, in his work *On the Reckoning of Time*, which was widely copied across Western Europe.

We could argue, then, that the Roman syllabus of the Seven Liberal Arts was reorganised in the Christian-dominated scholarship of Western Europe in terms of three essentially practical arts: first, grammar to permit understanding of the Bible and other Christian texts; secondly, music to permit the development of church services; and, thirdly, compute to permit the fixing and prediction of the date of Easter and other Church festivals. To these areas of scholarship were added others which had begun in the Roman period but which were quintessentially Christian, such as the writing of saints' *Lives* (hagiography) which derived from describing the deaths of martyrs such as Polycarp, and the study of the Bible to produce commentaries (exegesis) as Bede did.

Educational system

We could argue further that this Church-dominated development of scholarship was based on Church dominance of the educational system. Secular schools had existed in the Roman period, at any rate for the upper orders of society, and these continued to exist for a time after the end of the Roman Empire in the west, probably being referred to, for example, in Gregory of Tours's *History of the Franks* (V.44). According to this, King Chilperic (561–84) 'added certain letters to our alphabet' and, in an early piece of educational control, 'sent instructions to all the cities in our kingdom, saying that these letters should be taught to boys in school, and that books using the old characters should have them erased with pumice-stone and the new ones written in'. But for most of our period the only schools were those in monasteries, churches, and bishops' residences. These were sometimes open to those not destined to be monks or priests, as seems to have been the case with the biographer of the Frankish ruler Charlemagne, Einhard, who was educated in the monastery of Fulda (Germany) before becoming a courtier. But overwhelmingly they seem to have been intended for the education of churchmen. It is true that Charlemagne's capitulary called *The General Admonition* (789) orders:

> And let schools for teaching boys the psalms, musical notation, singing, computation and grammar be created in every monastery and episcopal residence.
>
> (*Capitularies*, no. 5, sec. 72)

Whether this was actually done and whether, if it was, schools with a curriculum so obviously ecclesiastical were for the education of anyone but aspirant monks and priests are issues open to discussion. It is possible that from this time on monasteries routinely had external as well as internal schools, the former for lay boys; and that this is what is shown by the building on the Plan of St Gall which is labelled 'House of the common school' (Horn and Born, 1979, II, 168–75); but it is not easy to show this, and, even if that was the intention of Charlemagne's *General Admonition*, there is a subsequent edict in 817 in the reign of Louis the Pious (814–40) which stipulates that 'there should be no school other than in the cloister'. This is not clear, but it could be interpreted as meaning that the only school in the monastery should be one within the inner part of such an institution, the part that was strictly for monks.

We have been arguing so far for a Church monopoly on scholarship, but that was not strictly the case because there was also considerable scholarly activity in the palaces of at least some of the kings of our period. Charlemagne is well known for having assembled at his palace at Aachen an impressive community of scholars, including the Englishman Alcuin, whom he had 'head-hunted' while Alcuin was travelling through Italy, the Lombards, Paul the Deacon, Peter of Pisa, and Paulinus of Aquileia, and the Visigoth Theodulf, who became bishop of Orléans. A scholarly court was not, however, an innovation of Charlemagne's. The court of the kings of the Lombards had similarly been adorned with scholars. Moreover, there was a tradition of scholar-kings. Charlemagne himself, although he could not write, appears in contemporary sources as engaging in scholarly activity with his palace-circle of luminaries, and he built up a library which appears in his will as Einhard records it. But the scholar-king had appeared in Western Europe much earlier. Gregory of Tours records that King Chilperic had written 'a number of books of poetry' in imitation of the fifth-century Christian poet Sedulius (Gregory, *Hist. Franks*, V.44). Gregory did not approve of Chilperic's scholarship, since his poetry did not follow the rules of metre, but we should perhaps be impressed with the extent of that scholarship. A little later, we know that the king of Northumbria in the late eighth century, Aldfrith, was a scholar (poetry was later attributed to him), and that he exchanged an estate of land with Benedict Biscop, abbot of Monkwearmouth-Jarrow, in return for a manuscript of the *Cosmographer* (probably the Roman writer Pliny). His successor, Ceolwulf, was clearly also a scholar, for it was to him that Bede sent the draft of his *Ecclesiastical History of the English People*.

Charlemagne's successors, his son Louis the Pious (814–40) and grandson Charles the Bald (840–70), continued the tradition of maintaining scholars in the palace, but the pinnacle of this was probably attained by Alfred the Great, king of Wessex (871–99), who not only assembled at his palace an international group of scholars, including his biographer Asser from St David's (Wales), Grimbald of Saint-Bertin (Flanders), and John the Old Saxon (from Saxony), as well as scholars from Mercia. Unlike Charlemagne, Alfred could not only write but also translate out of the Latin, and he actually contributed to the scholarly translations undertaken in his reign, including Orosius's fifth-century Christian history and Gregory the Great's *The Pastoral Care*.

You could interpret this royal scholarship as aimed at raising the prestige of rulership itself, by making the scholar-kings appear to be imbued with the scholarship of the Roman Empire and of more recent Christian history. Just as the Sun-King, Louis XIV of France, steeped his court at Versailles in art and music to enhance his standing in the world, so – you could argue – these kings of our period made their palaces foci of scholarship for the same sort of reason. There may be some truth in this, but you should also consider the extent to which the Church dominated palace-scholarship just as it did scholarship elsewhere. The great majority of palace-scholars were churchmen, and many went on to Church positions, as when Theodulf became bishop of Orléans and Alcuin became abbot of St Martin's Abbey at Tours. Moreover, the scholarship of the palaces can often be shown to have grown up in association with royal cooperation with the Church in ecclesiastical reform and missionary work. Charlemagne's father, Pippin III, also had a palace-circle of scholars including the Irish bishop, Virgil, and the English missionary-reformer Boniface. Alfred the Great's scholarly activity seems to have been explicitly intended to correct the weaknesses of the contemporary Church following the Viking attacks of the ninth century. As the king himself wrote in his translation of *The Pastoral Care*, he had been galvanised into action with regard to scholarship because:

> Learning had declined so thoroughly in England that there were very few men on this side of the Humber who could understand their divine services in English, or even translate a single letter from Latin into English: and I suppose that there were not many beyond the Humber either.
>
> (Keynes and Lapidge, 1983, p. 151)

It may be, then, that you will want to interpret royal scholarly activity not so much as scholarship being promoted other than by the Church, but rather as a demonstration of the strength of the Church's grip, not only over society at large (or its literate elite at any rate), but also over kings themselves. We saw in Chapter 4 how Christianity shaped the institution of kingship itself, and you may want to argue that in promoting scholarship these kings were simply acting as agents of the Church.

So you can argue for seeing Western European scholarship and culture in our period as in the first place an inheritance from the classical scholarship and culture of Rome, itself modified by Christianity, especially from the time of the imperial adoption of that religion in the fourth century. Further, you can argue that this Roman scholarship and culture was drawn into the service of the Church, so that it came in effect to characterise that Church as it was in Western Europe. The Church too dominated schooling, with the disappearance of the Roman public schools and the limitation of formal schooling to monasteries and other ecclesiastical sites.

This did not necessarily mean, however, that the Church established a total monopoly over scholarship and culture, for there must have been a flourishing lay scholarship and culture for which our evidence is inevitably much poorer. In the case of the Old English epic *Beowulf*, it cannot be doubted that, Christian as it may be in the form that we have it, behind it lay a whole series of narratives and motifs, which may never have been written down in our period but which circulated orally, perhaps being sung by the minstrels (or *scopas* in Old English) in the mead-halls of the kings and the aristocracy, and perhaps at lower levels of the social scale. The figure of the hero Beowulf himself, for example, seems clearly to be related to a whole group of stories about a uniquely strong figure, sometimes called Little Bear (*Böðvarr bjarki*), which appear in Scandinavian sagas, for example *Grettís Saga*, and other writings. The name Beowulf, which literally means 'wolf (or enemy) of the bee', is probably an allusive Old English means of referring to the bear (a kenning in technical terms). Behind all this must lie a lay tradition of story-telling and oral composition which we can only glimpse dimly. In Ireland too, we have further glimpses of a lay culture represented by oral tales which happen to have been written down at some point, notably those known as *The Cattle Raid of Cooley*, which describe raiding in an entirely secular context in the Irish countryside.

You need then to think critically about how far Church writers, whose work constitutes most of the evidence we have, are misleading us into seeing the scholarship and literature of this period as much more Roman and Christian than, if we could see it across the whole range of society, it really was.

Research and study

Broad research questions

How far were scholarship, learning, and literature merely a continuation of their Roman equivalents?

How far, on the other hand, did they represent significant innovation?

How far were these activities suborned to the purposes of the Church

How far did there continue to exist a distinctively lay culture?

Books and papers to begin with

Two classic studies by Laistner (1957) and Riché (1976) argue that the Roman tradition of scholarship persisted well into our period, although neither go to the end of our period. For the various period subdivisions, Fouracre (2005, chs 26–7), McKitterick (1995, chs 25, 28–9), and Reuter (2000, ch. 7) are helpful as surveys. For scholarship in the British Isles, very useful are Ó Cróinín (1995) and Blair (1976). For the Carolingian Renaissance, there are excellent discussions by Bullough (1973, ch. 4, 1991a). Also useful are the papers edited by McKitterick (1994). Her book (McKitterick, 1977) is especially good on the use of scholarship for Christian preaching and teaching. Ullmann (1969) is a very important book on the purposes of the Carolingian Renaissance in the context of rulership. There is an interesting discussion of the limits of that Renaissance by Nelson (1977). Hildebrandt (1992) discusses whether or not there were in that period 'external schools' in monasteries, open to boys not intending to become monks.

Pursuing more specific aspects

Career-patterns of individual scholars

How far was there consistency of pattern across the careers and works of individual scholars?

See, for example, Brown (1967) and Bonner (1963) on Augustine of Hippo; Lynn (1994) on Ambrose; Rebenich (2002) on Jerome; Gibson (1981) on Boethius; O'Donnell (1979) on Cassiodorus; Moorhead (2005), Straw (1988), and Markus (1997) on Gregory the Great; Mitchell and Wood (2002) on Gregory of Tours; Brown (1987, 2009) and De Gregorio (2010) on Bede; Bullough (2002) on Alcuin or (that work being large and difficult) the more accessible if less up-to-date works by Gaskoin (1904), Browne (1908), and Duckett (1951).

Handwriting

What does the type of handwriting (script) used or developed in our period show about cultural influences on scholarship and about its purposes?

This is not an easy area, but it is well worth understanding. The most accessible works are Bischoff (1990) and Brown (1990). These works deal mostly with handwriting in manuscripts. You must not be put off by the fact that they use different names for the different types of handwriting.

Vernacular literature

Vernacular homilies (i.e. sermons) and saints' *Lives* were obviously produced in a Church context, but they may nevertheless reflect strong lay influence on scholarship and learning. Works like the great Old English epic *Beowulf* may (or may not) cast light on purely lay areas of written culture.

How far does the existence of writings in vernacular languages (Old English, Continental Germanic, Old Norse) show that there was a tradition of learning and scholarship independent of the Church?

It is easiest to approach this issue through Old English literature, where early texts are most numerous and you can get to know many of them in modern English translation. See, for example, *Beowulf*, the very rich Old English poems translated by Hamer (2006) or Alexander (1991), and prose and verse translated by Raffel and Olsen (1998). Lapidge and Godden (1991) provide surveys and discussions, although you cannot expect them to answer the question directly. The question of what the audience of Old English literature was is discussed directly in two technical articles by Bullough (1993) and Wormald (1978).

For Continental Germanic, there is a discussion by McKitterick (1977, ch. 6), but it is very exciting actually to read the *Heliand*, an account of Christ in Continental Germanic from the ninth century (Murphy, 1992). There is a discussion by Murphy (1989).

The use of runes as a writing system in England and Scandinavia raises other issues about the function of writing, and you can pursue this in the work of the great runologist, Page (1987, 1999, 1995).

Compute and music

Was the development of compute (i.e. the calculation of the calendar) and of music aimed purely at providing the Church with practical tools for its services?

Compute is not the easiest subject to grasp, but it is fascinating and was clearly of great importance in our period, not least to Bede, whose great speciality it was. The best starting-point is Stevens (1985), but also very useful is the introduction to Wallis (1999). There is helpful background in Borst (1993).

For music, there is a good survey by Rankin (1994) and a very interesting discussion of the origin of Gregorian Chant by Levy (1998).

14

Art and architecture

We have been asking of the development of scholarship and literature how far it was just a continuation of Roman scholarship, for most of our period taken over and modified by the Church for its own purposes; and we have also raised the question of the importance of distinctively lay culture. We need now to ask these questions of the development of art and architecture, as visual forms of culture.

Architectural forms

Secular basilicas

If we want to argue for the strength of Roman influence, a key piece of evidence is provided by the role in early medieval architecture of the basilica, which was the dominant form of Roman buildings. A basilica is a rectangular building, generally with a rounded end (or apse) at one of the short sides. A spectacular surviving example is the emperor's basilica in the Roman city of Trier (Germany), now used as a Protestant church, but in the Roman period a meeting-hall, in which the emperor's throne was located in the apse to give it greater grandeur (Fig. 31).

This building has only a single central space (the nave), but even grander basilicas could have aisles, or corridors running parallel to the nave and separated from it by columns (which made up the nave arcade). A spectacular example is the enormous basilica, called the New Basilica (*Basilica Nova*), completed by the first Christian emperor Constantine on the forum in Rome.

How influential were such basilicas on the buildings of rulers and potentates in the barbarian kingdoms which were the immediate successors of the Roman Empire

Figure 31 Interior of the Roman basilica at Trier (Germany). Although this building has been much restored and is now used as a church, the basic form and scale of the Roman architecture is still clearly evident. The lines of round windows are original in form, as the masonry on the exterior demonstrates. Notice the rectangular shape of the basilica, with the great arch opening into the semi-circular apse, or termination of the building, where the emperor would have sat to preside over meetings and trials.

in the west? The closest we can come to one is a representation on a mosaic in the church of San Apollinare Nuovo in Ravenna of a building labelled *palatium* ('palace'). The mosaic belongs, like the church, to the reign of Theoderic, king of the Ostrogoths, who (we know from a contemporary source called the *Anonymus Valesianus*) had built a palace in Ravenna. There seems little doubt then that this is what the mosaic shows, and it is evident that it was a basilica with aisles, and a triangular pediment entirely in the Roman manner. The next basilica used in a royal palace we can identify is that at Naranco near Oviedo in northern Spain, dating from the eighth century, and there too we have a basilica without an apse admittedly, but with Roman-type columns, a Roman-type semi-circular vault, and a triangular pediment on the short side just as appears in a sixth-century mosaic of Theoderic's palace at Ravenna.

The use of the basilica in palaces is even more obvious at Charlemagne's great palace at Aachen of the late eighth century, where the great hall (*aula*), the basic form of which is preserved to this day as the Renaissance-style town-hall into which it was converted, is a basilica with an apse resembling in its proportions the Roman basilica at Trier. And we find a similar basilica at the Carolingian palace of Ingelheim on the River Main (Fig. 8 above), although at the other Carolingian palaces which are known from archaeological excavation at Frankfurt-am-Main and Paderborn (Germany) the great halls are rectangular in shape but have no apse. Nevertheless, we have here strong evidence for the continuation of a Roman form in the successor-states of the Roman Empire in the west.

The stone basilica was not, however, the only form of royal hall in early medieval Western Europe. As we have seen in Chapter 6, timber halls, the mead-halls of *Beowulf*, were characteristic of royal sites in Scandinavia and in northern Britain, where the classic example is the halls at the seventh-century Northumbrian royal palace of Yeavering. These timber halls have often been regarded as deriving from barbarian, Germanic or Scandinavian, traditions of building, and perhaps they did. But we might be struck by the fact that their rectangular proportions were not so different from those of Roman basilicas, and we might want to argue that these timber buildings were just as much a continuation of Roman architecture, but in wood rather than in stone.

Ecclesiastical basilicas

We could argue that the most striking aspect of the history of the Roman basilica, however, is the way in which it was so completely taken over as the principal plan for Christian churches. In the second half of the seventh century, we find in northern Spain the church of San Pedro de la Nave, the central space of which is a Roman-type basilica, with a nave and an apse at the east end, in which the high altar was placed. At about the same time was built in Mercia the great church of Brixworth (Northamptonshire; Fig. 32). This had a strikingly Roman basilican plan, with an apse at the east end as at San Pedro de la Nave, and with a great nave arcade of arches opening out into aisles flanking the nave which have disappeared since it was built. We could turn too to the church which Charlemagne's biographer Einhard built at Steinbach (Germany). The surviving stonework shows that this was a Roman-style basilica, with an apse and a nave arcade opening originally into aisles.

The basilica could of course take different forms, and its proportions and details were modified across the centuries until a church like Durham Cathedral (begun 1093), basilican in form as it is, nevertheless does not look Roman in its proportions. The link with Rome, however, was strikingly demonstrated in the Carolingian period by the construction of what the great art historian Richard Krautheimer (1942) called T-basilicas. The label referred to the fact that these basilicas, which included the Carolingian churches of Fulda (Germany) and Saint-Denis (France), had a nave and a long transept (i.e. that part of the church running from north to south at 90° to the nave), giving the plan a 'T' shape. These churches, Krautheimer showed, were

Figure 32 The nave of Brixworth church (Northamptonshire), interior looking west. The large arches to either side would originally have opened into lines of side-chapels or *porticus*. Notice how Roman they are in style with their radiating lines of tiles, and notice too the rectangular shape of the church itself, which (when still complete) would have resembled a Roman basilica, but one with aisles to either side of the central nave.

direct imitations of those built by the emperor Constantine in Rome, especially that of St Peter's in the Vatican and St John's in the Lateran.

Centrally planned churches

We could extend our line of argument to include buildings other than those based on the basilica, which was not the only Roman building-plan. Some Roman buildings, such as the Pantheon in Rome, were what architectural specialists call centrally planned, that is, they were round or oval or polygonal. Such plans were used for Late Roman churches, such as that of St Gereo in Cologne (Germany), which has been miraculously restored after the Second World War bombing of the city, and that of the fifth-century church at Fréjus (southern France). They were used in the Byzantine Empire, not least for the great church of the Haghia Sophia which the emperor Justinian (527–65) built in Constantinople, and the church of San Vitale which the same emperor built at Ravenna, the centre of Byzantine power in Italy. It was probably this last church which influenced the design of the church at Charlemagne's palace at Aachen, for both churches are polygonal and they share architectural details, such as the first-floor gallery (Fig. 7 above).

We could argue, further, that the dominance of Roman architectural forms over ecclesiastical architecture was as great as Roman influence over their plans. In Gaul, the baptistery (a church specially designed for the rite of baptism) of St John at Poitiers (France) dates probably from the seventh century. Aside from its Roman proportions, its exterior is Roman in detail. In Spain, the wall-painting (now largely destroyed) in the early ninth-century Santullano Church at Oviedo is strikingly Roman in the architectural decorative details it represents. In England, the possibly seventh-century church of Escomb (County Durham) has an arch between the nave and the eastern part (the chancel or sanctuary) which is so Roman in form that some scholars have argued it must have been re-used from a Roman building.

Sculpture, decoration, and painting

We could assemble further evidence for the adoption of Roman forms by the Church, which is very obvious in these areas of artistic expression. In Italy, the church of Santa Maria in Valle at Cividale, dating probably to the eighth century, is strikingly Roman, not only in its architectural form but also in its decoration, including a series of lifelike figures executed very much in the Roman naturalistic manner. We have already had occasion to look at the *Codex Amiatinus*, which was an imitation of Cassiodorus's *Codex Grandior*, itself entirely in the Roman tradition of art as well as writing. Another very striking example is a manuscript illuminated in the early ninth century in the context of the Carolingian Renaissance, namely the Gospels of St Médard of Soissons. Here the Roman style of the representation of the Fountain of Life, with animals and birds surrounding it, is arresting, as also is the representation of the Lamb of God from the biblical Book of Revelation (i.e. the Apocalypse).

To that we could add the crypt of the seventh-century Frankish abbey of Jouarre near Paris, which contains a series of tombs, including that of Bishop Agilbert of Paris. The walls were decorated with geometric, multi-coloured stonework derived from Roman decoration called *opus reticulatum*; the columns with their Roman-style capitals (technically called Corinthian capitals), and the tombs themselves all breathe the Roman character of this seventh-century ecclesiastical building. Bishop Agilbert's own tomb is remarkable for being carved with a series of human figures on either side of Christ, their arms raised upwards in the early Christian posture of praying (art historians call figures praying in this way *orantes*). These figures are represented in a very naturalistic way, entirely in line with Roman sculpture, and we see the same thing in the very rich stone sculpture from early medieval England, especially from Northumbria and Mercia. The pre-eminent example is the great cross (or perhaps monument, for it is not certain that it was a cross), probably of the eighth century, at Ruthwell, which is situated on the north coast of the Solway Firth in south-west Scotland, but was when it was erected in the kingdom of Northumbria (Fig. 33).

The narrow sides of the cross are decorated with a naturalistic vine-scroll, itself derived from Roman art such as the mosaic covering the vault of the fourth-century church of Santa Constanza in Rome.

Figure 33 Ruthwell Cross, Dumfriesshire. Detail of the inhabited vine-scroll with a version of the Old English poem, *The Dream of the Rood*, inscribed in runes beside it. You can see a bird in the lower frond of the vine-scroll with a mammal in the upper frond biting at the vine. The Latin inscription on the right of the photograph relates to the biblical and other scenes carved on the adjacent face.

The vine represented Christ feeding the faithful with wine, as is made explicit at Santa Constanza by the inclusion of his head in the vine. At Ruthwell, naturalistic small mammals and birds are carved as feeding on the grapes of the vine, and presumably symbolise the faithful feeding on the blood of Christ's body, as in the Mass. The margins are inscribed in runes with an early version of *The Dream of the Rood*. The long sides of the cross have naturalistic figures representing a series of scenes primarily from the Bible, including Christ in the wilderness with beasts at his feet, Mary Magdalen cleaning His feet, and Christ healing the blind man. These scenes have been extensively discussed by modern scholars and it is clear that they were intended to convey quite a sophisticated Christian message, whether about the nature of monasticism and its origins in the desert (the desert hermits Anthony and Paul are the figures in another of the scenes), or about the nature of Christ. So the cross, along with other English crosses such as those at Bewcastle (Cumbria) and the one which was at Easby (North Yorkshire), are a continuation of essentially Roman figure-sculpture and Roman decoration pressed into the service of the Church.

Such sculpture was also a feature of religious art in Ireland, where the great high crosses of Kells and Monasterboice are fine examples, and also in the kingdom of the Picts. In the case of the latter, sculpture in the form of the so-called 'Pictish stones' is one of the principal pieces of evidence which that kingdom has left us. In this most northern Christian kingdom in Britain, beyond the bounds of the former Roman Empire, we cannot help but be struck by the Roman style of the scenes sculptured on crosses, grave-markers, and tombs. The great carved sarcophagus of the eighth century at St Andrews is a very fine example, with its scene of a hunt to the left of the main panel, and a great, bearded, classically draped figure of the biblical David fighting the lion (as in the Bible) with his hands forcing open the beast's jaws (Fig. 34). The corner posts of the shrine, like other examples of Pictish sculpture, have vine-scrolls very much in the Roman manner.

Figure 34 St Andrew's Sarcophagus, David fighting the lion.

Against all this, however, we could argue that Roman styles were not the only ones pressed into service by the Church. The Pictish sculptures, for example, show other elements, such as geometrical patterns apparently derived from decorative metalwork of the Germanic barbarians but also of the Celtic inhabitants of Western Europe reaching back in date to the pre-Roman period. The same can be seen very clearly in manuscripts from the British Isles, and a particularly clear example is the Book of Durrow, a copy of the gospels made perhaps in Ireland, perhaps in Northumbria, in the seventh century. The representation of the man-symbol of St Matthew is especially striking, since it is one-dimensional, eschewing the Roman style of modelling a rounded human form, and the patterning of its cloak is strongly reminiscent of the so-called cloisonné work in barbarian metalwork, where geometrically shaped cells of gold were filled with coloured stones such as garnet or patterns of coloured glass called millefiori.

We could argue that we can see the Roman style and this use of barbarian decorative motifs side by side in a somewhat later manuscript of the early eighth century, the Lindisfarne Gospels. At the beginning of each Gospel is a portrait of the evangelist in question, represented very much in the Roman style (Fig. 35). Alongside each of these,

(a)   **(b)**

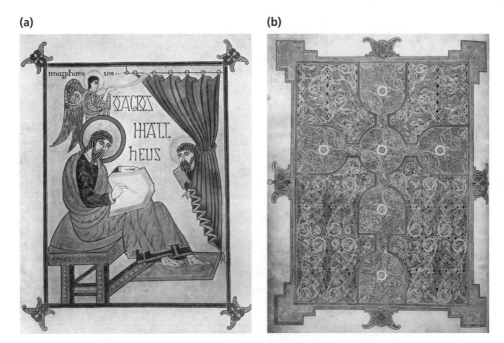

Figure 35 Lindisfarne Gospels, preliminary pages to the Gospel of St Matthew. In the left-hand miniature, notice Matthew's classical drapery, and the representation of depth in his footstool (all features of Roman painting). In the right-hand miniature, notice the range of geometrical patterns and interlace. The outer margins are in fact made up of interlaced animals and birds, all forms derived from barbarian and Celtic art. (London, British Library, MS Cotton Nero D.iv, fols 25b, 26b)

Figure 35a source: © INTERFOTO/Alamy.
Figure 35b source: Courtesy of Heritage Images.

however, is a so-called carpet-page, decorated with a whole range of geometrical patterns and animal patterns derived from barbarian and Celtic art. The cross around which it is all arranged offers strong evidence in favour of the takeover of this art by the Church.

The use of such forms continued even in periods such as that of the Carolingian Renaissance when imitation of the Roman past was especially emphasised. One of the earliest manuscripts produced for Charlemagne's court-school, for example, was a book of gospel-readings called by scholars the Godescalc Evangelistiary after its scribe, who is named. In this, the representation of Christ, seated and blessing, combines Roman and Byzantine influences with those from the British Isles (Fig. 36).

Figure 36 The Godescalc Evangelistiary, miniature of Christ enthroned. Christ is robed and holds in his left hand a bible, while he makes the symbol of blessing with his right. He has a halo with a cross in it, which marks him out as Christ. The staring eyes looking out from the picture with an ethereal gaze may be the result of Byzantine influence, but influence from the British Isles is apparent in the winding interlace on the front of Christ's footstool and also on either side of the low wall behind him. *Source*: © The Art Archive/Alamy.

A similar Christian takeover of barbarian art-forms is apparent in Viking art of the tenth and eleventh centuries, especially in the style of stone-carving known as the Jellinge Style. The style, the name of which derives from the fact that metalwork decorated with it was found at the pagan Viking site of Jellinge, is characterised by the use of two-dimensional animal-motifs, their bodies indicated by a double outline, and their jaws often long and trailing like streamers. This style too was used on Christian stone-carving, especially in England in the period when that country was much under the influence of Viking culture as a result of Viking raids and ultimately of the Viking dynasty of King Cnut and his sons.

Barbarian styles

The Church, then, may not have limited itself to Roman forms, but may have drawn in also the art and culture of the Germanic (and Scandinavian) barbarians and of the Celtic inhabitants of Western Europe, in stone-carving, in ecclesiastical metalwork like that recently discovered in an Irish bog at Derry Na Flan, and in manuscript illumination. But did the Church blot out all other traditions of artistic expression, or was there a distinctively lay artistic culture throughout our period, which represented different traditions and ideas, independent of those of the Church? We are handicapped in pursuing this by the fact that, although we know a fair amount about pre-Christian barbarian art as we find it in the grave-goods of the pagan period, we know much less about secular art after the conversion to Christianity than we do about Church art, because so much more of the latter has survived. Nevertheless, the surviving grave-goods from burials belonging to the post-conversion period suggest the continuation of barbarian and Celtic artistic styles in lay Christian contexts. If an apparently royal grave like Prittlewell in Essex, with its gilt crosses, is really a Christian grave, then the grave-goods represent a continuation of pre-Christian barbarian traditions of art. And this is certainly the case with the graves under Cologne Cathedral, which unquestionably belong to the Christian period of Frankish history and yet have grave-goods in a markedly barbarian style.

Most striking of all in this respect, we may think, are the helmets recovered from early medieval graves. These are found across Western Europe, notably in Mound 1 at Sutton Hoo, but also at the Scandinavian burial-sites of Vendel and Valsgärde. They are generally constructed around an iron framework, often attached to which are decorated plates to cover the head, with equally decorated cheek-guards and neck-protectors. The decoration is often markedly barbarian in character, like the images of naked berserker warriors on the Sutton Hoo Mound 1 helmet; but the most striking thing about the whole group is that it seems to derive from Roman helmets, especially those worn by cavalry soldiers on parade. Even in this superficially barbarian type of object, found as it is especially in pagan Scandinavia, we can argue that the influence of Roman culture was very pronounced.

But to an extent we can argue too for the same Christian takeover of artistic forms which we have proposed elsewhere in our discussion. Just over twenty years

Figure 37 The Coppergate Helmet (Yorkshire Museum, York). Notice the very fine workmanship of the metal plates of the helmet, and notice too the intricate interlace decoration on the nose-guard, and the monster's head with the fine gold eyebrows to either side of it. The inscription with the name Oshere occurs twice: once from the back to the front of the head, terminating with the monster's head, and once from ear to ear (not visible here).
Source: Courtesy of York Archaeological Trust.

ago, a mechanical digger working on the edge of the Viking site of Coppergate in York unexpectedly uncovered a richly decorated helmet of the ninth century, now preserved as the Coppergate Helmet in the Yorkshire Museum in York (Fig. 37). This had the same structure and cheek-plates as we have noted as being derived from Roman helmets, and it had the barbarian-style decoration of interlaced patterning with animal-forms. But across the metal ridges running from front to back and from ear to ear as additional protection was a very remarkable inscription:

> In the name of our Lord Jesus Christ and of the Spirit of God, let us offer up Oshere to All Saints. Amen.

Oshere was evidently the owner of the helmet, which had a Christian inscription aimed presumably at interceding with All Saints for his welfare. It is another striking example of the cultural dominance of Christianity, in this case the adornment of what is at first glance a characteristically barbarian object, but was in fact another derivative from the Roman period.

There is, then, a strong case to be made for the view that art and architecture in our period were derived from Roman culture and shaped by Christian influence. But there may be enough evidence to suggest that there was more to it than that. As you go forward with your research and reading, you need to be alert to the possibility that, alongside what appear to us the mainstream developments of Romano-Christian culture, there was a distinctively lay art, and perhaps also an architecture – if we cast our minds back to the great timber palaces such as Yeavering and Lejre (see above, p. 125) – which were just as vigorous even if they have left fewer traces.

Research and study

Broad research questions

How far were early medieval art and architecture just a continuation of Roman art and architecture?

What was the role of barbarian Germanic and/or Celtic culture in the evolution of early medieval art and architecture?

How far were early medieval art and architecture innovative?

How far were there distinctive non-ecclesiastical forms of art and architecture in the Early Middle Ages?

Books and papers to begin with

We need to approach these questions above all by getting to know in as much detail as possible individual art-objects and buildings, and using them as evidence. Magnificently illustrated surveys with very helpful appendices for this purpose are Grabar, Gilbert, and Emmons (1967), Hubert, Porcher, and Volbach (1969 and 1970). Other excellent surveys are by Beckwith (1964) and Henderson (1972), the latter especially thought-provoking. There is a more up-to-date survey by Nees (2002), who also provides a discussion in McKitterick (1995, ch. 30).

English art is accessible through rich surveys by Wilson (1984) and Dodwell (1982). There are two extremely useful exhibition catalogues, which include buildings as well as objects and allow really specific study of individual items (Backhouse, Archibald, Turner, et al., 1984, Webster and Backhouse, 1991).

Pursuing more specific aspects

Church-building

How innovative was church-building in its use of particular Roman forms and in its development of new ones?

The fullest study, although focused on the latter part of our period, is Conant (1959). The argument that Carolingian architecture imitated that of the first Christian emperor Constantine to make a deliberate statement is made by Krautheimer (1942), although doubts about his thesis are set out by Goodson (2010).

There are very useful studies of English architecture by Clapham (1930) and Fernie (1983).

Manuscript illumination

What light does the development of manuscript illumination cast on the cultural importance of the British Isles on the one hand, and the desire to imitate Roman culture on the other?

Very useful for getting to know the most important manuscripts are the excellently illustrated guides by Weitzmann (1977), Nordenfalk (1977), and Mütherich and Gaehde (1977). If you want to go further on manuscripts from the British Isles, there is a brilliant book by Henderson (1987).

For the *Codex Amiatinus*, which is so important for the influence of Roman culture in Northumbria, there is a detailed but lucid study by Bruce-Mitford (1967). For the Lindisfarne Gospels, which are important also for the innovative culture of the British Isles, there is a readable and popular book by Backhouse (1981), with many illustrations, and a research book (if you really want to pursue the manuscript in depth) by Brown (2003). For the Book of Durrow and the Book of Kells, there are excellent introductions by Meehan (1996, 1994).

For Ottonian manuscripts, there is a stimulating study, which explores their historical as well as their artistic significance by Mayr-Harting (1991b).

Stone-sculpture

What was the purpose and the audience of stone crosses and sculptured stones?

Such monuments are most frequently found in the British Isles, where they are very common and very important, especially in northern England, eastern Scotland (the

Pictish kingdoms), and Ireland. For England, there is a basic survey by Lang (1988), and an excellent discussion of Viking-period sculpture, including its representation of pagan myths, by Bailey (1980). If you want to pursue two of the greatest crosses (or maybe monuments rather), Ruthwell and Bewcastle, there is a recent, very detailed study by Lees, Orton, and Wood (2007) and a brilliant discussion by Ó Carragáin (2005). The astonishingly rich, but mysterious, carved stones of the kingdoms of the Picts are discussed with lavish illustrations by Henderson and Henderson (2004), although there is a briefer survey by Ritchie (1989). The equally rich carved crosses of Ireland can be studied in Harbison (1992).

Decorated metalwork and ivory-carving

What light does decorated metalwork throw on the priorities and practices of the Church?

The best survey of the second half of our period, richly illustrated, is Lasko (1994). To look in more depth at the British Isles, there is a beautiful study of ivory carvings by Beckwith (1972), and for Irish metalwork, there is a superbly illustrated catalogue of an exhibition edited by Youngs (1989). Metalwork was also produced in non-ecclesiastical contexts, and it is an interesting question as to what the relationship was between ecclesiastical and secular art in this medium. See, for example, Wilson (1984) and, for the recently discovered Staffordshire hoard, Leahy (2009).

Conclusion

We have been concerned in this part of the book with the extent to which the scholar-ship, literature, art, and architecture of our period were an inheritance of the Roman world, or an adaption of the culture of that world in the interests of the Christian Church, or rather something quite new coming from barbarian traditions and culture beyond the reach of Roman influence. These are clearly important questions for our understanding more widely of what Western Europe in our period was like, and how it related to what had come before.

But, as you go forward with your research and reading, so you need also to think beyond these discussions. We have in the preceding chapters not had the opportunity to look, for example, at the question of how homogenous scholarship, literature, art, and architecture were across Western Europe. Yet this is an important question to consider if we want to assess how far the various regions and kingdoms were united by common interests and common types of artistic endeavour. As regards learning, we may perhaps be impressed by the spread of Latin in scholarly contexts, so that quite early in its Christian history Ireland's scholars were writing grammars of that language, even though it had never been spoken in their country. We may also be impressed by the way in which scholars were able to move across Europe, as Alcuin moved from York to Aachen, or scholars like Clement the Irishman or Columbanus transferred their learning effortlessly from Ireland to the Continent. But we may equally wonder what was the significance for our question of areas of Western Europe where scholarship was also pursued in vernacular languages, especially England, but also Ireland (where Old Irish texts appeared quite early), Saxony (with the *Heliand*), and Scandinavia. Was the use of these languages an indication that some areas of Western Europe were much less immersed in Roman culture? Does it indicate at the least a fusion with barbarian culture? Or were the texts in the vernacular just as much products of a homogenous fusion of Roman and Christian culture as were the Latin texts, but directed at those who were unable to learn Latin?

We could ask of art too how far it points to homogeneity of culture across Western Europe. Certainly, the forms of architecture, especially the dominance of the basilica, may point in this direction. But what of the riot of geometrical and animal patterns in the great manuscripts of the British Isles? Do they represent a culture, perhaps more influenced by non-Roman traditions, specific to that area? Also, what does barbarian metalwork, such as the magnificent items of jewellery recovered from early graves, contribute to this question? Does it derive from a quite different, barbarian world? Or is it too an element in the adaptation of essentially Roman culture to new situations?

There is, in addition, a quite different question that we ought to think about, a question which – like so many others in this book – requires us to widen our chronological perspective. How far did the achievements in this period in learning and art amount to a turning-point in Western European culture? How far did they set the pattern for future centuries, or how far were they superseded and swept away by developments after the end of our period? We could argue, for example, that what really mattered to Western European learning was the rise of cathedral schools, such as that of Chartres (France) in the eleventh and especially the twelfth centuries, and then the development of universities, the first charters for which date from the early thirteenth, including Paris, Bologna, Oxford, Cambridge, and Montpellier (Ridder-Symoens, 1992). It could also be argued that the real turning-point in the development of Western European culture was the introduction of Greek learning, almost unknown in our period, in the course of the twelfth century. This, together with developments in other areas of study such as law and history, can be argued to make of the twelfth century a 'renaissance' comparable to that of the fifteenth and sixteenth centuries (Brooke, 1969, Swanson, 1999). How did this compare, on the other hand, with developments of our period? Was the progress made under the Carolingian rulers, for example, equally a 'renaissance', as it has sometimes been called?

The same question can be applied to art, and especially to architecture. If we look ahead beyond 1050, the scale of church-building in Western Europe is breathtaking. Everywhere we see enormous cathedrals and abbeys, often dwarfing what came before them, and sometimes showing technical breakthroughs such as the introduction of stone-vaulting with ribs, as we find it in Durham Cathedral (Coldstream, 2002). Yet, we may want to argue that the essence of such architecture was nevertheless developed in our period with, for example, the adaptation of the Roman basilica to the needs of the Christian Church. It is, needless to say, a matter for your judgement, but, as you go forward, to widen your perspective can only give greater weight to that judgement.

Time-line: Part VI

306–37	Reign of Emperor Constantine
	Basilica Nova, Rome
	Church of St Peter in the Vatican
	Church of St John in the Lateran
	Church of Santa Constanza, Rome
c.311–83	Ulfilas, missionary to the Goths, translator of the Bible into Gothic
354–430	Augustine of Hippo
	395–8 The *Confessions*
	416–22 The *City of God*
5th century	Martianus Capella, author of *The Marriage of Philology and Mercury*
417	Orosius, author of *History against the Pagans*
480–524	Boethius, author of *The Consolation of Philosophy*
485/90–c.580	Cassiodorus, author of the *Variae*, *History of the Goths* (lost), founder of Vivarium
527–65	Reign of Emperor Justinian
	San Vitale, Ravenna (Italy)
	Haghia Sophia, Constantinople (Istanbul, Turkey)
c.540–94	Gregory of Tours, author of the *History of the Franks* (*Ten Books of Histories*), and the *Lives of the Fathers*
c.530–c.600	Venantius Fortunatus, author of Latin poetry and a *Life of St Martin*
590–604	Pope Gregory the Great, author of *The Pastoral Care*, the *Dialogues*, the *Commentary on Job*
c.560–636	Isidore of Seville, bishop of Seville, author of the *Etymologies*, and the *Great Chronicle*
7th century	Book of Durrow
?–689	Benedict Biscop, abbot of Monkwearmouth-Jarrow (England)
	673/4 founds Monkwearmouth
	681/2 founds Jarrow
688–716	Ceolfrith, abbot of Monkwearmouth-Jarrow
c.673–735	Bede, monk of Monkwearmouth-Jarrow, author of the *Reckoning of Time*, and the *Ecclesiastical History of the English People*
Early 8th century	Lindisfarne Gospels
8th century	Buildings and sculpture
	Naranco, palace near Oviedo (Spain)
	Ruthwell Cross (Scotland)
	Bewcastle Cross (or monument; Cumbria)
	St Andrews sarcophagus (Scotland)
	Church of Santa Maria, Cividale (Italy)

c.675–754	Boniface (Wynfrith), missionary, archbishop of Mainz (Germany)
c.700–84	Virgil, missionary, bishop of Salzburg (Austria)
768–814	Charlemagne, king and emperor
	789 *The General Admonition*
c.720–c.800	Paul the Deacon, scholar at Charlemagne's court, author of the *Deeds of the Bishops of Metz*, and the *History of the Lombards*
c.730–802	Paulinus of Aquileia, scholar at Charlemagne's court
c.740–804	Alcuin of York, scholar at Charlemagne's court, abbot of St Martin's, Tours (France)
c.750–821	Theodulf, bishop of Orléans, scholar at Charlemagne's court, author of the *Caroline Books*
814–40	Reign of Emperor Louis the Pious
c.810–c.877	John the Scot, Eriugena, author of *On the Division of Nature*
871–99	Alfred the Great, king of Wessex
	887 Grimbald of Saint-Bertin at King Alfred's court
	890 John the Old Saxon at King Alfred's court
	893 Asser of St David's writes the *Life of King Alfred*
902	Death of Hoger, abbot of Werden, author of *Musica enchiriadis*
c.950–c.1010	Ælfric of Eynsham, author of homilies and saints' lives in Old English

PART VII

Conclusion

We began this book with a question: was the period from 300 to 1050 one of the most formative in Western Europe's history? Did it see, as the subtitle of this book has it, the 'birth of western society'? We have attempted, in the chapters which have followed, to explore various ways in which we might break that question down into subsidiary questions. What were the nature and significance of the formation of states in the wake of the dissolution of the Roman Empire in the west? How much like peoples we would recognise as such were the ethnic groupings which emerged, such as the Franks, the Visigoths, and the English? How varied and sophisticated was the exercise of power, whether ideological, bureaucratic, or personal power, within society? How formative were the changes which took place in the economic foundation of Western Europe, that is, in its rural, commercial, and urban life? What were the processes by which Christianity became the universal religion, and how effective were its mechanisms of government and control? And, finally, how innovative and coherent a culture emerged in terms of learning and art?

It is not at all the intention of this book to answer either the overarching question or these subsidiary questions, but rather to offer you some guidance on how they might be approached – indeed how they have been approached – and what evidence and arguments you might bring to bear in order to answer them. It is up to you to develop your own discussions, to use the evidence as you think it should be used, and to defend your conclusions with your own arguments, while being aware – in a critical way – of what others before you have written. It is up to you, in other words, to answer the questions, and if in your research and reading you find reason to disagree strongly with the ways I have suggested approaching them, no one could be better pleased than myself.

As you look at the subsidiary questions, you may, as I have repeatedly commented in the conclusions to the different parts of the book, wish to finesse them, especially from a chronological or a geographical point of view. This book has often, although not always, treated Western Europe and the period we are dealing with as entities, not only because of the constraints of space and time, but also because it seems to me that there is a case to be made that Western European history was in many respects characterised by a coherence of forms and structures across widely separated areas, and also by continuity across time. So that it is not unreasonable, for example, to relate at least some aspects of the power of Charlemagne, ruler of much of Continental Western Europe, to that of an Irish ruler, king of little more than a modern county. But, as you go forward in your research and reading, you may want to question this, and to explore our period much more in terms of variation between areas, and change between chronological subdivisions of it, than this book has attempted. Was the period of the Carolingian rulers, for example, the real period of change? Was England in the tenth and eleventh century much more advanced in government organisation than most of the Continent? Was the depth in which Christianity was established greater in the former Roman lands than outside them?

Underlying such questions is a general issue, for the tension between continuity and change in history becomes very apparent when we range across as many centuries as this book does. How important, in other words, are the changes within a particular period, such as this one, compared with the continuities – bearing in mind always that periods themselves are creations of modern scholars rather than those of contemporaries? We have suggested in the conclusions to the various parts of the book that one way of assessing the importance of what we are seeing in the period we are studying is to move beyond it, and if you are also studying later periods of the Middle Ages, or if you are going on to do so, you will inevitably have the opportunity to look back at our period in the light of what you know about them. How important was it in comparison?

We can finish with an exciting book, which you need not agree with, but which shows what you might do by following this comparative approach. It is R. I. Moore's *The First European Revolution c.970–1215* (Moore, 2000), the title of which shows at once the drift of his argument. For him, the real turning-point in Western European history was not our period, or at least it occurred at the very end of it and in the course of the following century. According to Moore, the revolution he has identified involved many of the aspects we have ourselves been considering. It involved a revolution in urbanisation, which resulted in more numerous and larger towns. These made demands on the food supply, which encouraged lords to make changes in rural life by which even free peasants were reduced to serfdom, and were organised in ways which made them utterly dependent on those lords. So the real emergence of the servile peasantry of the Middle Ages took place in the eleventh century, and was associated with the clearing of new land, closer control of the peasantry, and the shaping of the rural economy in new ways. Aristocratic society was itself transformed at the same time by the introduction of primogeniture as the manner of inheritance, which profoundly altered the structure of aristocratic families, producing a group of landless younger sons who were responsible for much of the violence that we see in medieval society. Learning too underwent a revolution, with the formalisation of subjects like rhetoric, and with the emergence of educational institutions, the universities and their precursors. Moreover, a new court culture emerged, in which education was driven by the needs and ambitions of governments, which themselves came to be greatly influenced and changed by the participation in them of men trained in schools and universities. Europe, for Moore, was born 'in the second millennium of the Common Era, not the first', while our period only 'provided an essential stock of materials, certainly – social, economic and institutional as well as cultural and intellectual – but from that stock . . . the men and women of the eleventh and twelfth centuries took what they wanted for their own intricate and highly idiosyncratic construction, and discarded what they did not want' (pp. 1–2).

We cannot do justice here to Moore's book. But, if you read it, or other books concerning later centuries, you need to ask as you do so, how do the developments of the period 300–1050 compare with those of such later periods? Were those of the eleventh and twelfth centuries as formative as Moore maintains compared with those of the period 300–1050 as a whole? Did that period, in other words, see the 'birth of western society', or should that label more properly be applied to the eleventh and twelfth centuries, so that it would only impinge on the very end of the period we have been discussing, or indeed to some other period altogether? I can do no more than to wish you good reading, good thinking, and good discussing!

Original sources

Abbreviations used and translations available

Abbreviations	Translations
Alcuin, *Letters*	Allott, Stephen, ed., 1974. *Alcuin of York c. AD 732 to 804: His Life and Letters*. York: William Sessions.
Ammianus	Hamilton, Walter and Andrew Wallace-Hadrill, ed., 1986. *Ammianus Marcellinus: The Later Roman Empire (A.D. 354–378)*. Harmondsworth: Penguin.
Aneirin, *Gododdin*	Jackson, Kenneth Hurlstone, ed., 1969. *The Gododdin: The Oldest Scottish Poem*. Edinburgh: Edinburgh University Press.
	Jarman, A. O. H., ed., 1988. *Aneirin: Y Gododdin. Britain's Oldest Heroic Poem*. Welsh Classics, 3. Llandysul: Gomer Press.
Anglo-Saxon Chronicle	Swanton, Michael J., ed., 1996. *The Anglo-Saxon Chronicle*. London: Dent.
Annals St Bertin	Nelson, Janet L., ed., 1991. *The Annals of St Bertin*. Manchester Medieval Sources. Manchester: Manchester University Press.
Asser	Keynes, Simon and Michael Lapidge, ed., 1983. *Alfred the Great: Asser's 'Life of King Alfred' and Other Contemporary Sources*. Penguin Classics. Harmondsworth: Penguin.
	Smyth, Alfred P., ed., 2002. *The Medieval Life of King Alfred the Great: A Translation and Commentary on the Text attributed to Asser*. Basingstoke: Palgrave.
Battle of Maldon	Alexander, Michael, ed., 1991. *The Earliest English Poems*. Penguin Classics. Harmondsworth: Penguin.
	Scragg, Donald, ed., 1991. *The Battle of Maldon AD 991*. Oxford: Blackwell.

Abbreviations	Translations
Bede, *Eccl. History* Bede, *Letter to Ecgbert*	McClure, Judith and Roger Collins, ed., 2008. *Bede: The Ecclesiastical History of the English People, the Greater Chronicle, Bede's Letter to Egbert*. Oxford World's Classics. New edn. Oxford: Oxford University Press.
	Sherley-Price, Leo, R. E. Latham, and David H. Farmer, ed., 1990. *Bede, Ecclesiastical History of the English People with Bede's Letter to Egbert and Cuthbert's Letter on the Death of Bede*. Penguin Classics. Revised edn. Harmondsworth: Penguin.
Bede, *History of the Abbots* Bede, *Life of St Cuthbert*	Webb, J. F. and D. F. Farmer, ed., 1983. *The Age of Bede: Bede, Life of Cuthbert; Eddius Stephanus, Life of Wilfrid; Bede, Lives of the Abbots of Wearmouth and Jarrow, with the Voyage of St Brendan*. 2nd edn. Harmondsworth: Penguin.
Beowulf	Alexander, Michael, ed., 2003. *Beowulf: A Verse Translation*. Penguin Classics. Revised edn. Harmondsworth: Penguin.
	Heaney, Seamus, trans., 1999. *Beowulf*. London: Faber and Faber.
Brevium Exempla	Loyn, Henry R. and John Percival, ed., 1975. *The Reign of Charlemagne*. Documents of Medieval History, 2. London: Arnold, pp. 98–105.
Burgundian Laws	Fischer Drew Katherine, ed., 1972. *The Burgundian Code: Book of Constitutions or Law of Gundobad: Additional Enactments*. Philadelphia: University of Pennsylvania Press.
Capitularies	King, P. D., ed., 1987. *Charlemagne: Translated Sources*. Kendal: P. D. King, sec. 8.
Cassiodorus, *Variae*	Barnish, S. J. B. ed., 1992. *Cassiodorus: Variae*. Translated Texts for Historians, 12. Liverpool: Liverpool University Press.
Charters	Whitelock, Dorothy, ed., 1979. *English Historical Documents, I, c.500–1042*. 2nd edn. London: Eyre and Spottiswoode, section II.B.
Customs of the Monastery of Corbie	Horn, Walter and Ernest Born, 1979. *The Plan of St Gall*. 3 vols. Berkeley: University of California Press, II, 91–126.
Cuthbert, *Death of Bede*	McClure, Judith and Roger Collins, ed., 2008. *Bede: The Ecclesiastical History of the English People, the Greater Chronicle, Bede's Letter to Egbert*. Oxford World's Classics. New edn. Oxford: Oxford University Press.
Deeds of the Franks	Hill, Rosalind M. T., ed., 1962. *Gesta Francorum et aliorum Hierosolimitanorum: The Deeds of the Franks and the Other Pilgrims to Jerusalem*. London: Thomas Nelson.

Abbreviations	Translations
Domesday Book	*Domesday Book: A Complete Translation*, 2002. Harmondsworth: Penguin.
Einhard, *Life Charl.*	Thorpe, Lewis, ed., 1969. *Two Lives of Charlemagne*. Penguin Classics. Harmondsworth: Penguin.
	Ganz, David, ed., 2008. *Two Lives of Charlemagne*. Penguin Classics. London: Penguin.
Fredegar, *Chronicle*	Excerpts in Murray, Alexander Callander, ed., 1999. *From Roman to Merovingian Gaul: A Reader*. Broadview: Letchworth, no. 58 (book IV), no. 79 (II, 4–6, 8–9, III, 2, 9), nos. 86–9 (III, 7, 11, 12, 18, 19, 21, 56, 57–9, 70–2, 93).
Ger. Wales, *Ireland*	O'Meara, John, ed., 1982. *Gerald of Wales, The History and Topography of Ireland*. Penguin Classics. Harmondsworth: Penguin.
Gildas, *Ruin and Destruction of Britain*	Winterbottom, Michael, ed., 2002. *Gildas, The Ruin of Britain and Other Works*. Arthurian Period Sources, 7. Augmented edn. Chichester: Phillimore.
Gregory, *Hist. Franks*	Thorpe, Lewis, ed., 1974. *Gregory of Tours: The History of the Franks*. Penguin Classics. Harmondsworth: Penguin.
Heliand	Murphy, G. Ronald, ed., 1992. *The Heliand: The Saxon Gospel*. Oxford: Oxford University Press.
Hincmar, *Organisation of the Palace*	Herlihy, David, ed., 1970. *History of Feudalism*. London: Macmillan, pp. 208–27.
Ibn Fadlan, *Journey*	Frye, Richard N., ed., 2005. *Ibn Fadlan's Journey to Russia: A Tenth-Century Traveler from Baghdad to the Volga River*. Princeton: Markus Wiener Publishers.
Jonas Orl., *Royal Institution*	Dyson, Robert W., ed., 1983. *A Ninth-Century Political Tract: The De Institutione Regia of Jonas of Orléans*. New York: Exposition.
Jordanes, *Gothic History*	Mierow, Charles Christopher, ed., 1915. *The Gothic History of Jordanes*. 2nd edn. Cambridge: Speculum Historiale.
Life of Gregory the Great	Colgrave, Bertram, ed., 1968. *The Earliest Life of Gregory the Great by an Anonymous Monk of Whitby*. Kansas: University of Kansas Press.
Life of Guthlac	Colgrave, Bertram, ed., 1956. *Felix's Life of Saint Guthlac: Introduction, Text, Translation and Notes*. Cambridge: Cambridge University Press.
Life of John the Almsgiver	Dawes, Elizabeth and Norman H. Baynes, ed., 1977. *Three Byzantine Saints: Contemporary Biographies Translated from the Greek*. 2nd edn. London and Oxford: Mowbrays, pp. 195–262.

Abbreviations	Translations
Nennius, *History of the Britons*	Morris, John, ed., 1980. *Nennius: British History and the Welsh Annals*. History from the Sources. London and Chichester: Phillimore.
Notker the Stammerer, *Life of Charlemagne*	Thorpe, Louis, ed., 1969. *Two Lives of Charlemagne*. Penguin Classics. Harmondsworth: Penguin. Ganz, David, ed., 2008. *Two Lives of Charlemagne*. Penguin Classics. London: Penguin.
Paul the Deacon, *History of the Lombards*	Foulke, William Dudley, ed., 1907. *Paul, the Deacon, History of the Langobards*. Philadelphia: Department of History, University of Pennsylvania (reprinted Kessinger Publishing's Rare Reprints).
Procopius	Dewing, H. B., ed., 1916–40. *Procopius*. Loeb Classical Library. 7 vols. London: William Heinemann.
Royal Frankish Annals *Revised Royal Frankish Annals*	Scholz, Bernhard Walter and Barbara Rogers, ed., 1972. *Carolingian Chronicles: Royal Frankish Annals and Nithard's Histories*. Ann Arbor: University of Michigan Press. King, P. David, ed., 1987. *Charlemagne: Translated Sources*. Kendal: P. D. King.
Rule of St Benedict	McCann, Justin, ed., 1976. *The Rule of St Benedict*. London: Sheed and Ward. Parry, Abbot and Esther de Waal, ed., 1990. *The Rule of Saint Benedict*. Leominster: Gracewing.
Sedulius, *Christian Rulers*	Doyle, E. G., ed., 1983. *Sedulius Scottus, on Christian Rulers and the Poems*. Medieval and Renaissance Texts and Studies, 17. Binghamton, New York: Medieval and Renaissance Texts and Studies. Dyson, R. W., ed., 2010. *Sedulius Scottus, De Rectoribus Christianis: An Edition and English Translation*. Woodbridge: Boydell Press.
Song of Roland	Sayers, Dorothy L., ed., 1957. *The Song of Roland*. Penguin: Harmondsworth.
Stephanus, *Life of Bishop Wilfrid*	Colgrave, Bertram, ed., 1927. *The Life of Bishop Wilfrid by Eddius Stephanus*. Cambridge: Cambridge University Press. Webb, J. F. and D. F. Farmer, ed., 1983. *The Age of Bede: Bede, Life of Cuthbert; Eddius Stephanus, Life of Wilfrid; Bede, Lives of the Abbots of Wearmouth and Jarrow, with the Voyage of St Brendan*. Penguin Classics. 2nd edn. Harmondsworth: Penguin.
Tacitus, *On Germany*	Mattingly, H. and Sallie A. Handforth, ed., 1970. *Tacitus: The Agricola and the Germania*. Penguin Classics. Revised edn. Harmondsworth: Penguin.

Abbreviations	Translations
Taliesin	Pennar, M., ed., 1988. *The Poems of Taliesin*. Lampeter: Llanerch.
Visigothic Code	Scott, S. P., ed., 1982. *The Visigothic Code (Forum Judicum)*. Littleton, Colo.: Rothman.
Will. Malm. *Kings*	Mynors, R. A. B., Rodney M. Thomson, and Michael Winterbottom, ed., 1998–9. *William of Malmesbury, Gesta Regum Anglorum, the History of the English Kings*. 2 vols. Oxford Medieval Texts. Oxford: Oxford University Press.

References

Abels, Richard P., 1988. *Lordship and Military Obligation in Anglo-Saxon England*. London: British Museum Publications.

Addyman, Peter V., 1973. 'Saxon Southampton: A Town and International Port of the Eighth to the Tenth Century', in *Vor und Frühformen der Europäischen Stadt im Mittelalter*, edited by Herbert Jankuhn. 2 vols. Göttingen, I, pp. 218–28.

Agache, Roger, 1978. *La Somme Pré-Romaine et Romaine d'après les prospections aériennes à basse altitude*. Amiens: Société des Antiquaires de Picardie.

Aillagon, Jean-Jacques, ed., 2008. *Rome and the Barbarians: The Birth of a New World*. Arte Antica. Venice: Skira.

Airlie, Stuart, 1995. 'The Aristocracy', in *The New Cambridge Medieval History. Vol. 2: c.700–c.900*, edited by Rosamond McKitterick. Cambridge: Cambridge University Press, pp. 431–50.

——, 2005. 'Charlemagne and the Aristocracy: Captains and Kings', in *Charlemagne: Empire and Society*, edited by Joanna Story. Manchester: Manchester University Press, pp. 90–102.

——, 2006. 'The Aristocracy in the Service of the State in the Carolingian Period', in *Staat im frühen Mittelalter*, edited by Stuart Airlie, Walter Pohl, and Helmut Reimitz. Forschungen zur Geschichte des Mittelalters 11. Vienna: Österreichische Akademie der Wissenschaften, phil.-hist. Klasse: Denkschriften, pp. 93–111.

Aitchison, N. B., 1994. *Armagh and the Royal Centres in Early Medieval Ireland*. Woodbridge: Boydell Press.

Alcock, Leslie, 1971. *Arthur's Britain: History and Archaeology AD 367–634*. Harmondsworth: Penguin.

Alexander, Michael, ed., 1991. *The Earliest English Poems*. Penguin Classics. Harmondsworth: Penguin.

Alföldi, Andreas, 1948. *The Conversion of Constantine and Pagan Rome*. Translated by Harold Mattingley. Oxford: Clarendon Press.

Almond, Mark, Jeremy Black, Felipe Fernandez-Armesto, et al., 1994. *The Times Atlas of European History*. London: Times Books.

Althoff, Gerd, 2004. *Family, Friends and Followers: Political and Social Bonds in Medieval Europe*. Translated by Christopher Caroll. Cambridge: Cambridge University Press.

Amory, Patrick, 1993. 'The Meaning and Purpose of Ethnic Terminology in the Burgundian Laws', *Early Medieval Europe* 2, 1–28.

——, 1994. 'Names, Ethnic Identity, and Community in Fifth- and Sixth-Century Burgundy', *Viator* 25, 1–30.

——, 1997. *People and Identity in Ostrogothic Italy, 489–554*. Cambridge: Cambridge University Press.

Anderton, Mike, ed., 1999. *Anglo-Saxon Trading Centres: Beyond the Emporia*. Glasgow: Cruithne Press.

Ando, Clifford, 2008. *The Matter of the Gods: Religion and the Roman Empire*. Berkeley: University of California Press.

Angenendt, Arnold, 1986. 'The Conversion of the Anglo-Saxons Considered against the Background of the Early Medieval Mission', in *Angli e Sassoni al di qua e al di là del mare*, 2 vols. Settimane di Studio sull'Alto Medioevo. Spoleto: Centro Italiano sull'Alto Medioevo, pp. 747–81.

Anon., 1997b. *Großer Atlas zur Weltgeschichte*. 2nd edn. Braunschweig: Westermann.

Arnheim, M. T. W., 1972. *The Senatorial Aristocracy in the Later Roman Empire*. Oxford: Clarendon Press.

Aston, T. H., 1958. 'The Origins of the Manor in England', *Transactions of the Royal Historical Society*, 5th ser. 8, 59–83.

Audouy, Michel and Andy Chapman, 2008. *Raunds: The Origin and Growth of a Midland Village, AD 450–1500*. Oxford: Oxbow.

Bachrach, Bernard S., 2002. *Warfare and Military Organisation in Pre-Crusade Europe*. Variorum Collected Studies. Aldershot: Ashgate.

Backhouse, Janet, 1981. *The Lindisfarne Gospels*. Oxford: Phaidon.

Backhouse, Janet, Marion Archibald, D. H. Turner, et al., ed., 1984. *The Golden Age of Anglo-Saxon Art, 966–1066*. London: British Museum for the Trustees of the British Museum and the British Library Board.

Bailey, Richard N., 1980. *Viking Age Sculpture in Northern England*. London: Collins.

Bak, János M., ed., 1990. *Coronations: Medieval and Early Modern Monarchic Ritual*. Berkeley: University of California Press.

Barnish, Samuel, 1986. 'Taxation, Land and Barbarian Settlement in the Western Empire', *Papers of the British School at Rome* 54, 170–95.

Barnish, Samuel and Federico Marazzi, ed., 2007. *The Ostrogoths from the Migration Period to the Sixth Century*. Woodbridge: Boydell Press.

Barnwell, S. and Marco Mostert, ed., 2003. *Political Assemblies in the Earlier Middle Ages*. Studies in the Early Middle Ages, 7. Turnhout: Brepols.

Barraclough, Geoffrey, 1968. *The Medieval Papacy*. London: Thames and Hudson.

——, 1990. *The Times Atlas of World History*. London: Times Books.

Barthélemy, Dominique, 2009. *The Serf, the Knight, and the Historian*. Translated by Graham Robert Edwards. Ithaca: Cornell University Press.

Bartlett, Robert, 1986. *Trial by Fire and Water: The Medieval Judicial Ordeal*. Oxford: Oxford University Press.

——, 1993. *The Making of Europe: Conquest, Colonization and Cultural Change 950–1350*. London: Allen Lane.

——, 2001. 'Medieval and Modern Concepts of Race and Ethnicity', *Journal of Medieval and Early Modern Studies* 31: Winter, 39–56.

——, 2007. 'From Paganism to Christianity in Medieval Europe', in *Christianization and the Rise of Christian Monarchy: Scandinavia, Central Europe and Rus, c.900–1200*, edited by Nora Berend. Cambridge: Cambridge University Press, pp. 47–72.

Bazelmans, J., 1999. *By Weapons Made Worthy: Lords, Retainers and their Relationships in Beowulf*. Amsterdam: Amsterdam University Press.

Beck, Roger, 2006. *The Religion of the Mithras Cult in the Roman Empire: Mysteries of the Unconquered Sun*. Oxford: Oxford University Press.

Beckwith, John, 1964. *Early Medieval Art: Carolingian, Ottonian, Romanesque*. London: Thames and Hudson.

——, 1972. *Ivory Carvings in Early Medieval England*. London: Harvey, Miller, and Medcalf.

Behringer, Wolfgang, 2010. *A Cultural History of Climate*. Cambridge: Polity Press.

Berend, Nora, ed., 2007. *Christianization and the Rise of Christian Monarchy: Scandinavia, Central Europe and Rus, c.900–1200*. Cambridge: Cambridge University Press.

Beresford, Maurice W., 1967. *New Towns of the Middle Ages*. London: Lutterworth Press.

Beresford, Maurice W. and John Hurst, 1991. *Wharram Percy: Deserted Medieval Village*. New Haven: Yale University Press.

Bernhardt, John W., 1993. *Itinerant Kingship and Royal Monasteries in Early Medieval Germany c.936–1075*. Cambridge: Cambridge University Press.

Bhreathnach, Edel, ed., 2005. *The Kingship and Landscape of Tara*. Dublin: Four Courts.

Biddle, Martin, 1973a. 'The Development of the Anglo-Saxon Town', in *Settimane di Studio sull'Alto Medioevo*, edited by Anon. 2 vols. Spoleto: Centro Italiano sull'Alto Medioevo, 21, I, 203–30, II, 99–312.

——, 1973b. 'Winchester: The Development of an Early Medieval Capital', in *Vor- und Frühformen der Europäischen Stadt im Mittelalter: Bericht über ein Symposium in Reinhausen bei Göttingen in der Zeit vom 18.–24. April 1972*, edited by H. Jankuhn, W. Schlesinger, and H. Steuer. 2 vols. Göttingen: Vandenhoeck and Ruprecht, 229–61.

——, 1975. 'Felix Urbs Wintonia: Winchester in the Age of Monastic Reform', in *Tenth-Century Studies: Essays in Commemoration of the Millennium of the Council of Winchester and Regularis Concordia*, edited by David Parsons. London and Chichester: Phillimore, pp. 123–40.

——, 1976a. 'The Evolution of Towns: Planned Towns before 1066', in *The Plans and Topography of Medieval Towns in England and Wales*, edited by Maurice W. Barley. CBA Research Report, 14. London: Council for British Archaeology.

——, 1976b. 'Towns', in *The Archaeology of Anglo-Saxon England*, edited by David M. Wilson. Cambridge: Cambridge University Press, pp. 99–150.

Biddle, Martin and David Hill, 1971. 'Late Saxon Planned Towns', *Antiquaries Journal* 51, 70–85.

Binchy, D. A., 1970. *Celtic and Anglo-Saxon Kingship*. Oxford: Clarendon Press.

Bischoff, Bernhard, 1990. *Latin Palaeography: Antiquity and the Middle Ages*. Cambridge: Cambridge University Press.

Bitel, Lisa M, 2002. *Women in Early Medieval Europe, 400–1100*. Cambridge Medieval Textbooks. Cambridge: Cambridge University Press.

Blackburn, Mark, 1995. 'Money and Coinage', in *The New Cambridge Medieval History. Vol. 2: c.700–c.900*, edited by Rosamond McKitterick. Cambridge: Cambridge University Press, pp. 538–59.

Blackmore, Lyn, 2002. 'The Origins and Growth of *Lundenwic*, a Mart of Many Nations', in *Central Places in the Migration and Merovingian Periods: Papers from the 52nd Sachsensymposium, Lund, August 2002*, edited by Brigitte Hårdt and Lars Larsson. Acta Archaeologica Lundensia 8/39. Stockholm: Almqvist and Wiksell International, pp. 273–301.

Blair, John, 1988. *Minsters and Parish Churches: The Local Church in Transition 950–1200*. Oxford: Oxford University Committee for Archaeology.

——, 1995. 'Ecclesiastical Organization and Pastoral Care in Anglo-Saxon England', *Early Medieval Europe* 4, 193–212.

——, 2005. *The Church in Anglo-Saxon Society*. Oxford: Oxford University Press.

Blair, John and Richard Sharpe, ed., 1992. *Pastoral Care before the Parish*. Leicester: Leicester University Press.

Blair, Peter Hunter, 1976. *Northumbria in the Days of Bede*. London: Book Club Associates.

Bloch, Marc, 1961. *Feudal Society*. Translated by L. A. Manyon. 2 vols. London: Routledge and Kegan Paul. Originally published as *La Société féodale*. Paris: Michel. 1939–40.

Boardman, Steve, John Reuben Davies, and Eila Williamson, ed., 2009. *Saints' Cults in the Celtic World*. Woodbridge: Boydell and Brewer.

Bolin, Sture, 1953. 'Mohammed, Charlemagne and Ruric', *Scandinavian Economic History Review* 1, 5–39.

Bonnassie, Pierre, 1991. *From Slavery to Feudalism in South-Western Europe*. Translated by Jean Birrell. Cambridge: Cambridge University Press.

Bonner, Gerald, 1963. *St Augustine of Hippo: Life and Controversies*. London: SCM Press.

Borst, Arno, 1993. *The Ordering of Time: From the Ancient Computus to the Modern Computer*. Chicago: University of Chicago Press.

Bowman, Alan K., Averil Cameron, and Peter Garnsey, ed., 2005. *The Cambridge Ancient History. Vol. 12: The Crisis of Empire, A.D. 193–337*. Cambridge: Cambridge University Press.

Brandenburg, Hugo, 2004. *Ancient Churches of Rome from the Fourth to the Seventh Centuries: The Dawn of Christian Architecture in the West*. Turnhout: Brepols.

Breuilly, John, 2005. 'Changes in the Political Uses of the Nation: Continuity or Discontinuity?', in *Power and the Nation in European History*, edited by Len Scales and Oliver Zimmer. Cambridge: Cambridge University Press, pp. 67–101.

Brooke, Christopher, 1969. *The Twelfth Century Renaissance*. London: Thames and Hudson.

Brooks, Nicholas, 1984. *The Early History of the Church of Canterbury: Christ Church from 597 to 1066*. Studies in the Early History of Britain. Leicester: Leicester University Press.

——, 2000. *Bede and the English*. Jarrow Lecture. Jarrow: St Paul's Jarrow.

Brown, George Hardin, 1987. *Bede the Venerable*. Twayne's English Authors Series. Boston: Twayne.

——, 2009. *A Companion to Bede*. Woodbridge: Boydell and Brewer.

Brown, Michelle P., 1990. *A Guide to Western Historical Scripts: From Antiquity to 1600*. London: British Library Publications.

——, 2003. *The Lindisfarne Gospels: Society, Spirituality and the Scribe*. British Library Studies in Medieval Culture. London: British Library Publications.

Brown, Peter, 1967. *Augustine of Hippo: A Biography*. London: Faber.

——, 1971. *The World of Late Antiquity*. London: Thames and Hudson.

——, 1978. *The Making of Late Antiquity*. Cambridge, Mass.: Harvard University Press.

——, 1981. *The Cult of Saints: Its Rise and Function in Latin Christianity*. Haskell Lectures on History of Religions, New Series, 2. London: SCM Press.

——, 1989. *The Body and Society: Men, Women and Sexual Renunciation in Early Christianity*. London: Faber.

——, 2002. *The Rise of Western Christendom: Triumph and Diversity, AD 200–1000*. 2nd edn. Oxford: Blackwell.

Browne, George Forrest, 1908. *Alcuin of York: Lectures Delivered in the Cathedral Church of Bristol in 1907 and 1908*. London: SPCK.

Bruce, J. Collingwood and David J. Breeze, 2006. *Handbook to the Roman Wall*. 14th edn. Newcastle-upon-Tyne: Society of Antiquaries of Newcastle-upon-Tyne.

Bruce-Mitford, Rupert L. S., 1967. *The Art of the Codex Amiatinus*. Jarrow Lecture. Jarrow: St Paul's Jarrow. Reprinted in Michael Lapidge, ed., *Bede and his World. Vol. I: The Jarrow Lectures 1958–78*. Variorum: Aldershot, 1994, pp. 185–234.

——, 1975–83. *The Sutton Hoo Ship-Burial*. 3 vols. London: British Museum Publications.

Brühl, Carl-Richard, 1988. 'Problems of the Continuity of Roman *Civitates* in Gaul, as Illustrated by the Interrelation of Cathedral and *Palatium*', in *The Rebirth of Towns in the West*, edited by Richard Hodges and Brian Hobley. CBA Research Report. London: Council for British Archaeology, pp. 43–6.

Brunner, Karl, 1995. 'Continuity and Discontinuity of Roman Agricultural Knowledge in the Early Middle Ages', in *Agriculture in the Middle Ages: Technology, Practice and Representation*, edited by Del Sweeney. Philadelphia: University of Pennsylvania Press, pp. 21–40.

Buc, Philippe, 2000. 'Ritual and Interpretation: The Early Medieval Case', *Early Medieval Europe* 9: 2, 1–28.

——, 2001. *The Dangers of Ritual: Between Early Medieval Texts and Social Scientific Theory*. Princeton: Princeton University Press.

Bullough, Donald A., 1973. *The Age of Charlemagne*. London: Ferndale.

——, 1975. '*Imagines Regum* and their Significance in the Early Medieval West', in *Studies in Memory of David Talbot Rice*, edited by George D. S. Henderson and Giles H. Robertson. Edinburgh: Edinburgh University Press, pp. 223–76.

——, 1991a. *Carolingian Renewal: Sources and Heritage*. Manchester: Manchester University Press.

——, 1991b. *Friends, Neighbours and Fellow-Drinkers: Aspects of Community and Conflict in the Early Medieval West*. H. M. Chadwick Memorial Lectures, 1. Cambridge: Department of Anglo-Saxon, Norse and Celtic, University of Cambridge.

——, 1993. 'What has Ingeld to do with Lindisfarne?', *Anglo-Saxon England* 22, 93–125.

——, 2002. *Alcuin: Achievement and Reputation, being Part of the Ford Lectures Delivered in Oxford in Hilary Term 1980*. Education and Society in the Middle Ages and Renaissance. Leiden: Brill.

Burns, T. S., 1984. *A History of the Ostrogoths*. Bloomington, Ind.: Indiana University Press.

Cameron, Averil, 1993. *The Later Roman Empire, AD 284–430*. London: Fontana.

Cameron, Averil and P. Garnsey, ed., 1998. *The Cambridge Ancient History. Vol. 13: The Late Empire, A.D. 337–425*. Cambridge: Cambridge University Press.

Cameron, Averil, Bryan Ward-Perkins, and Michael Whitby, ed., 2000. *The Cambridge Ancient History. Vol. 14: Late Antiquity: Empire and Successors, A.D. 425–600*. Cambridge: Cambridge University Press.

Campbell, James, 1973. 'Observations on the Conversion of England', *Ampleforth Journal* 78, 12–26. Reprinted in James Campbell, *Essays in Anglo-Saxon History*. London and Ronceverte: Hambledon, 1986, pp. 49–68.

——, 1975. 'Observations on English Government from the Tenth to the Twelfth Century', *Transactions of the Royal Historical Society* 25, 39–54. Reprinted in James Campbell, *Essays in Anglo-Saxon History*. London and Ronceverte: Hambledon, 1986, pp. 155–70.

——, 1987. 'Some Agents and Agencies of the Late Anglo-Saxon State', in *Domesday Studies: Papers Read at the Novocentenary Conference of the Royal Historical Society and the Institute of*

British Geographers Winchester, 1986, edited by J. C. Holt. Woodbridge: Boydell Press, pp. 201–18. Reprinted in James Campbell, *The Anglo-Saxon State*. London: Hambledon, 2000, pp. 201–26.

Carver, Martin O. H., ed., 1992. *The Age of Sutton Hoo: The Seventh Century in North-Western Europe*. Woodbridge: Boydell Press.

——, 1995. 'Roman to Norman at York Minster', in *Excavations at York Minster. Vol. I: From Roman Fortress to Norman Cathedral*, edited by Derek Phillips, Brenda Heywood, and Martin O. H. Carver. London: HMSO, 1, pp. 177–221.

——, 1998. *Sutton Hoo: Burial Ground of Kings?* London: British Museum Publications.

Carver, Martin O. H. and Angela Care Evans, 2005. *Sutton Hoo: A Seventh-Century Princely Burial Ground and its Context*. London: British Museum Publications.

Chadwick, Owen, 1968. *John Cassian*. 2nd edn. Cambridge: Cambridge University Press.

Chaney, William A., 1970. *The Cult of Kingship in Anglo-Saxon England*. Manchester: Manchester University Press.

Charles-Edwards, Thomas M., 2000. *Early Christian Ireland*. Cambridge: Cambridge University Press.

Chitty, Derwas J., 1966. *The Desert a City: An Introduction to the Study of Egyptian and Palestinian Monasticism under the Christian Empire*. Oxford: Blackwell.

Christie, Neil, 1995. *The Lombards: The Ancient Longobards*. Oxford: Blackwell.

——, ed., 2004. *Landscapes of Change: Rural Evolutions in Late Antiquity and the Early Middle Ages*. Aldershot: Ashgate.

Clanchy, Michael, 1993. *From Memory to Written Record: England 1066–1307*. 2nd edn. Oxford: Blackwell.

Clapham, A. W., 1930. *English Romanesque Architecture. 1: Before the Conquest*. Oxford: Oxford University Press.

Clark, Gillian, 2004. *Christianity and Roman Society*. Cambridge: Cambridge University Press.

Clarke, Helen and Björn Ambrosiani, 1991. *Towns in the Viking Age*. Leicester: Leicester University Press.

Clarke, Howard Brian and Mary Brennan, ed., 1981. *Columbanus and Merovingian Monasticism*. British Archaeological Reports, International Series, 113. Oxford: British Archaeological Reports.

Coates, Simon J., 1996a. 'The Bishop as Benefactor and Civic Patron: Alcuin, York, and Episcopal Authority in Anglo-Saxon England', *Speculum* 71, 529–58.

——, 1996b. 'The Bishop as Pastor and Solitary: Bede and the Spiritual Authority of the Monk-Bishop', *Journal of Ecclesiastical History* 47, 601–19.

Coldstream, Nicola, 2002. *Medieval Architecture*. Oxford History of Art. Oxford: Oxford University Press.

Colgrave, Bertram, ed., 1940. *Two Lives of St Cuthbert: A Life by an Anonymous Monk of Lindisfarne and Bede's Prose Life*. Cambridge: Cambridge University Press.

Collins, Roger, 1983. *Early Medieval Spain: Unity in Diversity 400–1000*. London: Methuen.

——, 1999. *Early Medieval Europe 300–1000*. 2nd edn. London: Macmillan.

Conant, Kenneth John, 1959. *Carolingian and Romanesque Architecture*. Harmondsworth: Penguin.

Coupland, Simon, 2003. 'Trading Places: Quentovic and Dorestad Reassessed', *Early Medieval Europe* 11: 3, 210–32.

Cramp, Rosemary J., 1976. 'Monastic Sites', in *The Archaeology of Anglo-Saxon England*, edited by David M. Wilson. Cambridge: Cambridge University Press, pp. 201–52, 453–62.

——, 1994. 'Monkwearmouth and Jarrow in their European Context', in *Churches Built in Ancient Times: Recent Studies in Early Christian Architecture*, edited by E. Painter. London: Society of Antiquaries, pp. 279–94.

Cramp, Rosemary J., G. Bettess, F. Bettess, et al., 2005–6. *Wearmouth and Jarrow Monastic Sites*. 2 vols. Swindon: English Heritage.

Crumlin-Pedersen, Ole, 1990. 'The Boats and Ships of the Angles and Jutes', in *Maritime Celts, Frisians and Saxons*, edited by Seán McGrail. CBA Research Report, 71. London: Council for British Archaeology, pp. 98–116.

Cusack, Carole M., 1998. *Conversion among the Germanic Peoples*. Leicester: Leicester University Press.

——, 1999. *The Rise of Christianity in Northern Europe, 300–1000*. London: Cassell.

Daniels, Charles, 1962. *Mithras and his Temples on the Wall*. Durham: University of Durham Museum of Antiquities.

Dark, Kenneth R., ed., 1996. *External Contacts and the Economy of Late-Roman and Post-Roman Britain*. Woodbridge: Boydell Press.

Davidson, Hilda Roderick Ellis, 1964. *Gods and Myths of Northern Europe*. London: Penguin.

——, 1976. *The Viking Road to Byzantium*. London: G. Allen and Unwin.

——, 1993. *The Lost Beliefs of Northern Europe*. London and New York: Routledge.

Davies, Rees, June 2003. 'The Medieval State: The Tyranny of a Concept?', *Journal of Historical Sociology* 16: 2, 280–300.

Davies, Wendy, 1988. *Small Worlds: The Village Community in Early Medieval Brittany*. London: Duckworth.

——, 2011. 'Where are the Parishes? Where are the Minsters? The Organization of the Spanish Church in the Tenth Century', in *England and the Continent in the Tenth Century: Studies in Memory of Wilhelm Levison*, edited by David Rollason, Conrad Leyser, and Hannah Williams. Turnhout: Brepols, pp. 379–98.

Davis, R. H. C. and Robert I. Moore, 2006. *A History of Medieval Europe from Constantine to St Louis*. 3rd edn. London: Longman.

De Gregorio, Scott, ed., 2010. *The Cambridge Companion to Bede*. Cambridge: Cambridge University Press.

De Jong, Mayke, 1995. 'Carolingian Monasticism: The Power of Prayer', in *The New Cambridge Medieval History. Vol. 2: c.700–c.900*, edited by Rosamond McKitterick. Cambridge: Cambridge University Press, pp. 622–53.

Deliyannis, Deborah Mauskopf, 2009. *Ravenna in Late Antiquity*. Cambridge: Cambridge University Press.

Dill, Samuel, 1926. *Roman Society in Gaul in the Merovingian Age*. London: Macmillan.

——, 1933. *Roman Society in the Last Century of the Western Empire*. London: Macmillan.

Dobat, Andres Siegfried, 2006. 'The King and his Cult: The Axe-Hammer from Sutton Hoo and its Implications for the Concept of Sacral Leadership in Early Medieval Europe', *Antiquity: A Quarterly Review of Archaeology* 80, 880–93.

Dodwell, C. R., 1982. *Anglo-Saxon Art: A New Perspective*. Manchester: Manchester University Press.

——, 1993. *The Pictorial Arts of the West 800–1200*. Pelican History of Art. New Haven and London: Yale University Press.

Doherty, Charles, 1985. 'The Monastic Town in Early Medieval Ireland', in *The Comparative History of Urban Origins in Non-Roman Europe*, edited by Howard Brian Clarke and Angret Simms. 2 vols. British Archaeological Reports, International Series, 255. Oxford: BAR, 1, pp. 45–76.

Dolley, Reginald Hugh Michael and D. Michael Metcalf, 1961. 'The Reform of the English Coinage under Eadgar', in *Anglo-Saxon Coins: Studies Presented to F. M. Stenton on the Occasion of his 80th Birthday, 17 May 1960*, edited by R. H. M. Dolley. London: Methuen, pp. 136–68.

Dopsch, Alfons, 1937. *The Economic and Social Foundations of European Civilization*. Translated by M. G. Beard and Nadine Marshall. London: Kegan Paul, Trench, Trubner and Co.

Dowden, Ken, 2000. *European Paganism: The Realities of Cult from Antiquity to the Middle Ages*. London: Routledge.

Drinkwater, J. F. and Hugh Elton, 1992. *Fifth-Century Gaul: A Crisis of Identity?* Cambridge: Cambridge University Press.

Driscoll, S. T., 2004. 'The Archaeological Context of Assembly in Early Medieval Scotland – Scone and its Comparanda', in *Assembly Places and Practices in Medieval Europe*, edited by Aliki Pantos and Sarah Semple. Dublin: Four Courts, pp. 73–94.

Duby, Georges, 1968. *Rural Economy and Country Life in the Medieval West*. London: Arnold.

——, 1974. *The Early Growth of the European Economy: Warriors and Peasants from the Seventh to the Twelfth Century*. Translated by Howard B. Clarke. London: Weidenfeld and Nicolson.

Duckett, Eleanor S., 1951. *Alcuin, Friend of Charlemagne: His World and his Work*. New York: MacMillan.

Dunn, Marilyn J., 2000. *The Emergence of Monasticism: From the Desert Fathers to the Early Middle Ages*. Oxford: Blackwell.

——, 2008. *The Christianization of the Anglo-Saxons c.597–c.700: Discourses of Life, Death and Afterlife*. London: Continuum.

Dutton, Paul E., ed., 2004. *Carolingian Civilisation: A Reader*. 2nd edn. Peterborough, Ont.: Broadview.

Edwards, Nancy, 1990. *The Archaeology of Early Medieval Ireland*. London: Batsford.

Edwards, P., 1980. 'Art and Alcoholism in Beowulf', *Durham University Journal* 72, 127–31.

Ellmers, Detlev, 1990. 'The Frisian Monopoly of Coastal Transport in the Sixth–Eighth Centuries AD', in *Maritime Celts, Frisians and Saxons*, edited by Seán McGrail. CBA Research Report, 71. London: Council for British Archaeology, pp. 91–2.

Elsner, Jaś, 1998. *Imperial Rome and Christian Triumph: The Art of the Roman Empire, AD 100–450*. Oxford: Oxford University Press.

Elton, Hugh, 1996. *Frontiers of the Roman Empire*. London: Batsford.

Enright, Michael J., 1985. *Iona, Tara and Soissons: The Origin of the Royal Anointing Ritual*. Berlin: Walter de Gruyter.

——, 1996. *Lady with a Mead Cup: Ritual, Prophecy and Lordship in the European Warband from La Tène to the Viking Age*. Dublin: Four Courts Press.

——, 2006. *The Sutton Hoo Sceptre and the Roots of Celtic Kingship Theory*. Dublin: Four Courts Press.

Evans, Angela Care, 1986. *The Sutton Hoo Ship Burial*. London: British Museum Publications.

Evans, Joan, 1931. *Monastic Life at Cluny, 910–1157*. London: Oxford University Press.

Everett, Nicholas, 2003. *Literacy in Lombard Italy, c.568–774*. Cambridge Studies in Medieval Life and Thought. Cambridge: Cambridge University Press.

Faith, Rosamond, 1997. *The English Peasantry and the Growth of Lordship*. London: Leicester University Press.

——, 1999. 'Estate Management', 'Manors and Manorial Lordship', 'Peasants', in *The Blackwell Encyclopedia of Anglo-Saxon England*, edited by Michael Lapidge, John Blair, Simon Keynes, and Donald Scragg. Oxford: Blackwell, pp. 175–6, 300–1, 359–61.

Fell, Christine, 1984. *Women in Anglo-Saxon England*. London: British Museum Publications.

Fernie, Eric, 1983. *The Architecture of the Anglo-Saxons*. London: Batsford.

Ferrill, Arther, 1986. *The Fall of the Roman Empire: The Military Explanation*. London: Thames and Hudson.

Fichtenau, Heinrich, 1991. *Living in the Tenth Century: Mentalities and Social Orders.* Translated by Patrick J. Geary. Chicago: Chicago University Press.

Finley, Moses I., 1992. *The Ancient Economy.* London: Penguin.

Fletcher, Richard, 1997. *The Conversion of Europe: From Paganism to Christianity 371–1386 AD.* London: Harper Collins.

Folz, Robert, 1964. *The Coronation of Charlemagne.* London: Routledge and Kegan Paul.

Foot, Sarah, 1996. 'The Making of Angelcynn: English Identity before the Norman Conquest', *Transactions of the Royal Historical Society*, 6th series, 6, 25–49.

——, 2006. *Monastic Life in Anglo-Saxon England, c.600–900.* Cambridge: Cambridge University Press.

Fouracre, Paul, ed., 2005. *The New Cambridge Medieval History. Vol. 1: c.500–c.700.* Cambridge: Cambridge University Press.

Fox, Cyril Fred, 1955. *Offa's Dyke: A Field Survey of the Western Frontier-Works of Mercia in the Seventh and Eighth Centuries A.D.* London: Oxford University Press.

France, John and Kelly DeVries, ed., 2008. *Warfare in the Dark Ages.* Aldershot: Ashgate.

Francovich, Riccardo and Richard Hodges, 2003. *Villa to Village: The Transformation of the Roman Countryside in Italy, c.400–1000.* London: Duckworth.

Franklin, Simon and Jonathan Shepard, 1996. *The Emergence of Rus 750–1200.* Harlow: Longman.

Frodsham, Paul and Colm O'Brien, ed., 2005. *Yeavering: People, Power and Place.* Stroud: Tempus.

Ganshof, François-Louis, 1968. *Frankish Institutions under Charlemagne.* Translated by Bryce Lyon and Mary Lyon. Providence, Rhode Island: Brown University Press.

——, 1971a. *The Carolingians and the Frankish Monarchy.* Translated by Janet Sondheimer. London: Longman.

——, 1971b. 'The Use of the Written Word in Charlemagne's Administration', in *The Carolingians and the Frankish Monarchy.* Translated by Janet Sondheimer. London: Longman, pp. 125–42.

Garipzanov, Ildar H., 2008. *The Symbolic Language of Authority in the Carolingian World (c.751–877).* Leiden: Brill.

Garipzanov, Ildar H., Patrick J. Geary, and Przemysław Urbańcyk, ed., 2008. *Franks, Northmen, and Slavs: Identities and State Formation in Early Medieval Europe.* Cursor Mundi 5. Los Angeles: UCLA Center for Medieval and Renaissance Studies.

Gaskoin, C. J. B., 1904. *Alcuin, his Life and Work.* London: C. J. Clay and Sons.

Gautier, Alban and Stéphane Lebecq, 2011. 'Routeways between England and the Continent in the Tenth Century', in *England and the Continent in the Tenth Century: Studies in Memory of Wilhelm Levison*, edited by David Rollason, Conrad Leyser, and Hannah Williams. Turnhout: Brepols.

Geary, Patrick J., 2002. *The Myth of Nations: The Medieval Origins of Europe*. Princeton and Oxford: Princeton University Press.

Gellner, Ernst, 1983. *Nations and Nationalism*. Oxford: Basil Blackwell.

Gerrard, Christopher, Mick Aston, Andrew Reynolds, et al., 2007. *The Shapwick Project, Somerset: A Rural Landscape Explored*. London: Society for Medieval Archaeology.

Gibson, Margaret, ed., 1981. *Boethius: His Life, Thought, and Influence*. Oxford: Oxford University Press.

Gillett, Andrew, ed., 2002. *On Barbarian Identity: Critical Approaches to Ethnicity in the Early Medieval Ages*. Studies in the Early Middle Ages, 4. Turnhout: Brepols.

Gillingham, John, 1989. 'The Most Precious Jewel in the English Crown: Levels of Danegeld and Heregeld in the Early Eleventh Century', *English Historical Review* 104, 373–84.

Goetz, Hans-Werner, Jörg Jarnut, Walter Pohl, et al., ed., 2003. *Regna and Gentes: The Relationship between Late Antique and Early Medieval Peoples and Kingdoms in the Transformation of the Roman World*. The Transformation of the Roman World, 13. Leiden: Brill.

Goffart, Walter, 1980. *Barbarians and Romans AD 418–584: The Techniques of Accommodation*. Princeton: Princeton University Press.

——, 1981. 'Rome, Constantinople and the Barbarians', *American Historical Review* 86, 275–306. Reprinted in Walter Goffart, *Rome's Fall and After*. London and Ronceverte: Hambledon Press, 1989, pp. 1–32; and in *Warfare in the Dark Ages*, edited by John France and Kelly DeVries. Aldershot: Ashgate, 2008, pp. 1–32.

——, 1988. *The Narrators of Barbarian History (A.D. 550–800)*. Princeton: Princeton University Press.

——, 2006. *Barbarian Tides: The Migration Age and the Later Roman Empire*. Philadelphia: University of Pennsylvania Press.

Goldsworthy, Adrian Keith, 1999. *Roman Warfare*. Smithsonian History of Warfare. London: Cassell.

Goodson, Caroline J., 2010. *The Rome of Pope Paschal I: Papal Power, Urban Renovation, Church Rebuilding, and Relic Translation, 817–824*. Cambridge: Cambridge University Press.

Grabar, André, Stuart Gilbert, and James Emmons, 1967. *The Beginnings of Christian Art, 200–395*. The Arts of Mankind. London: Thames and Hudson.

Granger-Taylor, Hero, 1989. 'The Inscription on the Nature Goddess Silk', in *St Cuthbert, his Cult and his Community to AD 1200*, edited by Gerald Bonner, David Rollason, and Clare Stancliffe. Woodbridge: Boydell Press, pp. 339–41.

Grant, Michael, 1998. *The Emperor Constantine*. London: Phoenix Giant.

Green, Dennis H. and Frank Siegmund, ed., 2003. *The Continental Saxons from the Migration Period to the Eighth Century: An Ethnographic Perspective*. Woodbridge: Boydell Press.

Grierson, Philip, 1959. 'Commerce in the Dark Ages', *Transactions of the Royal Historical Society*, 5th series, 9, 123–40. Reprinted in Philip Grierson, *Dark Age Numismatics: Selected Studies*. Collected Studies, 96. London: Variorum, 1979, no. II.

——, 1965. 'Money and Coinage under Charlemagne', in *Karl der Grosse: Werk und Wirkung*, edited by Wolfgang Braunfels. Düsseldorf: Schwann, pp. 501–36. Reprinted in Philip Grierson, *Dark Age Numismatics: Selected Studies*. Collected Studies, 96. London: Variorum, 1979, no. XVIII.

——, 1967. 'The Volume of the Anglo-Saxon Coinage', *Economic History Review*, 2nd series, 20, 153–60. Reprinted in Philip Grierson, *Dark Age Numismatics: Selected Studies*. Collected Studies, 96. London: Variorum, 1979, no. XXVII.

——, 1979. *Dark Age Numismatics: Selected Studies*. Collected Studies, 96. London: Variorum.

Grierson, Philip, 1990. 'The *Gratia Dei rex* Coinage of Charles the Bald', in *Charles the Bald: Court and Kingdom*, edited by Margaret T. Gibson and Janet L. Nelson. Revised edn. Aldershot Variorum, pp. 52–64.

——, 1991. *The Coins of Medieval Europe*. London: Seaby.

Grierson, Philip and Mark Blackburn, 1986. *Medieval European Coinage with a Catalogue of the Coins in the Fitzwilliam Museum, Cambridge. I: The Early Middle Ages (5th–10th Centuries)*. Cambridge: Cambridge University Press.

Hall, John A. and Ralph Schroeder, ed., 2006. *An Anatomy of Power: The Social Theory of Michael Mann*. Cambridge: Cambridge University Press.

Hall, Richard A., 1996. *English Heritage Book of York*. London: Batsford.

Halphen, Louis, 1977. *Charlemagne and the Carolingian Empire*. Translated by Giselle de Nie. Amsterdam: North-Holland Publishing Company. Originally published as *Charlemagne et l'empire Carolingien*. Paris: Albin Michel. 1947.

Halsall, Guy, 1992. 'The Origins of the *Reihengräberzivilisation*: Forty Years On', in *Fifth-Century Gaul: A Crisis of Identity?*, edited by J. F. Drinkwater and Hugh Elton. Cambridge: Cambridge University Press, pp. 196–207.

——, 1995. *Early Medieval Cemeteries: An Introduction to Burial Archaeology in the Post-Roman West*. Skelmorlie: Cruithne Press.

——, 1998. *Violence and Society in the Early Medieval West*. Woodbridge: Boydell Press.

——, 2005. *Barbarian Migrations and the Roman West, 376–568*. Cambridge Medieval Textbooks. Cambridge: Cambridge University Press.

Hamer, Richard, ed., 2006. *A Choice of Anglo-Saxon Verse*. London: Faber.

Hamerow, Helena, 1994a. 'Migration Theory and the Migration Period', in *Building on the Past*, edited by Blaise Vyner. London: Royal Archaeological Institute, pp. 164–77.

——, 1994b. 'Review Article: The Archaeology of Rural Settlement in Early Medieval Europe', *Early Medieval Europe* 3, 167–79.

——, 2002. *Early Medieval Settlements: The Archaeology of Rural Communities in North-West Europe 400–900*. Oxford: Oxford University Press.

Hannestad, Niels, 1988. *Roman Art and Imperial Policy*. Aarhus: Aarhus University Press.

Harbison, Peter, 1992. *The High Crosses of Ireland: An Iconographical and Photographic Survey*. Bonn: Habelt.

Hårdt, Brigitte and Lars Larsson, ed., 2002. *Central Places in the Migration and Merovingian Periods: Papers from the 52nd Sachsensymposium, Lund, August 2002*. Acta Archaeologica Lundensia 8/39. Stockholm: Almqvist and Wiksell International.

Haslam, Jeremy, ed., 1984. *Anglo-Saxon Towns of Southern England*. Chichester: Phillimore.

——, 1985. *Early Medieval Towns in Britain c.700 to 1140*. Princes Risborough: Shire Publications.

Havighurst, Alfred F., 1969. *The Pirenne Thesis: Analysis, Criticism and Revision*. Boston, Mass.: Heath.

Haycock, Marged, 1999. *'Where Cider Ends, There Ale Begins to Reign': Drink in Medieval Welsh Poetry*. H. M. Chadwick Memorial Lectures, 10. Cambridge: Department of Anglo-Saxon, Norse and Celtic.

Heather, Peter J., 1996. *The Goths*. Oxford: Blackwell.

——, 2006. *The Fall of the Roman Empire: A New History of Rome and the Barbarians*. Oxford: Oxford University Press.

——, 2008. 'Ethnicity, Group Identity, and Social Status in the Migration Period', in *Franks, Northmen, and Slavs: Identities and State Formation in Early Medieval Europe*, edited by Ildar H. Garipzanov, Patrick J. Geary, and Przemysław Urbańcyk. Cursor Mundi 5. Los Angeles: UCLA Center for Medieval and Renaissance Studies.

——, 2009. *Empires and Barbarians: Migration, Development and the Birth of Europe*. London: Macmillan.

Heather, Peter J. and John Matthews, ed., 1991. *The Goths in the Fourth Century*. Liverpool: Liverpool University Press.

Hedeager, Lotte, 1992. *Iron-Age Societies: From Tribe to State in Northern Europe, 500 BC to AD 700*. Translated by John Hines. Oxford: Blackwell.

——, 2001. 'Asgard Reconstructed? Gudme – A "Central Place" in the North', in *Topographies of Power in the Early Middle Ages*, edited by Mayke De Jong, Franz Theuws, and Carine Van Rhijn. Transformation of the Roman World, 6. Leiden: Brill, pp. 467–507.

Hedstrom, Darlene L. Brooks, 2006. 'Redrawing a Portrait of Medieval Monasticism', in *Medieval Monks and their World: Ideas and Realities: Studies in Honor of Richard E. Sullivan*, edited by David Blanks, Michael Frassetto, and Amy Livingstone. Brill's Series in Church History, 25. Leiden: Brill, pp. 11–34.

Henderson, George, 1972. *Early Medieval*. Harmondsworth: Penguin.

——, 1987. *From Durrow to Kells: The Insular Gospel-Books 650–800*. London: Thames and Hudson.

Henderson, George and Isobel Henderson, 2004. *The Art of the Picts: Sculpture and Metalwork in Early Medieval Scotland.* London: Thames and Hudson.

Hendy, Michael F., 1988. 'From Public to Private: The Western Barbarian Coinages as Mirror of the Disintegration of Late Roman State Structures', *Viator* 19, 29–78.

Henning, Joachim, 2007. 'Early European Towns: The Development of the Economy in the Frankish Realm between Dynamism and Deceleration AD 500–1100', in *Post-Roman Towns, Trade and Settlement in Europe and Byzantium. Vol. 1: The Heirs of the Roman West*, edited by Joachim Henning. Millennium Studies in the Culture and History of the First Millennium CE. Berlin and New York: Walter de Gruyter, pp. 3–40.

Herity, Michael, 1989. 'Early Irish Hermitages in the Light of the Lives of Cuthbert', in *St Cuthbert, his Cult and his Community to AD 1200*, edited by Gerald Bonner, David Rollason, and Clare Stancliffe. Woodbridge: Boydell Press, pp. 45–63.

——, 1995. *Studies in the Layout, Buildings and Art in Stone of Early Irish Monasteries.* London: Pindar.

Herlihy, David, ed., 1970. *History of Feudalism.* London: MacMillan.

Higgins, Clare, 1989. 'Some New Thoughts on the Nature Goddess Silk', in *St Cuthbert, his Cult and his Community to AD 1200*, edited by Gerald Bonner, David Rollason, and Clare Stancliffe. Woodbridge: Boydell Press, pp. 329–37.

Hildebrandt, M. M., 1992. *The External School in Carolingian Society.* Leiden: Brill.

Hill, Boyd H., ed., 1972. *Medieval Monarchy in Action: The German Empire from Henry I to Henry IV.* London: George Allen and Unwin.

Hill, David, 1981. *An Atlas of Anglo-Saxon England.* Oxford: Blackwell.

Hill, David and Robert Cowie, ed., 2001. *Wics: The Early Mediaeval Trading Centres of Northern Europe.* Sheffield: Sheffield Academic Press.

Hill, David and Alex Rumble, ed., 1996. *The Defence of Wessex: The Burghal Hidage and Anglo-Saxon Fortifications.* Manchester: Manchester University Press.

Hill, David and Margaret Worthington, 2009. *Offa's Dyke: History and Guide.* 2nd edn. Stroud: Tempus.

Hines, John, ed., 1997. *The Anglo-Saxons from the Migration Period to the Eighth Century: An Ethnographic Perspective.* Woodbridge: Boydell Press.

Hodges, Richard, 1982. *Dark Age Economics.* London: Duckworth.

——, 1997. *Light in the Dark Ages: The Rise and Fall of San Vincenzo al Volturno.* London: Duckworth.

——, 2000. *Towns and Trade in the Age of Charlemagne.* Duckworth Debates in Archaeology. London: Duckworth.

——, 2004. 'The Cosmology of Early Medieval Emporia?', *Archaeological Dialogues* 10, 138–44.

Hodges, Richard and Catherine M. Coutts, ed., 1993–. *San Vincenzo al Volturno: The 1980–86 Excavations*. London: British School at Rome.

Hodges, Richard and Brian Hobley, ed., 1988. *The Rebirth of Towns in the West AD 700–1050*. London: Council for British Archaeology.

Hodges, Richard and John Mitchell, 1985. *San Vincenzo al Volturno: The Archaeology, Art, and Territory of an Early Medieval Monastery*. British Archaeological Reports (International Series), 252. Oxford: BAR.

Hodges, Richard and David Whitehouse, 1983. *Mohammed, Charlemagne and the Origins of Europe*. London: Duckworth.

Holloway, R. Ross, 2004. *Constantine and Rome*. New Haven: Yale University Press.

Hooper, Nicholas, 1989. 'The Anglo-Saxons at War', in *Weapons and Warfare in Anglo-Saxon England*, edited by Sonia Hawkes. Oxford University Committee for Archaeology Monograph, 21. Oxford: Oxbow, pp. 191–202.

Hope-Taylor, Brian, 1977. *Yeavering: An Anglo-British Centre of Early Northumbria*. London: HMSO.

Horden, Peregrine and Nicholas Purcell, 2000. *The Corrupting Sea: A Study of Mediterranean History*. Oxford: Blackwell.

Horn, Walter and E. Born, 1979. *The Plan of St Gall*. 3 vols. Berkeley: University of California Press.

Howard-Johnston, James and Paul A. Hayward, ed., 2000. *The Cult of Saints in Late Antiquity and the Middle Ages: Essays on the Contribution of Peter Brown*. Oxford: Oxford University Press.

Howe, Nicholas, 2001. *Migration and Mythmaking in Anglo-Saxon England*. Revised paperback edn. Notre Dame: University of Notre Dame Press.

Hubert, Jean, Jean Porcher, and W. F. Volbach, 1969. *Europe in the Dark Ages*. London: Thames and Hudson.

——, 1970. *Carolingian Art*. The Arts of Mankind. London: Thames and Hudson.

Hübinger, P. E., ed., 1968. *Bedeutung und Rolle des Islam beim Übergang vom Altertum zum Mittelalter*. Darmstadt: Wissenschaftliche Buchgesellschaft.

Hughes, Kathleen and Ann Hamlin, 1977. *The Modern Traveller to the Early Irish Church*. London: SPCK.

Innes, Matthew, 1998. 'Memory, Orality and Literacy in Early Medieval Society', *Past and Present* 158, 3–36.

——, 2000. *State and Society in the Early Middle Ages: The Middle Rhine Valley, 400–1000*. Cambridge: Cambridge University Press.

——, 2003. *An Introduction to Early Medieval Western Europe, 400–900*. London: Routledge.

Isbell, Harold, ed., 1971. *The Last Poets of Imperial Rome*. Harmondsworth: Penguin.

James, Edward, 1981. 'Archaeology and the Merovingian Monastery', in *Columbanus and Merovingian Monasticism*, edited by Howard Brian Clarke and Mary Brennan. British Archaeological Reports, International Series, 113. Oxford: BAR, pp. 33–55.

——, 1982. *The Origins of France: From Clovis to the Capetians, 500–1000*. London: Macmillan.

——, 1988. *The Franks*. Oxford: Blackwell.

——, 2009. *Europe's Barbarians, AD 200–600*. Harlow: Pearson Longman.

Jewell, Helen, 1996. *Women in Medieval England*. Manchester: Manchester University Press.

——, 2006. *Women in Dark Age and Early Medieval Europe c.500–1200*. European Culture and Society. Basingstoke: Palgrave Macmillan.

John, Eric, 1964. *Land Tenure in Early England: A Discussion of Some Problems*. Leicester: Leicester University Press.

——, 1966. 'English Feudalism and the Structure of Anglo-Saxon Society', in *Orbis Britanniae*, edited by Eric John. Leicester: Leicester University Press, pp. 128–53.

Johnson, Stephen, 1983. *Late Roman Fortifications*. London: Batsford.

——, 1989. *English Heritage Book of Hadrian's Wall*. London: B. T. Batsford Ltd./English Heritage.

Jolly, Karen Louise, 1996. *Popular Religion in Late Saxon England: Elf Charms in Context*. Chapel Hill: University of North Carolina Press.

Jones, A. H. M., 1962. *Constantine and the Conversion of Europe*. Harmondsworth: Penguin.

——, 1964. *The Later Roman Empire, 248–602: A Social, Economic and Administrative Survey*. 2 vols. Oxford: Blackwell.

——, 1966. *The Decline of the Ancient World*. London: Longman.

Joranson, Einar, 1923. *The Danegeld in France*. Augustana Library Publications, 10. Rock Island, Ill.: Augustana Book Concern.

Jørgensen, L., 2003. 'Manor and Market at Lake Tissø in the Sixth to the Eleventh Centuries: The Danish "Productive" Site', in *Markets in Early Medieval Europe: Trading and 'Productive' Sites, 650–850*, edited by Tim Pestell and Katharina Ulmschneider. Macclesfield: Windgather, pp. 175–207.

Kelly, Christopher, 2004. *Ruling the Later Roman Empire*. Cambridge, Mass.: Belknap Press of Harvard University Press.

Kelly, Susan E., 1992. 'Trading Privileges from Eighth-Century England', *Early Medieval Europe* 1: 1, 3–28.

Kent, John Philip Cozens, 1978. *Roman Coins*. London: Thames and Hudson.

Keynes, Simon and Michael Lapidge, ed., 1983. *Alfred the Great: Asser's 'Life of King Alfred' and Other Contemporary Sources*. Penguin Classics. Harmondsworth: Penguin.

Knowles, David, 1963. *The Monastic Order in England: A History of its Development from the Times of St Dunstan to the Fourth Lateran Council, 940–1216*. 2nd edn. Cambridge: Cambridge University Press.

Kowaleski, Maryanne, ed., 2006. *Medieval Towns: A Reader*. Peterborough, Ont.: Broadview Press.

Krautheimer, Richard, 1942. 'The Carolingian Revival of Early Christian Architecture', *Art Bulletin* 24, 1–38. Reprinted in Richard Krautheimer, *Studies in Early Christian, Medieval, and Renaissance Art* (New York, 1969), pp. 203–54 with 'Postscript', pp. 254–6, and in his *Ausgewählte Aufsätze zur Europäischen Kunstgeschichte* (Cologne, 1988), with 'Postscript', pp. 272–6.

——, 1980. *Rome: Profile of a City, 312–1303*. Princeton: Princeton University Press.

Laing, Lloyd R., 1969. 'Timber Halls in Dark Age Britain – Some Problems', *Transactions of the Dumfriesshire and Galloway Natural History and Antiquarian Society*, 3rd series, 46, 110–27.

Laiou, Angeliki E., 2008. 'The Early Medieval Economy: Data, Production, Exchange and Demand', in *The Long Morning of Medieval Europe: New Directions in Early Medieval Studies*, edited by Jennifer R. Davis and Michael McCormick. Farnham: Ashgate, pp. 99–104.

Laistner, Max Ludwig Wolfram, 1957. *Thought and Letters in Western Europe 500–900*. Revised edn. Ithaca, New York: Cornell University Press.

Lamb, Hubert Horace, 1966. *The Changing Climate: Selected Papers*. London: Methuen.

Lane Fox, Robin, 1988. *Pagans and Christians*. Harmondsworth: Penguin.

Lang, James T., 1988. *Anglo-Saxon Sculpture*. Aylesbury: Shire Publications.

Lapidge, Michael and Malcolm Godden, ed., 1991. *The Cambridge Companion to Old English Literature*. Cambridge: Cambridge University Press.

Lasko, Peter, 1994. *Ars Sacra: 800–1200*. 2nd edn. Pelican History of Art. New Haven: Yale University Press.

Latouche, Robert, 1967. *The Birth of the Western Economy: Economic Aspects of the Dark Ages*. 2nd edn. London: Methuen.

Lawrence, C. H., 2001. *Medieval Monasticism: Forms of Religious Life in Western Europe in the Middle Ages*. 3rd edn. London: Longman.

Lawson, M. K., 1984. 'The Collection of Danegeld and Heregeld in the Reigns of Ethelred II and Cnut', *English Historical Review* 99, 721–38.

Le Jan, Régine, 2000. 'Frankish Giving of Arms and Rituals of Power: Continuity and Change in the Carolingian Period', in *Rituals of Power: From Late Antiquity to the Early Middle Ages*, edited by Janet L. Nelson and Frans Theuws. The Transformation of the Roman World, 8. Leiden: Brill, pp. 281–309.

——, 2002. 'Personal Names and the Transformation of Kinship in Early Medieval Society (Sixth to Tenth Centuries)', in *Personal Names Studies of Medieval Europe: Social Identity and Familial Structures*, edited by George T. Beech, Monique Bourin, and Pascal Chareille.

Studies in Medieval Culture, 43. Kalamazoo: Medieval Institute Publications, pp. 31–50.

Leahy, Kevin, 2009. *The Staffordshire Hoard*. London: British Museum Press.

Lebecq, Stéphane, 1990. 'On the Use of the Word "Frisian" in the Sixth–Tenth Centuries Written Sources: Some Interpretations', in *Maritime Celts, Frisians and Saxons*, edited by Seán McGrail. CBA Research Report, 71. London: Council for British Archaeology, pp. 85–90.

——, 1997. 'Routes of Change: Production and Distribution in the West (5th–8th Century)', in *The Transformation of the Roman World AD 400–900*, edited by Leslie Webster and Michelle Brown. London: British Museum Press, pp. 67–78.

——, 2005. 'The Northern Seas (Fifth to Eighth Centuries)', in *The New Cambridge Medieval History. Vol. 1: c.500–c.700*, edited by Paul Fouracre. Cambridge: Cambridge University Press, pp. 639–59.

Lees, Clare A, Fred Orton, and Ian Wood, 2007. *Rethinking the Ruthwell and Bewcastle Monuments*. Manchester: Manchester University Press.

Levison, Wilhelm, 1946. *England and the Continent in the Eighth Century*. Oxford: Clarendon Press.

Levy, Kenneth, 1998. *Gregorian Chant and the Carolingians*. Princeton: Princeton University Press.

Leyser, Henrietta, 1996. *Medieval Women: A Social History of Women in England, 450–1500*. London: Weidenfeld and Nicolson.

Leyser, Karl J., 1979. *Rule and Conflict in an Early Medieval Society: Ottonian Saxony*. London: Edward Arnold.

——, 1981. 'Ottonian Government', *English Historical Review* 96, 721–53. Reprinted in Karl J. Leyser, *Medieval Germany and its Neighbours 900–1250*. London: Hambledon, 1982, pp. 69–102.

——, 1983. *Medieval Germany and its Neighbours 900–1250*. London: Hambledon.

——, 1993. 'Early Medieval Warfare', in *The Battle of Maldon*, edited by Janet Cooper. London: Hambledon Press.

Liebeschuetz, John Hugo Wolfgang Gideon, 1979. *Continuity and Change in Roman Religion*. Oxford: Clarendon Press.

Little, Lester K., ed., 2007. *Plague and the End of Antiquity: The Pandemic of 541–750*. Cambridge: Cambridge University Press.

Llewellyn, Peter, 1971. *Rome in the Dark Ages*. London: Faber and Faber.

Lobbedey, Uwe, 2002. 'Carolingian Royal Palaces: The State of Research from an Architectural Historian's Viewpoint', in *Court Culture in the Early Middle Ages: The Proceedings of the First York Alcuin Conference*, edited by Catherine Cubitt. Studies in the Early Middle Ages, 3. Turnhout: Brepols, pp. 129–53.

Lombard, Maurice, 1972. *Espaces et réseaux du haut moyen âge*. Paris: Mouton.

Loseby, Simon T., 1998. 'Gregory's Cities: Urban Functions in Sixth-Century Gaul', in *Franks and Alamanni in the Merovingian Period: An Ethnographic Perspective*, edited by Ian N. Wood. Woodbridge: Boydell Press, pp. 239–84.

——, 2005. 'The Mediterranean Economy', in *The New Cambridge Medieval History. Vol. 1: c.500–c.700*, edited by Paul Fouracre. Cambridge: Cambridge University Press, pp. 605–38.

Lynch, Joseph H., 1992. *The Medieval Church: A Brief History*. Harlow: Longman.

Lynn, Neil B., 1994. *Ambrose of Milan: Church and Court in a Christian Capital*. The Transformation of the Classical Heritage, 22. Berkeley: University of California Press.

Mackay, Angus and David Ditchburn, 1997. *Atlas of Medieval Europe*. London: Routledge.

MacLean, Simon, 2003. 'Queenship, Nunneries and Royal Widowhood in Carolingian Europe', *Past and Present* 178, 3–38.

Mann, Michael, 2003. *The Sources of Social Power. Vol. 1: A History of Power from the Beginning to A.D. 1760*. Cambridge: Cambridge University Press.

Markus, Robert Austin, 1990. *The End of Ancient Christianity*. Cambridge: Cambridge University Press.

——, 1997. *Gregory the Great and his World*. Cambridge: Cambridge University Press.

Matthews, John, 1990. *Western Aristocracies and the Imperial Court 364–425*. Revised edn. Oxford: Oxford University Press.

Mauss, Marcel, 2002. *The Gift: The Form and Reason for Exchange in Archaic Societies*. London: Routledge. Originally published as *Essai sur le don*. Paris: Presses Universitaires de France, in *Sociologie et Anthropologie*. 1950.

Mayr-Harting, Henry, 1991a. *The Coming of Christianity to Anglo-Saxon England*. 3rd edn. London: Batsford.

——, 1991b. *Ottonian Book Illumination: An Historical Study*. 2 vols. London: Harvey Miller.

——, 1992. 'The Church of Magdeburg: Its Trade and its Town in the Tenth and Early Eleventh Centuries', in *Church and City 1000–1500: Essays in Honour of Christopher Brooke*, edited by David Abulafia, M. J. Franklin, and M. Rubin. Cambridge: Cambridge University Press, pp. 129–50. Reprinted in Henry-Mayr Harting, *Religion and Society in the Medieval West, 600–1200: Selected Studies*. Collected Studies, 942. Aldershot: Variorum, 2010, no. IX.

McClure, Judith, 1983. 'Bede's Old Testament Kings', in *Ideal and Reality in Frankish and Anglo-Saxon Society: Studies Presented to J. M. Wallace-Hadrill*, edited by Patrick Wormald, Donald A. Bullough, and Roger Collins. Oxford: Blackwell, pp. 76–98.

McCormick, Michael, 1986. *Eternal Victory: Triumphal Rulership in Late Antiquity, Byzantium and the Early Medieval West*. Cambridge: Cambridge University Press.

——, 2001. *Origins of the European Economy: Communications and Commerce AD 300–900*. Cambridge: Cambridge University Press.

——, 2002. 'New Light on the "Dark Ages": How the Slave Trade Fuelled the Carolingian Economy', *Past and Present* 177, 17–54.

——, 2007. 'Where do Trading Towns Come from? Early Medieval Venice and the Northern *Emporia*', in *Post-Roman Towns, Trade and Settlement in Europe and Byzantium. Vol. 1: The Heirs of the Roman West*, edited by Joachim Henning. Millennium Studies in the Culture and History of the First Millennium CE. Berlin and New York: Walter de Gruyter, pp. 41–68.

McCormick, Michael, Edward James, Joachim Henning, et al., 2003. 'Origins of the European Economy: A Debate with Michael McCormick', *Early Medieval Europe* 13: 3, 259–323.

McGrail, Seán, 1987. *Ancient Boats in North-West Europe: The Archaeology of Water Transport to AD 1500*. London: Longman.

——, 2001. *Boats of the World: From the Stone Age to Medieval Times*. Oxford: Oxford University Press.

McKitterick, Rosamond, 1977. *The Frankish Church and the Carolingian Reforms 789–895*. London: Longman.

——, 1983. *The Frankish Kingdoms under the Carolingians 751–987*. London: Longman.

——, 1989. *The Carolingians and the Written Word*. Cambridge: Cambridge University Press.

——, ed., 1990. *The Uses of Literacy in Early Medieval Europe*. Cambridge: Cambridge University Press.

——, 1991. 'Latin and Romance: An Historian's Perspective', in *Latin and the Romance Languages in the Early Middle Ages*, edited by Roger Wright. London: Routledge, pp. 130–45.

——, ed., 1994. *Carolingian Culture: Emulation and Innovation*. Cambridge: Cambridge University Press.

——, ed., 1995. *The New Cambridge Medieval History. Vol. 2: c.700–c.900*. Cambridge: Cambridge University Press.

——, 2008. *Charlemagne: The Formation of a European Identity*. Cambridge: Cambridge University Press.

McLaughlin, Megan, 1994. *Consorting with Saints: Prayer for the Dead in Early Medieval France*. Ithaca: Cornell University Press.

McLynn, Neil, 2009. 'Pagans in a Christian Empire', in *A Companion to Late Antiquity*, edited by Philip Rousseau and Jutta Raithel. Blackwell Companions. Oxford: Blackwell, pp. 572–87.

McNamara, Jo-Ann, J. E. Halborg, and E. G. Whatley, ed., 1992. *Sainted Women of the Dark Ages*. Durham, North Carolina: Duke University Press.

McTurk, Rory W., 1975–6. 'Sacral Kingship in Ancient Scandinavia: A Review of Some Recent Writings', *Saga-Book: Viking Society for Northern Research* 19: 2–3, 139–69.

——, 1994. 'Scandinavian Sacral Kingship Revisited', *Saga-Book: Viking Society for Northern Research* 24: 1, 19–32.

Meehan, Bernard, 1994. *The Book of Kells: An Illustrated Introduction to the Manuscript in Trinity College Dublin*. London: Thames and Hudson.

——, 1996. *The Book of Durrow: A Medieval Masterpiece at Trinity College Dublin*. Dublin: Town House.

Menghin, Wilfried, ed., 2007. *The Merovingian Period: Europe without Borders*. Wolfratshausen: Minerva Editions.

Metcalf, D. M., 1965. 'How Large was the Anglo-Saxon Currency?', *Economic History Review* 18, 475–82.

——, 1989. 'Large Danegelds in Relation to War and Kingship: Their Implications for Monetary History, and Some Numismatic Evidence', in *Weapons and Warfare in Anglo-Saxon England*, edited by Sonia Chadwick Hawkes. Oxford: Oxford University Committee for Archaeology, pp. 179–89.

——, 1990. 'A Sketch of the Currency in the Time of Charles the Bald', in *Charles the Bald: Court and Kingdom*, edited by M. Gibson and Janet L. Nelson. London.

Miller, J. Innes, 1998. *The Spice Trade of the Roman Empire, 29 B.C. to A.D. 641*. London: Sandpiper Books Ltd.

Mitchell, Kathleen and Ian Wood, ed., 2002. *The World of Gregory of Tours*. Cultures, Beliefs, and Traditions, 8. Leiden and Boston, Mass.: Brill.

Mitchell, Stephen, 2007. *A History of the Later Roman Empire, AD 284–641: The Transformation of the Ancient World*. Oxford: Blackwell.

Mitchell, Stephen and Geoffrey Greatrex, 2000. *Ethnicity and Culture in Late Antiquity*. London: Duckworth and the Classical Press of Wales.

Momigliano, A., ed., 1963. *The Conflict between Paganism and Christianity in the Fourth Century*. Oxford: Oxford University Press.

Moore, Robert Ian, 1987. *The Formation of a Persecuting Society: Power and Deviance in Western Europe, 950–1250*. Oxford: Oxford University Press.

——, ed., 1983. *The Newnes Historical Atlas*. London: Edward Arnold.

——, 2000. *The First European Revolution, c.970–1215*. Oxford: Blackwell.

Moorhead, John, 2001. *The Roman Empire Divided: The Post-Roman World, 400–700*. Harlow: Longman.

——, 2005. *Gregory the Great*. London: Routledge.

Moreland, John, 2000a. 'Concepts of the Early Medieval Economy', in *The Long Eighth Century: Production, Distribution and Demand*, edited by Inge Lyse Hansen and Chris Wickham. Transformation of the Roman World, 2. Leiden: Brill, pp. 1–34.

——, 2000b. 'The Significance of Production in Eighth-Century England', in *The Long Eighth Century: Production, Distribution and Demand*, edited by Inge Lyse Hansen and Chris Wickham. Transformation of the Roman World, 2. Leiden: Brill, pp. 69–104.

——, 2004. 'Objects, Identities and Cosmological Authentification', *Archaeological Dialogues* 10, 144–9.

Moss, H. St. L. B., 1935. *The Birth of the Middle Ages 395–814*. Oxford: Oxford University Press.

Murphy, G. Ronald, 1989. *The Saxon Savior: The Germanic Transformation of the Gospel in the Ninth-Century Heliand*. Oxford: Oxford University Press.

——, ed., 1992. *The Heliand: The Saxon Gospel*. Oxford: Oxford University Press.

Mütherich, Florentine and Joachim E. Gaehde, 1977. *Carolingian Painting*. London: Chatto and Windus.

Muthesius, Anna, 1999. *Studies in Silk in Byzantium*. London: Pindar.

——, 2004. *Studies in Byzantine, Islamic and Near Eastern Silk Weaving*. London: Pindar.

Nees, Lawrence, 2002. *Early Medieval Art*. Oxford History of Art. Oxford: Oxford University Press.

Nelson, Janet L., 1977. 'On the Limits of the Carolingian Renaissance', *Studies in Church History* 14, 51–77. Reprinted in Janet L. Nelson, *Politics and Ritual in Early Medieval Europe*. London and Ronceverte: Hambledon Press, 1986, pp. 49–68.

——, 1978. 'Queens as Jezebels: Brunhild and Balthild in Merovingian History', in *Medieval Women: Essays Dedicated to Professor Rosalind M. T. Hill*, edited by Derek Baker. Studies in Church History: Subsidia, 1. Oxford: Blackwell, pp. 31–77. Reprinted in Janet L. Nelson, *Politics and Ritual in Early Medieval Europe*. London and Ronceverte: Hambledon Press, 1986, pp. 1–48.

——, 1986. *Politics and Ritual in Early Medieval Europe*. London and Ronceverte: Hambledon Press.

——, 1987. 'The Lord's Anointed and the People's Choice: Carolingian Royal Ritual', in *Rituals of Royalty: Power and Ceremonial in Traditional Societies*, edited by David Cannadine. Cambridge: Cambridge University Press, pp. 137–80. Reprinted in Janet L. Nelson, *The Frankish World 750–900*. London and Rio Grande: Hambledon Press, 1996, no. 6.

——, 1988. 'Kingship and Empire', in *The Cambridge History of Medieval Political Thought c.350–c.1450*, edited by J. H. Burns. Cambridge: Cambridge University Press, pp. 211–51.

——, 1994. 'Kingship and Empire in the Carolingian World', in *Carolingian Culture: Emulation and Innovation*, edited by Rosamond McKitterick. Cambridge: Cambridge University Press, pp. 52–87.

——, 1995. 'Kingship and Royal Government', in *The New Cambridge Medieval History. Vol. 2: c.700–c.900*, edited by Rosamond McKitterick. Cambridge: Cambridge University Press, pp. 383–430.

Nicholas, David, 1997. *The Growth of the Medieval City: From Late Antiquity to the Early Fourteenth Century*. London: Longman.

Niles, John D., 2007. 'Beowulf and Lejre', in *Beowulf and Lejre*, edited by John D. Niles. Turnhout: Brepols, pp. 169–234.

Nock, Arthur Darby, 1998. *Conversion: The Old and the New in Religion from Alexander the Great to Augustine of Hippo.* 2nd edn. Baltimore: Johns Hopkins University Press.

Nordenfalk, Carl, 1977. *Celtic and Anglo-Saxon Painting: Book Illumination in the British Isles 600–800.* London: Chatto and Windus.

North, J. J., 1994. *English Hammered Coinage. Vol. I: Early Anglo-Saxon to Henry III, c.600–1272.* 3rd edn. London: Spink.

Ó Carragáin, Éamonn, 1995. *The City of Rome and the World of Bede.* Jarrow Lecture. Jarrow: St Paul's Jarrow.

——, 2005. *Ritual and the Rood: Liturgical Images and the Old English Poems of the Dream of the Rood Tradition.* London: British Library.

Ó Carragáin, Éamonn and Carol Neuman de Vegvar, ed., 2008. *Roma Felix: Formation and Reflections of Medieval Rome.* Aldershot: Ashgate.

Ó Cróinín, Daibhi, 1995. *Early Medieval Ireland 400–1200.* London: Longman.

O'Donnell, J. J., 1979. *Cassiodorus.* Berkeley: University of California Press.

Oakley, F., 1973. 'Celestial Hierarchies Revisited: Walter Ullmann's Vision of Medieval Politics', *Past and Present* 60, 3–48.

Oakley, Francis, 2006. *Kingship: The Politics of Enchantment.* New Perspectives on the Past. Oxford: Wiley-Blackwell.

Odegaard, Charles Edwin, 1941. 'Carolingian Oaths of Fidelity', *Speculum* 16, 284–96.

——, 1945. *Vassi and Fideles in the Carolingian Empire.* Harvard Historical Monographs, 19. New York: Octagon.

Oleson, T. J., 1955. *The Witenagemot in the Reign of Edward the Confessor.* Oxford: Geoffrey Cumberlege/Oxford University Press.

Olson, Lynette, 2007. *The Early Middle Ages: The Birth of Europe.* Basingstoke: Palgrave Macmillan.

Orwin, Charles Stewart and Christabel Susan Orwin, 1967. *The Open Fields.* Oxford: Clarendon Press.

Ottaway, Patrick, 1992. *Archaeology in British Towns: From the Emperor Claudius to the Black Death.* London: Routledge.

——, 1993. *English Heritage Book of Roman York.* London: Batsford.

Owen, Gale R., 1981. *Rites and Religions of the Anglo-Saxons.* London: David and Charles.

Page, Raymond I., 1987. *Runes: Cuneiform to the Alphabet.* London: British Museum Press.

——, 1995. *Runes and Runic Inscriptions: Collected Essays on Anglo-Saxon and Viking Runes.* Woodbridge: Boydell Press.

——, 1999. *An Introduction to English Runes.* 2nd edn. Woodbridge: Boydell Press.

Palliser, David M., 2000. *The Cambridge Urban History of Britain. Vol. 1: c.600–c.1540.* Cambridge: Cambridge University Press.

Pantos, Aliki and Sarah Semple, ed. 2004. *Assembly Places and Practices in Medieval Europe*. Dublin: Four Courts Press.

Paolucci, Antonio, 1978. *Ravenna*. London: Constable.

Parkins, Helen M., 1997. 'The "Consumer City" Domesticated', in *Roman Urbanism: Beyond the Consumer City*, edited by Helen M. Parkins. London: Routledge, pp. 83–111.

Partner, Peter, 1972. *The Lands of St Peter: The Papal State in the Middle Ages and the Early Renaissance*. London: Eyre Methuen.

Peacock, D. P. S., 1982. *Pottery in the Roman World: An Ethnoarchaeological Approach*. London: Longman.

Peacock, D. P. S. and D. F. Williams, 1991. *Amphorae and the Roman Economy: An Introductory Guide*. London: Longman.

Pearce, Susan, 2003. 'Processes of Conversion in North-West Roman Gaul', in *The Cross Goes North: Processes of Conversion in Northern Europe, AD 300–1300*, edited by Martin O. H. Carver. York Medieval Press. Woodbridge: Boydell Press, pp. 61–78.

Pearson, Andrew, 2002. *The Roman Shore Forts: Coastal Defences of Southern Britain*. Stroud: Tempus.

Pelteret, David E., 1995. *Slavery in Early Medieval England: From the Reign of Alfred to the Twelfth Century*. Woodbridge: Boydell Press.

Percival, John, 1966. 'Ninth-Century Polyptyques and the Villa System: A Reply', *Latomus* 25, 134–8.

——, 1969. 'Seigneurial Aspects of Late Roman Estate Management', *English Historical Review* 84, 449–73.

——, 1976. *The Roman Villa: An Historical Introduction*. London: Batsford.

Pirenne, Henri, 1925. *Medieval Cities: Their Origins and the Revival of Trade*. Princeton: Princeton University Press.

——, 1939. *Mahommed and Charlemagne*. London: George Allen and Unwin.

Pohl, Walter and Helmut Reimitz, ed., 1998. *Strategies of Distinction: The Construction of Ethnic Communities, 300–800*. The Transformation of the Roman World, 2. Leiden: Brill.

Pohlsander, Hans A., 1996. *The Emperor Constantine*. London: Routledge.

Pollington, Stephen, 2003. *The Mead-Hall: The Feasting Tradition in Anglo-Saxon England*. Hockwold-cum-Wilton: Anglo-Saxon Books.

Pounds, N. J. G., 1994. *An Economic History of Medieval Europe*. 2nd edn. London: Longman.

Prestell, Tim and Katharina Ulmschneider, ed., 2003. *Markets in Early Medieval Europe: Trading and 'Productive' Sites, 650–850*. Macclesfield: Windgather.

Pryce, Huw, 1998. *Literacy in Medieval Celtic Societies*. Cambridge Studies in Medieval Literature. Cambridge: Cambridge University Press.

Raffel, Burton and Alexandra H. Olsen, ed., 1998. *Poems and Prose from the Old English*. New Haven: Yale University Press.

Rankin, Susan, 1994. 'Carolingian Music', in *Carolingian Culture: Emulation and Innovation*, edited by Rosamond McKitterick. Cambridge: Cambridge University Press, pp. 274–316.

Rapp, Claudia, 2005. *Holy Bishops in Late Antiquity*. Berkeley: University of California Press.

Rebenich, Stefan, 2002. *Jerome*. London: Routledge.

Reece, Richard, 1978. *Roman Coins: An Introduction*. Cirencester: Corinium Museum.

——, 1999. *The Later Roman Empire: An Archaeology, AD 150–600*. Stroud: Tempus.

Rees, Sian E., 1981. *Ancient Agricultural Implements*. Shire Archaeology. Princes Risborough: Shire Publications.

Reuter, Timothy, ed., 1979. *The Medieval Nobility: Studies on the Ruling Classes of France and Germany from the Sixth to the Twelfth Century*. Europe in the Middle Ages Selected Studies, 14. Amsterdam: North Holland.

——, 1982. 'The "Imperial Church System" of the Ottonian and Salian Rulers: A Reconsideration', *Journal of Ecclesiastical History* 33, 347–74. Reprinted in Timothy Reuter, *Medieval Polities and Modern Mentalities*, edited by Janet L. Nelson. Cambridge: Cambridge University Press, 2005, pp. 324–54.

——, 1985. 'Plunder and Tribute in the Carolingian Empire', *Transactions of the Royal Historical Society*, 5th series 35, 75–94. Reprinted in *Warfare in the Dark Ages*, edited by John France and Kelly DeVries. Aldershot: Ashgate, 2008, pp. 271–90; and in Timothy Reuter, *Medieval Polities and Modern Mentalities*, edited by Janet L. Nelson. Cambridge: Cambridge University Press, 2005, pp. 231–50.

——, 1991. *Germany in the Early Middle Ages c.800–1056*. Harlow: Longman.

——, 1999. 'Carolingian and Ottonian Warfare', in *Medieval Warfare: A History*, edited by Maurice Keen. Oxford: Oxford University Press.

——, ed., 2000. *The New Cambridge Medieval History*. Vol. 3: *c.900–c.1024*. Cambridge: Cambridge University Press.

Reynolds, Susan, 1984. 'Medieval Origines Gentium and the Community of the Realm', *Journal of the Historical Association* 68, 375–90. Reprinted in Susan Reynolds, *Ideas and Solidarities of the Medieval Laity: England and Western Europe*. Collected Studies, 495. Aldershot: Variorum, 1995, no. II.

——, December 2003. 'There were States in Medieval Europe: A Response to Rees Davies', *Journal of Historical Sociology* 16: 4, 550–5.

Richards, Jeffrey A., 1979. *The Popes and the Papacy in the Early Middle Ages, 476–752*. London: Routledge and Kegan Paul.

——, 1980. *Consul of God*. London: Routledge and Kegan Paul.

Riché, Pierre, 1976. *Education and Culture in the Barbarian West: From the Sixth through the Eighth Century*. Columbia: University of South Carolina Press.

Ridder-Symoens, Hilde de, ed., 1992. *A History of the University in Europe. Vol. 1: Universities in the Middle Ages.* Cambridge: Cambridge University Press.

Ritchie, Anna, 1989. *Picts: An Introduction to the Life of the Picts and the Carved Stones in the Care of Historic Scotland.* Edinburgh: HMSO.

Robinson, I. S., 1988. 'Church and Papacy', in *The Cambridge History of Medieval Political Thought c.350–c.1450*, edited by J. H. Burns. Cambridge: Cambridge University Press, pp. 252–305.

Rodwell, Warwick and Trevor Rowley, ed., 1975. *The 'Small Towns' of Roman Britain: Papers Presented to a Conference, Oxford 1975.* British Archaeological Reports, British Series, 15. Oxford: BAR.

Roesdahl, Else, 1982. *Viking Age Denmark.* Translated by S. Margerson and K. Williams. London: British Museum Publications.

——, 1987. *The Vikings.* London: Penguin.

Rollason, David, 1982. *The Mildrith Legend: A Study in Early Medieval Hagiography in England.* Studies in the Early History of Britain. Leicester: Leicester University Press.

——, 1986. 'Relic-Cults as an Instrument of Royal Policy c.900–c.1050', *Anglo-Saxon England* 15, 91–103.

——, 1989. *Saints and Relics in Anglo-Saxon England.* Oxford: Blackwell.

Rollason, David and Eric Cambridge, 1995. 'The Pastoral Organization of the Anglo-Saxon Church: A Review of the "Minster Hypothesis" ', *Early Medieval Europe* 4, 87–104.

Rollason, David, A. J. Piper, Margaret Harvey, et al., ed., 2004. *The Durham Liber Vitae and its Context.* Regions and Regionalism in History. Woodbridge: Boydell Press.

Rosenthal, J. T., 1964. 'The Public Assembly in the Time of Louis the Pious', *Traditio* 20, 25–40.

Rosenwein, Barbara H., 2009. *A Short History of the Middle Ages.* Toronto: University of Toronto Press.

Rostovtzeff, Michael Ivanovitch, 1957. *The Social and Economic History of the Roman Empire.* Translated by P. M. Fraser. Oxford: Oxford University Press.

Rowley, Trevor, ed., 1981. *The Origins of Open Field Agriculture.* London: Croom Helm.

Russell, James C., 1994. *The Germanization of Early Medieval Christianity: A Sociohistorical Approach to Religious Transformation.* Oxford: Oxford University Press.

Russell, Josiah Cox, 1958. *Late Ancient and Medieval Population.* Philadelphia: American Philosophical Society.

——, 1969. 'Population in Europe 500–1500', in *The Middle Ages. Part 1: Population in Europe, 500–1500*, edited by Josiah Cox Russell and C. M. Cipolla. Fontana Economic History of Europe, Vol. 1, Part 1. London: Collins, ch. 1.

Sarris, Peter, 2004. 'The Origins of the Manorial Economy: New Insights from Late Antiquity', *English Historical Review* 69, 279–311.

Sawyer, Peter Hayes, 1971. *The Age of the Vikings.* 2nd edn. London: Edward Arnold.

Sawyer, Peter Hayes and Bridget Sawyer, 1993. *Medieval Scandinavia: From Conversion to Reformation 800–1500.* Minneapolis: University of Minnesota Press.

Scull, Christopher, 2002. 'Ipswich: Development and Contexts of an Urban Precursor in the Seventh Century', in *Central Places in the Migration and Merovingian Periods: Papers from the 52nd Sachsensymposium, Lund, August 2002,* edited by Brigitte Hårdt and Lars Larsson. Acta Archaeologica Lundensia 8/39. Stockholm: Almqvist and Wiksell International, pp. 301–16.

Skre, Dagfinn, 2007. 'Towns and Markets, Kings and Central Places in South-Western Scandinavia *c.* AD 800–950', in *Kaupang in Skiringssal,* edited by Dagfinn Skre. Kaupang Excavation Project Publication Series, 1. Aarhus: Aarhus University Press, pp. 445–69.

Slicher van Bath, Bernard Henrik, 1966. *The Agrarian History of Western Europe, A.D. 500–1850.* Translated by O. Ordish. London: Arnold.

Smith, Anthony D., 1986. *The Ethnic Origins of Nations.* Oxford: Blackwell.

——, 1995. 'National Identities: Modern and Medieval?', in *Concepts of National Identity in the Middle Ages,* edited by S. Forde and A. V. Murray. Leeds Texts and Monographs, 14. Leeds: School of English, University of Leeds.

——, 2000. *The Nation in History: Historiographical Debates About Ethnicity and Nationalism.* Hanover, NH: University Press of New England.

Smith, Julia M. H., ed., 2000. *Early Medieval Rome and the West: Essays in Honour of Donald A. Bullough.* Leiden: Brill.

——, 2005. *Europe after Rome: A New Cultural History 500–1000.* Oxford: Oxford University Press.

Smyth, Alfred P., ed., 1998. *Medieval Europeans: Studies in Ethnic Identity and National Perspectives in Medieval Europe.* London: Macmillan.

Southern, Pat and Karen R. Dixon, 2000. *The Late Roman Army.* London: Routledge.

Stafford, Pauline, 1998. *Queens, Concubines and Dowagers: The King's Wife in the Early Middle Ages.* Revised edn. London: Leicester University Press.

Stancliffe, Clare, 1982. 'Red, White and Blue Martyrdom', in *Ireland in Early Medieval Europe: Studies in Memory of Kathleen Hughes,* edited by Dorothy Whitelock, Rosamond McKitterick and David Dumville. Cambridge: Cambridge University Press, pp. 21–46.

Stark, Rodney, 1996. *The Rise of Christianity: A Sociologist Reconsiders History.* Princeton: Princeton University Press.

——, 2007. *Cities of God: The Real Story of how Christianity Became an Urban Movement and Conquered Rome.* New York: HarperOne.

Stenton, Frank Merry, 1971. *Anglo-Saxon England.* 3rd edn. Oxford: Oxford University Press.

Stephenson, Paul, 2009. *Constantine: Unconquered Emperor, Christian Victor.* London: Quercus.

Stevens, Wesley M., 1985. *Bede's Scientific Achievement.* Jarrow Lecture. Jarrow: Jarrow Parish Council. Reprinted in Wesley M. Stevens, *Cycles of Time and Scientific Learning in Medieval Europe.* Collected Studies, 482. Aldershot: Variorum, 1995, no. II; and in Michael Lapidge, ed., *Bede and his World: The Jarrow Lectures 1958–93.* 2 vols. Aldershot: Variorum, 1994, II, 645–88.

Stevenson, J. and W. H. C. Frend, ed., 1987. *A New Eusebius: Documents Illustrating the History of the Church to AD 337.* Revised edn. London: SPCK.

Stoodley, Nick, 2002. 'The Origins of Hamwic and its Central Role in the Seventh Century as Revealed by Recent Archaeological Discoveries', in *Central Places in the Migration and Merovingian Periods: Papers from the 52nd Sachsensymposium, Lund, August 2002,* edited by Brigitte Hårdt and Lars Larsson. Acta Archaeologica Lundensia 8/39. Stockholm: Almqvist and Wiksell International, pp. 317–31.

Straw, Carole, 1988. *Gregory the Great: Perfection in Imperfection.* The Transformation of the Classical Heritage. Berkeley: University of California Press.

Strömbäck, Dag Alvar, 1975. *The Conversion of Iceland: A Survey.* Translated by Peter Foote. London: Viking Society for Northern Research, University College London.

Sullivan, Richard E., 1953. 'The Carolingian Missionary and the Pagan', *Speculum* 28, 705–40. Reprinted in Richard E. Sullivan, *Carolingian Missionary Activity in the Early Middle Ages.* Collected Studies, 431. Aldershot: Ashgate/Variorum, 1994, no. II.

——, 1956. 'Carolingian Missionary Theories', *Catholic Historical Review* 42, 273–95. Reprinted in Richard E. Sullivan, *Carolingian Missionary Activity in the Early Middle Ages.* Collected Studies, 431. Aldershot: Ashgate/Variorum, 1994, no. I.

Swanson, Robert, 1999. *The Twelfth-Century Renaissance.* Manchester: Manchester University Press.

Talbot, C. H., ed., 1954. *The Anglo-Saxon Missionaries in Germany, being the Lives of SS Willibrord, Boniface, Sturm, Leoba, and Lebuin, Together with the Hodoeporicon of St Willibald and a Selection of the Correspondence of St Boniface.* London: Sheed and Ward.

Tellenbach, Gerd, 1993. *The Church in Western Europe from the Tenth to the Early Twelfth Century.* Cambridge: Cambridge University Press.

Theuws, Frans, 2004a. 'Closer to the Essence of the Early Middle Ages: A Reply', *Archaeological Dialogues* 10, 149–59.

——, 2004b. 'Exchange, Religion, Identity and Central Places in the Early Middle Ages', *Archaeological Dialogues* 10, 121–38.

Thirsk, Joan, 1966. 'The Origin of the Common Fields', *Past and Present* 29, 3–25.

Thomas, Charles, 1981. *Christianity in Roman Britain to AD 500.* London: Batsford.

Thomas, Mark G., Michael P. H. Stumpf, and Heinrich Härke, 2006. 'Evidence for an Apartheid-Like Social Structure in Early Anglo-Saxon England', *Proceedings of the Royal Society, B* doi: 10.1098/rspb.2006.3627.

Thompson, E. A., 1966. *The Visigoths in the Time of Ulfila.* Oxford: Clarendon Press.

Thompson, E. A. and Barbara Flower, ed., 1996. *A Roman Reformer and Inventor: being a New Text of the Treatise De Rebus Bellicis*. Chicago: Ares Publishers.

Turville-Petre, E. O. Gabriel, 1964. *Myth and Religion of the North: The Religion of Ancient Scandinavia*. London: Weidenfeld and Nicolson.

Tweddle, Dominic, Joan Moulden and Elizabeth Logan, ed., 1999. *Anglian York: A Survey of the Evidence*. Archaeology of York. York: York Archaeological Trust.

Ullmann, Walter, 1955. *The Growth of Papal Government in the Middle Ages*. London: Methuen.

——, 1969. *The Carolingian Renaissance and the Idea of Kingship*. London: Methuen.

Urbańcyk, Przemysław, 2003. 'The Politics of Conversion in North Central Europe', in *The Cross Goes North: Processes of Conversion in Northern Europe, AD 300–1300*, edited by Martin O. H. Carver. York Medieval Press. Woodbridge: Boydell Press, pp. 15–28.

Van Dam, Raymond, 1993. *Saints and their Miracles in Late Antique Gaul*. Princeton: Princeton University Press.

Van der Meer, F., 1966. *Atlas of the Early Christian World*. London: Nelson.

Verbruggen, J., 1996. *The Art of Warfare during the Middle Ages from the Eighth Century to 1340*. 2nd edn. Woodbridge: Boydell Press.

Verhulst, Adriaan, 1985. 'The Origins of Towns in the Low Countries and the Pirenne Thesis', *Past and Present* 122, 3–35. Reprinted in Adriaan Verhulst, *Rural and Urban Aspects of Early Medieval Northwest Europe*. Collected Studies, 385. Aldershot: Variorum, 1992, no. X.

——, 1990. 'The "Agricultural Revolution" of the Middle Ages Reconsidered', in *Law, Custom and the Social Fabric in Medieval Europe: Essays in Honour of Bryce Lyon*, edited by Bernard S. Bachrach and David Nicholas. Kalamazoo: Medieval Institute Publications, pp. 17–28. Reprinted in Adriaan Verhulst, *Rural and Urban Aspects of Early Medieval Northwest Europe*. Collected Studies, 385. Aldershot: Variorum, 1992, no. V.

——, 1999. *The Rise of Cities in North-West Europe*. Cambridge: Cambridge University Press.

——, 2002. *The Carolingian Economy*. Cambridge Medieval Textbooks. Cambridge: Cambridge University Press.

Verwers, W. J. H., 1988. 'Dorestad: A Carolingian Town?', in *The Rebirth of Towns in the West AD 700–1050*, edited by Richard Hodges and Brian Hobley. CBA Research Report, 68. London: Council for British Archaeology, pp. 52–6.

Vince, Alan, 1990. *Saxon London: An Archaeological Investigation*. London: Seaby.

Von Simson, Otto G., 1987. *Sacred Fortress: Byzantine Art and Statecraft in Ravenna*. Princeton: Princeton University Press.

Wade, Keith, 1988. 'Ipswich', in *The Rebirth of Towns in the West AD 700–1050*, edited by Richard Hodges and Brian Hobley. CBA Research Report, 68. London: Council for British Archaeology, pp. 93–100.

Walbank, F. W., 1969. *The Awful Revolution: The Decline of the Roman Empire in the West*. Liverpool: Liverpool University Press.

Wallace-Hadrill, John Michael, 1971a. 'A Background to St Boniface's Mission', in *England before the Conquest*, edited by P. Clemoes and K. Hughes. Cambridge: Cambridge University Press. Reprinted in John Michael Wallace-Hadrill, *Early Medieval History*. Oxford: Blackwell, 1975, pp. 138–54.

——, 1971b. *Early Germanic Kingship in England and on the Continent*. Oxford: Oxford University Press.

——, 1983. *The Frankish Church*. Oxford: Clarendon Press.

Wallis, Faith, ed., 1999. *Bede: The Reckoning of Time*. Translated Texts for Historians. Liverpool: Liverpool University Press.

Ward-Perkins, Bryan, 1996. 'Urban Continuity?', in *Towns in Transition: Urban Evolution in Late Antiquity and the Early Middle Ages*, edited by Neil Christie and Simon Loseby. Aldershot: Scolar, pp. 4–17.

——, 2005. *The Fall of Rome and the End of Civilization*. Oxford: Oxford University Press.

Weale, M., 2002. 'Y Chromosome Evidence for Anglo-Saxon Mass Migration', *Molecular Biology and Evolution* 19: 7, 1008–21.

Weber, Max, 1947. *The Theory of Social and Economic Organization*. Translated by A. R. Henderson and Talcott Parsons. Revised edn. London: William Hodge and Company.

——, 1948. *From Max Weber: Essays in Sociology*. Translated by Hans Heinrich Gerth and C. Wright Mills. London: Routledge.

——, 1968. *Economy and Society: An Outline of Interpretive Sociology*. Translated by Guenther Roth and Claus Wittich. 3 vols. New York: Bedminster Press.

Webster, Leslie E., 1999. 'The Iconographic Progamme of the Franks Casket', in *Northumbria's Golden Age*, edited by Jane Hawkes and Susan Mills. Stroud: Sutton, pp. 227–46.

Webster, Leslie and Janet Backhouse, ed., 1991. *The Making of England: Anglo-Saxon Art and Culture AD 600–900*. London: British Museum.

Webster, Leslie E. and Michelle P. Brown, ed., 1997. *The Transformation of the Roman World*. London: British Museum Press.

Weitzmann, Kurt, 1977. *Late Antique and Early Christian Book Illumination*. London: Chatto and Windus.

Welch, Martin, 1992. *English Heritage Book of Anglo-Saxon England*. London: Batsford.

Wemple, Suzanne Fonay, 1985. *Women in Frankish Society: Marriage and the Cloister 500 to 900*. Philadelphia: University of Pennsylvania Press.

Werner, Karl Ferdinand, 1979. 'Important Noble Families in the Kingdom of Charlemagne', in *The Medieval Nobility: Studies on the Ruling Classes of France and Germany from the Sixth to the Twelfth Century*, edited by Timothy Reuter. Europe in the Middle Ages Selected Studies, 14. Amsterdam: North Holland, pp. 137–202.

Wheeler, Robert Eric Mortimer, 1964. *Roman Art and Architecture*. London: Thames and Hudson.

White, Lynn W., 1962. *Medieval Technology and Social Change*. 2nd edn. Oxford: Oxford University Press.

White, Stephen D, 1989. 'Kinship and Lordship in Early Medieval England: The Story of Cynewulf and Cyneheard', *Viator* 20, 1–18. Reprinted in Stephen D. White, *Rethinking Kinship and Feudalism in Early Medieval Europe*. Collected Studies, 823. Aldershot: Variorum, 2005, no. IV.

Whitelock, D., ed., 1979. *English Historical Documents. I: c.500–1042*. 2nd edn. London: Eyre and Spottiswoode.

Whitman, F. H., 1977. 'The Kingly Nature of Beowulf', *Neophilologus: An International Journal of Modern and Mediaeval Language and Literature* 61: 2, 277–86.

Whittaker, Charles R., 1990. 'The Consumer City Revisited: The *Vicus* and the City', *Journal of Roman Archaeology* 3, 110–18.

——, 1994. *Frontiers of the Roman Empire: A Social and Economic Study*. Baltimore and London: Johns Hopkins University Press.

Whittaker, Charles R. and P. Garnsey, 1998. 'Rural Life in the Later Roman Empire', in *The Cambridge Ancient History. Vol. 13: The Late Empire, A.D. 337–425*, edited by Averil Cameron and P. Garnsey. Cambridge: Cambridge University Press, pp. 277–311.

Wickham, Chris, 1984. 'The Other Transition: From the Ancient World to Feudalism', *Past and Present* 103, 3–37.

——, 1995. 'Rural Society in Carolingian Europe', in *The New Cambridge Medieval History. Vol. 2: c.700–c.900*, edited by Rosamond McKitterick. Cambridge: Cambridge University Press, pp. 510–37.

——, 2005. *Framing the Early Middle Ages: Europe and the Mediterranean, 400–800*. Oxford: Oxford University Press.

——, 2008. 'Rethinking the Structure of the Early Medieval Economy', in *The Long Morning of Medieval Europe: New Directions in Early Medieval Studies*, edited by Jennifer R. Davis and Michael McCormick. Farnham: Ashgate, pp. 19–32.

——, 2009. *The Inheritance of Rome: A History of Europe from 400 to 1000*. Harmondsworth: Penguin.

Wilson, David, 1984. *Anglo-Saxon Art: From the Seventh Century to the Norman Conquest*. London: Thames and Hudson.

——, 1992. *Anglo-Saxon Paganism*. London: Routledge.

Wilson, David Raoul, 2000. *Air Photo Interpretation for Archaeologists*. Stroud: Tempus.

Wolfram, Herwig, 1988. *History of the Goths*. Berkeley, Los Angeles, and London: University of California Press.

——, 1997. *The Roman Empire and its Germanic Peoples*. Berkeley: University of California Press.

Wood, Ian N., 1994a. *The Merovingian Kingdoms 450–751*. London: Longman.

——, 1994b. 'The Mission of Augustine of Canterbury to the English', *Speculum* 69, 1–17.

——, 1995. 'Pagan Religions and Superstitions East of the Rhine from the Fifth to the Ninth Century', in *After Empire: Towards an Ethnology of Europe's Barbarians*, edited by G. Ausenda. Woodbridge: Boydell Press, pp. 253–79.

——, ed., 1998. *Franks and Alamanni in the Merovingian Period: An Ethnographic Perspective*. Woodbridge: Boydell Press.

——, 1999. 'The Missionary Life', in *The Cult of Saints in Late Antiquity and the Middle Ages: Essays on the Contribution of Peter Brown*, edited by James Howard-Johnston and Paul Antony Hayward. Oxford: Oxford University Press, pp. 167–83.

——, 2001. *The Missionary Life: Saints and the Evangelisation of Europe 400–1050*. London: Longman.

Wormald, Patrick, 1976. 'The Decline of the Western Empire and the Survival of its Aristocracy', *Journal of Roman Studies* 66, 217–26.

——, 1977. 'The Uses of Literacy in Anglo-Saxon England and its Neighbours', *Transactions of the Royal Historical Society*, 5th series, 27, 95–114.

——, 1978. 'Beowulf and the Conversion of the Anglo-Saxon Aristocracy', in *Bede and Anglo-Saxon England*, edited by R. T. Farrell. British Archaeological Reports, British Series, 46. Oxford: BAR, pp. 32–95.

——, 1994. '*Engla Lond*: The Making of an Allegiance', *Journal of Historical Sociology* 7, 1–24.

——, 2005. 'Kings and Kingship', in *The New Cambridge Medieval History. Vol. 1: c.500–c.700*, edited by Paul Fouracre. Cambridge: Cambridge University Press, pp. 571–604.

Yorke, Barbara, 2002. *Nunneries and the Anglo-Saxon Royal Houses*. Women, Power and Politics. London and New York: Continuum.

——, 2006. *The Conversion of Britain: Religion, Politics and Society in Britain c.600–800*. Harlow: Pearson Longman.

Youngs, Susan, ed., 1989. *'The Work of Angels': Masterpieces of Celtic Metalwork, 6th–9th Centuries AD*. London: British Museum.

Index

Abbreviations
c.: *circa*
d.: died
fl.: flourished
r.: reigned

Aachen (Germany), Map 6
  church, 82, 85, 325, Fig. 7
  coronations, 85
  Gospels, 88–9, Fig. 11
  hall, 82, 85, 87, 125, 324
  in itinerary, 104, Map 7
  town, 224
Ælfric, abbot of Eynsham (*c.*950–*c.*1010),
    312, 313, 339
Æthelberht, king of Kent (d. 616), 66, 246
  conversion, 242–3, 288
  laws, 47, 97
Æthelflæd, 'lady of Mercia' (d. 918), 132,
    141
Æthelfrith, king of Northumbria (r. 604–16),
    57
Æthelred the Unready, king of England
    (r. 978–1016), 141
Aetius, patrician (d. 454), 27, 290
agriculture, 175–96
  agri deserti, 24, 184
  Carolingian, 176–8, Map 11
  polyptychs, 97, 176–7, 184, 184–5, 191,
    226, 227, Map 11
  Roman, 24, 175–6, 179–83
  technology, 187–91
    horse-collar, 189–90
    ploughs, 187–9, 190, Figs 18–19
    rotation of crops, 190
    water-mills, 190

Aidan, missionary, bishop of Lindisfarne
    (d. 651), 243, 246, 259
Alamans, *see* peoples
Alcuin, scholar, abbot of St Martin's, Tours
    (*c.*735–804), 287, 289, 315, 317,
    318, 336
Alfred the Great, king of Wessex
    (r. 871–99)
  army, 127
  attitude to Christianity, 91, 244
  burhs, 216
  law-code, 97
  scholarship, 312, 318, 339
Ambrose, St, bishop of Milan (*c.*339–97),
    237, 280, 302
Anglo-Saxons, *see* peoples: English
Anskar, archbishop of Hamburg (r. 831–65),
    253, 304
Anthony, St, of Egypt (d. 356), 258, 260,
    261
Arabs, *see* Moslems
Arcadius, eastern Roman emperor
    (395–408), 27, 66
archbishops, *see* prelates
architecture, 322–6, 337
  churches
    basilicas, 322–5
    centrally planned, 325–6
  palaces and halls, 82–4, 87–8, 323–4
    See also Aachen, Ingelheim, Lejre,
      Naranco, Nijmegen, Paderborn,
      Pfalzel, Ravenna, Split, Theoderic,
      Trier, Westminster, Winchester,
      Yeavering
Arianism, *see* Christian Church
Arles, Council of (314), 280

art, 326–33, 337
  barbarian styles, 331–3
  manuscript illumination, 326, 329–30,
      Figs 35–6
    Aachen Gospels, 88–9, Fig. 11
    Book of Durrow, 329
    Codex Amiatinus, 311–12, Fig. 30
    Godescalc Evangelistiary, 330, Fig. 36
    Golden Book of St Emmeram, 88
    Gospels of St Médard of Soisson, 326
    Lindisfarne Gospels, 329–30, Fig. 35
    Sacramentary of Metz, 85–6, Fig. 9
    Stuttgart Psalter, 244
  sculpture, 326–9, 331, Fig. 33
    Gosforth (Cumbria), 251, Fig. 27
    Ruthwell (Dumfries), 314, Fig. 33
  See also helmets
Attila, king of the Huns (435/40–453), 25,
    49, 66, 289–90
Augustine, archbishop of Canterbury
    (r. 597–604 × 609), 204, 242, 246,
    288, 289, 296
Augustine, bishop of Hippo (354–430), 264,
    308, 310, 338

barbarians
  cemeteries, 26, 43–4, Fig. 3
  hair-styles, 48, Fig. 4
  in Roman armies, 20, 199, 239–40
  invade Roman Empire, 25–6, 50–1
  settlement, 32–3
  See also peoples
Basil, St, 'the Great', monk and bishop
    (*c*.330–79), 259, 260, 302
basilicas, *see* architecture
Bede, monk of Monkwearmouth-Jarrow
    (*c*.673–735)
  life, 159, 184, 288, 312
  writings, 133, 140, 261, 316
    Ecclesiastical History of the English People, 9,
      45, 49–50, 52–3, 57, 59, 74, 90, 314,
      318
    Letter to Ecgberht, 272–3
Benedict Biscop, monastic founder (d. 689),
    133, 310–11, 318, 338
Birinus, missionary (d. 650), 199, 226, 246,
    289

Birka (Sweden), *emporium*, 213, 253, 304
bishops, *see* prelates
Bobbio (Italy), monastery, 259
Boethius (480–524), 303, 309, 310
Boniface, archbishop of Mainz, missionary
    (d. 754), 288, 289, 303, 318
Brandon (Suffolk), ? monastery, 265
British, *see* peoples
Brittany (France), rural settlement, 170
Brixworth (Northants.), 324, Fig. 32
Brunhild, queen of the Franks (d. 613),
    131, 140
Bruno, archbishop of Cologne (*c*.925–65),
    99, 295, 296
Burford (Oxon), planned town, 209,
    Fig. 22
Burgundians, *see* peoples
burhs, *see* urban centres

Cædmon, poet (fl. *c*.670), 45
Cædwalla, king of Gwynedd (d. 634),
    57, 58
Canterbury (Kent), 204, 287
Carloman, brother of Pippin III
    (*c*.708–54), 285
Cassian, John, monastic founder
    (*c*.360–after 430), 260, 302
Cassiodorus, senator, founder of Vivarium
    (485/90–*c*.580), 32, 52, 80, 96–7,
    264, 309, 310, 311
Cenwalh, king of Wessex (r. 642–72),
    199, 226
Charlemagne, king of the Franks
    (768–814), emperor (800–14),
    140–1, 148, 226, 303
  conquests, 54–5, 127, 215, 226,
    253
  coronation, 81–2, 84–5
  cultural policy, 287, 289
  image, 88, 91, Fig. 10
  relations with popes, 289
  reputation, 128, 122, 262
  royal style, 87
  scholarship, 317
  See also Einhard
Charles Martel, mayor of the palace (d. 751),
    134, 270, 271

Charles the Bald, king of West Frankia
        (840–77), emperor (875–7), 55, 141
    as lay abbot, 271
    coins, 158
    fortifications, 219
    image, 88
    inauguration, 85
    laws, 185
    scholarship, 318
Chaussy-Épagny (France), 182, Fig. 17
Childeric, king of the Franks (d. 486), 75, 40,
        140, 249, Fig. 5
Chlotar III, king of the Franks (657–73), 160,
        226
Christian Church, 231–304
    attitude to the dead, 283
    conversion, 232–3, 234–57, 288–9
        barbarian, 242–51
        Irish, 252
        missions, 244–6, 288–9
        outside Roman Empire, 251–4
        Roman, 234–42
    councils, 280
        See also Arles, Nicaea, Orléans
    doctrinal disputes
        Arianism, 29, 80, 235, 248, 280, 302
        Donatism, 235, 280, 302
    liturgy, see 'Gelasian of the Eighth
        Century', Hadrianum
    organisation, 246–7, 279–80
    purgatory, 262
    rise, 7, 231–3, 238–9, 243–4
    rituals, 278–9
    visions, 262
        See also prelates; Peace and the Truce of
            God; saints and martyrs; sanctuary;
            Vulgate Bible
cities, see urban centres
Cividale (Italy), Santa Maria in Valle, 326
climate change, 11, 185–6
Clonmacnoise (Ireland), monastery, 265
Clovis, king of the Franks (486–511), 140
    conquests, 40, 54
    conversion, 242, 247, 303
    Roman elements, 29, 81, 146
Cnut (d. 1035), king of England and
        Denmark, 141, 304

Code of Theodosius (Codex Theodosianus), 33
coins, 151, 154, 155, 156–8, 180
    Arab, 165, 166, 167
    Carolingian, 108–9, 158, 167, 226, Fig. 13
    Constantine's, 19, 241
    hoards, 157–8, 165–6, 167
    minting, 108–9, 157, 214, Fig. 13
    Offa's dinar, 167
    ships on, Fig. 16
    used by Rus, 165
Coldingham (Borders), monastery, 262, 268,
        271, 273
Cologne (Germany), 203, Map 6
    cathedral, 132, 203, 295, 331
    St Gereo, 325
Columba, St, monastic founder (c.521–97),
        259, 265, 271
Columbanus, monastic founder (d. 615), 259,
        265, 303, 336
Columella, Lucius Junius Moderatus (d. 70),
        'On Agriculture', 175, 226
Constantine, emperor (r. 306–37), 27, 29, 65,
        302, 338, Fig. 10
    buildings, 23, 29, 236–7, 294, 308, Fig. 25
    coins, 19, 241
    conversion, 23, 234–7, 241, 242
    Donation of, 294
    establishes Constantinople, 28, 65
    made emperor at York, 199–200
    military reorganisation, 20
Constantinople (Istanbul), 3, 15, 28, 65, 165,
        Map 5
    besieged, 158–9
    economic activity, 151, 152, 161
    Haghia Sophia, 325
Corbie (France), monastery, 160, 162
Corvey (Germany), monastery, 88, 268
culture, 307–39
    See also art and architecture; scholarship
Cuthbert, St, hermit, bishop of Lindisfarne
        (d. 687)
    asceticism, 261, 262, 296
    authority, 295
    coffin, 314
    silks, 159
    social status, 293–4, 273–4
    translations, 284

Danevirke (Germany), linear earthwork, 111, 212

Dienheim (Germany) , rural settlement, 179

Dinas Powys (Wales), reused hillfort, 155

Diocletian, emperor (284–305), 19, 23, 27, 65, Map 1

Dionysio-Hadriana, compilation of canon law, 289

Dionysius Exiguus (*c.*470–before 544), lawyer and mathematician, 288

Donation of Constantine, 294

Donatism, *see* Christian Church

Donatus (fl. 4th century), *Ars Maior*, 312

Dorestad (Netherlands), *emporium*, 210, 211, 212, 213, 214, 216, Fig. 16

Durham (County Durham)
    cathedral, 324, 337
        treasury, 159, 314
    foundation, 284

Easter, date of, 57, 281, 316

Ebo, archbishop of Rheims (d. 851), 293

economics, *see* agriculture; trade; urban centres

Edmund, king of England (r. 939–46), 58

Edward the Confessor, king of England (r. 1042–66), 79, 141

Edward the Elder, king of Wessex (r. 899–924), 58, 216

Edwin, king of Northumbria (r. *c.*586–633), 226, 303
    church at York, 201, 202
    conversion, 243, 246

Egeria, pilgrim (fl. 381–4), 260

Emma (Ælfgifu), queen of England (r. 1012–16, 1017–35), 132

emporia, see urban centres

English (Anglo-Saxons), *see* peoples

Escomb (County Durham), 326

Eugenius, Roman emperor (r. 392–4), 23, 27, 65, 237

Flixborough (Lincs.), ? monastery, 265

Fossa Carolina, canal, 111

Franks, *see* peoples

Franks Casket, 9, 249–51, Fig. 26

Fredegund, wife of King Chilperic I (fl. late 6th century), 131, 132

Fulda (Germany), monastery, 265, 267, 270, 303, 324

'Gelasian of the Eighth Century', liturgical book, 289

Gelasius I, pope (r. 492–6), 88, 281, 288

genealogies, 74, 128

Gerald of Wales (1146–1223), 76–7

gift-giving, *see* government

Godefrid, king of the Danes (d. 810), 214–15, 226, 255

Goths, *see* peoples

government
    assemblies, 105, 127, 254
    capitularies, 97, 99, 112, 141, 267
        General Admonition, 91, 317
    charters, 97, 99, 105, 272
    finances, 102–3
        gift-giving, 102, 213
        taxes, 102–3, 290, 291
        tolls, 104, 214, 215, 218, 270
    gift-giving, 102, 119, 123, 213, 241–2
    government through monasteries, 267–71
    law-codes, 47, 55, 97, 98
    military organisation, 110–13, 127–8, Fig. 14
    missi dominici, 98, 99, 105, 108
    ordeal, judicial, 101
    palace organisation, 98, 101–2, 102, 104, 123, 124–5, 131, 133
    regional government, 103–4
    writs, 97
    See also prelates; coins; Roman Empire

Gregory I the Great, pope (r. 590–604)
    at Rome, 291, Fig. 29
    holiness, 296
    Life, 285, 288, 289, 338
    mission to England, 246, 288–9,
    relic-distribution, 285
    scholarship, 309–10, 312, 318

Gregory VII, pope (r. 1073–85), 282, 297

Gundioc, king of the Burgundians (d. 469/70), 27

Guntram, king of the Franks (r. 561–92), 79, 150, 226

Guthlac, St, hermit (*c.*674–714), 261–2

Hadrian's Wall, 20

Hadrianum, liturgical book, 289

Haithabu (Germany), *emporium*, 210–11, 214–15, 216, 226, 227, Figs 16, 23, Map 13

halls, *see* architecture

Hamwih (Southampton, England), *emporium*, 161, 210, 213, 214, 227

Harald Bluetooth, king of Denmark (r. *c*.958–*c*.987), 254, 304

helmets, 126, 331–3

    Coppergate Helmet, 201, 226, Fig. 37

Henry I the Fowler, king of Germany (r. 919–36), 87, 141, 218

Henry II, king of Germany (r. 1002–24), emperor (r. 1014–24), 86, 141

Hexham (Northumberland), monastery, 268, 294

Hlothhere (r. 673–85) and Eadric (r. 685–? 686), kings of Kent, laws, 211

Honorius, western Roman emperor (r. 395–423), 27, 65

Huns, *see* peoples

Ine, king of Wessex (r. 688–726), laws, 191

Ingelheim (Germany), palace, 84, 125, 253, Map 6

'Instructions to the Merchants', 212

Iona (Scotland), monastery, 259, 265, 271

Ipswich (Suffolk), *emporium*, 213

Isidore of Seville, scholar (*c*.560–636), 47–8, 287, 303, 310, 338

Istanbul, *see* Constantinople

James the Great, apostle, 284–5

Jarrow, *see* Monkwearmouth-Jarrow

Jelling (Denmark), 254

Jerome, scholar and translator (*c*.345–420), 26, 259, 260, 287–8, 302, 308

Jews, *see* peoples

John the Almsgiver (d. 619), *Life*, 155

Jonas, bishop of Orléans (r. *c*.818–43), 91, 141

Jordanes, writer (fl. *c*.551), 52, 309

Jouarre (France), crypt, 326

Julian, Roman emperor (r. 360–3), 20, 23, 65, 235, 283

Julius Nepos, Roman emperor (r. 474–5), 66

Justinian, east Roman emperor (r. 527–65), 66

    buildings, 82, 308, 325,

    conquests, 28, 29, 32

Jutes, *see* peoples

Kenelcunill (Ireland), inauguration site, 76–7

Kiev (Ukraine), 165, Map 10

kings

    appearance

        hair-styles, 75–6, Fig. 4

        regalia, 77–9, 81, 86, Fig. 6

        representations of, 88–92, Fig. 9–11

    ideology

        Christian, 84–92, Fig. 9

        pagan, 72–80, 81, Fig. 5

        Roman, 80–4, Figs 7–8

    itineration, 104–5, 268, Fig. 28, Map 7

    relationship to aristocracy, 132–4

    rituals

        entry ceremonies, 81

        inaugurations, 7, 76–7, 81–2, 84–7, 279, Fig. 9

        See also Kenelcunill, Kingston-on-Thames, Navan Fort, Scone, Tara

    royal styles, 87

    See also government

Kingston-on-Thames (Surrey), inauguration site, 77

La Graufensque (France), 152, industrial site, Map 9

Lactantius (*c*.240–*c*.320), *Deaths of the Persecutors*, 234–5

land-holding, 272–3

language, 45–7, 312–14

    Continental Germanic, 45, 312

    Latin, 8, 98, 312, 313, 336

    Linguistic Frontier, 46–7

    Old English, 8, 45, 46, 98, 312–13

    Old French, 8, 122

    Old Norse, 8, 45, 73–4, 75

Lastingham (Yorks.), monastery, 261

Latimer (Bucks.), villa, 180

Le Mans, wills of bishops, 179
Lejre (Denmark), ? royal halls, 125
Leo I, east Roman emperor (r. 457–74), 27, 288
Leo I, pope (r. 440–61), 281, 291
Leo III, pope (r. 795–816), 81–2, 88, 140, 148, Fig. 10
Lérins (France), monastery, 259, 261, 266, 302
Licinius, east Roman emperor (r. 308–25), 23, 29, 238
Ligugé (France), monastery, 259
Lindisfarne (Holy Island, Northumberland), bishopric and monastery, 243, 259, 261, 265, 269, 284, 289, 303
   Gospels, 329–30, Fig. 35
literacy, 9, 45, 96–9, 111, 113
Loki, pagan god, 251
Lombards, 28, 32, 55, 66, 75, 215, 291
London (England), 7, 210, 211, 219
Lorsch (Germany), monastery, 98, 268, Fig. 28
Louis the German, king of East Frankia (840–76), 66
Louis the Pious, king and emperor (r. 814–40), 66, 165, 226
   baptism of King Harald, 253
   division of realm, 55
   scholarship, 318
Luxeuil (France), monastery, 259, 265

Martin, St, bishop of Tours (c.315–c.336–97), 296
   church, 284
   tomb, 283
Merovech, founder of Merovingian dynasty (fl. mid-5th century), 74
metropolitans (archbishops), see prelates
Milan, Edict of (313), 235
Milvian Bridge, battle (312), 29, 65, 234–5
Minster-in-Thanet (Kent), monastery, 270, 271, 274
Mithraism, 240, 302
monasteries, 233, 258–77
   archives, 98
   as episcopal centres, 265
   as towns, 265–6

as wergilds in bloodfeuds, 274
   burial at, 263–4
   consumption, 191
   early history
      Egyptian influence, 260–1
      origins, 258–9, 327
      rise, 7–8
   economic power, 269–70
   education, 266
   lands granted to vassals, 270
   obtaining prayers and masses, 263
   pastoral functions, 266–7
   religious and spiritual attractions, 259–64
   relationship to aristocrats, 272–4
   relationship to kings, 88, 105, 267–71
   rules
      Benedict, 259, 261, 263, 264, 267, 271, 273, 303, 309
      Chrodegang, 296
      Columbanus, 259
      the Master, 259
   schools, 317
   See also Bobbio, Coldingham, Corbie, Corvey, Fulda, Hexham, Lastingham, Lérins, Ligugé, Lindisfarne, Lorsch, Luxeuil, Minster-in-Thanet, Monkwearmouth-Jarrow, Monte Cassino, Nendrum, Ripon, St Gall, Saint-Denis, Westminster
money, see coins
Monkwearmouth-Jarrow (Northumbria), joint monastery, 148, 184, 265, 268, 270, 274, 311–12, 314
Monte Cassino (Italy), monastery, 259
Moslems
   coins, 165, 166, 167
   economic influence, 156–61, 163, 167
   expansion, 3, 28, 146–8, Maps 2, 8
   travellers, 165, 227

Naranco (Spain), palace, 323
Navan Fort (Ireland), inauguration site, 77
Nendrum (Ireland), monastery, 265
Nennius (fl. early 9th century), History of the Britons, 57, 168

Neoplatonism, 241
Nicaea, Council of (325), 280
Nijmegen (Netherlands), palace, 213, 214
Nottingham (Notts.), *burh*, 219
Novgorod (Russian Federation), trading
    centre, 165, Map 10
Nydam (Denmark), ship, 169

Odoacer, king of Italy (475–89), 25, 27, 80,
    66, 140
Offa, king of Mercia (757–96)
    dinar, 167
    Offa's Dyke, 9, 58, 111, 140, Fig. 14
Olaf Haraldsson, king of Norway (d. 1030),
    141, 254, 304
Olaf Tryggvason, king of Norway (995–9),
    254, 304
Olof Skötkonung, king of Sweden
    (*c*.995–1022), 254, 304
'On Military Matters', tract, 22, Fig. 2
Orléans (France), siege, 289–90
Ostia (Italy), 151
Ostrogoths, *see* peoples
Oswald, king of Northumbria (r. 634–42),
    243, 246, 268–9, 303
Oswine, king of Deira (d. 655), 274
Oswiu, king of Northumbria (r. 642–70),
    281, 303
Otto I, king of Germany (r. 936–73),
    emperor (r. 962–73), 82, 85, 99, 141,
    270
Otto II, king of Germany (r. 961–83),
    emperor (r. 967–83), 82, 141
    see also Theophanu
Otto III, king of Germany (r. 983–1002),
    emperor (r. 996–1002), 82, 89, 141,
    Fig. 11
Oviedo (Spain), Santullano Church, 326

Pachomius, monastic founder (*c*.290–346),
    258
Paderborn (Germany), palace, 81, 87, 125,
    324
paganism
    barbarian, 72–80, 240, 247, 248–51
    eastern cults, 240–1
    English, 248–9

Roman, 242
    Altar of Victory, 29, 237
    place in Roman life, 237, 238, 239
    prohibited, 23, 65
    Scandinavian (Norse), 248, 251, Fig. 27
    See also Mithraism, Neoplatonism,
        Unconquered Sun
palaces, *see* architecture; government: palace
    organisation
Paschal I, pope (r. 817–24), 284
Patrick, St, evangelist of Ireland (mid-/late
    fifth century), 252, 260, 302
Paul the Deacon (*c*.720–99), 75
Paulinus of Nola (353/5–431), 264
Paulinus of Pella (fl. *c*.460), 237
Pavia (Italy), industrial centre, 152
Peace and Truce of God, 291
Penda, king of Mercia (d. 655), 58
peoples, 37–59, Map 5
    Alamans, 20, 50, 55, 243
    British, 52–3, 57, Map 5
    Burgundians, 65
        conversion, 247
        law-codes, 47, 55, 97
        kingdom, 15, 27, 32, 40, 54, 66, Map, 3
        kings, 80
    English (Anglo-Saxons), 59
        conversion, 245–6, 248, 288–9
        hostility to British, 57–8
        paganism, 248–9
        settlement, 40, 44, 46, 49–50, 53, 54,
            66, Fig. 3, Maps 3, 5
    Franks
        civil wars, 55–7
        coins, 108–9
        conquests, 54–5, 146
        conversion, 247, 248
        francisca, 48
        law-codes, 47, 55, 97
        long-haired kings, 75–6, Fig. 5
        settlement, 15, 28, 40, 44, 52, Maps 3, 5
    Goths, 25, 29, 37, 43, 48–9, 50, 52, 65,
        Map 5
        See also Ostrogoths, Visigoths
    Huns, 25, 29, 37, 40, 49, 65, 66, 291,
        Map 5
Jews, 150

peoples (*continued*)
  Jutes, 40, 53, 66
  Ostrogoths,
    conversion, 247
    settlement, 15, 29, 32, 37, 40, 66,
      Maps 3, 5
  Picts, 53
  Rus, *see* peoples: Vikings
  Saxons, 40, Map 5
    conquered by Franks, 253
    conversion, 253
    sax, 48
  Scandinavians
    conversion, 253–4
    paganism, 248, 251, Fig. 27
  Suebi, 15, 40, 48, 65, Fig. 4, Maps 3, 5
  Vandals, 15, 26, 27, 32, 40, 51, 65, 66,
    Maps 3, 5
  Vikings
    'Danegeld', 103
    'Great Army', 58, 66
    'Norman Tribute', 103
    Rus (Swedish Vikings), 165, 227
    trade, 163–8
  Visigoths
    conversion, 244–5, 248
    disappearance, 54
    kings, 85
      See also Theoderic, Wallia
    law-codes, 32, 55, 97
    settlements, 15, 25, 27, 28, 32, 37, 40,
      65, Maps 3, 5
Peter, apostle, 281, 284, 285, 287, Fig. 29
Pfalzel (Germany), palace, 180–1
Piazza Armerina (Italy), villa, 25
Picts, *see* peoples
Pippin III, king of the Franks (751–68), 140
  accession, 75, 85
  coins, 108–9,
  conquests, 55, 214, 226
  Plectrude, wife of Pippin III, 203
  regulates markets, 192
  scholarship, 318
plague, 184, 226, 239
Poitiers (France), St John's, 326
Polycarp, St, martyr (d. *c.*155), 282
Pont l'Arche (France), *burh*, 219

popes, 279
  appeals, 289
  authority, 281–2
  'Book of the Popes', 288
  'Day Book', 288
  decretals, 288
  Gregorian Reform, 282
  individuals, *see* Gelasius I, Gregory I,
    Gregory VII, Leo I, Leo III,
    Paschal I
  pallium, 279, 281
  Patrimony of St Peter, 294
  'Peter's Pence', 289
  Petrine succession, 281
  relic-policy, 285–6
  rise, 280–2
  See also prelates
population, 24, 183–5
  See also plague
Portchester (Hants.), Saxon Shore fort, Fig. 1
prelates (bishops, archbishops, popes), 238,
    278–80, 282–304
  building, 294–5
  governmental role, 108, 289–93, 296–7
  hierarchy, 279
  holiness, 296–7
  immunities, 291
  individuals, *see* Ambrose, Augustine of
    Canterbury, Augustine of Hippo,
    Basil, Boniface, Bruno, Ebo, Le
    Mans, Wulfstan; *see also* popes
  military activity, 295–6
  relations with kings, 295–6
  rituals
    anointing kings, 279
    chrism distribution, 278–9
    dedicating churches, 279
    scholarship and expertise, 287–8
    social status, 126, 293–4
    wealth, 294
  See also popes
Prittlewell (Essex), burial, 331
Procopius, Byzantine historian
    (*c.*500–after 542), 26, 32, 184, 308
'productive sites', 214

Quentovic (France), *emporium*, 192

Radagaisus, barbarian leader (fl. early
    5th century), 26
Ravenna (Italy), 15, 294, 310, Maps 5, 6
    palace, 80, 323
    San Vitale, 82, 295, 325, Fig. 7
Rendlesham (Suffolk), royal vill, 213, 249
Reric (Groß Strömkendorf, Germany),
    trading centre, 214–15, 226
Ripon (Yorks.), monastery, 294
Robert II the Pious, king of France
    (r. 996–1031), 79, 141, 268
Rök (Sweden), runestone, 81
Roman Empire
    agriculture, 24, 175–6, 179–83
    aristocracy, 24–5, 29, 32–3, 129–30
    army, 19–20, 29
        cataphracts, 20
    barbarians, policy towards, 26–33
    cities, 28, 197, 198–206, 239, Map 4,
        Fig. 21
    citizenship, 42
    disintegration, 3, 18–36
    fortifications, 20–2, 198, 201, Fig. 20
        Saxon Shore forts, 21, Fig. 1
    frontiers, 3, 15, 23, Map 1
    government, 20, 279
        annona, 24, 152, 154, 161
        Edict of Prices (301), 19
        emperors, 22–3
        See also Constantine, Eugenius, Julius
            Nepos, Romulus Augustulus,
            Justinian, Theodosius I, Theodosius II,
            Trajan, Valens
        Notititia Dignitatum, 19–20
        taxes, 24, 176
    population, 24, 184
    revolts, 24
    technology, 22, Fig. 2
    trade, 151–6
    usurpers, 29
    villas, 25, 175–6, 180–2, Fig. 17
Rome (Italy), Map 6
    coronation of Charlemagne, 81–2,
        84–5
    imperial residence, 280
    monuments and sites
        Arch of Constantine, 236–7, Fig. 25
        Crypta Balbi, 155, 216
        forum, 204–5, Fig. 21
        Lateran, 88, 294, 325
        New Basilica (of Constantine), 23, 323,
            Fig. 21
        San Adriano, 295
        San Prassede, 294
        Santa Maria Antiqua, 295
        SS Cosmas and Damian, 294–5
        St Cecilia, 284
        St Peter in the Vatican, 281, 283, 285,
            294, 308, 325, Fig. 29
    paganism, 29
    pilgrimage centre, 285–6
    population, 24, 280
    relics, 285–7, Fig. 29
    sack of, 25, 40, 65, 308
    swamps, 280
Romulus Augustulus, Roman emperor
    (deposed 475), 25, 27, 66
Rus, see peoples: Vikings
Russian Primary Chronicle, 164–5

Saba, St, Passion of, 244–5
Saint-Denis (France), monastery, 263,
    269–70, 271, 324
Saint-Germain-des-Prés (France), rural
    settlement, 185
saints and martyrs, 260
    canonisation, 287
    cult, 242, 282–7
    martyrs
        in Roman army, 237–8
        Passions, 282
    relics, 99–100, 160–1, 264, 279, 283,
        285–7, Figs 12, 29
San Juan de las Abbadessas (Spain), rural
    settlement, 185, 227
San Pedro de la Nave (Spain), 324
San Vincenzo al Volturno (Italy), monastery,
    265
sanctuary, 291, 293
Santiago de Compostella (Spain)
    pilgrimage to St James, 284–5
Saxons, see peoples
Scandinavians, see peoples
scholarship, 8, 309–21, 336–7

scholarship (*continued*)
    educational system, 316–19
    scholars, 309–12, 315
    scripts, 314, Fig. 30
    syllabus, 315–16
    See also literacy
Scone (Scotland), inauguration site, 77
Seven Liberal Arts, 315–16
Shakenoak (Oxon), villa, 180
Shapwick (Somerset), rural settlement, 182–3
Sidonius Apollinaris, bishop of the Auvergne
    (*c.*430–*c.*486), 180, 293
Sigibert, king of the Ripuarian Franks
    (d. 508 × 511), 203
Skellig Michael (Ireland), hermitage, 261
society
    aristocracy, 125–30, 132–4
    marriage, 131
    names, 128–9
    oaths, 99–101
    peasants, 176, 178–9, 189, 215, 225
    slaves, 101, 165, 176, 177, 225
    war-bands, 117–25, 294
    women, 130–2
South Cadbury (Somerset), reused hillfort,
    155
Southampton, *see* Hamwih
Split (Croatia), palace, 23
St Albans (Herts., Verulamium), 245, 284
St Andrews (Fife)
    bishops, 284
    sarcophagus, 328, Fig. 34
St Gall, Plan, 263, 265–6, 268, 317
Suebi, *see* peoples
Sutton Hoo (Suffolk), burial-mounds, 126, 303
    baptismal spoons, 249
    helmet, 331
    ship, 120–1, 169–70, Fig. 15
    whetstone-sceptre, 77–9, Fig. 6
Swein Forkbeard, king of Denmark and
    England (d. 1014), 304
Symmachus, Roman senator (*c.*345–402),
    25, 65, 237
Syrians, 150–1

Taliesin, poems, 57
Tara (Ireland), inauguration site, 77

Theoderic, king of the Ostrogoths
    (r. 471–526), 140, 309
    accession, 27
    government, 29,
    palace, 323
    religious policy, 80
    reputation, 81
    written documents, 96
Theodosius I the Great, Roman emperor
    (379–95), 23, 28, 65, 302
    invades Italy, 27, 237
    religious policy, 29, 235
Theodosius II, emperor (408–50), 19, 66
Theophanu (d. 991), wife of Otto II, 132, 141
Thor, pagan god, 249
Tintagel (Cornwall), 155
towns, *see* urban centres
trade, 150–74, 192, 207
    Arab influence, 156–61, 163
    commodities
        amber, 158
        beeswax, 270
        furs, 165
        glass, 166
        honey, 270
        incense, 159–60
        ivory, 160
        papyrus, 151, 152, 158–9
        pottery, 152–3, 154–5, 156, 166, 180,
           183, Map 9
        silks, 151, 152, 159, 162
        slaves, 165, 270
        spices, 151, 152, 159–60
        swords, 166
        wine, 192
    Frisian, 168
    merchants, 104
    monasteries, 269–70
    northern seas, 163–70
    Pirenne Thesis, 145–51, 166, 197, 206–8,
        210, 215, 219
    Roman, 151–6
    routeways, 161–3
    ships, 168–70, 249, Fig. 16, Map 10
    trans-Mediterranean, 150–63, 166
    Viking, 163–8
Trajan, Roman emperor (r. 98–117), 176

Trier (Germany), Map 6
  basilica, 125, 323, Fig. 31
  baths, 205
  immunity, 291, Map 15
  layout, 203–4
  palace, 23

Ulfilas, missionary and translator (*c*.311–83),
    45, 245, 248, 302, 312
Unconquered Sun, cult of, 240, 241
Uppsala (Sweden), burial-mounds, 213
urban centres, 197–223
  functions, 204–6
  growth, 206–8
  influence of Christianity, 283–4
  new towns, 208–20, Fig. 22
    burhs, 216–20
    emporia (wics), 170, 210–16
    See also Dorestad, Durham, Hamwih,
      Nottingham, Novgorod, Quentovic,
      Winchester, Wallingford
  Roman cities, 28, 197, 198–206, 239,
      Map 4, Fig. 21
    See also Canterbury, Rome, St Albans,
      Trier, York
Urgell (Spain), rural settlement, 179

Valens, Roman emperor (364–78), 25, 50, 65
Vandals, *see* peoples
Varro, Marcus Terentius (d. 27 BC), 'On the
    Affairs of the Countryside', 175, 226
Vatican City, *see* Rome: St Peter in the
    Vatican
Venice (Italy), 158, 166, 206, 215, 226,
    Map 6
Verdun, Treaty of (843), 55, 66, Map 6
Verulamium, *see* St Albans
Villa Romana del Casale, *see* Piazza Armerina
villas, *see* Roman Empire
Visigoths, *see* peoples
Vorbasse (Denmark), rural settlement, 127
Vortigern, British leader (fl. mid-5th century),
    53
Vulgate Bible, 287, 312

Wallia, king of the Visigoths (415–18), 27
Wallingford (Oxon), *burh*, 217–18, Fig. 24
Wearmouth, *see* Monkwearmouth
Westminster (England), monastery and
      palace, 88, 104, 264
Weyland, legendary blacksmith, 9, 249,
      Fig. 26
Wharram Percy (Yorks.), rural settlement,
      182
Whitby (Yorks.), monastery, 266, 270,
      271
Whitby, Synod of (664), 281
wics, see urban centres
Widukind of Corvey, historian
      (*c*.925–*c*.1004), 218–19, 254
Wilfrid (634–709), bishop of the
      Northumbrians, 126, 269, 281, 289,
      293, 294, 295
Willibald (*c*.700–*c*.787), missionary, 162,
      226
Willibrord (658–739), missionary, 253,
      289
Winchester (Hampshire), 198–9, 213, 214,
      224
  burials, 198, 199
  churches, 198–9, 216, 226, 263, 295
  fortifications, 21, 198, 216
  layout, 216, 218, Map 14
  palace, 216
Woden, pagan god, 249
Woodchester (Gloucs.), villa, 181
Wulfstan I, archbishop of York, 296

Xanten (Germany), 283–4

Yeavering (Northumberland), palace, 84,
      125, 249, 324
Ynglingatal, Old Norse poem, 75
York (Yorkshire), 7, 199–202
  burials, 199
  finds, 201, 332–3, Fig. 37
  fortifications, 21, 199, Fig. 20, Map 12
  layout, 200–1, Map 12
  school, 287